"I'm deeply proud to be British, not least because of the extraordinarily brave, funny, brilliant, kind and talented people who call these small islands home. In particular, I'm proud of Britain's history of engaging in the challenges people face, not just at home but around the world. It has inspired and supported the work of my AIDS Foundation, which aims to help end this devastating pandemic around the world. A book examining what it means to be British and Britain's potential to be a force for good in the world is timely. Penny and Chris should be congratulated on seizing the opportunity to look forward in this interesting and enjoyable book."

SIR ELTON JOHN

"In her maiden speech to Parliament, my sister Jo Cox MP said, 'We are far more united and have more in common than that which divides us.' Sadly, it hasn't always felt like it in recent years. At her murder trial, the judge said that Jo was 'a true patriot' and that when she was killed 'the tributes to her from across the political spectrum were spontaneous, sincere and fulsome'. Indeed, our family saw, and felt, the best of humanity and the best of British at that unbelievable time. Britain is great, but we know to our cost that it can also be greater, and the themes explored in this excellent book give us all an opportunity to reflect on what we can do to play our part in the journey to make it so. I hope we do. Well done, Penny and Chris."

KIM LEADBEATER MBE, AMBASSADOR FOR
THE JO COX FOUNDATION

"This is a really important book. Because whatever disagreements there are about the recent political past, there is no doubt at all that the spirit Britain needs for its future is one that is optimistic, outward-looking, innovative and inclusive. And that is the spirit of the book Penny and Chris have written, which makes it both uplifting and highly readable."

RT HON. TONY BLAIR, FORMER PRIME MINISTER OF THE UK

"This really readable and funny book reminds me of so many of the things I love about the UK and gives me high hopes for the future."

RICHARD CURTIS, SCREENWRITER, PRODUCER AND DIRECTOR

GREATER
BRITAIN AFTER THE STORM

PENNY MORDAUNT AND CHRIS LEWIS
FOREWORD BY BILL GATES

Biteback Publishing

First published in Great Britain in 2021 by
Biteback Publishing Ltd, London
Copyright © Penny Mordaunt and Chris Lewis 2021

ISBN 978-1-78590-609-1

10 9 8 7 6 5 4 3 2 1

A CIP catalogue record for this book is available from the British Library.

Set in Minion Pro and Montserrat

Printed and bound in Great Britain by
CPI Group (UK) Ltd, Croydon CR0 4YY

MIX
Paper from
responsible sources
FSC
www.fsc.org   FSC® C020471

For our families and the people of Portsmouth

'National pride is to countries what self-respect is to individuals: a necessary condition for self-improvement.'

RICHARD RORTY

'We are far more united and have far more in common with each other than things that divide us.'

JO COX MP

This book was written after I left my role in government as Secretary of State for Defence in July 2019 and was updated prior to publication. It is a personal view.
THE RT HON. PENNY MORDAUNT MP

I have a different political opinion to Penny, especially on Brexit, but we both share the view that without dialogue, there can be no progress. Our future depends on it.
CHRIS LEWIS

CONTENTS

FOR THOSE WITH NEITHER THE TIME NOR THE PATIENCE...

This book is about how Britain can be better. It doesn't argue for a new role on the world stage. Britain's character is its destiny. By turns, it is industrious, cautious, creative, caring, trusted, frugal, fair, selfless and modest. Of course it has less attractive qualities; chief among them: dwelling on its less attractive qualities.

The notion of a country – or individuals – being 'Greater' is found in them rising above their differences and working together. Each of us is a set of skills and experience. But we are also an attitude.

As an ancient country, Britain's history, culture and traditions are vivid. Trust remains ascendant in the British brand. It's an asset, but it needs to be defended, in part because we don't have a plan. We never did. We don't really know what we're good at, what we're up against or how we can succeed. That last sentence was a test. If you bridled, good. It is precisely because the British character is so enduring that it is sceptical, even cynical, of those peddling panaceas.

Throughout its history, Britain hasn't always embraced the future because it values the tried and tested. This caution served the country well when faced with gradual change. As the pace of change has quickened, however, this approach needs to be updated. When the majority of parliamentarians are appointed by a handful of people, when certain seats are still reserved for men only, our political structures need modernisation.

Over decades, the apathy generated by this ossification has led to 'us'-and-'them' politics. This division has been deepened by the financial crisis, Brexit and Covid.

Dialogue is the only way to understand and deal with these divisions, but our freedom of speech is under threat. Parliament should defend the standards of public discourse. Free speech in a free press is not censored, but it is subject to the law. Free speech on social media should be no different. It should be subject to laws made by elected representatives, not heads of corporations.

The financial crisis and other scandals damaged trust in all our institutions. Britain needs to modernise its infrastructure, education, industry and economy as well. So often, government has confused legislation with real change. It is no substitute for a clear, well-executed national mission. This should not be a top-down plan, but one that enables everyone to help. Government needs to do less, better.

Britain is bound by bonds of mutuality, embodied in culture, commerce, welfare and education. We should use our most trusted organisations as a template for the teamwork, professionalism and innovation we need to rebuild Britain.

The state of national finance brought about by Covid will take years to fix. If we are to meet ambitions, money has to go further and be more sustainable. That means we must do more with the third sector and civil society. We will need energy, generosity, imagination, experience and attitude from people of all backgrounds who want to get it done.

FOREWORD

Fourteen years ago, I left my first career at Microsoft to begin a second one in philanthropy. Since then, I've worked with dozens of nations to fight poverty and disease, and Britain is easily one of the most effective at delivering development aid and articulating why it's important.

The UK is a force for good. This book tries to explain why, and what Britain must do to stay that way. The subject has never been more important.

First and foremost, Britain is a force for good because of its strong institutions which are devoted to helping fellow nations, particularly with regard to their health. No one knows this better than Penny Mordaunt.

Prior to this year, global health didn't get much attention in the news. Now, I expect that we'll (rightly) be hearing about new diseases, treatments and the health of people around the world for some time. What shouldn't be lost in this story is the fact that even before Covid, Britain was at work building institutions to fight viruses and other diseases on a global scale – institutions that, if they did not exist today, would need to be invented.

Look at Gavi, the Vaccine Alliance, for example. Surveys show that only a small portion of the general public knows about it, yet it has transformed healthcare for more than a tenth of the global population. Twenty years ago, before Gavi was founded, the vaccine market was broken. Hundreds of thousands of children in low-income countries were dying of entirely preventable diseases. Vaccines existed to keep them from getting sick, but they weren't being sold or distributed where the children lived. Gavi fixed that. Today, when new vaccines are introduced, kids in low-income countries get them at the same time as kids in wealthy ones. Plus, Gavi has vaccinated more than 760 million children – and saved 13 million lives.

If you are looking for reasons to be proud of Britain, look no further than this. Over the past thirty years, the number of children to die before the age of five has gone down by over 50 per cent – even as the population of that age group has gone up by 50 per cent. That wouldn't have happened without Britain's generosity and expertise. The UK has been Gavi's largest funder since its founding.

Of course, there is more that Britain and all nations must do. As I write this, the world is racing to develop vaccines for Covid. It's a reminder: countries need to constantly build and maintain their capacity to innovate.

Innovation thrives in places that welcome students and scientists and that allow them to collaborate with their colleagues around the world. The UK has been exactly that kind of place, and, in fact, outside of the United States, it's the nation where the Bill & Melinda Gates Foundation invests most in research and development. If the UK wants to remain a hub for innovation, then it must continue to welcome students and scientists to its shores post-Brexit.

This will be crucial not only to prevent future pandemics and health crises, but to solve many other global challenges. When it comes to climate change, for example, we need to drive the world's net carbon emissions down to zero. To do that, we'll need to invent and deploy new ways of doing things across virtually the entire physical economy – including how we generate electricity, grow food, move people and goods around the world, and make materials like cement and steel. We have some of the tools we need, but far from all of them, and countries like the UK need to help create the environment where innovators can take brilliant ideas out of the lab and into the marketplace.

There are also innovative methods that the UK can use to help the current victims of climate change. Some 2 billion people are either smallholder farmers or part of a smallholder's family. In most countries, being a smallholder farmer is a risky business. Most struggle to produce enough food to feed their families, and very few have the benefit of insurance or advanced crop strains that are more resistant to environmental disasters. So, when a drought or a flood hits, they're wiped out.

Climate change is making these droughts and floods more frequent and intense, meaning that more farmers are having their livelihoods ruined and struggling to feed their children. Malnutrition is a serious risk.

The UK should do what it can to help these farmers adapt. That includes investing in research to develop more heat-resistant crops or in technologies that help governments better track farm productivity.

It's easy to watch the news and feel pessimistic. Viruses are spreading. The planet is heating up. But I remain hopeful about the world because I know that humans – and, in particular, the British – have the ability to change it.

The past two decades have taught me that the world can out-innovate its greatest problems so long as there are nations that are willing to devote both their money and brainpower to the task. I am glad that people like Penny and Chris are making the case, too.

This book shines a spotlight on why Britain is a great nation and points the way ahead for it to become greater still.

Bill Gates
April 2021

PROLOGUE

It's a sticky summer evening in London in 2019. The sort of heat where make-up slides. The sky is growing darker. Above a weary city, the rain clouds, heavy and grey, jostle to decide which will be first to inundate the sweating bustle below.

On the terrace of the US ambassador's residence in Regent's Park, a group of twenty or so suited guests are making small talk while overlooking the largest private garden in London after Buckingham Palace. Some are politicians. They do small talk. They do big talk. There's not much in between; those are the only settings. There are also journalists. They don't converse; they probe.

The twelve acres of gardens around Winfield House are impressive. It looks like a giant garden, but on the Fourth of July, it transforms into a venue for bands like Duran Duran to play as guests admire American cars, jukeboxes and diner food. It's *the* ticket in town on the day. It highlights one of the differences between America and Britain: America has fun. Laugh-out-loud, whooping fun. The Brits only go in for that sort of thing two beers in. Most often, they just pass the time.

Half a century before the Norman conquest, this land belonged to the Abbey of Barking. Over the years, Henry VIII hunted there and Elizabeth I used it for entertaining. In 1936, the site was bought by 24-year-old heiress to the Woolworth fortune Barbara Hutton, who commissioned the mansion. Having decided to return to America on the outbreak of the Second World War, she later donated the house to the US government as the official residence of the American Ambassador to the Court of St James's.

This particular evening, the host is another American from another dynasty: philanthropist, businessman and diplomat, US Ambassador Robert 'Woody' Johnson. He's also owner of New York's American football team the Jets. His family business, Johnson & Johnson, is one of the world's largest healthcare companies.

He moves easily and quickly among the various groups and he's comfortable on the ball. A mic appears and suddenly he's speaking. But what he's about to say surprises, then angers, the group: 'Two years ago, when my family and I arrived in Britain, we were talking about Brexit,' he says, looking around the group, fixing them with his eyes. 'Two years on, we're still talking about Brexit.' His nostrils are flaring. He sighs. 'What sort of country is this?'

There's a rumble above. The clouds collide and conspire.

It's a bad start. There's subcutaneous harrumphing. The assembled Brits shift their feet, sticky in the fug. Truth be known, they're a bit prickly about the never-ending tantric politics of Brexit – and with good reason. It's been four years since it all started, including the announcement, the debate, the vote, the aftermath, the back and forth: the general election and the subsequent deadlock. The crowd is thinking: 'It's OK for *me* to criticise my country, but I'm not sure I like an American doing it...'

The cosmic grumble above echoes the mood and rolls across the terrace. A few are already shuffling their feet awkwardly, examining their shoelaces. Others find the distant trees of sudden interest. Woody is undaunted: 'I mean, what sort of country turns its back on its closest allies?' The mood darkens. 'What sort of country tears up every trade agreement it's ever made and heads off in a completely different direction?'

Those not embarrassed already are starting to bridle. The rain is threatening, but he ploughs on: 'You turn your back on history and set out in a completely different direction, prepared to take your fate into your own hands. Your approach divides communities.' Closer observers can detect a smirk playing on his face. He's enjoying this, the bloody madman. 'What sort of country does this?'

By this stage, something unusual is happening. The audience is starting to divide. Some are openly looking at their watches, but some are smiling. The quicker among them are already grinning widely.

'What sort of country...' he asks, pausing for effect. 'What sort of country takes this approach? Who in their right mind would do what you are doing? What sort of country declares their independence and takes their destiny in their own hands?'

'We would. We did. America did. What you're doing is a very American thing. It's a belief in self-determination and liberty.'

OK, we get it now. The rain and relief are now palpable. But some of us also know that a divided Europe is not necessarily a disadvantage to America.

He finishes with a smile on this face. His arms open. His eyes twinkling. Siegfried and Roy.[1] The elephant has vanished. It's clever stuff. Shorter than the Gettysburg Address and just as powerful. And funny, because he's pricked British pomposity.

The point is made. Britain and America have more in common than they do with their immediate neighbours. It is true of Britain and it is true of America. The US has more in common with Britain than it has with Mexico. It's no surprise that more than 750,000 British people feel at home there[2] (almost twice the number living in Spain, the next largest expat community).[3] It is logical to suggest some of our characteristics are common in spite of the ocean that divides us.

When Brits and Americans get together, something happens. There's the mutual admiration of an older nation for a younger one. There's the rivalry we reserve for family members. There's the accentuation of our differences because it's the only way we can really deny our similarities. Woody Johnson says it is time for Britain to behave just a little more like America. It's time to regain some self-confidence, belief and, above all, a mission in the world.

INTRODUCTION

Three great storms engulfed Britain in the ten years between 2010 and 2020: the financial crisis, the Brexit referendum and the global pandemic. They were similar in the following respects: they were unlike anything in living memory; they derailed longer-term government plans; they required unprecedented, profound and prolonged intervention; they were all eclipsed by each other; they exposed vulnerable communities; they revealed the British character; and they happened because Britain was more connected to the world than ever before. They were completely unexpected, but they were foretold by minorities.

The last of the events – the pandemic – was the greatest crisis the country faced since the Second World War. It changed the country in ways we're still trying to understand.

We now find ourselves blinking in brightly lit newness. We have a new decade, a new US president, new medicines and a new appreciation of all that we previously took for granted. We have a new debt-burdened economy. We have new ways of living and working. We have new inequalities and new threats to address. We have a new government, with a newly won majority and a new relationship with Europe. We have new fears and new hopes.

There are many questions about what lies ahead, both short and long term. Will we continue to trust capitalism? Does democracy still work? What can Britain still learn from its past? What can Britain still show the world? How will we use the 2020s? Will they be a re-run of the 'roaring' '20s, starting with disease and ending in depression? What will we do with our newness? Where will we go? What is our plan?

Although this book is about Britain, it investigates the qualities that make any country great. It also proposes what is needed to make them greater. Some might say that nations such as Britain and America cannot be great because they are so divided, as if somehow division should be considered embarrassing, feeble or shameful. Certainly, there are countries where there is no dissent. But their utter consensus is no more a sign of strength than lively disagreement is a sign of our weakness. If there is diversity of thought and opinion, how could that ever make a nation weaker? Strength is vested in diversity and democracy. America chose *e pluribus Unum* (out of the many, one) as its motto for good reasons. It's supposed to be diverse. It's about recognising that diversity is a source of strength and that problems are solved best from many points of view. Diversity is not just about race or provenance. It's about representation, character, freedom of speech, thought and action.

In any case, it's simply untrue that the autocracies are doing better than liberal democracies. In 1945, there were just eleven; now, there are seventy-six. They overtook autocracies at the end of the millennium and the long-term trend is clear.[1]

Democracies are winning, because nations that deny free speech are afraid of ideas. Their peoples are infantilised and diminished by their fear of the state. All progress is based on dissent. Even uncontroversial new ideas begin life as a minority voice. Philosopher and political economist John Stuart Mill warned against the 'tyranny of the majority'.[2] This is an important concept in democracy and one that governments with big majorities should be sensitive to. As American anthropologist Margaret Mead agreed: 'Never doubt that a small group of thoughtful, committed citizens can change the world; indeed, it's the only thing that ever has.'[3]

Does anyone seriously think the warnings of global warming would ever have come to light from climate scientists within totalitarian regimes? Or that institutional wrongdoing would ever be exposed by state-controlled media? Yet many still point, openmouthed, at the scale of what central planning can achieve. But what if the plan is wrong? For instance, what good is all the physical infrastructure coming out of China's Belt and Road Initiative if political factors erode the trust required for trade? Or if the carbon output of such infrastructure renders it unusable? Or the world moves products in the form of data not physical items? How many thirty-year plans can be successful in an age of rapid, unpredictable technical and cultural change? You wouldn't do it militarily, commercially or culturally. So, why do we think it's a good idea politically? Plans are useless, but *planning* is important.

Some say Britain is an ordinary and mediocre nation because it can't do these big visions, but the world is moving away from just quantity as a measure. Quality matters, too. Of all the countries in the world that migrants want to move to, Britain remains in the top five.[4] British democracy may have its challenges, but it remains a strong pull factor for those who were not born here. According to the World Economic Forum, 35 million people would like to move permanently to Britain.[5] They may be escaping from conflict, famine, disaster or high unemployment. It's not difficult to understand. Prior to the pandemic, the country had almost full employment. It's the sixth largest economy in the world and the largest investor into America. It's also the largest receiver of inbound investment in Europe. Globally, only Singapore is ranked higher than Britain as a country to invest in. Funding from Japan and America eclipsed EU investment several times over in 2017, despite the Brexit vote. Maybe *because* of the Brexit vote. Britain is the fifth biggest exporter in the world and has a stock market that's trusted the world over.[6]

Britain is wealthy, but it's also generous. A quarter of all British people volunteer at least once a month and it is listed among the top ten most charitable nations and overseas aid donors.[7,8] The country is also remarkably well educated. It has four of the top ten universities globally.[9] It has the world's oldest scientific academy, the Royal Society, with 1,600 fellows, including around eighty Nobel Laureates.[10] Britain is creative. It has the first billionaire book author, J. K. Rowling, twelve of the top fifty bestselling recording artists of all time and the largest theatre-going audience in the world.[11]

Britain also cares. It has a near-religious commitment to the NHS. Why? Because it's like a wedding vow. Britain promises to care for its citizens in sickness and in health. Home is where people are willing to look after you. It's about trust. The NHS is home. It also has to do with our sense of fairness. Illness and accidents can touch anyone, but if they do, in Britain, health and welfare safety nets ensure your life chances are improved. It's about justice: everyone is equal in health as they are before the law. The pandemic has shown just how proud the country is of the NHS. It's a wonderful, liberating thought to know that your nation cares about you enough to look after you in your time of need and it won't cost you a thing. Although the NHS is by definition a national system, its popularity is ultimately rooted in its local communities. It's the institution where we are born, where we go in emergencies and where many of us will die. Is it any wonder the British people identify so strongly with it? It's an act of faith.

The system is not just based on sentiment, either: the NHS also provides better value than almost any other service. In 2019, the US-based Commonwealth Fund, a respected global health think tank, ranked the British health system as the best of eleven other wealthy countries.[12] In the past twenty years, British life expectancy has increased another three years.[13] Like many other countries, the British are living longer, healthier, wealthier lives than ever before, and the Happiness Index is on the rise, too.[14]

Yet there remains a widespread belief that Britain is living in the worst of times, that these storms have brought only bad things. As Steven Pinker and many others have pointed out, this is also untrue: 'People today live far more years in the pink of health than their ancestors lived altogether, healthy and infirm years combined.'[15] The problem is, the facts are no longer enough. How Britain *feels* is important, too.

That's where this book comes in. It's here to argue that the British have much to be proud of and grateful for, but there's much to be modernised and rethought. Perhaps the most extraordinary thing about Britain is that there's never been a clearly identified mission to modernise. Harold Wilson hinted at the idea. Tony Blair was known as a moderniser. David Cameron became leader on a promise to modernise. Did they manage to? Did they have a mission to? Some would ask whether it really matters. I mean, who cares if Britain slips off the world stage and becomes another Rowley Birkin chuntering in a winged armchair of a retired nations care home?[16] What difference does Britain make to the world?

In Frank Capra's *It's a Wonderful Life*, George Bailey gets a chance to see how the world would have turned out had he never been born. Britain can also be seen in that way. If Britain had never happened, the world would be less compassionate, less wealthy, less successful, less funny, less connected, less international, less equal, less eccentric, less organised, less democratic, less consistent, less traditional, less entertaining, less inspirational and, in fairness, less pompous, less stuffy and less nostalgic.

And yet, despite all this, there is no such country as Britain. There is the United Kingdom. There is even an island called Great Britain. But there is no such nation as Britain, Great or otherwise. There never has been. And despite being a famous nation, Britons have never been quite sure what being British means. There's no evidence, however, that this ambiguity is a disadvantage. Indeed, it has been a powerful draw among migrants who have come to Britain for liberty, stability, opportunity, infrastructure, capital and education. It should not be forgotten that, way before America, Britain was America. People came for possibility. People came to blend in. People came to connect.

All character is destiny, and that is where the book begins in Chapters 1 and 2. This book asks what qualities make up the British character and why does it matter? Who do the British think they are? What are they good at? And what is their actual position in the world? Is there a difference between Britain's view of itself and that outside? The pandemic allowed us to see ourselves in action. We shopped for each other. We cheered the NHS. We did what we could. We shouted at the telly. We did what we were told. Our scientists went to work on a vaccine and found one faster than ever before.

Understanding the character of Britain is something leaders ignore at their peril. Everybody just seems to get the wrong idea about us. This has been going on for a while. Britain got its name from the Romans, who described the indigenous peoples of these islands as 'pretani', the Celtic word for the 'painted' or the 'tattooed' ones.[17] Despite David Beckham's valiant efforts, the country now ranks only eighth in the world's most tattooed nations behind Italy, Sweden, America, Australia, Argentina, Spain and Denmark.[18] But we still love our tats.

Life in Britain is not as it appears. Take the media for instance. Despite the tabloid press, most of us don't go around 'guzzling', 'romping', 'snubbing', 'storming', 'slamming', 'ousting', 'axing', 'blasting', 'perving' or 'probing' despite the 'chaos', 'meltdown' and 'Hell'. We don't burn with 'fury' or 'outrage' or 'despair'. Nor are we like the BBC imagines us to be. We don't suddenly change to show how in tune we are with the latest fashion. In fact, we're a bit suspicious of people that do. Nor are we relentlessly negative. We tend to keep away from those people. Similarly, with people that see politics in everything. No, if you're looking for the character of the British, the media isn't really the place.

So very often the British approach is prosaic, pragmatic and rooted in common sense, born not of preference but necessity. It is the character of going out come rain or shine. Of inconvenience. Of routine. Of the matter-of-fact. Of the stoic. Of putting up with things. Of shared burden. Of smiling through. Of drinking and laughter. Of small everyday kindnesses. Of shared anxieties. Of aches and pains. It is the stuff of the weekly budget. Of saving up. Of the Saturday and Sunday rituals. Of bearing regular burdens cheerfully. Of exasperation with those who seem divorced from these realities. Of practical, everyday, mundane clear-up-the-mess care. It's a place where, when honours or medals are awarded, recipients are often dumbfounded and even embarrassed. 'Someone had to do it' is a frequent reply.[19] Chapter 2 sense-checks these characteristics against a global panel of movers and shakers and international indices.

Chapter 3 explains how the country came to leave the European Union. This is explored in the story of the general election of 2019 and how the British public insisted that politicians honoured the result of the European referendum. You can claim the people were misled, but to do so undermines all elections. In democracies, the will of the people is the law of the land – not the will of *all* of the people, mind – but a *majority* of the people. Now, the majority of the people may not be the majority of the media or the majority of the people you know. The majority may not be the majority of the comfortably-off or the loudest or the most aggressive. It's the majority of ordinary people that choose to vote in a secret ballot. We don't even insist that they all vote. We can agree it's a terrible system, but it's the least worst we've found *in the long term*.

One of the best ways of seeing the British culture is to look at it through another nation's eyes. In Chapter 4, the book looks at America and China as the two superpowers that will shape Britain's future. It examines the relationships and history between the two.

Chapter 5 asks why Britain has never had a plan. It explains how Britain's mission will be formed, whether consciously or not, by what other nations are unwilling or unable to do. This is the very definition of a challenger. Trust is central to the British brand and something all nations, no matter how powerful, need. Subjugation through might is never sustainable nor efficient. Only cooperation through trust can endure.

Chapter 6 looks in detail at the first part of the modernising mission – the modernisation of Parliament and representative democracy. We currently tolerate an anachronistic parliamentary system which apes a feudal aristocracy where the majority of its representatives are unelected. Appointments are not open or based on skills or knowledge. In among this antiquity, politicians are drawn from ever-narrower backgrounds. What effect does this have?

Above all, Britain must be clear about its mission, at the local, regional and national levels. We look in detail at structures in Chapter 7 and examine how the mandate affects the management of the nation through government. It asks why government reform has failed many times over the years and why there are long-term challenges in funding. How can these bonds be strengthened? This book showcases the people and the organisations that are making a difference. How can we deliver for these people? Of course, the government has to *do* things, but it has to *be* them as well. Government has convening power. It can focus energy, but it has to recognise its limitations.

If the country wants a modern, aspirant and representative economy, then it needs to understand that equality, aspiration and economic growth feed off each other. A positive attitude towards repeated failure is the secret to success. This is the substance of Chapter 8, which explores our enduring concept of mutuality. Britain is the nation of Wilberforce, Leonard Cheshire and the NHS. It was the cradle of the anti-slavery movement, the Paralympics and Live Aid. The sense of duty that drives us towards each other is at the heart of Britain. The concept of different people working towards a unified goal is the foundation of the United Kingdom, and we should never forget it.

This is not just about gender, ethnicity, disability or class background. Our NHS is about equality of health. Our schools and universities are about equality of opportunity. Our welfare systems are designed to mitigate inequality. Equality is at the heart of mutuality. Better decisions are made when a wider variety of people are consulted and represented. It may make the process slower initially, but it's faster in the longer run.

The basis of Chapter 9 is an examination of capitalism, its leadership and the challenges it faces. This chapter documents how the private, public and third sectors have all struggled to cope with massive change. Since the financial crisis of 2010, leadership has been challenged across the board not just in politics but in finance, commerce, industry, utilities, entertainment, even in religion and charities. This has had a corrosive effect on public confidence, not just in national and international government but in leadership itself. School children, not politicians, have pointed the way. Leadership is in need of modernisation, and this is especially true in geopolitics, to help define and maintain the UK's position internationally. In this chapter, the reinvention of the Western world and the creation of new alliances is discussed.

There are many positives about capitalism and democracy. However, the constraints and pitfalls of capitalism undoubtedly affect the way democracies function. This is particularly true of stock markets and the ways in which public services are funded. We look in detail at the relationship between democracy and capital. Shrinking the state was the theme of the past forty years, but the problems caused by this require investigation. We have seen a battle fought out since the Second World War between mutuality and the markets. Each has been a 35-year tide, first flowing one way, then ebbing back again.

We examine the most effective way to support people and communities and how growing expectations might be met from dwindling coffers.

Chapter 10 is entitled 'What *Is* Britain?' because the country is so much more than what it does. You can't 'do' trusted; you can only *be* trusted. Integrity, sacrifice, honesty, modesty, loyalty, humour, compassion, generosity, love, courage and defiance are core British qualities. Britain believes in fairness. This means that as individuals or a nation state, the wealthiest should help the poorest. This is the bond of mutuality. Britain cares for its environment, whether it be the preservation of woodland or the global climate. Britain is suspicious of narrow self-interest. There are more important things than money, such as honouring those who serve communities. This is especially the case with the military, who can be called upon to defend both our markets and our mandate. They stand ready to defend us while we sleep, while we read and write books like this.

Finally, we look at what Britain means. In a new age, post-financial crisis, post-EU, post-pandemic, there is an opportunity for modernisation and new ideas in Britain that could spread around the world. This opportunity might not recur for another generation. A world darkened by fear and autocracy needs trust and leadership. Who will defend capitalism and democracy? America is a great ally and both countries should show the courage to defend human rights, democracy and free speech. These are systems that create the necessary conditions where humanity can be fully grown.

Britain's democracy is beautiful and simple and complex and timeless and fragile and frustrating and confusing and paradoxical. But through every storm, for the best part of a thousand years, it has demonstrated its durability. Will we celebrate this anniversary? Of course not. It's just not who we are.

Notwithstanding all of Britain's problems, in this ancient way of thinking, in this even older land, in this independent attitude, in this deep compassion, there remains something mysterious and precious about this place. So very much has changed, but the idea of Britain endures, waiting for each new generation to discover and reinvent it.

Penny Mordaunt and Chris Lewis
April 2021

PART ONE

US

1

WHO ARE WE?

The political polemicist Roger Scruton was that most typically British of things: Marmite. A philosopher and born controversialist, he loved to be hated by the left as much as he hated to be loved by the right. Whatever you thought of him, though, he really did his homework. In one of his numerous books, *England: An Elegy*, he depicted the UK as a lost country disappearing into a dystopian future.[1]

Divisive though he was, Scruton was right, but only because the future has *always* been dystopian. From Fritz Lang's *Metropolis* and Mary Shelley's *Frankenstein* to *Westworld* and *The Stepford Wives*, the future is endlessly frightening. It holds fears for all of us. We will get old and die in that future. Who's looking forward to that? It's tragic, but in typically British style, it's also comic. In David Renwick's sitcom *One Foot in the Grave*, the lead character is Victor Meldrew, who has taken involuntary early retirement. The series focuses on his hapless misunderstandings and misadventures, often as he tries to deal with the new. He has found all of life's big answers. The problem is, nobody ever asks him a question.

Britain is suspicious about change. It likes tried and tested. It likes incremental. Why? Because successful change is seldom radical. It's gradual. The British prefer a future that looks very much like the past, only a lot better.

Roger Scruton was right about something else, too. A type of Britain *is* disappearing from view – but that's only because a country is *always* disappearing from view. A country is its people. And those people are constantly disappearing; like Scruton, for instance. Was Scruton right; is there such a thing as the British character? And, if so, how has it changed since his time? You could compile an enormous great *British Book of Myths* about this, but there are universal traits exhibited by the British. Let's look at some.

THE BRITISH LOVE 'OLD'

Nostalgia is big business in the UK. Pandemic permitting, the Goodwood Revival, held in September every year, is the perfect illustration. It's an Indian Summer event for those in their own Indian Summer. Fifty thousand nostalgics descend on the motor-racing circuit and aerodrome in Sussex for three days of in vitro retro. Everything from Aermacchi to Zagato. There are desmodromic valves and bucket shim tappets. There's lookie-likie Birkin, Faithfull, Shrimpton and Twiggy. In the 1960s, everything shrank – the cars, the clothes, the computers, the comedians,[2] the currency,[3] even the Commonwealth. Monroe was out and the Mini was 'in' – skirt, car, calculator, van, bus, roundabout. Everything went mini-mad. The atmosphere at this annual event is part Woodstock, part car-boot sale and part *The Good Old Days*. Everyone dresses as their grandparents, even their grandparents' grandparents. There is contempt for the contemporary.

The Revival is quintessentially British. The truth is, though, it's not real at all. It's a memory. It's not the real past. It's the past confectioned, redacted and redux. The present is infinitely, unrecognisably, incomprehensibly better than the reality of the past. There's no rationed, crap, greasy food. No pint of sludge, Ted. No Vesta Chow Mein. No Mateus Rosé. No Austin Princess. No penneth of chips. No early closing Wednesday. No job demarcation. No Spanish customs. No diabolical liberties. No pea-soupers. No bomb sites. No jumble sale. No rag-and-bone man. No slums. No TB. No emphysema. No ringworm. No polio. No nutty slack. No pneumoconiosis. No all-day dusk. No nit nurse. No iron lungs. No leg irons. No greyed-out national health glasses. No Spastics Society orthopaedic-girl piggy banks. No sweet cigarettes (presumably providing Type II diabetes until you're old enough to get bronchitis from the real thing). No Green Shield Stamps. No muddy goalmouths. No Billy Bremner. No 'Chopper' Harris. No Tommy Smith. No 'get a reducer in early doors'. No pissing in someone's pocket with a rolled-up match-day programme. No Millwall Brick. No ICF. No Mick McManus. No Larry Grayson. No Arthur Askey. No Aberfan. No *Torrey Canyon*. No national service. No ''ands off cocks; on socks'. No 'get some in'. No corporal punishment. No bogus Majors. No *Merchant* class (wine, bank, scrap, tailor, navy). No Borstal. No body odour. No accusations of wearing 'poof juice' (aftershave). No male cosmetics of any kind. No bath once a week whether you need it or not. No snotty sleeves. No skid marks. No priapic priests. No Catholic guilt. No 'fallen' women. No 'Loony Bin'. No rhythm method. No Kotex Wonderform menstruation belts. No circle-stitched bras. No imminent threat of nuclear death. No Black Panther. No Moors murderers. No Yorkshire Ripper. No Ruth Ellis. No Reg Christie. No Timothy Evans. No 'He slipped on the way to the cell, sarge'. No Kray Twins. No bent coppers. No Bakelite handles. No 'I can't speak now, the pips have gone'. No 405- or 625-line TVs. No 'wait for it to warm up'. No 'pink' paraffin heaters. No two-bar electric 'log-effect' fires. No Baby Belling cookers. No hand-me-downs. No gabardine raincoats. No knit-one, purl-one. No 'have fun'. No 'join in'. No 'Paki-bashing'. No Black and White Minstrels. No winceyette pyjamas. No 'he knocks me about a bit when 'e's 'ad a few, but 'e loves me really'. No hire purchase. No 'never-never'. No streets full of dog shit. No coal in the bath. No off-licence. No St Bruno 'ready rubbed' that smelled like smouldering socks. No White Horse liniment oil. No BBC RP. No Muffin the Mule. No 'wait till we're married'. No cop a feel. No *heavy* petting. No *Saturday Night and Sunday Morning*. No 'If you *really* loved me, you'd let me'. No 'something for the weekend, sir'? No predatory history teachers on the qui vive in the changing rooms. No coat-hanger back-street abortions. No maiden aunts. No antimacassars. No Palais de Danse. No 'she's had it all taken away down below' and silent pointing. No terry-towelling nappies. No farty lodger. Thank Christ it's over. Some of us were there and remain so today. It's not a swansong this needs, it's a celebration.

Of course, we still feel the legacy of the past in our dental care, drinking habits, pub opening times, football racism, casual violence, 'We're closed' signs, 'That's not on the menu', motorway 'services' and endless your-call-is-important-to-us-customer-care-Vivaldi-induced-on-hold rage. Notwithstanding Covid, life is immeasurably, inconceivably, incomparably, quantum-leap better than in the decades before it. Maybe now, we'll appreciate it a little more.

Why do the British indulge in nostalgia? Because the past is the place to escape to when faced with itchy uncertainty. The Goodwood Revival is thus an amalgam of old and young fogeys. Sweet bird of youth meets the Owl of Minerva. No wonder the *Daily Telegraph* sponsors it. For all its twitchy net curtain, tartan, tweed and thermoses, it's an important political descant, socially, culturally, economically and arthritically.

It may be the case that the younger voices dominate the obloquy, but the older ones decide the country's future. They turn out. There are loads of them as a result of the post-war existential-survival baby boom. And they don't like revolutions. They don't want the future to be futuristic. They want it to be previous. They want it set in a place called St Broadband-on-Poundbury.

The British capacity for reinventing the past is literally the stuff of legend. For instance, you would've thought the British had enough ancient ruins, but 'new' ones remain in high demand. The Abbey Gothic Garden Ruin Kit[4] (yes, really) costs £2,682 and you, too, can fulfil your desire for ruins. It's the Jacob Rees-Mogg of garden ornaments; an artifice of antiquity.[5] The automotive equivalent is the black cab or the big red London bus. It looks like the past, only better and more modern.

You can still wear a top hat in the back of an all-electric, battery-powered, zero-emissions, air-conditioned black cab, if you choose. Even London cabbies are endearingly traditional, largely unchanged from the Mk I Sid James model featured in *Carry On Cabby* (Slogan: It's What's Up Front That Counts), a parable of women making their way in the workplace in the early 1960s. The cabs in this classic film are of clearly recognisable lineage. Sid James plays Charlie Hawkins, and his boys go everywhere in their old Austin FX3s to flutes, violins, harmonicas and the odd upward glissando on the slide whistle. His overweight wife Peggy Hawkins, played by Hattie Jacques, goes everywhere accompanied by a bass tuba. Her undercover competitor 'Glamcabs', with the more modern Cortina Mk Is, are, of course, propelled by muted trumpets, saxophones and swing brass, thus proving that sounds can be sexist, too. Needless to say, the Goodwood Revival features a concours collection of Mrs Glam's Glamcabs and they're hugely popular.

Our taste for historical revivalism is also upheld in British road signs and markings, for example. The trains have changed, yet the sign remains.

Source: https://www.gov.uk/guidance/traffic-sign-images
Open Government Licence (OGL) image licensed under the Open Government Licence v3.0.
(http://www.nationalarchives.gov.uk/doc/open-government-license/version/3/)

Even one of our most modern signs, the speed camera, is depicted with what appears to be a Box Brownie c.1920.

Source: https://www.gov.uk/guidance/traffic-sign-images
Open Government Licence (OGL) image licensed under the Open Government Licence v3.0.
(http://www.nationalarchives.gov.uk/doc/open-government-license/version/3/)

Like rugby, we run forward into the future, passing the ball backwards. And then there are the red telephone boxes. And red pillar boxes. And the Tube map. And mock Tudor buildings. And walnut dashboards, hunting pink, beer taps, horse brasses, wooden beams, recessed-button sofas, flat caps and Parker pens. Every pair of stilettos, every rustically packaged food product and absolutely every pub.

BOOZING

Have you ever been in a 'new' one? Pubs are worth a special mention, because Covid stopped the beating heart of the community. The British pub is one of the most reliable pieces of transport infrastructure in the country. In fact, the British pub is the *only* reliable piece of transport infrastructure in the country. Beer is a transformative, ancient trick. It confers temporary mythical power, a brief substitution of logic for haptic. And there'll be another one along in just a moment. Is it any surprise that the British have a reputation for their love of alcohol? Everything is funnier and everyone more attractive with beer goggles on. And pubs themselves have Einsteinian qualities; they slow down time then accelerate it again – specifically time of the opening and closing varieties. Most of all, though, they return the British to themselves. No one exits a pub in the same state of mind that they entered.

Jonathan Meades is a sort of human Geiger counter for bollocks. He has pointed out that newness is a type of heresy in the pub trade, especially for premium beers. There's Old Peculier, Old Bircham, Old Luxters, Old Jones, Owd Rodger, Old Devil, Old Growler, Old Smokey, Old Bill, Old Speckled Hen, Old Jock, Old Bushy Tail, Old Masters, Old Maidstone, Old Lubrication, Old Tom, Owd Tom, Old Hooky, Old Strong, Old Horizontal, Olde Suffolk, Old Stock, Old Brown Dog (really), Old Navigation, Old Curmudgeon, Old Thumper, even the presciently named Old Fart.[6]

It's also a sign of celebrity to be known by your name in your local pub. In an American bar, only the drinks are the celebrities. A Cuba Libre summons the image of Al Pacino and his 'lil friend', for instance; in Britain, it's a rum and coke. In America, a screwdriver is a cocktail worthy of Bogart and Bacall; in Britain, a vodka and orange. In America, it's 'up', and all that suggests; in Britain, it's 'neat', as in stationery organiser. In the UK, booze is nowhere near as glamorous. It's habitual, ipso facto dipso. Anyone seeking to understand the difference between America and Britain can find it right here. In America, there are 62,000 bars[7] and 384,000 churches.[8] It's a ratio of more than six to one in favour of churches. In Britain, there are 47,000 pubs[9] and 16,000 churches.[10] It's a ratio of almost three to one in favour of pubs. If that's not a source of national pride, nothing is.

The British turn to drink more often than they do to divinity. It's just more reliable. And they live longer than Americans as a result.[11] Then again, maybe it just seems longer.

SAYING SORRY

The British also have an obsession with apologising. This is an endless source of amusement for Americans.[12] We're aware of it ourselves, and there's even a UK website that tracks the number of times train companies apologise: sorryfortheinconvenience.co.uk. (Southwest Trains apologised 11,000 times in the first nine months of 2020.) Regular users of the Portsmouth-to-Waterloo 'service' will realise this is nowhere near enough.

According to a 2015 poll from YouGov, the British say 'sorry' a lot more than Americans, but not as an apology – for situations like getting past someone in the way, correcting someone who is wrong, or sneezing in the presence of others.[13]

What the Americans don't understand is that there are literally dozens of meanings of the word sorry when used by the British. It can mean 'pay attention'. It can mean 'no'. It can mean 'oops'. It can mean 'excuse me'. It can mean 'I'm interrupting you'. It can mean 'hello'. It can mean 'I can't help you there, mate'. It can mean 'I don't agree'. It can mean 'I didn't mean to do that but I'd do it again'. It can mean 'I didn't hear you'. It can mean 'I can't do that'. It can mean 'my mistake'. The social scientist Kate Fox, author of *Watching the English: The Hidden Rules of English Behaviour*, decided that if she really wanted to understand the English national character, she would have to do the research.[14] She spent a great deal of time deliberately bumping into people at railway stations. Despite her deliberate rudeness, more often than not she was the one who received an apology. The British commuter has a season ticket to sorry.

RECYCLING (AGAIN)

The golden age of nostalgia and unconscious austerity was the 1960s to the 1990s. It was a sort of sticky-backed British *trente glorieuses* for crap. *Blue Peter*, the longest-running children's TV show in the world, was famous for making stuff out of rubbish: a washing-up liquid bottle, some leftover wool, a cotton reel and toilet roll tube. With this, you could make an animal that looked nothing like your TV favourite. America had commercial merchandising to accompany children's shows like *Sesame Street*; British children preferred to make their toys out of what Americans called garbage.

In a particularly dark moment in 1965, Christopher Trace demonstrated how to make an Advent crown.[15] (There was no 'Happy Holidays' stuff then. It was the BBC of E.) To construct this masterpiece, Trace used tinsel, two coat hangers, some bottle tops and candles. The result was lethal. If the child did not manage to self-harm, self-puncture or self-immolate, the result was a merry adornment in the run-up to Christmas. The idea was to light one candle a week. The concept of a risk assessment never occurred to them. The tinsel was highly flammable for one thing, and that's before you even consider that the crown dropped hot wax onto the head of its owner, the whole rig becoming more and more lop-sided every day a new candle was lit. It was a class-action lawsuit waiting to happen.

It culminated in 1993 with Anthea Turner making a model of Thunderbirds' Tracy Island out of old newspapers (*The Guardian*, natch), some flour, a discarded box of 'soft cheese' (Philly with the name taped over), a crisp tube (thinly disguised Pringles) and, yes, another toilet roll tube. This was all before BBC Enterprises and its branding baksheesh.

The golden age of papier mâché came to an end on 9 September 1995 when Sony launched PlayStation in the UK. So central, however, was the obsession with recycling to the national psyche that in 2010, Procter & Gamble brought back the original washing-up liquid bottle, after it had been retired in 2000, to celebrate the brand's fiftieth anniversary. A spokesperson explained, 'The bottle became an essential part of any child's make-and-do kit. Now children who weren't around when the bottle was on the shelves have got their own chance to get inventive.'[16] A generation in America was constructing real space shuttles with NASA – another one in Britain was skip diving.

This obsession with garbage spawned another low-budget children's show: *The Wombles*. This programme concerned a gang of burrowing bear-like creatures who lived in suburban London, like real bears don't. They spent their time obsessively picking up rubbish and making it into furniture for their underground home. Had it been real, this would actually have been a useful public service.

The union-controlled 'binmen' of the time were on strike along with everyone else and the Wombles were probably the only sanitary option available. The Wombles made the big time following the popularity of the more wholesome Paddington Bear, who by then had turned into a merch superstar. The Wombles went one better, though, spawning a pop group of man-bears that featured what would later become the whizzed-up, greased-down, soft-rock, hard-man Chris Spedding, of *Motorbikin'* fame, on lead guitar. His career spanned Jack Bruce, Roxy Music, Dusty Springfield, the Sex Pistols and, eventually no doubt, an answer in an *Only Connect*[17] sequence.

By the mid-'70s, with the three-day week, endless strikes, power cuts, the failure of British Leyland, top-rate taxes of 98 per cent and the International Monetary Fund (IMF) bailout, many Brits wanted to drop out of the 'rat race' completely. The result was Esmonde and Larbey's sitcom *The Good Life*. It was a twee suburban insurrection of a professionally trained draughtsman and 'his housewife' deciding to abandon traditional life and live off the land. It became emblematic of a type of native dogma, perhaps the closest the British would ever get to revolution – a sort of BBC version of the *Battleship Potemkin*, without the mutiny, maggots or Mensheviks.

The theme, though, once again, was self-sufficiency through recycling. The stars of the show represented quintessentially British characters of the time. Tom Good was by turns depressive and cheerful – what you'd get by mating Arthur Askey with Tony Hancock. His wife Barbara, played by Felicity Kendal, was at the time considered the 'perfect' wife: she was wellington-booted, cheerful, supportive, practical, protective and attractive.

To add some drama to the comedy, Tom Good's neighbour, Jerry Leadbetter, was a scheming, intelligent, corporate executive who had risen to senior management through cunning and self-promotion rather than talent. He was married to a socially ambitious wife, Margo, who was an obsessive suburban snob. The snob is a favourite in British comedy: this sort of priggish British character is so embedded in our national consciousness that Chaucer and Shakespeare would have recognised it.

This nostalgic focus on a time gone by continued in the BBC's light entertainment output, with sitcoms set in what was even then considered to be a 'better' past. These now 'classic' shows were churned out by two of the most prolific comic writers in British history, David Croft and Jimmy Perry, who created *Dad's Army*, *Hi-de-Hi* and their embarrassing Bertha Rochester, still locked in the BBC's secret attic, *It Ain't Half Hot, Mum*. This featured a full-house bingo card of what is now known as casual racism, homophobia, white privilege, colonialism, transphobia, bullying, misogyny and sexual harassment.

This 'the past was so much better' theme was also notably reflected in films, by David Lean's *Great Expectations*, *Lawrence of Arabia* and *This Happy Breed*, the latter featuring Frank Gibbons's pithy observation: 'What works in other countries won't work in this one. We've got our own way of settling things. It may be a bit slow and it may be a bit dull … but it suits us all right and always will.'[18] And by Michael Anderson in *The Dam Busters* and *Yangtse Incident* (both stoic, dutiful and self-sacrificing and featuring real wartime para Richard Todd). It should be noted that Anderson's only films about the future were dystopics like *1984*, made in, err, 1956, and *Logan's Run*, made in 1976. The obsession with the past continues on TV today, with *Downton Abbey*, *The Durrells*, *The Last Post*, *Home Fires* and *The Crown* being notable examples of rose-tinted, revisionist, retro-representation.

At the top of the list of TV programmes that symbolised the British phlegmatic approach was proto-consumer rights show of the early '70s *That's Life!* In many ways, it was ahead of its time. It was crowd-sourced, with vox pops and newspaper clippings sent in by the public and presented principally by a woman – unusual at the time. The show took on bureaucracy and companies for poor service and, surprise surprise, there was no shortage of stories.

Everything was government-run back then – British Airways, British Telecom, British Steel, British Rail, British Leyland, the banks, the travel agents, all the utilities. Any organisation that was 'British' was state-run – then a by-word not just for poor but for aggressively stuff-you service. At the time, people waited a minimum of six months for a phone. Everyone was on strike, so customer service was on a wipe-your-nose-on-a-sleeve, take-it-or-leave-it basis. The show had a traditional British sense of humour, though. It featured elderly people whose false teeth fell out, novelty acts, eccentrics, performing animals – most memorably a dog that could say 'sausages'. The smutty humour was there. It laughed at vegetables shaped like breasts, bottoms or penises. It was one of the most popular shows on TV. Why? Because it captured the embarrassment the British had then about complaining and turned it into humour. It was very British.

QUEUES

We queue up at school, in Parliament to vote, at Glastonbury (indeed, all festivals and sports events), at the pub, to get into clubs, to get the latest bargain, at the bank, at the Post Office, on parents' evenings, in A&E, at petrol stations, at cash machines, for changing rooms, on the phone, in fast-food restaurants, in supermarkets, for public toilets, at Hamleys for the latest Christmas gift, outside the royal palaces, for amusement park rides, at football grounds, for the dole, for social housing, even at the crematorium. Covid introduced yet more opportunities to queue offline at 'drive-thru' test centres or online to get on to the Ocado website. It's all tied up with patience, manners, decency, fair play and democracy. That's why the country hated the stockpiling that preceded the pandemic (even as people were doing it themselves). That's why they allow vulnerable people to go ahead of them in supermarkets. There is evidence that the British will spend almost six months of their entire lives queuing up for stuff.[19] In some places, like Wimbledon or for royal weddings, it's even seen as part of the 'fun' to queue outside all night in a tent.

Just about the worst thing you can do in Britain is jump the queue. It's like farting in a lift. Or not buying a round. Or not being friendly to the vicar's dog when it's dry-humping your ankle and its mouth is clamped to your shin. Or criticising the NHS. Or, even worse, Sir David Attenborough. It's instant pariah status. The really weird thing is that 88 per cent of us have admitted to giving up in a queue and going home empty-handed.[20] A quarter of Brits say they hate doing it, yet they keep coming back for more. Why? British people are often shy, well-mannered and modest. There's a long list of things the British never discuss: constipation, sex, depression, relationships, thrush, money, toilets, feelings, seborrhoea, logorrhoea, gonorrhoea, Chris Rea, diarrhoea, duty or death. And they like personal space. During Covid, the World Health Organization only required social distancing to one metre.[21] The British chose two metres. Consequently, all Covid queues were colossal – past Nando's and several times round the car park.[22]

THE DOUBLE ENTENDRE AND EUPHEMISMS

The apologising, the embarrassment about complaining, the use of humour as a palliative are also present in the British approach to sex. Again, embarrassment and humour embrace. The British both recoil from and are magnetically attracted to smutty innuendo. In this, the two most unlikely bedfellows were James Bond and Benny Hill.

In comparison with Bond, Benny Hill was a sort of living Donald McGill seaside postcard. Following a bloodline that goes all the way back to music hall comedy, Hill usually played hapless little men who were responsible for accidentally-on-purpose removing women's clothing (it was funny then). He was also the master of visual innuendo and his sketches contained variants of the following: two bald men forming an image of cleavage, any amount of water jets coming out from groin level, a large selection of vegetable gags (again) and male sidekicks Bob Todd and Jackie Wright dressing as women. As Hill famously never said: 'She wanted a double entendre, so I gave her one.'

In a further example of this very British characteristic of using language to skirt around a subject, why can't the British call their toilets toilets? This is another thing we have really struggled with over the years, especially in the suburbs. The alternatives include going to the: smallest room in the house, little boys'/little girls' room, bog, throne, khazi, loo, lavatory, old house down the lane, ladies' room/men's room, restroom, 'the facilities' and plain old WC.

The act of going to the toilet is similarly euphemised: we spend a penny, go for a wee/pee, take a slash, pass water, drain the spuds, water the horses, go for a waz, splash our clogs, shake hands with the unemployed, go to see a man about a dog, take a pit stop, get caught short, inspect the plumbing/porcelain, syphon the python or point Percy. The British are so embarrassed about bodily functions that only humour permits any form of reference.

PLUCKY BRITS

Sometimes being British is difficult to explain. Failure is not good, but magnificent failure is brilliant. Here, plucky is the usual term applied to losers who persist in the face of overwhelming odds or multiple cock-ups. Think: the Black Knight in Monty Python's *Holy Grail*. Scott of the Antarctic. George Mallory on Everest. The Charge of the Light Brigade. Dunkirk. The Somme. Gallipoli. Pretty much any battle in the First World War. Gordon of Khartoum. Isandlwana. The *Titanic*. Frank Spencer.[23] Eddie 'The Eagle' Edwards, whose main achievement was to avoid being maimed.

Edwards was a real-life Norman Wisdom. He learned to ski jump by borrowing other people's equipment (he had to wear six pairs of socks to make his boots fit) and he was the only Brit to compete in the 1988 Winter Olympics ski jump, the first to do so for sixty years. And despite breaking the British record, he came last.

The attention Edwards received so embarrassed the ski jumping establishment that in 1990 the entry requirements were tightened to make it impossible for anyone to follow his example. Ski jumping is serious, after all, and we can't have anyone taking the piss. Speed skating isn't funny either, and nor is curling, nor the luge, which basically involves hurtling down a frozen mountain toes-first on a tea tray. In 2016, Eddie the Eagle's story was told in a feature film starring Taron Egerton. It made £35 million and cost £17 million to make, and was rated excellent by an international audience.[24] In Britain, magnificent failure can be a huge success.

The plucky Brit is also a recurring theme in both film and TV, all the way from Willie Mossop in David Lean's *Hobson's Choice*, via every Norman Wisdom film, to Henry Palfrey in *School for Scoundrels* and Richard Lester's *The Mouse on the Moon*. Then there's the

BBC's *Doctor Who* and Del Boy in *Only Fools and Horses* and Wallace of *Wallace and Gromit*.

Explaining Norman Wisdom is a challenge in the third decade of the twenty-first century. His usual role was that of a well-meaning but excitable man-child to whom everything bad happened. Perhaps a comparison would help here? In America in 1966, they were making films like *Riot on Sunset Strip*, about how LSD led to gang rape among youths. At the same time, the British response was to administer the drug to Wisdom in *The Early Bird*. His milkman character Pitkin works for Grimsdale's, a small family firm up against the might of evil empire Consolidated Dairies. It is trying to strong-arm Pitkin off his patch with its 'new-fangled' milk floats. Grimsdale's cart is drawn by Nellie. Seeing an opportunity for sabotage, they lace Nellie's Pippins with LSD. Pitkin and Mr Grimsdale eat them by mistake and the whole affair culminates in the two of them going off on one. The former is later discovered sleeping next to Nellie. This isn't helping, is it? Well, needless to say, Consolidated Dairies – and their condescending chief executive played by Jerry Desmonde – is later destroyed by Pitkin in an act of what would today be called wilful arson. Obviously.

British favourite comic heroes have in common that they are determined, cheerful, innocent, hopelessly ill-equipped, ingenious and thrifty. They are underdogs up against some kind of threat from authority or adversity. (And speaking of dogs, they often have a more intelligent canine sidekick, like *Blue Peter*'s John Noakes with Shep, Doctor Who with K9 or Wallace with Gromit.)

Only Fools and Horses featured perhaps the most popular and durable of plucky Brits. Again, it's difficult to explain Del Boy's get-rich-quick schemes. They involved everything from promoting singers who couldn't pronounce their 'r's to dealing in second-hand satellite dishes and exploding blow-up sex dolls.

Not to be confined to Earth, plucky Brits spread into space. In *The Mouse on the Moon*, the Duchy of Grand Fenwick (an obviously British government headed by Margaret Rutherford – a sort of prototype Ann Widdecombe) embarks on a race to the moon. Bernard Cribbins (Vincent Mountjoy) teams up with David Kossoff playing the questionably named Professor Kokintz. With superior but old-fashioned technology, Mountjoy and Kokintz (hmm) beat the Americans and Russians to the moon, rescuing the former and bringing them back to earth safely.

For his part, Doctor Who, a sort of DIY enthusiast from the future armed with a sonic screwdriver, was always ably assisted by yet another plucky Brit. Brigadier Lethbridge-Stewart was a moustachioed officer who commanded the British Army contingent of UNIT (United Nations Intelligence Taskforce), an international organisation that defended the earth from alien threats. When faced with alien invasion, his men could be relied upon to die valiantly while confronting the high-tech ray guns and impervious space craft with Series II Land Rovers and short Lee–Enfield rifles. However, a more typical mission was to investigate reports of a yeti in the London Underground. No, really.

The Doctor's other habitual nuisance was the Daleks. BBC budget restrictions mandated that his arch enemy was a sort of aggressive, home-made, speech-defective wheelie bin adorned with car-parking lights and armed with a sink plunger and an egg whisk that could render you 'exterminated'. (Indeed, in leaked blueprints, Raymond Cusick's design for the original Dalek[25] reveals the total cost was, even then, a very reasonable £15.) The main way to avoid being omeletted by these most high-tech of villains, it seemed, was to run up some stairs. There are no stair lifts on Skaro. This anomaly was finally addressed in 1988 when the creatures were given the power to levitate, apparently through some form of unexplained Dalek flatulence.

Some more plucky Brits in outer space were the BBC's *Blake's 7*. That programme fared little better on budget restrictions. Here, political dissident Roj Blake commands a group – from what appeared to be a socialist clique in north London – rebelling against the forces of the totalitarian Terran Federation, which rules the earth. Avon, the character played by Paul Darrow, delivered his lines like Richard Burton with all the happy, self-effacing, easy-going cheerfulness squeezed out. No doubt, this was done to distinguish Avon from the amiable, door-to-door cosmetic sales personnel of the time. And as for the rest of the over-permed, over-acting, bolshy crew, they spent as much time fighting themselves as they did their spectacularly touchy ship-board computer, Orac, a sort of earlier, more cynical version of Apple's Siri. *Blake's 7* was so bad it was good. Critic Clive James described it as 'classically awful'. In the *Daily Telegraph*, Tim Stanley described the show's spaceship, the *Liberator*, as a cross between Star Trek's *Enterprise* and the ever-popular, mallard-based khazi cleaner, Toilet Duck.[26]

THE HOPE THAT SPRINGS ETERNAL

Plucky Brits always bring the prospect of hope, and this is important in Britain. It's ever-present in British sporting tournaments. Many of the most famous FA Cup moments, for instance, are acts of so-called Giant Killing. This can refer to any lower-league side beating a 'better' team. Thus a dream came true when the plucky Leicester won the Premier League in 2016. Not Liverpool. Not Manchester United. Not Arsenal. Leicester, who had come up from the Championship two years before.

The British belief in the underdog is what powers schemes like the National Lottery and the football pools. The idea that the lowly can win is enduring and powerful not necessarily for how often it occurs but because it happens at all. And, really, our belief in the underdog makes sense; the real miracles are part of our history. See: Agincourt, Drake and the Armada, Waterloo, the Battle of Britain and the Falklands War. Maybe you wouldn't bet on Britain, but it came through in the end.

THE BRITISH DO COMPLICATED

The British love complicated rules and protocol. The terms of etiquette in Britain are difficult to explain. There is no rule book, so some of the basics are here. It is complicated:

- The British don't leave a pub without buying a round.
- The British don't order at the bar if someone else is waiting and got there first.
- The British always say please and thank you (often several times in one transaction).
- If the British complain, they say sorry first.
- The British hold up a hand if someone lets them into the traffic line. And they expect it back if they let someone else in.
- The British pedestrian thanks drivers for stopping on a Zebra crossing, even though they have right of way.
- The British always say sorry if they bump into someone, even if it is an inanimate object.
- The British always say excuse me when approaching a stranger.
- Before the pandemic, the British would shake someone's hand for just the right amount of time and with exactly the right pressure.
- The British always offer to pay half.

- The British don't make eye contact or talk on the Tube.
- The British always hold the door open for the person behind them.
- The British still offer their seat to an elderly/pregnant/disabled person on the bus.

Anyone breaking these rules can expect to disappear into a vast, steaming fissure of social opprobrium. And if you thought all that was complicated, here is an extract from the rules of croquet:

If a ball goes through a hoop in the wrong direction, it cannot run that hoop until the ball has passed fully through the hoop in the wrong direction. Alternatively, it can go around the hoop and enter it from the correct side. Once a ball has gone through the final, 'rover', hoop, the ball is a 'rover'. It is usually best not to peg out immediately but to leave the ball 'roving' so that it can be used to assist the partner ball to finish. The game is won when both balls have pegged out. Even moderately skilful players can peg out both balls in one turn.

And this is the offside rule, as explained by the Football Association:

A player in an offside position at the moment the ball is played or touched by a team-mate is only penalised on becoming involved in active play by: interfering with play by playing or touching a ball passed or touched by a team-mate or interfering with an opponent by: preventing an opponent from playing or being able to play the ball by clearly obstructing the opponent's line of vision or challenging an opponent for the ball or clearly attempting to play a ball which is close when this action impacts on an opponent or making an obvious action which clearly impacts on the ability of an opponent to play the ball…

In situations where: a player moving from, or standing in, an offside position is in the way of an opponent and interferes with the movement of the opponent towards the ball this is an offside offence if it impacts on the ability of the opponent to play or challenge for the ball; if the player moves into the way of an opponent and impedes the opponent's progress (e.g. blocks the opponent) the offence should be penalised under Law 12; a player in an offside position is moving towards the ball with the intention of playing the ball and is fouled before playing or attempting to play the ball, or challenging an opponent for the ball, the foul is penalised as it has occurred before the offside offence; an offence is committed against a player in an offside position who is already playing or attempting to play the ball, or challenging an opponent for the ball, the offside offence is penalised as it has occurred before the foul challenge.[27]

Cricket is simple in comparison. There are only eleven ways of being out: Bowled, Caught, Stumped, Hit the ball twice, Hit wicket, Obstructing the field, Timed out, Leg before wicket (LBW), Handled the ball, Run out and Retired.

Still, calculating the target score in a limited-overs match is a little more complicated:

The Duckworth–Lewis–Stern method (DLS) is a mathematical formulation designed to calculate the target score for the team batting second in a limited-overs cricket match interrupted by weather or other circumstances. The method was devised by two English statisticians, Frank Duckworth and Tony Lewis. It was formerly known as the Duckworth–Lewis method. It was introduced in 1997 and adopted officially by the ICC in 1999. After the retirements of Duckworth and Lewis, Professor Steven Stern became the custodian of the method and it was renamed to its current title in November 2014. When overs are lost, setting an adjusted target for the team batting second is not as simple as reducing the run target proportionally to the loss in overs, because a team with ten wickets in hand and twenty-five overs to bat can play more aggressively than if they had ten wickets and a full fifty overs, for example, and can consequently achieve a higher run rate. The DLS method is an attempt to set a statistically fair target for the second team's innings, which is the same difficulty as the original target. The basic principle is that each team in a limited-overs match has two resources available with which to score runs (overs to play and wickets remaining), and the target is adjusted proportionally to the change in the combination of these two resources.

Much more important than cricket, Parliament itself is no less complicated in its rules and procedures. Erskine May's treatise on the law, privileges, proceedings and usage of Parliament was first published in 1844. Now available online and in its twenty-fifth edition, it contains forty-five chapters and a hardback copy runs to over 1,000 pages. Why the extent and resulting precision? Because the British are sticklers for the rules. Without rules, there can be no fairness. Especially for people who write them.

Some have made our complicated rules into a living. According to the TaxPayers' Alliance, the size of *Tolley's Tax Guide*, the publication explaining the tax codes, has increased greatly over the past two decades. Its corporation tax guide is now 1,897 pages long, more than double the length it was in 1999/2000. Its income tax guide is now 1,801 pages long, 54 per cent longer than it was in 1999/2000. And, not to be outdone, its inheritance tax guide is now 958 pages long, 63 per cent longer than it was in 2001/2002.[28]

We will complicate and bureaucratise things to a point where it's impossible for anyone to make it happen. Prohibition is too draconian, so we complicate it as a prophylactic.

THE BRITISH HATE NEW, THEN THEY LOVE IT

British psychology is strange sometimes. New things can be resisted, then hated and then loved. Take the London Eye, for instance. Higher than Big Ben and St Paul's Cathedral, it was the largest Ferris wheel in the world until 2006, when a bigger one was built in China. It was opened on 31 December 1999 and was supposed to be demolished five years later. It now receives around 3.5 million visitors a year, its familiar image has become representative of Britain and it is the site of London's annual New Year firework display.[29]

When it was posited that the wheel should remain in place, not everyone supported the idea. In March 2002, in a piece entitled 'Pull Down the London Eye', Giles Worsley, the *Daily Telegraph*'s architecture critic, argued that

> to make the London Eye permanent would be to undermine the transience – a quality we find increasingly hard to value, at least in buildings – that made the idea so appealing in the first place. It would also devalue the planning system ... the London Eye is, ultimately, a giant fairground attraction dropped into the centre of London. Like a great cuckoo in the nest, it distorts and devalues everything around it. It is inescapable in key views of

London, especially from the Royal Parks, and above all, it reduces the Palace of Westminster, the symbol of British parliamentary democracy, to insignificance ... The way the London Eye seems gently to mock the Palace of Westminster could be read as a symbol of the growing irrelevance of the Houses of Parliament...[30]

Ultimately, though, he said, 'If there is one thing the English hate more than a new building going up, it is the idea, once they have got used to it, that it might come down.' Now, the Eye is London's number-one tourist attraction. Five thousand people have even become engaged on it.

FRUGALITY

Perhaps the defining quality of British people is that of frugality, and this increases with distance from London. The British are used to doing more with less. Despite the fact that they're frugal, they are also generous and cooperative in helping each other. One of the most rec- ognisable features of post-war life in terraced houses was neighbours borrowing from each other. That still happens today, believe it or not.[31]

This leads to another stand-out quality found in British people: a kind of improvised creativity made all the more inspirational by its modest provenance. The British are incredibly inventive, be that with rubbish, euphemisms, innuendo, engineering, food, trans- port, humour, entertainment, games or stories. The stories that sometimes do the rounds of British people inventing things in their sheds are endless.

There's also an instinct for fairness, backing the little guy against the system because they strive and they struggle. They display the right stuff. Ranged against superior forces, there's also an implicit suggestion, they might win. Leonidas confronting the wealth and power of Persia.

Closely related to this is the belief that might is not always right and that just because you've got money and resources you don't always get the right outcome. This is at the root of pluckiness. Not every problem can be solved just by throwing money at it. There has to be a will to change.

Powerful, wealthy forces are also inherently weakened by the fact that they have something to lose. They are more political and less unified. Thus, a small, disciplined force with self-belief can defeat superior resources, wealth and entitlement. As we've discussed, the lesson is important because all progress starts in a minority group.

It's peculiarly British given the rights of individuals that have existed since Magna Carta. After the Great Fire of London, Christopher Wren wanted to build open boulevards all pointing to St Paul's. The land-owning rights in Magna Carta stopped this *grand projet*. This attitude exists today and frustrates new airports, motorways and train lines. The British hold the rights of the individual high.

The British respect fair play. It is better to lose as an amateur and do the right thing than to win with professional or learned skills. In *School for Scoundrels*, for instance, Henry Palfrey is (he thinks) outmanoeuvred for his girl by cad Raymond Delauney. The latter has all the impressive moves, but Palfrey finds out that he has learned them. Once Palfrey has learned the skills, he finds they work and he has got the object of his affection where he wants her. Right at that moment, Palfrey has an epiphany and confesses. He wins the girl and the moral is that an honest man playing by the rules will always win. It is the idea of the gentleman's superiority to the player. Or the Cavalier's superiority over the Roundhead. It is quintessentially British and seen in every walk of life and every profession.

CONCLUSIONS

It is a challenge to highlight the British character, because it's paradoxical. It's frugal but generous. It's traditional yet modern. It's serious but has a sense of humour. It values fairness but lives with inequality. It's sober but loves a drink. It changes fast but doesn't like revolution. The British know what works and what doesn't, after all, and don't go looking to change what they don't think is broken. The British have a love of the familiar and a scepticism of the new-fangled.

From the neo-classical to the neo-gothic, the British just don't like anything new. They never did. They like evolution; they like nostalgic 'old'; they like an organic, gradual movement from one era to the next. The impact? Creating architecture in Britain is like trying to harmonise a brass band with Brahms or Beethoven.

British values are a matter of character. They can be summarised as a 'crown' of values.

THE BRITISH CHARACTER

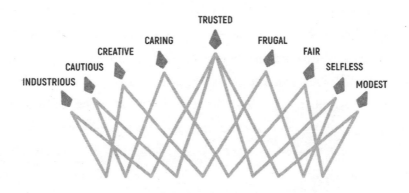

We like what we had before, only better than it actually was. When Nigel Farage, tweed-clad, gripping fags and beer, won some fans and influence in the early part of the 2010s, he channelled 'bogus Major' to an older generation. What he failed to achieve with personal appeal, nonetheless, had widespread effect. He secured a referendum. Huge efforts were made by MPs to ensure he and his networks did not run the Leave campaign. Had he done so, it would have surely lost.

Despite our cutting-edge science and technology, culturally the British have never much cared for the future. The new Globe theatre looks exactly like the old one. The British are the world's best cultural recyclers in fashion, architecture, music and newspaper stories.

Britons cheer for the underdog and are on the side of the little guy against the system; they love someone who keeps trying no matter how hopeless it seems.

Brits care about each other and do more with less. The British attitude is frugal and has been intrinsically recycling-minded for a long time with their culture and love for a time gone by. Latterly, this has been turned towards saving the planet. The British are, on the whole, tolerant and judge people by who they are (for more on this see Chapter 8).

Perhaps most importantly, British people laugh at themselves. Being British is, above all, about having a sense of humour. Paradoxically, it's something that's taken very seriously indeed. It indicates judgement, timing, intelligence, confidence and shows whether the person will be relaxed, a good colleague, friend or partner. The British have had much to put up with in the past, but a sense of humour has always helped. Even if it is innuendo and toilet-based.

2

WHAT ARE WE GOOD AT?

So, we now have a sense of the British character. There are so many myths, even among the British, about what we're good at. In this chapter, those beliefs are examined and compared to reality. We turn to a panel of both British nationals and others from around the world. What do they think Britain is good at? What, if anything, does Britain stand for? More than just character, what defines the country?

For each theme the panel raises, we examine the facts. We look at where Britain scores on international indices and what those nations that score higher are doing differently. We look at the performance of UK plc and the challenges it faces to improve the quality of life for its citizens and how well it lives up to those values the public holds dear. Finally, we look at what matters to the British people themselves. What do they care about most? What do they want their leaders to focus on? What are their ambitions for their country?

We were never short of opinions. Some of which we even asked for. In true *Play Your Cards Right* tradition, we asked 100 movers and shakers from around the world what Britain meant to them and what were their hopes for its future. They were asked under 'Chatham

House rules', meaning they would not be named or described in this text so they could speak freely. The sample included a wide variety of backgrounds and walks of life, representing the worlds of sport, exploration, business and trade, the third and social sectors, the clergy (of a number of faiths), the military, academia, museums and libraries, music, art, film, theatre, design, education, medicine, politics, finance, construction, transport, the media and science. The panel included people of all political persuasions and none. They came from all points of the compass. They spoke of Britain's capabilities, particularly innovation and creativity, and of the country's opportunities and potential. Values were a consistent theme, in particular trust, a love of freedom, fairness and generosity. Leadership abroad and quality of life at home were focused on as well as attitudes and the social fabric of the UK. What follows is the results of that survey. Warts and all, explained through the quotes of panel members, together with an assessment of whether those beliefs were accurate.

INNOVATION AND CREATIVITY

Many of the panel described the UK as 'pioneering innovation'. They pointed to achievements compared to Britain's size. That 'we've given birth to the second highest number of Nobel Prize winners, topped only by the US'. Our inventions and the impact they have had on the world, 'from inventing the World Wide Web to bringing about new industrial and manufacturing processes that have raised the living standards of literally billions of people around the world'.

Others focused on consistency and longevity:

> For centuries, we've been at the heart of technological innovation. Through figures like Charles Babbage, Ada Lovelace and, more recently, Tim Berners-Lee, we've pioneered computing, algorithms

and cyberspace. These are breakthroughs that have changed the world as we know it beyond recognition, and they will continue to ensure that the UK shapes the direction of the world.

Our engineering skills were mentioned frequently, as were Britain's 'creativity and ingenuity'. Britain's

creative industries lead the way in music, architecture, television, film, gaming, fashion, publishing, design, craft, advertising, art and culture, and they contributed over £100 billion to the UK economy in 2017.[1] I am sure that this is due in large part to the diversity of our culture, which draws on influences from around the world.

Clearly, the country is highly inventive and creative. In 2015, a study ranked all nations for their creativity, including technology, talent and tolerance (diversity): the Global Creativity Index. Britain came twelfth.[2] The top three spots were taken by Australia, America and New Zealand. Six European nations performed better than the UK. We look later at how this translates to soft power.[3]

Britain ranks fifth for innovation in the world according to the Global Innovation Index. The UK is good at coming up with solutions to problems. However, other indices put us much lower. The 2020 Bloomberg Innovation Index, which scores nations against seven criteria, places the UK eighteenth. Britain scores best in the tertiary efficiency measurements. These look at the enrolment and graduation percentages in particular levels of education and subjects (engineering and science). In the 2020 index, Singapore came top. Britain was sixth. This, despite the UK being unable to produce the engineers or healthcare professionals it needs. On all other measures it fared considerably less well. For high-tech density (volume of domestically domiciled high-tech public companies), Britain was ranked fifteenth. The US came top. For research concentration, Britain was nineteenth. For patent activity and research and development intensity, twenty-first. For productivity, twenty-seventh. For manufacturing added value, forty-fourth.[4]

These indices tend not to capture productivity in the arts and creative industries. They do, however, give an indication of the presence of key factors in realising talents and opportunities. What they show is great potential but an inability to really capitalise on it. Britain is hampered by lack of targeted investment and planning; of sovereign capability and resilience; of consistent excellence and determination; of focus and follow-through; of appetite – and by an excess of complacency.

As one of the panellists said, Britain's 'skills are unmatched. But our maturity and careful approach are now holding us back as Britain becomes risk-averse. New ideas and concepts are over-evaluated, causing us to miss market opportunities and diluting our economic strength.'

OPPORTUNITY AND POTENTIAL

According to our panel, the British dream is alive and well. There may be some bias in the sample, however, as those included in the panel were prominent in their fields. They could not be described as underachievers, no matter what start they had.

> *I am proud to be British and no one will ever take that away from me. It's an amazing country with endless opportunities. When you're sick, the NHS is there to heal you, when you're vulnerable or elderly, the welfare system supports you and our*

amazing armed forces, police and emergency services protect you. As a country, the UK gives everyone the same opportunities and they are there for the taking. I am not saying for one minute that it is easy, but there are lots of opportunities. Just look at me: I left school without any qualifications and built up a top engineering firm, then broke thirty-seven world and national records in the process.

Gulp.

Many of those interviewed were determined strivers, focused on Britain's performance and reaching their full potential. Britain has been vocal and active on increasing economic participation and opportunity for all its citizens and in its international economic and development policies.

The good news is that Britain has been listed as the best nation in which to start a career[5] and one of the top ten for starting a business.[6] However, it does less well on social mobility. The 2018 OECD report on the subject measured the number of generations it would take for the descendants of a child born into the lowest 10 per cent of socio-economic groups to earn the national average wage. In the UK, it was five generations. In Denmark, just two.[7]

Your chances of increasing your income and opportunities diminish further if you are a woman, an ethnic minority or have a disability. The reasons for this in the UK are complex. Often policies, in welfare for example, have not just failed to address these obstacles but actually exacerbated them. They have disincentivised those on low pay from earning more. The UK has no national occupational health service, although there are moves to establish one. It is an area where the government has been right to urgently focus activity since the 2019 general election.

The panel thought that 'Britain has a resilient, hard-working population capable of great innovation', and there's much evidence to support that view. When it came down to it and the nation needed Brits to pick sprouts, or rather pick fruit and plant squash, they did so. The Pick for Britain scheme during the Covid crisis saw people step up to keep food production going when migrant labour was scarce, just as the land army had done decades before.[8] Those working from home during Covid increased their productivity (though with a corresponding increase in alcohol consumption, it has to be admitted).[9]

Britain's practicality, administrative capabilities and 'pragmatic approach to issues' were also praised. Britain is still helping strengthen the administrations of other nations, but this time in true partnership. Afghanistan's legal system, from the police to the courts to the prison system, has been designed and established with UK expertise and resources. Across the globe, from Pakistan's forensics capabilities to health partnerships with ministries in East Africa, to insurance systems to help hurricane-prone Caribbean Islands, the UK is there building capacity. It is in its interests to do so. It is not just government, its agencies and the armed forces providing these partnerships, but also the UK's institutions and the voluntary sector. For example, the Royal Horticultural Society is helping African farmers identify and map the approach of crop-munching bugs.

Others on the panel said that Britain was 'a reliable partner, a place that gets things done and a place that can be trusted'. British business and institutions were often cited as the reason. For example, 'every year almost 300,000 students around the world choose to take an exam with the Royal Academy of Dance. There are similar stories in a range of professions like the MRCP PACES exam for medicine.'

While the UK is happy to share its skills and expertise with others, there is still more to do at home. The UK ranks ninth in the Global Competitiveness Index, which assesses the skills of the national workforce.[10] There is much criticism, too, about the UK's productivity levels. In December 2019, the Royal Statistical Society chose as its 'Statistic of the Decade' the estimated average annual increase in UK productivity in the decade or so since the financial crisis, reflecting the significance of the unusual weakness observed since the 2008 economic downturn. The UK's productivity gap has been as much as 16 per cent below that of comparable nations, according to the Office for National Statistics (ONS).[11]

There has been much debate about the relevance and fairness of such comparisons, as well as the possible reasons why a gap exists. Low capital investment, skills shortages, employment and interest rates that, until Covid, have not challenged inefficient firms are some of the theories postulated. Professor Cary Cooper, president of the UK's Institute of Personnel Development, has pondered this problem alongside the top HR professionals from across the UK. He puts great emphasis on the skills and attitudes of line managers, arguing that an improvement in their training, confidence and ability to deploy gumption would make a difference.

Only in recent years has the government really examined the skills the UK needs. This is not about a paucity of education but, rather, the right education. By 2030, it is estimated that without better planning, 6 million Brits risk being in jobs for which they are overqualified or being unemployed.[12] Five million low-skilled workers will be chasing 2 million low-skilled jobs. Today, employers struggle to find high-skilled employees – at the time of writing there was an estimated shortfall of 3.4 million. Seventy-two per cent of UK businesses said they struggled to find people with the right skills.[13]

There are also gaps in basic literacy and numeracy. The OECD ranks the UK seventeenth (out of thirty-four nations) for literacy.[14]

The Joseph Rowntree Foundation ranks it fifteenth for numeracy.[15] The National Literacy Trust estimates that 5 million adults in England are functionally illiterate, meaning that they have a reading age of eleven or below. Sixty per cent of the prison population has difficulties with basic literacy and numeracy skills.[16] The Department for Education's (DfE) own statistics show that one-fifth of all children leaving primary school in 2018 could not read or write properly.[17] Autism and dyslexia are often diagnosed late in a person's life (see page 375 for an example). The DfE puts the cost of this failure to equip all its citizens with these basic skills at an estimated £37 billion to the UK economy. Many of the panel wanted further improvement in academic standards and in behaviour in our schools. Others pointed to the wasted talent and opportunities that were the result of children leaving school unable to read and write.

Tech skills are similarly wanting. Access to technology and good connectivity are clearly vital for a successful nation. In 2020, 96 per cent of UK households were able to access the internet.[18] According to a study published in October 2020, the UK had the forty-second fastest mobile broadband speed compared with other nations.[19] For fixed broadband it came forty-seventh. Not what you would expect from the fifth largest economy in the world, or a nation that has attracted so much inward investment in new tech companies. In 2014, a GCSE in computer science was introduced and a concerted effort made to train teachers with the establishment of the National Centre for Computing Education. In 2018, the Institute of Coding was established. In each case, credit goes to the Royal Society for booting the government into action. Business and civil society are also increasingly providing opportunities to learn basic coding or IT skills, such as the Google Digital Garage initiative.

The panellists wanted greater focus on educating and training people, not just in the skills needed for the future but in the ability to think and create. They praised other nations which had true collaborations between education and industries. 'We should provide an education system that can rival Singapore's.' That country's SkillsFuture movement was often cited, as was the importance of activities for young people. Schemes such as 'CatZero in Hull (a sailing programme for people from deprived areas) should be used to pick up those who are failing or likely to fail. This would help get them into jobs.'

Britain ranks sixteenth on the World Bank's Human Capital Index.[20] The index measures which countries are best at mobilising the economic and professional potential of their citizens. It tracks the investments a nation makes in its citizens and the return it gets for them. High-scoring nations invest effectively. While it is a fledgling index and therefore crude, it does show that there is room for improvement in the UK approach. The area where improvements would make the greatest difference to the UK's ranking are in the field of education.

Many on the panel also thought that Britain's geography and history as a trading and maritime nation were still important to its potential. 'We should become a maritime nation again. We live on an island.' 'The construction of a long-awaited replacement for *Britannia* could play a central role in this mission.' Not as a royal yacht but as a research, development and trade platform. 'We need to build up our merchant navy again and ensure we build those vessels in our own country.'

We need to provide a sufficiently large and effective navy to protect shipping and ensure it can reach our island in safety. The Royal Navy is hard pushed, with insufficient vessels for the demands and a shortage of seamen, leading to sailors having to work much harder and have their lives disrupted

more than is reasonable. That leads to a retention problem of
highly qualified and expensively trained personnel.

'It will be important to take advantage of the two new [aircraft] carriers to promote us. I know this is beginning to happen, but they need more escorts and we don't have enough.'

The panellists, whatever their views on Brexit, seemed to agree that the UK should take this moment to make the most of its assets and influence around the world, in order to forge an even more positive global future.

There were calls for Britain's 'development partners of today to become … trading partners of tomorrow'. 'Nothing matters other than making a success of Brexit and securing trade deals.' Britain should 'exploit the nation's full economic potential at home and abroad, not least by enhancing and expanding the nation's network of trading relationships across the globe'. There were suggestions for how to do this. From fully maximising multilateral relationships to ways of increasing reach and presence. The panel encouraged making a 'contribution to the preservation of international peace, security and prosperity by increasing the investment in Britain's armed forces, which would also help to counter the multiple threats posed by the increasingly volatile international climate'. Some panellists who were keen to see Britain more self-sufficient called for a gradual reduction of 'the dependence' on other nations, especially in the fields of energy, tech and military action. 'We must maintain an armed force capable of protecting our shores and trade and sustaining our position on the UN Security Council.'

A lack of focus on growth was another theme. 'We need to grow the economy instead of the government simply trying to ramp up taxes.' Many wanted an explicit connection between economic performance and public spending. A shift in attitudes so that business was really valued for the public services it helped provide. There were calls, too, that the 'taxation system needs to be simplified and made fairer for all'.

The panel's view and all the evidence point to middling performance and untapped potential. The lack of a plan to help focus the nation and to capitalise on British talent is clear. As one panellist put it:

> *Personally, I am not one for our habit of gazing nostalgically at our past. The world is dynamic, changing constantly, consistently and with complexity. Everyone needs to adapt. Britain needs to reinvent itself. The hard fact that many ignore is that we are failing on the world stage. A heavy dose of realism will tell you that we are ... showing a damning failure to get our act together, politically, academically and financially. Our industrial and manufacturing base has been gutted and what still exists is mostly foreign-owned. Now our financial and services industries will be similarly whittled down as our sphere of influence shrinks. We rank at or near the bottom in first-world education rankings and our universities only rank highly because of the huge foreign intake that we attract.*

TRUST AND LOVE OF FREEDOM

Many members of the panel who had international experience cited the feeling of trust which the country generates abroad. This was a marked trend compared with those whose experiences were primarily in the UK. Internationally, Britain is associated with a 'respect for fairness, decency and playing by the rules'. The UK's institutions, such as its 'highly evolved justice system, and the rule of law on which it's built, hold pride of place and have inspired countless other nations'.

Many saw the UK as 'an outward-facing, tolerant, compassionate, decent country that respects democracy, the rule of law (including the international rules-based system) and human rights'. Others cited the values they associated with the UK. 'Britain is a fundamentally honest and caring nation that sets the standards for democratic values and justice.' 'Britain stands for freedom, both of the individual and the community as a whole: freedom from oppression and from fear.' They thought Britain was reliable and 'trusted to pull its weight'.

According to the 2020 Best Countries report, Britain is among the most trusted nations on earth.[21] Britain ranks eighth on ease of doing business.[22] Apparently, it is one of the most straightforward, least bureaucratic places to establish and run a business. A 2019 Ipsos report found that 'in countries such as Britain, France, the US, Canada and Japan, for example, a clearly negative view of the government doesn't stop people having a more positive view towards public services'.[23] Others described 'an even-handedness in international affairs that is hugely valued'. Where Britain had been at her diplomatic best was when she 'was trusted to act as broker in international disputes', trusted by both sides.

There have of course been moments when that reputation has been called into question. But the trust seems to persist. Why? Could it be that these decisions have been taken alongside a long-held commitment to do the right thing by others over decades? Our role in the foundations of individual rights and freedoms? Ending slavery, the sacrifice of world wars and cold wars? The UK's commitment to NATO of spending 2 per cent GDP to support collective defence is evidence of that. One act of supposed mistrust does not change the aggregate view. It's a pattern of behaviour, not a single act.

Compassion was a consistent theme mentioned by the panel.

> *Britain is at the forefront of saving lives, alleviating poverty and bringing freedom, security and prosperity for those who need it most. The UK's response to the Ebola crisis in 2014 and 2015 was a great example of Britain at its best, putting our world-class scientists, nurses and armed forces personnel to the task of fighting a disease that was taking thousands of lives and setting development back years. We must always ensure that our development policy makes the best use of our country's talent, expertise and resources, making the difference that only Britain can make.*

The Charities Aid Foundation ranks the compassion of each nation based on analysing three questions: How likely are people to help a stranger? How many donate money? How many volunteer? The UK ranks sixth in the world.[24]

In contrast, the UK has been ranked as having 'low empathy' on the index of the world's most empathetic nations. Here, the researchers defined empathy as the tendency to be psychologically in tune with other people's feelings and perspectives. To measure this in the participants, the researchers asked them to complete a comprehensive list of questions drawn from several standardised tests.[25]

Do Brits have a hard time seeing others' point of view? Are they emotionally constipated? That has certainly been suggested as one reason for foreign policy gaffes. Do they lack a basic understanding about how people feel, or overlook the details of particular complex situations and dynamics? Or how another nation or region might respond?

FAIRNESS AND GENEROSITY

'Britain means kindness and empathy.' 'The UK is synonymous with ambition, opportunity, fairness, generosity of spirit and courage.'

Many were grateful that 'we live in a nation where we can enjoy freedom of speech, a national health service that is free at the point of use and an independent justice system'. Others spoke about the welfare state with pride: 'Despite all of the negativity and divisiveness going on in the world today, our welfare state was born of a desire to protect the vulnerable and ensure dignity for all.'

For many others this was Britain's key quality: 'When you travel around the world, you realise that it's the combination of the democratic traditions, culture and respect for fairness and justice that most characterises Great Britain.' As evidence for this, panel members cited the actions of the British people as least as much as they talked about government policies: 'the Live Aid concert, the actions to free Nelson Mandela and the Make Poverty History campaign' and more. One panellist said, 'It's remarkable that in the historical records of social change it is the legislative and political parties' role that is emphasised. The public agitation is ignored and yet this was often the most crucial part of the social changes that occurred.' Many spoke passionately about personal responsibility: 'Never underestimate the power of the individual to change their circumstances; every one of us has a personal responsibility to contribute to a better world; and when respect, kindness and courage combine, anything is possible.'

Many panellists spoke about these values being at the heart of what the UK should be focusing on as a nation. Our mission is

to unite around the things we have in common, to break down the things that divide us, to get beyond [party] politics, to collaborate with empathy, kindness and civility, to reconnect, to

*reconcile, to innovate and to drive growth (in all senses). To be
a prosperous, civil and reunited kingdom. To improve health
and well-being.*

The World Justice Project ranks Britain eighth in fairness.[26] For
healthcare, Britain ranks nineteenth.[27] The panel saw the links
between the two. Justice is not just something confined to jurisprudence. The British approach to justice is multivariate: quality
healthcare, housing, equality and education.

'Britain's balanced international judgement, which is based on
our past economic, industrial and military strength, is now at a
crossroads. We have a choice between increasing our concentration
on personal freedoms or resurrecting the strength of community
that made Britain great.'

For many members of the panel, a sense of determination went
alongside moderation, trust and reliability as being key values. 'We're
known for our tenacity in adversity and defending what is right.'

The UK was ranked tenth in the 2019 FM Global Resilience Index
of nations' business environments.[28] That dogged determination was
not always seen as a positive. 'British stoicism, inventiveness, innovation and adventurism (when it is not checked by bureaucracy)
are reasonable until pushed too far. Then it becomes stubbornness.'

The British like a laugh. 'We have an ability to take the mickey out
of ourselves in a manner that most overseas visitors do not understand until they have been here for a while.' According to international public polling, we rate as the best nation in Europe for having
a laugh.[29] Some panellists thought that this was key to our success. It
made the Brits likeable. However, 'humour, tolerance and common
sense are qualities always under threat from a range of people, such as
extremists, single-issue folk, virtue signallers and those who hate us.'

They appear to be self-deprecating, too. One panellist said, 'I don't know where the negativity comes from because people are polite, but other countries have always been nothing but applauding of the UK. The only people I've ever heard challenge me on Britain are British.'

Other panellists pointed to pessimism and a lack of confidence.

> *As a country, Britain should have a greater sense of ambition and stop selling itself short by allowing the nation's narrative to be dominated by negative individuals and groups that have no belief in the true potential of its people. Britain must show a greater willingness to exploit every advantage at the nation's disposal in pursuit of its wider political and economic interests. Innovation, hard work and achievement should always be a source of pride and celebration, rather than being quietly swept under the carpet.*

There's even an international index for being a misery. Britain remains one of the most pessimistic nations, notwithstanding all of its evident advantages. The country ranks fifteenth in overall optimism, coming in behind top-ranking China, India, South Africa, Russia, Brazil, America, Australia, Canada, Spain, South Korea, Turkey and Germany. Britain may have come in fifteenth, but there was a silver lining. The French came seventeenth.[30]

GLOBAL LEADERSHIP

'Britain is a global actor with a unique standing.' A 'soft-power superpower'. 'Britain has a long track record as an outward-looking nation that is prepared to play a leading role on the world stage.' These were consistent themes from our panellists, but there was also scepticism about how long this would continue:

*Britain is the global brand for strong leadership, integrity, in-
novation and tenacity. In the past, it has been the standard
by which other countries judge their industrial strength and
military capability, but one thing depends on the other and
both have been allowed to deteriorate to such a position that
our strength is now questionable.*

Our history and connections to other nations and their citizens
were frequently mentioned as laying the foundations for influence
and leadership. 'So many of the ministers I meet around the world
have spent time in the UK. A lot of people in Britain have also gone
back to the countries of their cultural heritage to help build them up
and those places have learned so much from Britain.'

Britain has

*been international for many hundreds of years. The legacy and
links that we've made mean that at our best we can plug in
and play with amazing ease. The Commonwealth is based on
this. Fifty-three countries share English as one of their official
languages,[31] English law, the rule of law, a common approach
to regulations, and for most, a shared history. Because of these
factors it's easier for Commonwealth business to trade within
the Commonwealth rather than outside it.*

According to the 2019 Best Countries report, Britain is ranked as
the second best-connected nation in the world.[32] The UK has the
second largest value international education market and the prized
Commonwealth and Chevening scholarship schemes.[33]

The US News & World Report ranks Britain third among the
most influential nations in the world, after America and China.[34]

However, it is not just emerging powers and growing economies that threaten to undermine the UK's leadership position. Again, there appears to be a lack of drive and understanding of how best to use the nation's assets, together with the absence of a clear long-term view about the national interest.

'I think we're extremely successful on the international stage, but truth be told, our influence is not what we think it is. What I see is that other countries are starting to be taken a lot more seriously than the UK.'

'Britain does such amazing work with the Department for International Development, but some of those countries [in receipt of effective UK support] prioritise those [countries] that aren't interested in helping them build their economy.'

> *A colleague from the Seychelles said to me: 'We thought when the British left, this was the next chapter for us, but we're a nation of 80,000 people and we now have to have an army, we now have to have embassies. We need representation at the UN and at the International Maritime Organization and the African Union and we need our own healthcare system. This small island nation is being destroyed by climate change, but we just don't have the resources politically to do anything about it. If Britain hadn't left, I think we would be in a better place.'*

The panel pointed to the UK 'needing to do more with the nations where they could make the most difference, to building a stronger union with our Commonwealth brothers and sisters, particularly the smaller countries'.

A GREEN, PLEASANT AND BEAUTIFUL LAND

'It would be hard to find another place I would prefer to live.' All panellists agreed that living in the UK was still to be prized, but the Brits were more critical than international residents. Perhaps the latter were just being polite? Perhaps the former were just being British?

The panel mentioned that the British landscape was worthy of note. For many, this applied to both urban and rural locations. Quality of life, culture and heritage were common themes.

'The sheer diversity of Britain's countryside and culture and the dynamism of our commercial, science and business landscape are amazing.'

> We think of Britain as a green and pleasant land. It is. But it's that combined with its people and communities, its culture and tradition that makes it truly great. It's a country that values its history and traditions, but it uses them to be innovative and entrepreneurial and able to embrace change.

'Being born in Britain is like winning the lottery of life.' But how well does the UK score on quality of life when rated against other comparable nations?

Britain ranks eleventh on Legatum's Prosperity Index, which measures quality of life as well as economic and social indicators.[35] Pre-Covid, the Office for National Statistics noted that people's satisfaction with life had deteriorated since 2011, especially in the north-east and south-east of England. This has been a gradual deterioration.[36] People were increasingly anxious and less content, especially in the north-east. Brits may have won the geography lottery, but they want more. So, what needs improving?

ENVIRONMENT

Just 5.9 per cent of the UK is built on; 2.5 per cent is green urban space; 34.9 per cent is natural green space and 56.7 per cent farm-land.[37] In recent years there has been a move towards supporting biodiversity on farmland. The importance of hedgerows, ponds and untidy corners in fields is appreciated. Species have returned or have been reintroduced. Britain is the twelfth greenest nation on earth and leads the world in the amount of renewable energy gener-ated through offshore wind.[38,39] The 2019 IQAir report places Britain as the seventy-eighth most polluted country and falling short of the World Health Organization target.[40] Government policy is to meet that target and achieve zero emissions by 2050.

On air quality and climate change, many of the panel pointed to the lack of a plan. That 'we should create a cross-departmental inte-grated plan to achieve zero emissions by 2050'. 'It is important that we push hard for a total reliance on sustainable energy. In particu-lar, since we are an island surrounded by tides, we should invest in research into how to harness this source of predictable power and then export that knowledge.' 'We must work to become the centre of clean energy industries by commercialising tidal stream energy.' In point of fact, the government already has a 25-Year Environment Plan,[41] which was put in place before the climate change conference COP 26 (COP = Conference of the Parties).

Many thought of the legacy for future generations. 'I'm watching my kids grow up in Cornwall by the sea and it breaks my heart … that they might not be able to breathe clean air or know that they can go to the beach without getting tangled in plastic.'

Britain has led the charge on environmental protection. Recently, it took a prominent role in securing the Paris Agreement on climate change and it galvanised many nations into supporting the Com-monwealth Blue Charter, protecting marine environments. It has impressively reduced and near removed its use of coal. Its planning regime has prevented many of the eyesores and safety hazards seen elsewhere. However, these actions are not those of a nation recently crawling to the cross. The UK's forestry programmes around the world are decades old. UK-funded schemes in Nepal were founded thirty years ago. They are also at scale. A protected forest the size of England in Indonesia is home to endangered tigers and orangutans courtesy of the British taxpayer. Mrs Thatcher – yes, her – was one of the first to raise the alarm on pollution and on climate change at the UN in 1989. Well, she was a scientist, the only Prime Minister ever to be so. The UK's instincts are right on these issues, perhaps because it is an island nation. However, there are areas it still wrestles with. Air quality is one. Capitalising on the full potential of renewables and new nuclear technology, much invented in the UK, is another. Again, huge potential not seized.

SAFETY AND SECURITY

Of the Brits we asked, their opinion on this was highly dependent on where they lived or had lived and what they did for a living. Many raised how safe they felt.

'It feels like we're becoming more lawless.' 'Violent crime is going up.' Many panellists were concerned about an intolerance in public discourse and divisions in society. Some blamed Brexit, others culture wars or social inequality.

The Community Life Survey of 2018/19 showed that our neighbourhoods are strong. Britain actually has one of the lower crime rates in the world, ranking 160 out of 210 for its murder rate, for instance.[42] Nevertheless, a OnePoll.com survey in the same year showed 31 per cent felt unsafe in their own home.[43] The research also examined crime rates across the UK and added them to perceptions of crime in those areas. These measures combined to give a safe city score. The safest cities were Edinburgh, with just 16 per cent experiencing crime and 90 per cent feeling safe, followed by Bristol, Brighton and Hove, Southampton and Cambridge. Birmingham came towards the bottom, with 42 per cent feeling at risk, followed by Leicester, Manchester, London and Sheffield. Those surveyed were of the view that better community policing and neighbourhood design improvements, such as good lighting at night, were the factors that would make them feel more secure. Dyfed-Powys is said to be the safest place in Wales and one of the safest places in the UK. Northern Ireland has moved on from the dark days of the Troubles. Today, it is the safest region of the UK and its capital, Belfast, is much safer to visit than other UK cities.

While some parts of Britain are beacons of tolerance and cohesion, our panellists noted that such experiences are not uniform across the country. Their view was that there is discrimination, although this is accompanied by a simultaneous recognition that it must be tackled. There was recognition that in some places communities live in fear.

According to the Office for National Statistics, a significant minority (4.2 per cent of men and 7.9 per cent of women) suffered domestic abuse. This increased during the Covid lockdown. Domestic violence murders were at a five-year high in 2019.[44] Hate crime is in sharp focus, too. Many people with disabilities, in particular those with learning disabilities, say bullying and discrimination are part of everyday life, according to the Crown Prosecution Service (CPS).[45] This translates into the structure of our society, too, as the current disability employment gap is 15 per cent.[46] Based on the same CPS report, homophobic and transphobic crime prosecution and conviction rates were also up in 2018/19.

In July 2017, the government published the largest survey in the world on the quality of life of LGBTQ+ people in Britain. More than two-thirds of respondents said they had avoided holding hands with a same-sex partner for fear of receiving a negative reaction from others. In the twelve months preceding the survey, at least 40 per cent of respondents had experienced an incident such as verbal harassment or physical violence because they were part of the LGBTQ+ community. Only 10 per cent of incidents were ever reported.[47]

Crime data is difficult to interpret. In 2019, the number of completed prosecutions for religiously motivated hate crime decreased to 605, down 26.2 per cent from the previous year.[48] There were also 9,931 prosecutions for racially aggravated hate crime – a decrease of 10.2 per cent on the previous year. This could mean many things about crime numbers, but also about the capabilities of the police and the CPS, the level of security at mosques and synagogues, with many having increased security in recent years, or changing attitudes.

Despite public perceptions, terrorism incidents are declining. However, there are new areas of sinister criminality. The National Crime Agency estimates that there are 300,000 paedophiles sharing sexual images or abusing children on the dark web.[49] Drug-related crime is starting to fall but is moving from London and other major cities into small towns and villages, especially in the east of England and the south-east.[50] Increasingly, children are being used in these distribution networks. Failing vulnerable children has been a recurring theme, as the girls and young women of Rotherham, Rochdale and Oxford will testify.

Many of the panel cited the UK's legal legacy to the world. British laws and its judicial system have been the foundation for so many others. The panel largely thought the UK system to be strong, but some did point to the absence of a 'constitution' making the UK more open to challenge on the grounds of international law. 'Countries with a constitution are more trusted to be able to sort out their own affairs robustly.' Access to the law was seen as important by the panel. Changes to legal aid, starting with the 1999 Access to Justice Act, have reduced the chance of legal representation in many cases, especially in the areas of family, welfare benefits and employment law.

The Institute for Government performance tracker highlights both the shortfall in funding provision for the criminal courts and that the prison service, dealing with a comparatively large prison population, is fragile.[51] Technology and the opportunity for online courts, accelerated by Covid, are one route to help support a system under strain.

WELL-BEING AND HEALTH

For our panel, the NHS was the pragmatic manifestation of British values. Its creation was a rare moment, outside of war, when there was a true national mission. The celebration of it alongside the countryside, the industrial revolution, James Bond, HM The Queen, Rowan Atkinson, Tim Berners-Lee and the Spice Girls during Danny Boyle's 2012 Olympic opening ceremony confirms this. Good health and good healthcare are consistently the prime care and concern of the British public. There are indices that show the NHS and wider UK healthcare services are the best in the world. There are also ones that will tell you its outcomes are poor. The barely concealed truth is that it's inconsistent. Every year, more people develop illnesses that would never have killed their parents simply because they wouldn't have lived long enough to get them. It's the only organisation in which the annual successes sow the seeds of tomorrow's challenges.

The NHS is acknowledged as a system that controls healthcare costs, is good on patient feedback and is evidence-led. The UK excels in particular clinical fields; the treatment of congestive heart failure, for example. However, prized above all of that is equality of access and experience. The Commonwealth Fund Equality of Experience Survey showed that the UK had the least cost-related obstacles in accessing healthcare among all the nations it surveyed.[52] However, the same research also showed that people in the UK often could not see a doctor on the same day.

On other international benchmarks such as waiting times and quality, the UK was, at best, average. The OECD found that in 2014, waiting times for cataract, knee and hip replacements were below the average among the fourteen countries for which it had data.[53] Despite screening programmes being in place, diagnostics are poor, and cancer survival rates are below the EU average, although they are improving.[54] We are right to set ambitious targets in this area.

Despite the equality of access, there is wide disparity of outcomes. There are massive differences in how healthcare organises itself in different parts of the UK and in clinical practice. Where good practice exists, it has been hard to roll out elsewhere, although initiatives through a non-departmental body, NHS Improvement, are working on that.

The differences in health outcomes are closely linked to people's socio-economic circumstances. This relationship is referred to as the 'Marmot Curve' after Sir Michael Marmot's important work in this field. For England, there are big geographical inequalities in life expectancy. There are more deprived areas in the north than in the south and, as you might have guessed, life expectancy is better in the latter.[55]

While this inequality had been improving, in recent years progress has stalled and the UK has the lowest life expectancy improvements of similar nations. Infant mortality rates are also poor against comparative nations.[56] Over a third of British women will have abortions.[57] And Britain ranks twenty-third among the countries with the highest abortion rates.[58]

British people's attitudes to the NHS are as mixed as international reviews. They treasure it and its equality of access and they also rate the quality of care they receive. For huge numbers it is their chosen profession, with the NHS alone accounting for a third of all public sector workers and 5 per cent of the UK workforce.[59] The country has a portfolio of patient organisations campaigning, delivering, caring, helping to improve care and assist research. The Charity Commission lists 620 cancer organisations alone. However, according to the King's Fund, the British public are among the most pessimistic about the future of the NHS.[60] As they are about pretty much everything else.

Perhaps pessimism is one of the reasons the Centre for Social Justice described the UK in 2013 as the 'addiction capital of Europe'.[61] At the time of filing its report, titled *No Quick Fix*, the UK had the highest rate of addiction and the highest lifetime use of drugs across Europe. Roughly 10 per cent of the population aged between sixteen and fifty-nine had taken drugs in the past twelve months (you may be tempted after reading this). For those aged sixteen to twenty-four, that figure doubled.[62] The Centre for Social Justice also pointed to the estimated 595,131 people suffering from alcoholism as well as the paucity of rehab programmes and facilities. Only 18 per cent were receiving treatment.[63] The rest presumably self-medicate.

According to an Opinions and Lifestyle Survey, 29 million people in the population aged over sixteen drink alcohol; 7.8 million people 'binged' on their heaviest drinking day. Higher earners, those aged over twenty-four and people from the north of England were more likely to have unhealthy drinking habits.[64] For men, the tipple of choice is beer. For women, wine (or 'lady petrol' in some northern locals). There are similar rates of people being overweight or obese across the four nations, at around 62 per cent for women and 67 per cent for men respectively.[65] Wales has a lower obesity rate but a higher rate of being overweight and a markedly lower number of adults getting their recommended daily physical activity.

In recent years, there has been a greater focus on preventative health and mental health. Covid has accelerated that trend. The NHS, though, is just one part of the health economy. Social care has suffered from a lack of a plan to put it on a sustainable footing, despite reviews, commissions, committees, features, articles, white and policy papers. The Institute for Government has the lack of a plan in adult social care and rising demand as one of its red ratings. In 2019, Age UK estimated that 1.5 million people in England between the age of sixty-five and eighty-nine had unmet social care needs.[66]

Social prescribing and the bringing together of services have been around for decades, but these have yet to break down the silos between public and community services and organisations that sit outside the public sector.

Those interviewed were just as proud of the welfare state but wanted it fit for the twenty-first century. 'We need to look at reinventing the welfare state for the digital age.' 'One of the questions we want to be part of answering is: "What would the welfare state look like if it was invented after the internet?" The short answer to that is, if the welfare state used the internet fully, it would be cheaper and it would have more effective and more personalised services.'

'We should be leading the world with innovation to end homelessness.' An estimated 320,000 people are homeless in the UK and between 4,000 and 5,000 people have slept rough on any one night in the past few years.[67] During the Covid crisis, many were brought in off the streets for the sake of public health. It remains to be seen whether the opportunity to support those individuals with highly complex problems has been seized.

Despite noting the fragility of such services, many on the panel were proud of Britain's safety nets. 'I work with people who don't have anything. You're given a lot in Britain and people should be reminded of that. You know the NHS needs investment and improving, but it's still amazing.'

They see health and welfare systems as viable candidates for one of the UK's national missions, if only political parties 'could put dogma aside', come together and focus on clinical outcomes. The panel was universally fed up with politicians making territorial claims for the NHS. 'We're the party of the NHS, they say. See my badge! What a load of bollocks. No, you are not "the party of the NHS". Nor are the other lot. It's all of us.'

Britain's support and care systems have their heart in the right place, achieve a great deal, but need considerable modernisation. There is clarity in understanding what needs to be done. Again, the lack of a focused national mission holds the nation back.

WEALTH AND FINANCIAL RESILIENCE

Pre-Covid, the ONS painted a picture of a fairly robust nation. In April 2016 to March 2018, 54 per cent of households with someone in work could cover a 75 per cent fall in income for three months.[68] So a majority of working households had financial resilience. Money worries, however, were a definite concern for a significant minority. A Social Market Foundation report pointed to low financial resilience as a significant cause of stress across the UK workforce, with a quarter of those surveyed 'just about managing'.[69]

Prior to Covid, 7.8 per cent of the UK's population were in

persistent poverty, that is experiencing relative low income both in the current year and in at least two out of the three preceding years.[70]

The take-up of the 'Tory Triumvirate' of pensions, share and home ownership is a good indicator of financial resilience. Recent policies have encouraged pension provision, especially in the private sector. According to the ONS, 76 per cent of UK employees were members of a workplace pension scheme in 2018, largely thanks to automatic enrolment.[71]

In 2020, the *Financial Times* estimated that 15 per cent of the UK stock market was held by individual shareholders.[72] In 1963, that number was 50 per cent. In contrast, the figure for the United States is 37.6 per cent. This is significant, as we shall discover in Chapter 9.[73]

The Money Charity estimated that pre-Covid, 12.8 million households had less than £1,500 in savings. Total debt per household was £60,363 and £2,595 was the average household credit card debt. The average time to pay off a credit card debt (if making minimum payments) was twenty-six years and eight months. 4.8 million households were without at least one essential household appliance or white goods.[74]

Home ownership reached an all-time high of 73 per cent in 2007, but the UK suffered the largest fall of any nation in the EU after the financial crash. In 2016, it started to climb again in part due to policies to assist first-time buyers, but for many, building up a property stake remains out of reach. There is a shortage of housing stock across the board. According to data from the Ministry of Housing, Communities and Local Government, house building is 60 per cent of what it was forty years ago.[75] The £4.5 billion Home Building Fund sounds massive, until you compare it with the £22 billion spent on housing benefit every year.[76,77]

For many of these new builds, too little was done too late to protect against sharp practice, such as the conditions placed on those buying leaseholds or retirement apartments, locking people into huge fees or unable to sell their properties. Good design standards, such as those showcased at the UK's Global Disability Innovation Hub, still evade many developers.[78]

The problem with housing is two-fold. Population is going up, sure enough. But the number of households is still increasing. Other notable trends are a decrease in household size. Of the 27 million households in 2015, 29 per cent of these consisted of just one person. This was up from 20.2 per cent in 1981.[79]

The delay in getting on the housing ladder is often cited as one reason people are also postponing childbirth. That, in turn, is resulting in an increased demand for fertility treatments on the NHS.

Women are also having fewer children. By the age of thirty, 53 per cent of women born in 1973 had at least one child, compared with 82 per cent for their mothers' generation, according to the ONS. That in turn has knock-on effects for those in the care system a generation on.[80]

According to the Association of British Insurers, even accounting for fluctuations in household numbers in the UK, there is a decline in the number of UK households with insurance products. This is true for all types of cover except motor and income protection.[81]

Access to low-cost credit is an issue for an estimated 8 million people.[82] 1.2 million are unable to access the potential for reduced utility bills that comes from traditional high-street banking.[83]

Britain should be proud of its safety nets. Universal Credit was increased and expanded during the pandemic, but there's much more to do to enable all of its citizens to be healthy and wealthy and to enjoy the best quality of life possible.

CONSTITUTIONAL AND ADMINISTRATIVE CHANGE

No part of the UK's constitution, governance or government systems escaped criticism from the panel. There were calls from the abolitionists to abolish pretty much everything. 'Abolish the Supreme Court and reinstate the Lord Chancellor.' 'Abolish the House of Lords, including the hereditary peers, and institute an elected Lords. It is ludicrous that pop stars, actors, sports folk and others of that ilk, ennobled by all parties, should have any say in how we are governed.' 'Abolish the National Security Council and revert to the well-tried system where defence and foreign policy are decided by the defence and overseas policy committee, consisting of the PM, Foreign Secretary and all four chiefs of staff.' Abolish 'the stovepipe nature of interdepartmental working by integrating the departments better, particularly in their approach to policy'. Abolish centralisation and 'delegate more authority to the regions'. 'Abolish separate organisations purporting to represent industrial sectors.'

A consistent theme was deep scepticism about how the government organises itself, lack of power at a local level and lack of competent management. The public appears to share the panel's concern about particular institutions. According to a 2017 ERS/BMG poll, almost two-thirds of the public now back an elected House of Lords. The public is also in favour of greater devolution.[84]

In recent years, there have been movements to renew democracy, to create consensus and centre ground or constructive dialogue between existing political parties: people feel that politics isn't working for them.

SOCIAL FABRIC OF THE UNION

If you're sat there reading this and you're angry, then you're not alone. Unionists are angry about nationalists who are angry about Westminster which is angry about 'woke' Remainers who are angry at Brexiteers who are angry about the BBC which is angry about the government which is angry about the public not giving them credit because Covid has taken away their civil liberties and made them angrier by forcing them to watch the telly which is full of angry people who are angry about absolutely everything especially unionists who are angry... It's an Escher diagram of the endlessly dyspeptic. Academics have taken to studying it.

Professor Erin Meyer is a Senior Affiliate in the Organisational Behaviour Department at INSEAD, specialising in the field of Cross-Cultural Management, Intercultural Negotiations, Multi-Cultural Leadership and Multisyllabic Departmental Taxonomy. She offered some advice on how to negotiate with particular nations via an axis drawn according to their propensity to be emotional, expressive and confrontational.[85]

People from the UK, along with those in Sweden, Korea and Japan, were emotionally inexpressive and avoided confrontation. Has she been watching the BBC News of an evening? Trying to get through a single bulletin without scenes of wailing, anger, starvation, tears and confrontation is a challenge. And that's just the international news. Presenter Orla Guerin is a sort of animated Edvard Munch painting. Available settings include 'Harrowing' or 'Off'. Does every BBC *News at 10* presenter have a default setting of miserable? More people prefer to watch *The Repair Shop* than the news. It's hardly surprising.[86]

Culture wars are on the rise. The issues might change from place to place but the temperature doesn't. Yet, really, anger doesn't sit well with Brits. Full-blown, foot-stomping, crockery-throwing door-slamming, tyre-squealing, they're-gonna-blow angry is actually quite a rare sight still in the UK. The British do finger drumming. They do peevish. They certainly do waspish. They do petulant. They do petty. They do sarky. They do bitchy. They get the hump. They even get the arse. Apart from that, they're too tolerant, too sensible and too shy to get really cross.

There is one notable exception. Brits only really do loss of control when they've properly been on the sauce. This phenomenon is called 'Saturday Night'. It's a British ritual that happens in most market towns and some cities. In Manchester, it's a meteorological condition known as 'The Deansgate Tornado', complete with strewn rubbish, 'pavement pizza' and people staggering about with torn clothes clinging to lampposts, etc. Also known as a Whitley Bay Whirlwind.[87] Participants limber up about five o'clock in the afternoon with pre-loading. Make-up, booze, *dernier cri* (her) and post-match pint to question the eyesight/parentage/sexual habits of the match officials (him). This results in getting mutually mortalled, trolleyed, shit-faced, sloshed, plastered, tanked, wasted, wankered, hammered, Badered (after the legless flying ace) and battered. In fact, you can play this game yourself. Basically, *any* verb, *any* past participle.

You see, according to the panel, there are serious pressures arising from just being British in Britain. The emotional constipation, the political incontinence of the media, the preference for bodging, the millions of ways the weather can 'spoil things', the 'fancying' of everything (horses, grub, cuppas, fags, pints, people), how no one is 'being funny, but', the carrying on calmly, the self-denial, the apologising, the deference (to everyone), the thousands of 'y'alrights?' to which the only answer must be positive, the 'sex-change vicar in midnight mercy dash to palace' red tops, the over-egging, the under-whelming, the budging up, the dressing down, the leaving out, the joining in, the skiving off, the holding on, the faffing around, the buggering up, the sprogging down, the tinkles on the blower, the chinwagging, the grinning and bearing of all sorts of 'it's, the nouns to which the adjectives 'cheeky' and 'lovely' can be applied, the number of times you need to 'turn around and say' something, the sentences that end with the word 'mate', the number of mother's brothers called Bob, the even larger number of lorry backs from which something fell, the men to be seen about dogs, the onions you need to know, Sod and his law, the necks that need to be 'wound in', the rogering, the wangling, the whingeing, the snogging, the tickety-booing, the injury time opposition goals (we wuz gutted) and, of course, the cheesing off, the mustn't grumbling, the sending to Coventry, the going to pot and the comparison of everything good and bad to the testicles of either dogs or men, the larger, the better. You may think you speak English, but you don't really learn how until you're forty.

The panel registered the pressures and sought to historically contextualise them.

> *Much of the recent debate on Brexit has been characterised by rancour and division, with little attempt to listen to opposing views or compromise. And yet in the broad sweep of British history, we have overcome such serious divisions before; we came through the turmoil of the reform of the corn laws, Catholic emancipation and Irish home rule. Those debates were just as fierce and often violent. It is notable that the divisions of Brexit have not spilled over into rioting or violence. I suspect this would have happened in so many other countries.*

The Saturday Night safety valve has its uses. It is, after all, something that all the home nations have in common.

Saturday Night is always followed by Full English. The Almighty makes herself known through the presence of breakfast. The British eat breakfast like it's their last meal on earth. Because of this, for many, it is.[88] Comedian Al Murray has spoken fondly of the bond formed by the British and their bacon at moments like this: 'Bacon means you can kill yourself with alcohol on a Friday night and be fully resurrected Saturday morning with the application of just one bacon sandwich and that's a fact.'[89]

These rituals are close to a unifying force if there ever was one. And they're not confined to either England or breakfast time. The 24-hour Market Diner in Brighton is home to the legendary 'Gut Buster', which comprises egg, bacon, sausage, burger, black pudding, beans, mushrooms, tomatoes, fried slices and chips with tea (£7.99). This has been recently superseded by the 'Mega Buster': two eggs, fried slice, bacon, two sausages, two black pudding, two burgers, beans, mushrooms, tomatoes, chips, bread, butter and tea OR coffee, which in many cases seldom actually sees the gut let alone busts it. When consumed at 2 a.m. after a gallon of beer, the meal is more a short-term rental than an outright freehold.

Full English allotropes are the 'Ulster Fry', that adds Irish potato bread, soda farl and black pudding, and the Welsh breakfast with laverbread and, err, cockles. In Scotland, it's the Full Scottish (natch) and can be bracketed by porridge, kippers and even a slice of haggis.

Not surprisingly, after such breakfast bowel-bashing there blossoms a stool of biblical proportions. Exodus by Caesarean section. The 'Full' in 'Full English' is in all respects a superlative.

The Market Diner is a slice of life missed by those who only dwell in daylight. Darkness is a disguise.

The best documentary evidence of Saturday Night comes from the full volumes and flat vowels of Sheffield's Arctic Monkeys. As lead singer Alex Turner says: 'Said, this town's a different town to what it was last night. You couldn't have done that on a Sunday.' The perspectives in Britain shift temporally as well as economically, socially and geographically.

There was recognition from the panel that attitudes and concerns varied wildly around the UK.

I feel in London we don't understand the UK as well as we should. We have a slightly different picture of the country here, and my view as someone from central and east London is that Britain is tolerant and open – it's a fair and just country. But that view is not the case in all parts of the country.

We may be a small island in the grand scheme of things, but we're not cut off from the world. We embrace distinctive cultures and we've always been very outward-looking and cosmopolitan in our approach to life. Our cultural identity as well as our language are rich and diverse and this is a huge part of what we stand for as a nation.

I lived on a street with Muslims on one side and Hindus on the other. The guy who lived opposite was from Jamaica, the other guy was Trinidadian. I had Scots on my street and I went to a school with people from a multitude of backgrounds. My local MP was a Jewish Labour member and there was a big Jewish community where I lived. It was so diverse and the question of colour or creed really never occurred to me or anyone on that street. But as I've gotten older and as I read the press as I travel around England, you do see there is an element of segregation that you don't have in London.

IS BRITAIN RACIST?

'The UK is stubborn, racist and intolerant. We are down on our-selves and we should be: we have a reputation for backwardness, bad grub and colonialism.'

In December 2018, *The Guardian* commissioned an ICM poll that compared the frequency of certain experiences between white and black and minority ethnic people. If you were from an ethnic minority, it was found that you were far more likely to have been wrongly suspected of shoplifting, with 38 per cent reporting having been wrongly accused, as compared with 14 per cent of white people. Those from ethnic minority backgrounds were three times more likely to be thrown out of or denied entry to bars or pubs for no good reason, at 25 per cent compared with 9 per cent of white people. Minorities were also twice as likely to receive abuse from a stranger.[90]

The 2017 Race Disparity Audit[91] showed the gap of outcomes in education, justice and employment between people of different ethnicities. People from black African, Bangladeshi and Pakistani ethnic groups are still today most likely to live in poverty and dep-rivation. Given the damaging effects of poverty on education, work and health, families can become locked into such disadvantage for generations.

It is on the football terraces, it is in the closed-shop entertain-ment industry and arguably extant in the term 'Black and Minority Ethnic' (BAME) itself and many other places besides. Racism is present – 71 per cent of people from ethnic minorities face discrimi-nation.[92]

Britain has been on a journey. Our history is one of reform and progress. We have moved from participation in slavery, through Wilberforce's reforms and then to the role of the Royal Navy in ending the trade. From race riots over the generations and test cases, through to the Race Relations Acts of 1965, 1968 and 1976, which outlawed discrimination in employment, housing and social services. Most recently, we have had the Equality and Human Rights Commission, established in 2006. Similarly, the Public Order Act 1986 covers stirring up hatred on the grounds of race, religion and sexual orientation. (Though, notably, there is no offence of stirring up hatred on the grounds of transgender identity or disability, yet.) In the wake of terrorist events and criminal acts, the British National Party (or its latest incarnation) has always tried to expand its ranks. It has always failed.

None of this is to say that we shouldn't be concerned. The volume of organisations monitored by the HOPE Not Hate campaign is disturbing. But it's worth noting the consistent rejection of such racism and phobia by the bulk of the British public. As the resurrected Beattie in Maureen Lipman's 2019 general election campaign advert said, 'My mother always used to say: "Britain is a kind and decent country, they will always do the decent thing."'

In the 1990s, the British Social Attitudes Survey found that 44 per cent of people would be upset if their children married across ethnic lines. Now, for younger generations, that figure is 5 per cent.[93] Collectively, we recognise that progress as good. Which is why the recent treatment of the Windrush generation and their children has been so shocking.

The 1948 British Nationality Act gave citizens of the UK and colonies status and the right to settle in the UK, by virtue of having been born in a British colony. They were given no documentation on entry to their new country and many did not accumulate any records; they had no need for them, since such papers weren't required. In 2018, the Windrush scandal saw many of these people and others wrongly deported, detained or refused re-entry to the UK. They were denied access to the public services to which they had been contributing for years. Everything was withheld because they had no papers to show.[94]

Their rallying together, their dedication and service to Britain, their determination to overcome so much (yes, including racism on arrival), their hopeful plans to make a better life – this all speaks to the heart of national values. The inept, unjust, impersonal bureaucracy and lack of care that resulted in the Windrush scandal do not. The lessons of what happened should be learned by the machinery of government.

THE BRITISH EMPIRE

Britain's view about its colonial past is being revised. We have not always taught the Empire in classrooms, leading some to accuse us of historical amnesia. But the truth is many of us did not know anything to forget. We haven't been informed and therefore we haven't had time to think or evaluate the bad and the good of our country's past.

At its height in 1922, the British Empire was the largest the world had ever seen, covering a quarter of the world's total land area and one fifth of humanity. Its decline was swift, but it left a mixed legacy. The panel spoke about both the good and the bad: 'In Britain, we're ashamed of our colonial past, but when I work with highly educated people from around the world, they often say the British system is why they are where they are today.'

A YouGov poll published on 19 January 2019 found that 43 per cent of Brits thought the British Empire was a good thing, while 32 per cent were proud of Britain's colonial history.[95,96] In the same poll, 19 per cent said it was bad. Although the proponents of the Empire say it brought various economic developments to the parts of the world it controlled, critics point to massacres, famines, the use of concentration camps. Even more recently, it took until 8 November 2018 to ensure that pre-independence Commonwealth veterans, those who had fought with Britain's armed forces, received support in their old age.[97] That legacy of destruction affects our relationships with those nations today.

With each passing year, we become more aware of inequality. We should also recognise that the UK has some of the strongest equalities legislation in the world. But racism exists in Britain. Inequality and discrimination, too. These issues are being tackled, slowly. Take the honours system. When George V created the Orders of the Empire, it was an imperial award, designed to reward civilians. Initially, this was for their wartime work in munitions production, logistics and community and voluntary service. Sir Kenneth Olisa's words here about context and intent are informative.[98]

In recent years, there has been debate about whether that gong ought to have a different name. Those who have turned down the honours recognition include Liverpool Football Club's first black player Howard Gayle, authors Doris Lessing, J. G. Ballard, Graham Greene, Benjamin Zephaniah, campaigner Peter Tatchell, and those from the arts, such as John Lennon, David Bowie, Danny Boyle and Henry Moore. L. S. Lowry holds the record for saying no the most times: five. When refusing an MBE for services to the arts, writer and spoken-word artist Jonzi D said, 'Man, I'm a *Star Wars* fan – Empire is bad.'[99]

Fellow spoken-word artist and podcaster George the Poet, aka George Mpanga, expressed similar sentiments when he rejected an honour in 2019, saying he had done so because of the 'pure evil' perpetrated by the British Empire. 'It's not fair that in order to accept this accolade, in order to accept this recognition, I have to submit to that interpretation of empire,' he said.[100]

We don't want to offend its existing recipients. We don't want to make a fuss; it is, after all, only 2 per cent who refuse. Yet, the fact that one in fifty do, for the reason George explained, should make us pause. Should the view of the refusers matter to the rest of us? To make a change, do we too need to think the Empire was 'pure evil'? Let's look at what has actually happened.

In 2004, Parliament's Public Administration and Constitutional Affairs Committee did examine the facts and recommended 'that there should be no further appointments to the Order of the British Empire. A new Order, the Order of British Excellence, should be founded in its place.'[101] It did consider the suggestion of creating an 'Order of Britain', as recommended in the Wilson Review, but dismissed it as sounding 'flat and flavourless'.[102] It had no heart. This was possibly because part of the recognition process is having an award that's, well, *recognisable*. The committee concluded that the new name had merits, solving the problems we have just noted: 'Perhaps most importantly, it would actually mean something, embodying our principle that only excellent service or achievement should be recognised in the honours lists.' The Empire was over. Excellence was in.

Eight years later, though, nothing had happened. A further hearing and report from the same committee concluded that the honours system should be reformed, but not before its centenary in 2017. Even when we recognise an issue, even when our leaders have decided on a course of action, we are slow to change. We hate letting go of the past. Especially when we are told we should take no pride in what previously made us proud.

Would such changes be unpatriotic? The Palace is involved, after all. Can refusing an honour be a patriotic act? Is wanting these changes incompatible with patriotism? In the 2020 Labour leadership contest there was a huge variety of flavours to choose from: 'progressive patriotism',[103] 'radical patriotism'[104] and 'pride in the national flag'.[105] Patriotism could mean pride in the NHS, the countryside, diversity, pubs, the armed forces or the BBC. It means different things to different people. The fact that patriotism is so diverse merely serves to show how much there is to be grateful for.

People therefore show patriotism and community pride in many different ways. Some with flags, others with service or activism or charity. Voters in Rochester may fly English flags to support the national team. The British Muslim Heritage Centre in Manchester exhibits the contribution it makes to our armed forces. For his part, Stormzy sponsors Cambridge students.

Patriotism is about the values a nation shares and its esteem of fellow citizens. It requires two things: first, a nation, and second, a people who are ready and willing to come together. Unless Britain means something to *all* its citizens, it won't have either. That is, each community. Each part of the United Kingdom.

WHAT DOES THE PUBLIC CARE ABOUT?

As we know from recent months, Britons do care about history, tradition and singing 'Land of Hope and Glory', but what is at the top of their list? In 2018, amid the Brexit impasse, Dr Christina Pagel and Christabel Cooper from University College London conducted a detailed survey about the priorities of the British.[106] Brexit loomed large, of course. But squinting past that, the collective priorities of the British people were primarily about growing the economy as the overall top concern, followed by sovereignty and securing trade deals. The study found that for Leave voters, sovereignty – or, put more simply, the idea of gaining control over law-making – was more important than either economic growth or controlled immigration. For the Remain vote, though, there was little common ground across the political spectrum. In fact, there were deep divisions about the nation's priorities across all Labour voters. For the nation as a whole, the top priorities were:

1. Ensuring strong economic growth.
2. Giving Britain control over its laws and regulations.
3. Allowing Britain to make its own trade deals.
4. Making sure there are enough jobs and that workers are paid fairly.
5. Reducing pressure on public services (e.g. by reducing demand, increasing the workforce, or with more money).
6. Ensuring everyone can afford decent housing.
7. Limiting immigration to high-skilled workers or where there are shortages.
8. Reducing the gap between richest and poorest people in the UK.
9. Reducing the gap between the richest and poorest regions of the UK.
10. Ensuring that state benefits are distributed fairly.
11. Maintaining the union of Northern Ireland, Scotland, Wales and England.
12. Preserving British culture.

One year later, heading into the 2019 general election, YouGov similarly captured the issues of greatest concern to the public, asking them to pick their top three concerns from a list of issues.[107]

Brexit (sovereignty) remained the top issue for the British public. Some 68 per cent of Britons ranked it within their top three, consistent with polling over the preceding two years. (Notably, though, it was found that Brexit meant the most to those communities that voted for it.) Healthcare came in second, with 40 per cent of the public placing it in their top three, again consistent with previous polls. Comparatively, focus on the economy had fallen nine percentage points since 2017, to 25 per cent.

In the same poll, crime had become an important issue. In May 2017, just 11 per cent of people listed this in their top three concerns, a figure that had risen to 28 per cent by November 2019. The environment was the other issue gaining significant traction with the public. In the two years between the 2017 and 2019 elections, this subject rose from being in 8 per cent of people's top three concerns to becoming a key issue for 25 per cent of people. And while immigration and asylum took the third spot in the lead-up to the 2017 election at 35 per cent, in 2019 it had dropped to 22 per cent.

CONCLUSIONS

The themes raised by the panel seemed to be a lack of practical focus on growth, human capital and capitalising on our talents. What you think of Britain is a function of where you are in it. This applies culturally, geographically, economically and politically. It's not a matter of dispute that Britain has a past. Again, what you think about that depends on where you are in the present. The most important thing the panel point to is a country obsessed by its past, like being trapped under a heavy object. We spend a lot of time talking about our history. We have so much of it, you see. We can argue over the facts of history, but there are no facts in the future. There's only faith. Do you think the country has a future? If you don't, then you have a lot in common with those who do. Because you're both right.

In the next chapter we look at how we got to where we are today.

3

HOW DID WE GET HERE?

There's no doubt that both government and media were wrong-footed in recent years by unexpected outcomes that fundamentally changed both national and international politics. Leadership is simply no longer just about facts but about feelings as well. Three dolly-zoom, double-take shocks illustrate this.

First, the candidate with the fewest nominations in the 2015 Labour Party leadership contest was Jeremy Corbyn. Very few expected him to follow Gordon Brown and Tony Blair as party leader: the betting odds were 100–1 against.[1] Even fewer expected him to win by a landslide, taking 60 per cent of the votes in the first round. We love an underdog. Only up to a point, though: he fought two elections and lost both, the latter marking Labour's worst defeat since 1935.[2]

Second, Britain voted to leave the EU in 2016. Again, the betting showed Remain as a strong favourite, reaching an 82 per cent chance of victory at one point.[3] The Remain vote had been an odds-on favourite for the majority of the campaign, but, again, the bookies and pollsters got it wrong. Why? Because Remainers patronised Brexiteers, saying they were Little Englanders/not well

educated/parochial/poor/northern/undesirable/racist/bigoted/
old-fashioned/failures etc. It was pillory without persuasion. Worse,
it pushed them firmly into the other camp. Intelligent Brexiteers
submerged out of sight. Unsurprisingly, they did not volunteer their
preferences to friends, colleagues, employers, neighbours, pollsters,
the BBC etc., for fear of identification, illumination, denunciation,
isolation or demotion. To demonise your opponent is thus to ultimately disguise them. The resulting incredulity of outcome doesn't
signal the sinister interference of a foreign power or underhanded
gerrymandering but merely the correct functioning of democracy
by secret ballot. Of course no one disagrees with you when you
threaten them. The ill-judged belligerent ones that do only con-
firm the lazy stereotype some always secretly prayed they would be
viz. Little-England lunatic, royal family fetishising, racist, fanatic,
geriatric, Union Jack-underpanted, chromatically indistinguish-
able, beige-clad, halitotic, expectorating, elasticated-trouser, grey
plastic shoe-wearing, flatulent, Steradent-addicted, stairlift-borne
psycho-gammon.

The really strange thing about voter vilification is why nobody
gets that it has completely the opposite effect. Far from persuad-
ing an opponent, it polarises them. There are so many examples
through history of peaceful, persuasive protest. It's why there are
more streets named after Martin Luther King than Malcolm X.
Demonising those with whom you disagree feels good, but it's cata-
strophically ineffective.

During the EU referendum campaign, there was an illustration
of this demonisation and social snobbery in a curious race up the
charts. The Remain campaign was not only ineffective; it actively
boosted Brexiteers with its bellicosity. Remainers emphasised their
cultural sophistication by endorsing a live version of the European

Union anthem *Ode to Joy* performed by Dutch conductor André Rieu with the Johann Strauss Orchestra. Brexiteer sentiment was best expressed in the lyrics of Dominic Frisby's song '17 Million Fuck Offs'.[4]

The song reached No. 43 on the UK chart. It later reached No. 1 on Amazon.

This sort of sentiment doesn't easily show through in opinion polls and voting intentions, possibly because there isn't a box marked 'Fuck Off'.

Finally, and arguably the largest shock of all, was the election of Donald Trump against all the predictions and forecasts to the US presidency in November 2016. He started his campaign with odds of 66–1.[5] Hillary Clinton's campaign fund was almost double Trump's. Politicians and celebrities lined up to declare that Trump would never, ever, under any circumstances, become President.[6] Multiple opinion polls showed Hillary Clinton at least ten points ahead. Many forecast her winning by a landslide. Some media channels had to remake front pages. Could this illustrate that some of the most powerful forces were listening to an echo chamber of their own views? Or was it that they were reluctant to report uncomfortable truths – that some people were just not persuaded by them? Or perhaps they didn't have the imagination to consider for one moment that so many people might actually be attracted to Trump?

None of these events was deemed likely, but Brexit especially surprised a lot of people. Some believe that the European referendum was the cause of division, but there's no evidence for that. The division existed way before a referendum was ever discussed in Downing Street. Some of the reasons related to the European Union and its inability to reform. The poor attitude to the security and prosperity of its member states, for example, had caused the EU to become a lightning rod for dissatisfaction in some quarters in Britain. The option for a reformed EU was not on the ballot paper, but many who voted either for the status quo or to leave would have chosen it. The reason was that it had already been rejected after the EU vetoed David Cameron's suggested reforms. And you can only have a binary question in the referendum.

What happened in Britain was similar to what occurred in the US. The gaps in society had opened up soon after the financial crisis of 2008. The hardship was felt by the most vulnerable and their reasonable conclusion was that parts of the country were being neglected. The bottom third felt ignored – worse than that, actually: patronised or despised. A questionable belief for this group was that greater priority for community resources was being given to 'outsiders', in the form of immigrants. Naturally, then, the European referendum and subsequent elections favoured those who wanted to control immigration, ergo the people knew exactly what they were voting for.

Instead of seeking to understand these regions, which contained many traditional Labour-voting areas, the Labour Party subjected them instead to a sort of middle-class Munchism. They variously mocked (and were shocked by) their 'bigotry' and their England-flag-football patriotism. They called them 'stupid'. OK, you could actually laugh about Lord Mandelson going into a northern chippy and mistaking the mushy peas for guacamole, but revulsion spilled from *their own party* was difficult for Labour voters to take. No wonder they were spitting tacks.

What happened next was in the British tradition of high farce. The Remain campaign tried to frighten those who'd become economically marginalised with the threat of becoming economically marginalised. It accelerated, concentrated and super-heated the

Brexit flame just before the vote. It was like the Trumpton fire engine filled not with water but with petrol. The effect was transformational. Jeremiahs catastrophised that there would be a war in Europe, no medicines, no vegetables, even.[7,8,9] The kedgeree would be cancelled. America reported that Britain would run out of salad. Shows how much they know about our pecking-order priority and preferences. In a YouGov survey in April 2019 of Britain's favourite foods, Yorkshire pudding, Sunday roast, fish and chips, full English and bacon sandwiches came out top, with bangers and mash, cottage pie and chicken tikka masala, Lancashire hotpot, steak and kidney pie not far behind. Kippers, haggis, black pudding and jellied eels also received an honourable mention. Salad did not feature.[10]

The majority of Britons eat meat pie at least once a month. Britain holds world records for its meat pies. It has the most expensive, the largest, and in 2014 Martin Tarbuck, author of *Life of Pies: In Search of Piefection*, ate 341 of them in 700 days, travelling over 10,000 miles in so doing. Finally, we know the answer to the question 'Who ate all the pies?' He did.[11]

At the height of the madness, the British were told they would be sent to the back of the queue for a trade deal if they didn't stay in line.[12] And the Bank of England rowed in behind all of it. At least it had the common sense and decency to later admit to a 'Michael Fish moment'.[13]

Outside the Westminster bubble, the vast majority watched the events unfold with astonishment. Part of the reason the campaign was so bitterly fought was because the people knew that whatever the outcome, it would be implemented. Unlike many other countries, it's still a newsworthy story in Britain when campaign pledges are broken. The British people felt the weight of responsibility for the vote in the 2016 referendum. They took it seriously. They knew the risks. They weighed them up and finally they voted. Some tried to undermine the validity of the referendum vote, saying that people had been confused, that they didn't know what they were voting for. How could anyone doubt the validity of the referendum while at the same time accepting a general election result? It's the same electorate. If you insult their understanding at the referendum, you insult them and their democratic will.

It illustrates the truth of the previous chapter when it comes to listening. A small group ended up as a majority. Whichever side of the argument you were on (and the authors of this book were on opposite ones), at the end of it all, Britons should be left with a residual feeling of pride. Not because of the result, but because of the democracy that delivered it. When the people choose what they want, all democrats can celebrate. If the people are wrong, then they can change it. Although there is already an active rejoin movement,[14] British politics has a settled view on Europe. A functioning democracy, whether you agree with the outcome or not, is no reason for despair. On the contrary, it is testimony to freedom of choice and the strength of democracy by secret ballot.

THE POWER OF DEMOCRACY

There are many areas of mutual self-interest in a democracy – sustainable economic growth without climate change, security, health, education, the economy. Everyone wants the NHS to be the best it can and free at the point of delivery. There's pride in key workers and in the serving military.

There is, however, a fundamental belief in the power of dissent. If there are more who disagree than those who agree, everyone defers to their judgement. This is not some utopian, theoretical experiment.

It's a voluntary system, just like traffic lights. The system works because we consent. Democracy prefers cooperation to coercion. But this is not a lightly held belief. It is democracy and liberty, and historically we've been prepared to die for it. Every city, town and village in the country has a memorial to prove it.

Democracy has stood the test of time across the world. In Britain's case, it's been evolved, tried and tested for the best part of a thousand years of uninterrupted sovereignty. It is not perfect. But it is the least imperfect system. Brexiteer and Remainer may not agree on the outcome, but they can all agree on the decision-making process.

Why does democracy matter? Because democratic countries are consistently healthier, richer and, ultimately, better at protecting human rights. They are also driven by democratic capitalism. The great experimental idea is that you can have capitalism without democracy. As the great Zen master said: 'We'll see.'

The British people know our ancient democratic institutions are strong. They may be old-fashioned and in need of modernisation. They don't change easily. This is precisely why they can absorb criticism in times of uncertainty. They are repositories of enduring values.

The warning from the EU was intended to belittle, scare and threaten. Again, pressing all the wrong buttons. The British live on an island. They're used to being surrounded. They don't respond well to diktats, threats or lectures from anyone, let alone from people who don't eat pie. They trust democratic accountability because it works. It's in tune with the people. To want to leave was thus not to be stuck in the past but to recognise that it's Europe, not Britain, that's diverging from democracy. Britain knows that Europe's strength is in part dependent on its contribution economically and politically.

This has been true throughout European history from the multiple congresses and treaties over the past 200 years, both before and after the European Union. Vienna, Versailles, Rome, Maastricht, Amsterdam, Nice and Lisbon all were key steps in the evolution of Europe. Britain still constitutes a beacon of global democracy and a powerful economy. Whether it is a part of a formal European Union or not, it plays (and will continue to play) a vital role in European success. In or out of a political union, Britain remains the third biggest market for French farm goods, the second biggest for French wine[15] and one-fifth of German car sales globally.[16] There are more scientists based in Britain than in any other European country.[17] It was the second largest contributor to the European budget and the largest to NATO, after America.[18,19]

Britain could, of course, reject America and vice versa. If it doesn't move closer to America, it could petition for re-entry to the EU with all the attendant loss of face that entails. Or it could cultivate a new relationship with America. The latter seems the most obvious and logical course of action. Much of what happens may be down to the next US administration. It will definitely be down to the UK's stubbornness.

It's often overlooked by Brits, but Europe also needs to find a way forward after the first of its membership leaves. As journalist and historian Simon Jenkins put it: 'Britain's departure could not be lightly dismissed. Its economy was second only to Germany's in size and contributed 20 per cent of the EU budget.'[20] And it may be the first, but will not necessarily be the last.

The European Union has to ask how and why it happened, but it probably won't. All evidence to date points to it continuing as it is, which is one of the reasons why the British left.

Britain leaving Europe is not like Zayn Malik leaving One

Direction to pursue a solo career. It's not even like Paul and John leaving the Beatles. It's much more like the Rolling Stones firing Brian Jones for his abuse of drugs and alcohol. Yes, you heard that right. Mick, Keith and the boys fired Jones for *over-indulgence*. This is high praise indeed from those so qualified in the art. Sure, Britain has its problems with democracy, but nothing like the European Union. This is why so many voted to leave it. They asked why hundreds of years of successful self-determination should be subordinated to a system barely seventy years old. Especially one with all its failed economic harmonisation and dystopian bureaucracy. It was incompatible with democratic values in both form and content. It forgot the first rule of democracy: the system serves the people, not the other way around.

The long-rooted trust in democracy links back to the British faith in the tried and tested, discussed earlier. There is always talk about 'revolutionary approaches' to this or that. Something *really* revolutionary in British politics would have been the politicians ignoring the result of the referendum. Parliament came close to this in the three years between 2016 and 2019. The outcome of the general election of December 2019 was driven by the people, who saved a pompous establishment from this predicament.

WHAT THE MANDATE MEANS

The directionless decade that started in 2010 with David Cameron as Prime Minister in a coalition government has gone. The government finally has a clear mandate. It also has new responsibilities in representation. With an eighty-seven majority, it has more power to legislate than any other government in the past thirty years. The pandemic has obscured this truth. It's hard to overstate the importance of this and the scale of the massive shift.

This matters because without a majority, governments can barely deal with day-to-day events. They can't do anything. This is where it had got to when Boris Johnson was elected leader of the Conservatives. In fact, it was worse than that. It was what is technically called a significant minority position. With a small majority (up to fifty seats), governments can pass budgets and set about running the country. In a house of 650 MPs, though, if one in thirteen, or 7 per cent, of your MPs rebel, then you've lost your small majority. With a moderate majority (of 50–100 seats, as now), then bolder, more effective reforms are possible, and, as we shall see, they are needed.

It's important to note that since the Second World War, only two political leaders have won more than 100-seat majorities. They were Margaret Thatcher in 1983 and 1987 and Tony Blair in 1997 and 2001.[21] People seem to forget that it was for good reasons that Tony Blair was the first and only Labour Prime Minister *ever* to be returned to office after not one election but three in a row. It's the only time it happened in one hundred years of the Labour movement. Just think about that for a second. All the way from Sidney and Beatrice Webb through Keir Hardie, Nye Bevan and Manny Shinwell to Barbara Castle, Tony Benn and Jeremy Corbyn. He was strong enough to fight the laziness of complacent thinking. It's important to understand that when the Labour Party learns nothing, forgets nothing and offers nothing dressed up as something, the result lets down progressively minded members in *both* parties.

THE DANGERS OF A LARGE MAJORITY

An essential hallmark of democracy is that all change initially begins as minority dissent. This is true even when the government itself decides on a definitive course of action; it then needs to sell its approach to backbenchers, the media, civil servants and its own voluntary party activists.

Of course, the position of a 'stonking' majority seems like a novel idea today, since the UK has experienced a decade with no significant majority in Parliament. When there is a large majority, though, the government still has a responsibility to listen to minority voices, not the least of which may bring solutions to intractable problems. Some of the best causes speak with the quietest voices.

This is where an effective opposition comes in. No court is truly balanced when only one side is making an argument. For this reason, when there is no effective opposition party, a number of other things can happen to ensure the government is challenged as it should be. For instance, a government may face opposition within its own party. There will be those who have been passed over for promotion, those who consider themselves wronged or who relish mischief. Within a large majority, there will be many not serving in government roles and many opinions about the right course of action.

Just like the more traditional opposition, this type of government can inflict wounds. Like those the Conservatives wreaked on themselves during the Brexit civil war, for example. In order to create unity, several experienced senior figures were defenestrated. There was a danger that this could become a rerun of the 'wets' and 'dries' of the Thatcher years, which culminated in the Heseltine/Lawson and Thatcher split. It was there, too, under John Major with the Eurosceptics, even when he had a workable majority. It's also been seen in the Labour Party, showing multiple times between Tony Blair and Gordon Brown, despite their majority of more than 100 seats. If the government is to bring unity to the country, a mandate is a start, but it is not enough in itself; the ruling party first has to unify itself.

Whitehall and the civil service can also become the opposition. The government can sometimes go as far as to perceive the civil service as the enemy – an idea that was famously satirised in the Thatcher years in the TV sitcoms *Yes, Minister* and *Yes, Prime Minister*.

Large majorities can also cause a government to over-reach itself. Being armed with a number of like-minded MPs and near-guaranteed support can be deceptive. The majority can be interpreted as carte blanche. The government can decide to settle old scores that the public either don't care about or which they are actively against. In the 1990s, the poll tax became a touchstone issue for the public while the Conservative government of the time was obsessed with in-fighting over Europe.

The government can become the target of the story arc during times of large majority, and the honeymoon period in media coverage for any new government does not often last long. The bigger the majority, the quicker the arc changes. It becomes fashionable to attack the government, and those with a large majority quickly acquire noisy media opponents.

VOTER TURNOUT

Parliament came dangerously close to ignoring a democratic mandate after the European referendum. There's evidence that many voters disengaged after this. Despite the wall-to-wall, three-year, constant mind-numbing, spleen-rupturing coverage of Brexit, the 2019 turnout was still the *fifth lowest* in 100 years. This lack of interest is echoed and amplified at the local level. We should be worried about participation rates.

2019 ELECTION VOTER TURNOUT

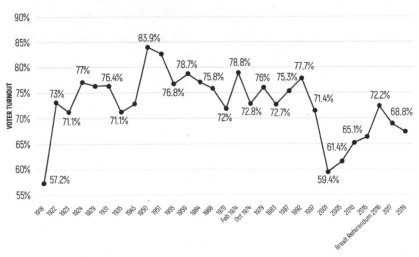

Source: 'Voter turnout in general elections and in the Brexit referendum in the United Kingdom from 1918 to 2019'
© Statista 2019

What are we to make of this graph? Well, we should start by noting that it is more interesting for what it doesn't say. The X axis is truncated, for one thing, indicating nothing below 50 per cent. In addition, and we'll come back to this later, it is notable that only about half of this number turn out at local elections. There's a lot less interest at that level.

Looking at what the graph indicates, the first conclusion is about the consistency of the figures. Between two-thirds and three-quarters of the population always vote. This has remained pretty much the same for 100 years. This remains true despite the number of graduates increasing from 4,357 annually in 1920 to 350,800 in 2011[22] (see below). So, either non-graduates have become less and less interested as more and more graduates join the voting pool, or the increasing number of graduates has had no effect on turnout. Whatever is the case, the most qualified young people are still less likely to turn out than the least qualified people aged fifty-five and over.[23] Student turnout is well below average.[24] This may account

99

for some of the long-term decline in voter turnout. In this respect, both capitalism and democracy need the young to believe in them, otherwise both systems will be seen as irrelevant.

STUDENTS OBTAINING UNIVERSITY DEGREES, UK

	FIRST DEGREES			HIGHER DEGREES		
	MEN	WOMEN	TOTAL	MEN	WOMEN	TOTAL
1920	3,145	1,212	4,357	529	174	703
1930	6,494	2,635	9,129	1,123	200	1,323
1938	7,071	2,240	9,311	1,316	164	1,480
1950	13,398	3,939	17,337	2,149	261	2,410
1960	16,851	5,575	22,426	2,994	279	3,273
1970	35,571	15,618	15,189	11,186	1,715	12,901
1980	42,831	25,319	68,150	14,414	4,511	18,925
1990	43,297	33,866	77,163	20,905	10,419	31,324
2000	109,930	133,316	243,246	46,015	40,520	86,535
2005	122,155	156,225	278,380	63,035	62,050	125,085
2010	144,980	185,740	330,720	93,375	89,235	182,610
2011	153,235	197,565	350,800	96,280	97,990	194,270

Notes:
All figures are for students from all domiciles
Full-time first degree students only

Major break in series
1925 - Excludes higher degree awarded without further study
1973 - Includes universities in Northern Ireland
1994 - Includes former Polytechnics and Open University from now on
2000 - Includes students qualifying from 'dormant' status - where a student is not actively studying for their qualification. This may be where there is an administrative delay between completion and award. These qualifications were not previously recorded. The main impact is on the number of doctorates.

Source: Statistical abstract for the United Kingdom 1935, Board of Trade
Annual abstract of statistics, ONS/CSO
Higher Education Statistics Agency.
House of Commons Library
Education, 'Historical statistics. Statistical abstract for the United Kingdom 1935, Board of Trade Annual abstract of statistics, ONS/CSO Higher Education Statistics Agency'

© Parliamentary Copyright, 2019
Contains public sector information licensed under the Open Government Licence v3.0.
http://www.nationalarchives.gov.uk/doc/open-government-licence/version/3/

Although the majority of people are turning out to vote, this obviously says nothing for the substantial minority that does not. There are any number of reasons as to why a person might not vote. Some are not interested or they don't understand politics (who does?); others don't think their vote will make a difference, for example, if they are a Labour voter in a safe Tory seat; or perhaps they just don't care. It could also be because they don't have time in the day. Let's be clear, this could also indicate contentment and/or satisfaction, but it's doubtful. We don't know what we don't know.

The great localism experiment pursued by successive administrations was designed to enthuse voters. It has not. We can also see that with an ageing population over this period of time (and the increased level of turnout that comes with that age group), the turnout has, perhaps unexpectedly, remained consistent. This possibly indicates that older voters have replaced younger ones. If this is the case, as the population ages, we would expect to see the turnout increase or remain at around the same level, though with an increased bias towards conservatism as the older among voters leave behind their more liberal youths. This, then, could explain the gap between the media/Westminster bubble that has a representative bias towards youth and the electorate at large. This will have implications for any government spending in the future.

THE AGE PIVOT

In a prescient piece in *The Guardian* just prior to the 2019 general election, Torsten Bell noted:

> In the same way that class dominated many elections of the twentieth century, age has increasingly come to dominate in the twenty-first. A voter's age wasn't a decisive factor in which party they opted for in the 1970s, but it has become increasingly important as a predictor in recent decades. In 2017, a thirty-year-old was twice as likely to back Labour as a seventy-year-old. The latter, in turn, was more than twice as likely to vote Conservative. Come polling day, our age will do a lot of work in explaining who we vote for.[25]

The dominant factor of age was illustrated by the 2019 election result:

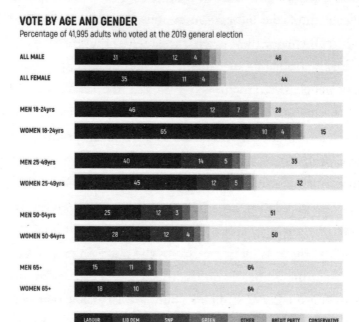

VOTE BY AGE AND GENDER
Percentage of 41,995 adults who voted at the 2019 general election

Source: 'How Britain voted in the 2019 general election', Adam McDonnell and Chris Curtis, YouGov, 13-16 December 2019

Discussing the election result in *The Times* on 17 December 2019, Matt Chorley said:

> The age at which voters are more likely to vote Tory than Labour dropped dramatically as younger people fell out of love with Jeremy Corbyn. In 2017, when Theresa May lost her majority, the crossover point at which people were more likely to be Conservatives occurred at age forty-seven. In [the 2019] election result this fell to thirty-nine.

So, in 2019, the crossover happened earlier and the age skew was bigger still. The political irony may be that while youth is no advantage, all representatives need a positive, future-orientated narrative.

The British Election Study[26] has produced data for every election since 1964. It shows an electoral view through the rear-view mirror. It specifically shows the 'baby boomers'. This really matters because there are more of them and they're also living longer. They turn out and vote. They are the backbone of Britain. They're the youngest generation of older people ever. There's never been a generation so politically powerful. They are the home-owning, garden-obsessed, community-focused, debt-free, index-linked, triple-locked, equity-released, disposable-incomed, NHS hip-replaced, happily married, politically organised, letter-writing, book-reading, telly-shouting, *Telegraph*-buying, meals-on-wheels volunteering, post-war, post-national service, *Question Time*-watching, statin-soaked, vitamin-pumped, Voltarol-eased, Viagra-fuelled, suburban-dwelling, hill-walking, always-voting, car-owning, *Archers*-listening, Titchmarsh-worshipping, broadband-enabled, baby boomers. They are the Guards Armoured Division of Waitrose, the Varangian Guard of the Royal Voluntary Service, the Hashishin of the Royal Horticultural Society, the Knights Hospitaller of the Anglican Church, the Berserkers of the British Legion and the Pennines of every county council, every village fete and every flower show. God bless them. They're the heart of the nation and we owe them a great deal.

The dynamics of age and character that drove the Brexit vote and the return to conservatism at the 2019 general election are significant because they reveal much about the British character. To many, turning our back on Europe is a risk, but by a majority we decided that it was a risk worth taking. This is where the British character reasserts itself. Without strong roots, you can't take big risks. It is precisely because Britain has a strong and flexible constitution that it can do something like this. The British have a sense of themselves in spite of changing demographics, technologies, behaviours and communities.

They were interested enough in the outcome to make it happen. There is an opportunity here. Once more, people are engaged in politics. So, what if this passion was applied across the country?

NATION, COUNTRY, IDENTITY AND BONDS

A national identity is formed by processes which are bottom-up as well as top-down. Strong brands have always been part of the British identity. These are often linked to the ancient accents, culture and traditions of a particular area. We have a strong sense of what it is to be from Scotland, Wales and Northern Ireland. In a similar way, we can recognise Cornwall, Lancashire or Yorkshire or the north-east. The closer to London, the more we see a top-down identity partly because of the national institutions and cosmopolitan cultures that reside there.

In a similar way, if the greatest aspect of the British brand is trust, how much of this comes from, say, the Yorkshire brand, for example? It has all the elements of trust, reliability and common sense, to which we could add frugality, robustness and plain speaking. In the same way, the union flag is a synergy of strands, a sort of British tartan, that forms our national identity.

If we know the qualities that Britain stands for, we should be able to say the same for the regions. Understanding this set of identities is vital. A national identity cannot be about one type of homogenised culture. It must be about understanding, respecting and celebrating regional and local cultures. They key to defeating nationalism paradoxically then comes from celebrating national diversity. Nationalism only emerges when cultures feel threatened. So, for example, if the centre only celebrates metropolitan culture, this will be perceived as a threat. This is why the Director-General of the BBC Tim Davie is right to champion local cultures.[27] This cannot just be about racial, sexual or political diversity. It must include regional and local diversity too.

Britain has always had a rich and diverse culture. If that is threatened, can anyone be surprised that it is robustly defended? National identity emerges from a synergy of local identities. The relationship between the two is linear and direct. One cannot sustainably succeed without the other.

Billy Connolly starts his book *Made in Scotland* by posing the question: 'What do you come from?'[28] Not where. His book is about history, his own seventy-five years and Scotland's millennia. It is a love letter to his country. His identity with it. His deep connection to it, even when he is living far away. He saw nothing incompatible with that sense of himself as a Scot and not a nationalist. He states that only one thing would cause him to change his position: his view that Britain might be turning its back on Europe.

He describes how many feel British, but also English, Welsh, Scottish and Irish. For some of our citizens this identity is complicated further still. In her book *Brit(ish)*, Afua Hirsch describes the exasperation of minority Brits continually being asked where they are from or facing the 'sense that there is some inherent conflict between white British values and accomplishments and those of everyone else'.[29] Her identity is threatened and misunderstood, so she defends it, and why not?

Top-down, the four devolved nations have shared missions in the creation of the NHS, the welfare state, shared defence and social reform. We could celebrate this more. Britain is unusual in not having either a national day of celebrations or distinct events around our great institutions. The instincts to do so are there. It happened spontaneously during Covid when communities clapped the NHS, so why can we not celebrate our national institutions, or even our devolved nations, formally? Let's look more closely at these.

Scottish nationalism grew up under Labour, digging in further post-devolution. It was turbo-charged when the Conservatives came to power. There is a strong anti-Westminster feeling in Scotland fuelled by what is on offer. It appears to lack understanding. Its priorities appear different. It appears obsessed with metropolitan matters. It is not loved. It is not even trusted.

It is said that the union prevents the progress of the Scottish nation – both materially and morally. We can do more to celebrate Scots culture perhaps in the way Canada and America do. Most English people would need no excuse to join in the drinking on St Patrick's or St David's Day. As for Burns Night, well, try stopping them. If we don't invest in relationships, why are we surprised when they atrophy through reciprocal disinterest? Scots may feel abandoned by London in the same way that provinces of England do.

Northern Ireland illustrates an extreme example of what happens when cultures appear to be existentially threatened – they defend themselves with violence. Devolution may have quelled this, but it did not automatically lead to a consistently functioning assembly. It took hard work to revive it after a three-year suspension when power sharing collapsed. There is a danger that the tools designed to promote cooperation will result in vetoing and paralysis. The divisions can be addressed with common culture. Perhaps the best example of this is the personal relationship between Martin McGuinness and Ian Paisley.[30] Whatever you thought of them, they both shared a passion, had a sense of humour and dedication to their cause.

Scotland's identity in the world is strong, as is Northern Ireland's; Wales, however, may appear the quieter sister. Until recent times, even its own language was in danger of becoming invisible, with Welsh school children being punished for speaking it. Legislation changed all that. Now, 19 per cent of Welsh people speak Britain's oldest language. It is the country of Dylan Thomas and Roald Dahl, of Brydon, Burton and Bassey. It has connections all over the world and a strong identity, too. For instance, 50,000 people in Patagonia claim Welsh heritage.[31] The British could celebrate Wales more.

The differences between the English and their neighbours are well documented by social anthropologists. Kate Fox identified what she called the English social disease, an awkwardness which does not afflict the other nations of the UK. Mr Bean, after all, is most definitely English.[32]

If the other nations are feeling hard done by because of devolution, then they can rest assured that England feels it, too. English nationalism has also been on the rise in recent years, although it is waning now, perhaps in part due to the introduction of English votes for English laws in 2015. In *England: An Elegy*, Roger Scruton sees a country being undermined:

When people are animated by an ideal … to whatever small degree, they endeavour to live up to it. It is not in the gross and material things that a national character is revealed, but in the superfluities, the places where people are at one with themselves and endeavour to be what they ought: the institutions of education, justice, religion and leisure. In these areas ideals make a difference. They do not become a reality, but they strain constantly to incarnate themselves, and act as 'regulative ideas' in the day to day conduct that invokes them. When this ceases to happen – when people discard, ignore, or mock the ideals which formed their national character – they no longer exist as a people, but only as a crowd. That is what is happening now in England.[33]

The point he fails to grasp here is that the English celebrate neither the devolved nations nor their own regions. If Scotland is turning its back on England, then how soon before Cornwall or Yorkshire slide into the same process?[34] Brexit may not be a single event. It may be the beginning of a process unless we reverse the drift.

The practical upside to the union is well understood, but the Brexit vote showed one thing clearly: even if people thought they might be worse off afterwards, there were other things that mattered more. Post-Brexit, Britain needs to examine why the union of the four nations matters and how to reverse the drift. If the union matters, it needs to be clear why. If the UK is to survive, its existence can't be taken for granted.

Former Stormont First Minister Lord Trimble, along with former First Ministers of Scotland and Wales Lord Jack McConnell and Carwyn Jones, proposed a new 'constitutional settlement' to help secure the future of the United Kingdom. What is it that binds us, ultimately? Have we become so selfish that we cannot enjoy or celebrate one another? All these questions must be answered.

We have much to unite our cultures. In our history, we've celebrated the military prowess of the Scots, the Welsh and the Northern Irish regiments. Many will remember Colonel Tim Collins's speech to the Royal Irish Regiment on the eve of battle in the Second Gulf War.[35] We are passionate about our sports. All parts of the union like their food and drink. Britain has ninety different beers,[36] hundreds of different types of bread,[37] 400 types of sausage[38] and 700 types of cheese.[39] But maybe we take them for granted? Maybe there is an opportunity for restaurateurs?

We all use humour as insurrection. Character always appreciates character. We moan about the weather. And it's not just the cultural similarities. It's the big stuff, too. All parts of the UK are generous, compassionate, open and global. Northern Ireland, for instance, took the highest proportion of Syrian refugees.[40] It is estimated that there are 20,000 refugees living in Scotland.[41]

Compare that to Japan, for example. According to the United Nations High Commissioner for Refugees (UNHCR), by the end of 2018 there were 126,720 refugees, 45,244 pending asylum cases and 125 stateless persons in the UK. That's around one-quarter of a per cent (0.26 per cent) of the UK's total population.[42] In 2017, Japan took in twenty.[43] This is true despite the fact that the country is a demographic time bomb, desperate for migrant workers. Being British is more than a nationality; it is an attitude.

SOCIAL FABRIC OF THE UK

What no one has started to look at is the impact that devolution has had on the social fabric of the UK. Let's take the issue of being able to marry the person you love. Until 2020, embarking on a relationship in the UK could be a complex issue. If you were gay, you could marry in England, Wales and Scotland, but not Northern Ireland. If you were straight you could have a civil partnership in England and Wales, but not Scotland because it chose to legislate separately. This had a more expansive impact than you might first think. Imagine the difficulties of being a British business, for instance, trying to figure out which among your employees are considered to have a spouse, and who is entitled to that aspect of your employment conditions.

Access to abortion is another issue that has resulted in huge inequalities between women and girls within the four nations. Despite knowing that harm was done to women and girls as a result of no access to legal abortions, the government was reluctant to act until a court ruled that Northern Ireland's abortion law was in breach of the Human Rights Act. In recent times, courts have ruled before politicians have acted. But 'change by judge' makes for bad law. The legislative processes of Parliament and assemblies are designed to hone solutions, create consensus, consult those affected. A court ruling does not do that. It's not meant to. And that is not to mention the trauma and expense we might be putting our citizens through if they wish to challenge legislation. Politicians must be more proactive on these social issues and keep pace with societal development and changing attitudes if we both value the union and want devolution to be a positive force for social progress.

The lowering of the voting age will become another matter of difference across the UK. Surely each of the countries that make up the nation should make reference to each other when devising these policies? Is there an incentive to perpetuate division and difference if you are a nationalist politician? Well, yes, there is. But surely the focus should be on what is in the best interests of all citizens, at least.

Covid brought out some of the advantages of the union. The British armed forces helped to deploy a vaccine which was approved faster and distributed quicker than almost anywhere in the world. The devolved nations benefited equally from this. Should we be investing more in those institutions that bring us together? These key issues, which define values and enshrine freedoms and obligations, must be at the heart of reviving the union.

CONCLUSIONS

In summary, if the government is going to deliver on a mandate to rebuild trust, modernisation must be considered, but only in parallel to other solutions. It has to be a top-down as well as bottom-up approach. The government can't rely on just changing structures at the local and regional levels because it has been tried on so many occasions and failed every time. The cynicism alone is a difficult hurdle to overcome. This opinion is especially present in places like Scotland, where Westminster long ago ceded the ground to nationalism. Devolution should not be an excuse for dismissal or disinterest.

People want to help. But they think they can't. That is why they're frustrated at politics. Not because others are wrong, but because they feel powerless. The nationalist solution is to seek to balance the needs of the head and the heart by tearing out the latter and expecting the former to prosper on its own. Overcoming this will require a genuine commitment to solving the problem, rather than the more common Westminster bait-and-switch, which promises delivery before drowning it in complications.

The key to gaining any locomotive momentum outside of London is in how finance can be raised to make change happen when so much is still required for basic public services. We look at this further in Chapter 7.

Britain arrived at this point via an extraordinary period which started with the European referendum in 2016 and culminated in the general election of 2019. It was ironic that for such a big international move, it was a period when the country was almost exclusively focused on domestic issues. Thus, Britain left the European Union at 2300 hours GMT on 31 January 2020, as a matter of fact. Its future cannot be fuelled by faith alone. We've looked at the internal forces that drove the outcome. Next, we need to understand the forces outside Britain that will shape our future.

4

WHO DO WE COMPETE WITH?

There was an element of Gloria Gaynor's 'I Will Survive' about Brexit. We went, went out the door, just turned around and were not welcome any more. Well, we're going to need a better long-term vision than that. In this chapter, we explore the ways in which Britain could develop a new relationship with the world after Brexit. Which countries have similar outlooks? What is the next step in the special relationship with America? What do we both believe in? What is the future of our European relationships? How will the rise of China change the world? Could new partnerships spark a resurgence in our democratic values and modernise our capital markets?

Countries are like couples. The relationship works best when they are different but complementary – when they can become more than just the sum of their parts. For a relationship to work, the parties don't have to be the same, but they must be looking in the same direction. They must each have qualities the other either admires or aspires to have. It really helps if one has something the other needs and vice versa. The table stakes for any relationship are trust and mutual self-interest. It helps if they have a shared history. Sometimes relationships can come back stronger after a dispute. Some relationships are formed and strengthened by a common threat.

THE SPECIAL RELATIONSHIP

The free world has a peculiar relationship with America. It relies upon it for protection, then criticises the way it provides it. The free world wants authority but not responsibility. And this is the chief source of disbelief and derision from the American point of view. How can an entire continent, let alone the free world, willingly accept its military protection, then still criticise it so stridently?

America historically has always been reluctant to get involved in wars. It joined the First World War three years after it started. It joined the Second World War three years after that one started as well. It's easy to understand why. The complications and futility of European wars were exactly what America was founded to avoid. This is why the rebellion and subsequent Civil War of 1861 was a traumatising tragedy for America.[1] The Union went to war with the Confederacy over the issue of slavery. The first and only time a Confederate flag flew in the Capitol building was 6 January 2021, when it was carried inside by rioters.[2] It was calculated to outrage and it did.

Notwithstanding the blood and treasure expended in all its wars, it was American generosity that funded $135 billion in today's currency for the Marshall Plan to rebuild Europe in 1947. It wrote off German sovereign debt in the 1950s.[3] It stood guarantor to Europe through fifty years of Cold War. In return, it got back a tsunami of anti-American sentiment.

It's the greatest paradox of all time. Democracies die to defend the denigration of democracy. It's why free speech carries responsibility. Or it should. Military cemeteries around the world are full of those who died on all sides for our right to speak our minds.

Our public discourse should therefore be worthy of their loss, their families' grief and their memories. Try this. Visit one of the American cemeteries at Madingley near Cambridge or at Colleville-sur-Mer in France. In the late afternoon quiet of a winter sunset, sit a while in these places among the long shadows. Breathe the freezing, deathly air. Touch the headstones. Here, you'll find hundreds of American boys thousands of miles away from homes to which they never returned. They didn't start the wars they fought in. They didn't know about concentration camps. They didn't get to live long enough to know why they had been sacrificed. Of course, you can point to the staggering scale of Russian sacrifice which was matched only by the territorial claims at Yalta. The only territory America claimed in Europe was the ground to inter these young men. This creates a special relationship, not just with Britain but with all the democracies they fought for.

Respecting democracy doesn't mean you can't question America or protest against its wars, only that when you tell the Americans to go home, you spare a thought for the ones that never will.

America remains the largest contributor to NATO and it has fought to preserve European freedoms three times in a hundred years. And when your biggest ally turns out for you in three world wars – one cold, two hot – if you're any sort of reliable ally, you have little real option but to reciprocate. This came to pass in the first and second Gulf Wars and 9/11. Tony Blair understood this. Thatcher did. Churchill, too. If you support your biggest and most powerful ally, it doesn't make you a neo-con nutter; it makes you a student of Bismarck's realpolitik. Nevertheless, Tony Blair was vilified by the very party he delivered three election victories for. In that respect, he and America have much in common. They're both subject to ingratitude and amnesia.

Of course, there are many familial clichés about the Anglo-American relationship. It's parent-to-child. We're cousins. We're brothers in arms. The UK is America's conscience. It's Ancient Greece to Rome. It's not clear what America means to Britain: protection, wealth, opportunity possibly. To Americans, though, it's obvious what Britain and Europe mean to them. It's family. Literally. Britain has family in America, but America has family across the world. These are the branches of a global family tree wanting to identify and connect with their provenance. We share sisters, daughters, wives, sons, brothers, fathers, uncles and aunts.

America was defined by its separation from Britain. It was rebelling against a lack of democracy. Thus, it was defined by Britain, or more truthfully by the defects in the British political system. When the United States chose self-determination, Britain learned little. Just as Europe is learning nothing as Britain chooses self-determination for pretty much the same reason. The British Empire and the European Union thus made the same mistakes of self-centricity and complacency at different times. And whether it likes it or not, Britain will be defined by its separation from Europe. How it will be defined is, as yet, unwritten. It needs no reminding of the shortcomings of Europe, but it should remember, for instance, that the EU contributed towards a settled peace in Northern Ireland and the successful reunification of a divided Germany. It wasn't all bad.

For both America and Britain, independence led to a renewed vigour. Both countries went on to great success. Both countries went on to develop their democracies and their economies. It's therefore clearly possible for Britain to leave the European Union to the enduring benefit of both parties. Furthermore, the existential shock caused by the rupture could well be the provenance of renewed energy and vigour. The Congress and the Senate were both illuminated as much by idealism as by the failure of the parliamentary system it left behind. This is where Britain needs to learn from the American experience and use the move towards independence from Europe to re-invigorate its democracy. It could start with the defence of free speech.

The first responsibility of government may be to defend the state, but a pretty close second is the defence of public discourse. This is now the daily frontline of defending democracy. It is the responsibility of the state to ensure free speech survives. It set standards of public discourse through our laws.

There's a reason the seats of democracies are at the brightly lit centre of our cities. They are places where no one is afraid to tread, where the standards of discourse are the highest, where people, no matter their disadvantages, can feel safe. Why should it be any different online? There is a direct, line-of-sight link between the standards of public discourse and the rising level of domestic extremism and international violence.

If we don't defend public discourse it will cost lives. It already has. Jo Cox's killer learned his extremism online. So did many other homegrown terrorists. The rioters that smashed up the Capitol Building in Washington DC and killed people were organised and marshalled through social media.

The preservation of democracy involves sacrifice. Should young men and women die to preserve the right to hurl abuse on social media? Even more so when it is facilitated and accelerated by private sector corporations solely for profit? Britain, America and all the world's democracies face the same challenge to their public discourse. There's an opportunity to show leadership here and it connects strongly to the equalities issues discussed later in this book.

This is not an argument to censor free speech, only that it be subject to the law. In any case, it would be like trying to hold back the sea. Without reform, we risk drowning our most sacred institutions in a cheese dream conspiracy theory of David-Icke-deranged evil space lizards torching 5G towers on behalf of The Bilderberg Group.[4] It would be deeply comic, but for its profoundly tragic consequences as we saw in the American Capitol in January 2021.

So far, the private sector has moved faster than democratic institutions to censor the most violent noises coming from the looneyverse. The social media companies began that finally when placed under pressure to remove Donald Trump from their platforms. If there is to be censorship, then it should be by elected and accountable representatives working in the public interest, not corporations facilitating ever more extreme content for profit. Social media companies have the power to facilitate bullying, hatred and violence, so shouldn't they be accountable in law for doing so? Protecting against online harms is difficult, but it's no reason not to try.

Social media needs and feeds division. It can do so with immunity because it is unfettered by the standards of truth the so-called mainstream media operate under. There's nothing mainstream about a media that operates within the parameters of the law. There's just potential redress when it libels someone or damages a reputation wrongly. Neither do the parameters that mainstream media operate under prevent free speech. If they did, why would they be enshrined in British law and the American First Amendment?

We have a mainstream media because we have mainstream lives, mainstream protections of minorities, mainstream transport in-frastructures, mainstream environmental regulations, mainstream food standards, mainstream medicines, mainstream corporations, mainstream schools and mainstream police services. Our civil society lives under a set of laws. Why should any organisation be allowed not to? There's really no argument for allowing social media to remain unregulated at the expense of mainstream media, at the expense of civil discourse, at the expense of so many vulnerable groups and at the expense of communities-supporting newspapers that hold local government to account. Newspapers are not doomed because of their economics. There are many parts of the world where they are still thriving.[5]

Totalitarianism is the suppression of free speech by the public sector. How different are we if we allow it by the private sector instead?

Niall Ferguson explains how social media escaped liability in his book *The Square and the Tower: Networks and Power, from the Freemasons to Facebook*. They were exempted from publishers liability under the American Telecommunications Act 1996, Section 230, which categorises them as telecommunications firms rather than publishers. He argues that companies are entitled to Section 230's protection – but only if they uphold the diversity of discourse envisaged by Congress.

A drive for the reinvention of public discourse could be at the centre of a drive to modernise our democracy to act as a rallying call for other areas of British life to follow suit.

Both Britain and America feel strongly about the issue of free speech. As we leave Europe, can we use the opportunity to show fresh leadership in this area? Independence is an argument about far more than politics. It's a different view of the universe. When Copernicus revealed his new heliocentric view of the world, it was a challenge to the Catholic Church, so they 'cancelled' it. They prohibited it because it was a threat to their authority. Free thinking should never be proscribed by power or provenance. Left unprotected by the law, we could end up with the freedom of an online mob to bully a minority.

It's difficult to understand why democratic nations aren't focused on common challenges like this. They seem too obsessed with their internal differences let alone the external ones. Could it be because they are so similar? After all, they are both founded on the same idea; for instance, that a union of states is stronger than a single one. Their flags contain similar stars albeit with different backgrounds. America modelled itself, initially at least, on the best aspects of British, French and even Roman government.[6] What was the Declaration of Independence if not an updated version of Magna Carta?[7] What is the European Union if not a tribute to America? What was Brexit if not a Declaration of Independence?

Europeans think that Americans are everywhere in Europe. Europe consumes American food, listens to American music, its businesses run on American software, it's even defended by Americans. Its defence systems and intelligence communities work closely together. America thinks the same. It thinks that Europeans are everywhere. Americans drive European cars, watch and listen to European entertainment, follow European soccer and eat European food.

If it's only chlorinated chicken that separates the UK from the US, then this illustrates how much our interests align. Freud called this phenomenon 'the narcissism of minor differences'.[8] This might explain the need Britain has to see America as a kind of exaggerated, more dramatic world of extremes, where the differences become caricature. In Chapter 1, we explored the notion of the British character, but to really understand America, we turn to American caricature.

THE SCOOBY-DOO MODEL OF ANGLO-AMERICAN RELATIONS

It's difficult to believe now, but there was a time when British TV culture was highbrow rather than monobrow. Men like Jeremy Isaacs (Oxford) made *The World at War*. It explained how superior the Allies were. Jacob Bronowski (Cambridge) made *The Ascent of Man*. It explained how superior humans were. Kenneth Clark (Oxford) made the 1969 TV series *Civilisation*. It explained how superior Oxford-educated British middle-aged white men were. Clark was presaged by stool-loosening organ music as he extolled the Apollo Belvedere. It was Presbyterian TV. Not necessarily appetising, but probably good for you. Televisual bran flakes. It reeked of Reith.

American culture of the time was unencumbered with such puritanical pieties. It did have Carl Sagan, a brilliant scientist who speculated about intelligent life in the cosmos (not to be confused with the very reasonably priced package holiday company with a similar name). He died prematurely, but not before he had popularised the baton phrase 'billions and billions'. This was later picked up as a tribute phrase by home-grown British TV all-round super-intelligent science-saucepot, Professor Brian Cox. He and David Attenborough show how great communicators create interest in science.

1970s American culture was really embodied in *Scooby-Doo, Where are you!*, which extolled the fun you could have with a cartoon dog. You can learn a lot about the relationship between America and Britain from its children's entertainment. There are differences and similarities. There's the shared obsession with bears, for instance. America has Baloo the Bear, Barney Bear, Blubber Bear (*Wacky Races*), Fozzie Bear, Fleegle (*The Banana Splits*), Smokey the Bear, Square Bear (*The Hair Bear Bunch*), Yogi Bear and Boo-Boo. The British have Biffo the Bear, Big and Little Ted (*Play School*), Bungle

(*Rainbow*), Nookie Bear, Paddington Bear, Pooh Bear, Rupert the Bear, The Three Bears, Sooty, Sweep and SuperTed.

Of course, this book is not going to gamble what little is left of its credibility discussing the relative IQ of Bungle versus Baloo the Bear, but there is a difference. Baloo is more glamorous, more knowing, more *racy*. We never saw any British bears dancing, singing or being hep. Bungle is not racy, but then nor are the British. Or so it first appears.

In a strong case of art imitating life, Bungle's post-TV panto career was destroyed following a devastating sex scandal when the presence of an 'X-rated' episode was revealed. It is still available on the less frequented parts of the internet.[9] Had a similar thing occurred to Baloo in America, the Disney Corporation would have sued everyone in the room. No one in Britain is planning to launch a class-action suit claiming damages from the legendary episode entitled: 'Have you seen Bungle's Twanger?'

Britain and America had their own foxes as well. America had Wile E. Coyote, who went from failure to failure armed only with an abundance of cunning, a box of bird seed and an anvil that would later crush him. The British in their turn had the ever-popular Basil Brush, who laughed a lot, was upbeat and enthusiastic. Sadly, he too was the subject of a scandal. Under a headline of 'Is Basil Brush Racist?',[10] *The Guardian* reported that 'Basil Brush is under investigation by the Hate Crimes Unit of Northamptonshire Constabulary'. Brush was accused of bigotry and of being 'a vulpine Terry-Thomas' and of 'stereotyping a recognised ethnic group'. He apparently had joked that a 'gypsy' fortune teller had stolen his wallet. You'd never be able to charge Wile E. Coyote with racism. Handling unauthorised Acme ballistics, maybe.

Despite this generally fun and carefree outlook on life, kids in both America and Britain (today's leaders) were busily preparing themselves for a lifetime of capitalism and warfare. Children were fed on a diet of war films and heavily militarised toys. The Johnny Seven OMA (One Man Army) was a good example. It was the first multifunction semi-automatic assault rifle toy weapon. Its 'seven functionality' was based on being able to fire bullets one at a time via a bolt-action spring mechanism through a silver barrel. There were three different rockets: a green armour-piercing shell – an anti-bunker device – a grenade launcher and the red anti-tank missile fired via spring action on the main barrel. The toy, when fully assembled, was over three feet long and weighed about four pounds. If all else failed, you could just club your brother senseless with it.

At the time, children's bedrooms resembled Fallujah. When you weren't simulating warfare yourself, there were dolls to do it for you. Launched as GI Joe in America and Action Man in Britain, it came in many variations. In 1976, a version was made that had swivelling eyes. They only went side to side, mind. Up and down would have presumably introduced a sense of ironic camp prejudicial to military discipline.

Guns and alcohol were everywhere, especially in children's advertising. A popular commercial of the time was for Nestlé's (at the time pronounced 'Nessels')[11] Milky Bars. This featured an NHS-bespectacled, prepubescent, philanthropic, vertically challenged cowboy (with the emphasis on boy) dispensing dental decay and discharging firearms in a saloon bar (yes, really). He pulled out a revolver, which curiously morphed into a belt-fed MG42, as he drilled the words MILKY BAR into any target of opportunity. Sadly, the Milky Bar Kid went the way of many of the other British childhood icons. Despite being the white chocolate Ganymede, he was jailed for robbery and died prematurely after leaving prison, where he'd got hooked on Spice. Thus proving Milky Bar to be the gateway drug we always believed at the time.[12]

This confrontational approach continued into outer space in transatlantic, quasi-military-themed children's shows like puppet-based *Fireball XL5*, *Thunderbirds* and *Stingray*. Despite being British productions, they featured almost exclusively American voices and scripts. The two exceptions to this were International Rescue's 'London' agent Lady Penelope and her ever-pliable chauffeur, the proboscitic Parker.

The Cold War inspired the darker *Captain Scarlet and the Mysterons* and proto-nerd *Joe 90*, where a Milky Bar Kid look-alike had his brain melted by a gigantic computer called 'BIG RAT' so he could indulge in murine espionage. The real brains behind it all were military man Gerry Anderson and his missus Sylvia, who voiced Lady Penelope. Together they went on to expand the militarism into space, first with *UFO* then *Space: 1999*. Both of these series featured a war against aliens who were apparently bent on invading 1970s austerity Britain, presumably to study Vesta Chow Mein, the three-day week and Bruce Forsyth's hair.

The 1980s heralded a new, more masculine era in American culture, and the cartoon world responded in sympathy. *He-Man* was laden with all sorts of testosterone-based, dominant imagery. He transformed his flaccid feline familiar Cringer into the ferociously brave and engorged Battle Cat with his mighty 'Power Sword'. This becomes *He-Man*'s fighting mount, powered purely by thinly masked penile metaphors.

The female spin-off of *He-Man*, *She-Ra: Princess of Power*, was similarly marinated in metaphor. When She-Ra mounts her faithful steed, Spirit, he becomes a winged unicorn with telepathic ability to communicate with other animals. Like the 1980s culturally, it proved equality after a fashion. The boys had 'the most powerful man in the universe'; the girls got a talking pony.

All of the above was the shared soundtrack that current leaders of the free world grew up to. British and American kids were fed pretty much the same diet. It was an exciting, militarised, masculine world full of possibilities, certainties and symmetries. There were clearly identifiable good guys and bad. The state was on your side. We knew who 'we' were. It was probably the last generation ever to be certain about anything. From the 1970s onwards, nothing was ever the same. Vietnam, Watergate, superpower confrontation, the IRA, OPEC, punk rock, morally debatable Middle Eastern wars, countless financial crises, political scandals, moral relativism, the collapse of the banks, the rise of nationalism, Covid and the rise of China have all contributed to the insecurities and paranoia.

The children of the new superpower had a very different upbringing.

THE RELATIONSHIP WITH CHINA

We cannot understand the trajectory of either Britain or the other democracies without understanding the challenge that China poses to them.

The democracies, despite their economic success – *because* of their economic success – look and feel weak. To understand what they have to offer, we need to thoroughly understand the alternative. Some say China is simply rising from poverty on a trajectory leading towards greater democracy and regional security.

In *The Plague*, Albert Camus says: 'There have been as many plagues as wars in history; yet always plagues and wars take people equally by surprise.'[13]

China has already been the provenance of a plague. Michael Pillsbury in *The Hundred-Year Marathon*[14] foretells a more sinister future. He points out five fundamental myths in the way that the democracies deal with non-democracies:

1. **Engagement brings cooperation**
   Pillsbury points out that no matter how hard America tried to engage over the problems with North Korea, China did nothing. The problem remains and poses a threat to America's regional allies.

2. **China is moving towards democracy**
   The recent events in Hong Kong, and China's internment of Uighur Muslims in 're-education' camps, show this to be untrue. China is pursuing a harder line with Hong Kong legislation and is prepared to use force on democratic protest.

3. **China is a fragile flower that might fall apart**
   This is the notion that China's internal forces may tear it apart and therefore it is no long-term threat. There is no sign of this happening. China is emerging from Covid as one of the stronger nations.

4. **China just wants to be like us**
   Simply not true. China looks upon the dissent and turmoil caused by Western democracies and is horrified at the lack of planning and the waste.

5. **The hawks in China are weak**
   This is the notion that China just wants to be friendly. Its action in the South China Sea shows this to be questionable.

If Pillsbury is wrong, democracy is safe. If he's right, it's about to face another global challenge.

WHAT THE DEMOCRACIES CAN LEARN FROM CHINA

Pillsbury believes that Beijing is pursuing a systematic campaign of anti-Americanism and the rewriting of history books that depict America and Britain as nations that tried to destroy China. As Pillsbury says: 'The frightening thing about their vision of the future isn't that they spout lies about the United States; the frightening thing is that they actually believe their own propaganda.'

In its defence, China is one of the most misunderstood countries in the world. Culturally, it tends to look at things from a 'we' rather than an 'I' viewpoint. The West can learn from this. Furthermore, about 20 per cent of the Chinese language is made up of identical characters which depend on pronunciation to clarify their meaning. To add to the complexity, there are instances where the same pronunciation of the same character is paired differently, which results in a different meaning. Chinese language is one of the most complex languages, due to both its written character system and tonal nature. Some say it's also one of the reasons English is still preferred as a language for the business world. Business is an uncertain activity. It requires trust and clarity. Without trust, higher levels of return are needed to offset risk. That creates a huge advantage for democracies. In every respect, China needs to be understood. Its geography, its supply chains, its hopes and its fears. The scope for misunderstanding is great.

What we're seeing in China is a re-run of a process we've seen in the West before in its attitude towards Asian nations. The first stage is to dismiss the country as irrelevant. The second stage is to belittle in

glorious complacency. In the third stage comes the shock. This is followed by the fourth stage: the tendency to believe they are supermen.
In the fifth stage, the West begins to assimilate some of the qualities.

Anyone who has travelled to China is in the fourth stage. They
are dazzled by what appears to be an incomprehensible amount of
success, often attributed to some confused notions. For instance:

- **'China is successful because it has an authoritarian government.'**
  Not true. If this were the case, then the likes of North Korea,
  Russia, Cuba and Iran would be leading the way economically.
  They aren't. Unless your country is resource-rich, an authoritarian
  regime is highly unlikely to be successful. This was true of China
  under Chairman Mao and the cultural revolution. Millions died
  of starvation. So, something changed. Its success must be down
  to something else. It used to be a very authoritarian state, but it
  has liberalised its regime *to an extent*. Of course, it is nowhere
  near as free as the democracies, but the direction of travel is clear.
  Or it was. In 1988, village elections were introduced, but under Xi
  Jinping the level of authoritarianism has increased. Sometimes,
  though, just the promise of better days to come is enough. After
  all, it's a principle that underpins all types of capitalism.

- **'China is successful because it has an infrastructure advantage.'**
  Not true. If this were the case, then India would be leading economic growth, not China. In 1950, India had the best infrastructure of all developing nations. It had thousands of miles of railways built by the British.[15] India is developing quickly, but not as
  fast as China. There's no doubt that China has an infrastructure
  advantage now and has used central government to leverage it,
  but its expansion is largely due to economic success. Nor could

China claim to be well connected geographically. To its west is desert and mountains. To the east is the Pacific Ocean, which became possible to cross much later than the Atlantic.

- **'China is successful because it has mineral resources.'**

  It does have natural resources, such as coal, oil and natural gas.[16] It's also consuming them four times faster than the United States.[17] It's a producer of aluminium, magnesium, antimony, salt, talc, barite, cement, fluorspar, gold, graphite, iron, steel, lead, mercury, molybdenum, phosphate rock, rare earths, tin, tungsten, bismuth and zinc. But that's been there for a long time. It doesn't explain the sudden acceleration in economic growth.

- **'China is successful because it has a big population.'**

  China's population is roughly the same as India's and around four times the size of America's (1.4 billion to 328 million[18]). About a third of the country is desert, around the same as America. Only half the land is habitable. That's the same in America. Ninety-four per cent of China's population lives east of the Hu Line, which notionally divides the country in two from the north-east to the south-west. The area west of the line remains underdeveloped and poor. The Isle of Man has a higher population density than China.[19] For many years the country had too many people and had a one-child policy. This ended as recently as 2015.[20] The demographic time bomb this created means that in the future there will be fewer of working age to support an ageing population.

There are the dazzled and then there are the dismissive:

- **'China's numbers are fabricated.'**

  It may be the case that some of the numbers are unreliable. This is especially true of those numbers reporting a downturn, but the scale of achievement is undeniable. The share of state-owned enterprises in industrial output continues to drop steadily, from 78 per cent in 1978 to 26 per cent in 2011.[21] Private industry far outstrips the value added in the state sector, and lending to private players is growing rapidly. It doesn't matter how the figures are manipulated, the scale of what's been achieved is a credit to the Chinese people. They have worked hard and made many sacrifices. Never before in human history has a country risen so far so fast by its own efforts. Of course, the human rights issues add more than just a dark cloud to the success. It may be that the repressive regime is a legacy of a less secure history, where governments felt they had to be strong. Whatever the reasons for the horrors and abuses, its economic achievements cannot be denied. China's place in history is secure. It now has no reason to feel that diversity and human freedom are necessarily weaknesses. After all, it never held Hong Kong back.

- **'China is no good at innovation.'**

The main argument for this notion is the rigid conformity of the education system, but there is no doubt China is good at copying technology, scaling and improving on it. Thus, the creativity is incremental rather than revolutionary, although it is now moving into completely new areas. It has the world's largest floating solar power plant, the largest waste-to-energy plant and a string of world firsts. It has the world's first passenger and delivery drone, trackless smart train, electromagnetic hypersonic cannon, forest city, solar motorway, 3D printed car, fully electric cargo ship, quantum satellite and unhackable computer.[22] Whether innovation in scaling or improving, it is churlish for the West to say that it doesn't exist in China. It does and it's everywhere.

- **'China has destroyed its own environment.'**
  China is spending heavily on an environmental clean-up. The nation's Airborne Pollution Prevention and Control Action Plan, mandating reductions in coal use and emissions, has earmarked an estimated $277 billion to target regions with the heaviest pollution.[23] It still has work to be done; for example, the policing of its fishing policies, which are doing enormous damage to the oceans.

  This needs to be seen in the context of its quest to find protein to feed a rapidly industrialising country. In 2014, China's WH Group (Shuanghui International Holdings) bought American group Smithfield Foods in Virginia for $4.7 billion. It is the world's biggest pork processing plant and slaughters around 10,000 pigs a day.[24] Arnold Silver, a director, said at a recent industry conference that sales to China could create bacon and ham shortages for Americans.

- **'China will collapse under a mountain of debt.'**
  China's debt has increased to some $28 trillion,[25] mostly secured against real estate, but this is only 55 per cent of national GDP, much lower than many other countries. In America, some 30 per cent of national wealth is related to stock markets; China is much less dependent on them, but this also may represent a lower level of trust.[26]

- **'The gap between rich and poor will tear China apart.'**
  There's evidence certainly of pressure between the urban, wealthier, younger Chinese and the rural, older generation, but it's difficult to gauge because of the lack of free speech. This is a valid problem, but then it also applies to just about every developed country on earth.

SO WHY HAS CHINA BEEN SO SUCCESSFUL?

In short, equality, discipline and investment in human capital. Its literacy rates are one of the highest in the region. In China, literacy means fluency with 1,500 Chinese characters. In India, it's the ability to write your name (in whatever your language is). China's success is also down to gender equality. Chinese manufacturing is built on working women. Up to 80 per cent of jobs are filled by women. India's story is that men still dominate manufacturing, especially in garment production, and women are less equal than in China.[27]

At the heart of China's power and authority is a simple gamble – that capitalism can thrive without democracy and accountability *in the long term*. Its proposition is that liberty does not need to be absolute, only sufficient or gradually improving.

Only history will say whether this can work in the longer term. Sure, it needs education and discipline, but ultimately its citizens will want to express themselves through something other than material choice. The Chinese people's work, resilience and intelligence have created one of the most remarkable stories of human economic success ever. But what happens when every person in China is raised to a Western standard of materialism; what then? Does anyone really think that the desire for material plurality will not then be superseded by the desire for political, religious and philosophical self-determination? Humans crave more than materialism. At what point does economic choice morph into political dissent? The answer to this is simple: when growth slows or stops. Dissent is integral to the long-term, sustainable progress of human capital. Of course, you can suppress dissent, but to do so denies human potential.

All progress begins with a minority that sees the future. At present this may be vested in a small elite who get to choose alternatives. We, in the democracies, have learned through bitter experience that utter conformity eventually results in the denial of human potential, or, put another way, a waste of human capital – and that's the very thing that China's success is built on.

WHAT DO AMERICA AND CHINA HAVE IN COMMON?

There are two ways of looking at America and China. We can identify the differences, or we can show the similarities. Here we do both.

The Similarities

America	China
Free speech restricted by the private sector	Free speech restricted by the public sector
Third largest country (9.8 million square km)	Fourth largest country (9.6 million square km)
Land use 45 per cent agriculture	Land use 55 per cent agriculture[28]
Median age thirty-eight years	Median age thirty-eight years (Britain is fifty years)[29]
Birth rate 11.9 per 1,000[30]	Birth rate 11.4 per 1,000[31]

It's easy to see why the two countries rival each other. They are similar in many respects. Both rely upon the Pacific Ocean for security and trade. Both have significant wealth inequality. Both are young compared with Britain.

The Differences

America	China
Urban population 82.5 per cent	Urban population 60.1 per cent
Electricity consumption 3.9 trillion kilowatts per day[32]	Electricity consumption 6.3 trillion kilowatts per day[33]
Petrol consumption 19.9 million barrels per day	Petrol consumption 3.4 million barrels per day[34]

$600 billion defence budget[35] (2020)	$200 billion budget[36] (UK = $53 billion)[37]
1.9 million annual graduates[38] (56 per cent female)[39]	7.5 million annual graduates[40] (51 per cent female)
Total government spending $7.3 trillion[41]	Total government spending $3.4 trillion[42]
Natural gas consumption 817 billion cubic metres	Natural gas consumption 243 billion cubic metres[43]
CO_2 emissions 5.1 billion metric tons[44]	CO_2 emissions 10.4 billion metric tons[45]
Obesity rate 36.2 per cent	Obesity rate 6.2 per cent[46]

This is a more striking picture. It shows greater education equality in China and a fitter, more disciplined population. It also shows that militarily, at present, China is of a different scale but growing fast. It definitely poses a threat to the rest of the world in carbon emissions alone. Together, America and China represent almost 40 per cent of global emissions.[47] On 1 April 2016, they issued a joint statement confirming that both countries would sign the Paris Climate Agreement. America withdrew under President Trump. President Biden brought the US back.

A NEW CHALLENGE TO DEMOCRACY

What is it that defines 'we' and 'they'? The bigot's answer would be to divide us on ethnic, racial, gender or geographic lines. But what if the answer has nothing to do with difference but with similarity? What if it was nothing to do with what was inside a community but something outside? When faced with a significant external threat, differences melt away and we find what we have in common.

The future relationship must be about more than just an Anglo-American alliance. It's about a much bigger shared goal and prize – the preservation of liberty, justice and human rights for all democracies. The differences between democracies may not disappear, but they're likely to become less important. Collectively, the democratic nations will need to make a stronger defence of democracy. They will need to spend more as well. The scale of this increase can be seen below.

WORLD MILITARY EXPENDITURE, BY REGION, 1988-2018*

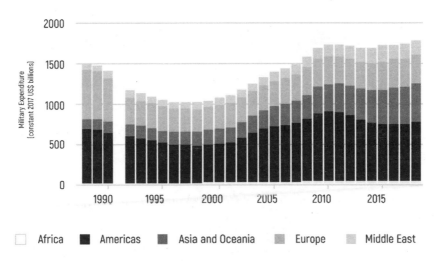

*No total can be calculated for 1991 as no data for the Soviet Union is available for that year
Source: SIPRI Military Expenditure Database (29 Apr. 2019)
© SIPIRI 2019

In 1945, there were eleven democracies; now there are seventy-six, according to *The Economist* Intelligence Unit's Democracy Index.[48] The growth of democracies has undoubtedly been good for the planet. Democracy is an efficient proxy for violence. The capitalism that attends such democracies has also been the greatest wealth-creating system ever known. Of course, there are problems associated with it, but with a political will, they are manageable. Countries with better levels of education historically are also more likely to be democracies today.

CORRELATION BETWEEN EDUCATION IN THE PAST AND DEMOCRACY TODAY

Average years of schooling for total population aged 25+ in 1970, and political regime according to the Polity IV assessment (ranging from -10 for 'Fully Autocratic' to +10 for 'Fully Democratic') in 2015

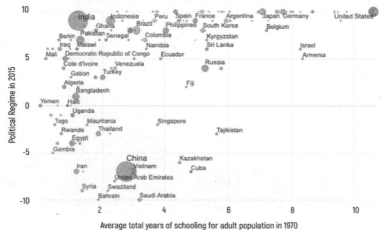

Source: Political Regime (OWID based on Polity IV and Wimmer & Min), Lee-Lee (2016), Barro-Lee (2018) and UNDP, HDR (2018), Population (Gapminder, HYDE (2016) & UN (2019))
Published online at OurWorldInData.org. Retrieved from:
https://ourworldindata.org/grapher/correlation-between-education-and-democracy-1

Let's be clear about this – democracies are better in many ways. They are better educated, richer, healthier and better at protecting human rights. They distribute wealth more equitably. They have better justice systems. They are less corrupt. If they are also noisy hotbeds of dispute on important issues, this does not make them weak or divided; it just makes them popular democracies.

And the democratic system is making progress around the world. In the 1960s and 1970s, three-quarters of African leaders were ousted by violence; in the period 2000 to 2005, this figure had dropped to one-fifth.

By the end of 2011, the only countries really considered autocracies were Azerbaijan, Bahrain, Belarus, China, Cuba, Eritrea, Iran, Kazakhstan, Kuwait, Laos, North Korea, Oman, Qatar, Saudi Arabia, Swaziland, Syria, Turkmenistan, United Arab Emirates, Vietnam and Uzbekistan.

Political participation is on the rise in almost every region of the world; the most striking advance has been in the extension of the franchise. HM The Queen and the royal family are eligible to vote, although they do not. Even astronauts aboard the International Space Station can vote. They send PDFs of the paper ballots they'd usually receive in the mail back down to Earth. Clerks open the encoded documents and submit a hard copy to be counted. Online voting is also making progress. Since 2005, Estonians have been able to vote online instead of going to polling stations. Although in-person voting is still popular, more than one-third of the people voted online in the last election. Estonia, though, has a population of only 1.3 million.

Democracies across the world are diverse. Take, for instance, the days upon which different nations vote. In most places, elections are held on Sundays, but there are several exceptions. Americans vote on Tuesdays because historically they needed enough time to make it back home in time for market day on Wednesday. Australians and New Zealanders vote on Saturdays. In Britain, workers were paid on Fridays, and if they went to drink in a public house it was thought that they would be subject to pressure from the Conservative brewing interests.[49] Comparatively, on Sundays it was felt that they would be subject to influence by Free Church ministers, who were generally Liberal in persuasion. It was therefore decided that voting would take place on the day furthest from influence by either Conservatives or clergymen: Thursday. For its part, India is the largest democracy in the world. It is home to more than 800 million eligible voters, and in order to run an election, the government holds the votes over the course of many weeks. The last major general election in 2019 took place on nine separate days over five weeks[50] and elected 543 Members of Parliament.

Turnout is equally diverse: according to a 2016 report,[51] a little over 50 per cent of Americans performed their civic duty during the 2012 election cycle, which places the US thirty-third out of thirty-seven OECD nations most likely to vote. Australia and Belgium see high turnout in elections, but then registration is compulsory.[52] As we've seen earlier, in the UK's December 2019 general election, the turnout was the fifth lowest of the past 100 years at 67.3 per cent.[53]

One-third of the world's rising democratic nations are in the Commonwealth.[54] It is home to 2.4 billion citizens (one-third of the planet) and the majority of these (60 per cent) are under the age of thirty. Member countries are supported by a network of more than eighty intergovernmental, civil society, cultural and professional organisations. The Commonwealth's main role is to strengthen governance, build inclusive institutions and promote justice and human rights. It helps to grow economies and boost trade, empower young people and address threats such as climate change, debt and inequality.

The West has 1,000 years of accumulated experience with capital. China did not really start growing until the free market reforms of 1980. So, the China experiment with capitalism is barely forty years old.

Of course, there may be room for better systems than democracy. Lord knows enough people have tried for enough time. Even now, China may not be moving towards democracy but is certainly moving towards equality, with a record number of women in its National Congress and more female graduates.[55]

History may well be on the side of the democracies, but the West has been complacent before. Think about the fall of Singapore, Hong Kong and the surprise attack on Pearl Harbor. If we truly believe that democracy is best, then we cannot afford to be complacent. So, what better way of benefiting both China and the West than by modernising capitalism and democracy?

The notion of a D10,[56] bringing together the world's leading democracies, is therefore an idea that has merit. It has been argued that the G7 is an outdated narrow grouping. The G20 spans too great a divide of fundamental values. In bringing together democracies, not only could a global approach to issues be developed as before but it may also help galvanise other global institutions to support freedom and human rights. This would comprise America, Australia, Britain, Canada, Germany, France, Japan, India, Italy and South Korea. The pivotal market for this alliance is neither the UK nor America; it is the world's largest democracy, India. It is growing fast, but because it's a democracy with common law rights and a free press, it cannot just sweep aside people in pursuit of economic growth.

India should be at the heart of a D10 alliance. Britain should rebuild its relationship with that country to help it succeed. By modernising capitalism and democracy, the D10 could create a world of free capital movement subject to common controls and accountability. This is why accounting and taxation policies need to be synchronised. The democracies are not strengthened by beggar-thy-neighbour taxation policies. Democracy and capitalism are both in need of significant reinvention.

If Britain is truly going to capitalise on the global trading opportunity, then we will need some answers. We need to and want to trade with China. Large parts of the UK economy depend on it. People might say that capital will cease to flow wherever it becomes unaccountable to the rule of law. That's true, but only of legitimate capital. There's plenty of capital circling the world which seeks out high risk and high return. Some investors will always take the risk if the returns are high enough. And so, in the high-growth years of China, global capital has been sucked in because the growth opportunity offsets the accountability issue. As China goes into a period of slower growth, that mechanism may no longer work.

For this reason, Britain and America must work together to create a level playing field for global capital. This means common accounting systems, regulation and taxation. It also means a collective resolve to prevent and punish Human Rights abuses and eradicate them from supply chains. It is the English common law and the English language that are the two greatest drivers of capitalism. If the system becomes too corrupt or ceases to work for all of the participants, then capitalism and democracy are at risk. It should be remembered that there are more people who speak English than Mandarin Chinese and this remains the trusted business language of the world.[57]

A NEW AGE OF VALUES

Of course, at present, China's philosophy is what used to dominate Britain and America – that of wealth built on resources. At the core of all economic policy is energy consumption and cost. Renewable energy costs have fallen consistently to already become lower than fossil fuel production.[58] With the world becoming more energy-efficient, long-term costs are only going in one direction. Plentiful, carbon-free energy will remove fossil fuels and create abundant potable water through cheaper desalination. The water will allow more land to be utilised. Countries like China could gain vast tracts of hitherto unusable land and become self-sufficient. Abundance of resource will replace scarcity. This will be powered by low-cost renewable energy. Thus, in the longer term, we will leave behind an age of resources and the wars they provoked. The new scarcities in an age of values will be consistency, trust, justice, accountability, altruism, reliability, and nobility of cause and purpose.

Capitalist economies rely upon the central principle of trust and accountability. Remove this and the returns need to be unsustainably high to bear the risk of total loss. Companies that operate within totalitarian regimes will do so if there are high-growth opportunities, but as these economies slow, the returns will normalise to those of other economies. When this happens, companies faced with a choice of a reasonable return in an unregulated world or a reasonable return in a regulated one will opt for the latter.

At the heart of this should be closer Anglo-American cooperation. The urge for liberty is infectious, peripatetic and Promethean in nature. It has moved back and forth from Britain to America, igniting many other freedom-loving peoples on the way. This partnership needs to be rekindled to show the world that mankind aspires to nobility. It will be a beacon for all the world to see.

At the core of this is the world's most elusive value, hard to win but easy to lose: who will be the most trusted on the world stage?

5

WHAT SHOULD WE
BE DOING?

We know what we're good at. We've explored that already in this book. So why has Britain never had a clearly defined national mission? Britain has evolved to meet the needs of a global market, but it's happened more by accident than by planning. Many large organisations have missions and long-term business plans. Indeed, the United Nations has seventeen global goals. Is there something in the British character or history that militates against consensus on longer-term objectives? Is it possible that the notion of planning became somehow discredited after the Second World War? It achieved miraculous outcomes then and the methodology was used extensively for strategic industries – coal, steel, railways, everything – during the following two decades. Did the notion of a national mission die with the rise of consumer sovereignty? Or was it strangled by the mediocrity and bureaucracy of organisations like the European Union? Are MPs so overwhelmed in their daily lives that they don't have time to build up a bigger vision? Our political parties produce a manifesto, but these are often put together at the last minute with little consultation. In any case, a national mission is different from a manifesto or a plan. It is not the government's mission; it's the nation's. A mission is something communicated so others can help. It helps focus national assets. Britain has identifiable long-term national assets and characteristics. It should therefore harness them to work towards identifiable missions. How should we equip Britain for the challenges ahead? Can Britain still compete on a global stage? It can, but not without a mission to provide leadership.

First, we look at why we've never had a long-term mission.

PRUSSIAN GENERALS, *DAD'S ARMY* AND THE CULTURE OF COCK-UP

We opened this book quoting Heraclitus: character is destiny. Single characteristics can lead to specific outcomes. Let's take some negative ones. If your character is untrustworthy and inconsistent, you might never be given responsibility. If your character is rude, you might never be invited to social gatherings. If your character is selfish, you may have few friends.

We concluded Chapter 1 looking at the British character; it is multifaceted, but a transcendent quality is trust.[1] If you're trusted, you will be given responsibility. By any measure, the trust vested in Britain's national institutions has been eroded in recent years and a priority must be to restore it. Parliament cannot credibly ask organisations like the BBC to change unless it is prepared to do so itself.

Some might say that Britain has done well despite the absence of an overall plan. If we've done well without a plan, how much better could we do with one? There are many people in this country who want to help, but without a clear, published plan, how can they? They can't see what the government is trying to do beyond slogans.

Governments get themselves into a pickle over a false dichotomy – do I have a command-and-control industrial strategy or do I just let enterprise get on with it? Having a national mission is about neither of these options. A mission is a vision: it describes what we all agree on and what is worth fighting for. It lets you decide how you contribute to it. That's why government needs to know enough about the other sectors to let them help.

To be fair, there have been stated missions in one area: industrial strategy. The strategy was set out in 2017 after much consultation. It had tangible aims. For instance, to 'Use data, artificial intelligence and innovation to transform the prevention, early diagnosis and treatment of chronic diseases by 2030'. Or 'Ensure that people can enjoy at least five extra healthy, independent years of life by 2035, while narrowing the gap between the experience of the richest and poorest'. Or 'At least halve the energy use of new buildings by 2030'.[2]

This is good as far as it goes, but they were too narrow, tactical and technical and no one knows about them. Nor were they integrated into the heart of business and public services. Worse, they didn't recognise what the British people would choose. These might include objectives such as homes for all or a more comprehensive social care system. The frustration so often felt by members of the public is because they want to help, and a successful nation should harness every resource at its disposal. That is what missions seek to achieve. Having a Whitehall plan/grant fund/implementation team objective/two-year tax break will only get you so far. To do more with less, you need long-term, local and national, cross-sector cooperation. You need strategies that last more than four years too: in 2021 the strategy was scrapped. This enables those with the ideas, funds, skills and innovation to help as well. Let's look at how it goes wrong. Then we can see how to fix it

Successive governments have said they have a mission to help the most disadvantaged into training or work. There have been numerous government schemes, from Department for Work and Pensions (DWP) health and work programmes, to Ministry of Justice (MoJ) pilot projects for ex-offenders, to equalities schemes like Disability Confident, which ask employers to sign up to good practice. But often, that's where it ends.

At the same time as running these schemes, the DWP, for example, was handing out contracts to firms which subscribed to none of the above. The coffee franchise in its lobby neither employed any disabled people nor signed up to its schemes. Its structure for programmes meant it had little power to influence who it worked with. It selected prime suppliers, who then subcontracted to smaller organisations. This meant that neither government nor local authorities had any direct say in how the services were delivered. The preference would always be for what was tried and tested and what could be easily measured. This was even after the Social Value Act (2012), which enabled value to be taken into account when awarding contracts.

Social enterprise was not understood by civil servants in procurement or finance. Many did not see a difference between these businesses and charities. Government should use the power of procurement to deliver on national missions by insisting suppliers work towards its fundamental goals.

Another example would be nuclear technology that has been invented in the UK. The snail's pace of the government's small reactor competition saw many British inventors forced to develop overseas. They wanted to share the intellectual property and were prepared to give the government shares. They just needed a regulatory framework that would enable them to make progress. It took too long, so they went elsewhere.

In addition to the slow pace of Whitehall, it is often easier to get seed funding overseas. The Treasury understandably does not want to step in where the private sector is willing and able to. For pioneering, high-risk technology, governments can do much to help attract finance with small stakes.

Mark Littlewood of the Institute of Economic Affairs (IEA) has cited the inability of Whitehall to move with the times as a factor in the failure to capitalise on new ideas. To give permission for a new venture to be regulated, you need to know what type of service/product it is. But Whitehall takes too long to define that. It should have an approach that says crack on until we stop you. But it's more likely to put the plans on ice until it figures out how to regulate.

Whitehall also has an ego. It's used to providing its own answers. It has a problem, it figures out what it needs to solve it – an aircraft or a mental health service, for example. It then designs the specification and estimates how much it thinks it will cost. It then procures it. This usually takes an age. It rarely posts the problem and asks for ideas to fix it, for fear of appearing inadequate. At a local government level, it commissions packages of services, driving down costs and usually quality, too. It does not commission for outcomes.

Start-ups, small and medium-sized enterprises (SMEs) and social ventures are where the ideas are. They, however, don't have the track record to get on supplier lists. If we want local communities to design what works for them, we need to be more nimble about how we procure. We also need to understand what drives people to help.

In her book *The Entrepreneurial State*, UCL professor Mariana Mazzucato has looked at what shapes investment behaviour. She said:

What is required is a mission-oriented approach which sets a clear direction for change, while at the same time using the full range of government instruments to crowd in bottom-up investments and innovation across the entire economy. The change must occur at all levels: local, regional, national and international. It must be guided not by fear but by a positive vision for change.[3]

Charities often encounter problems when competing with other organisations. One of the main benefits of Dementia UK, for instance, is that as well as providing day-care services it offers support for carers. Without carers, the state would have to provide more services. So, keeping carers strong and capable is a good thing. However, if you're procuring day-centre services for people with dementia, you are not able to take that obvious point into account. You can commission services for carers, but unless you have explicitly written that into your tender document, you cannot consider it when assessing who should get the contract. The fact that an organisation will provide such services, for no extra cost, is irrelevant. The lack of consideration of other unmet needs results in missed opportunities to lever more from budgets.

Francis Maude's reforms to procurement in 2015 helped social organisations to get a foot in the door with local authorities.[4] A level playing field for the third sector, however, is way off.

Whitehall loves pilots, targeted interventions and competitions for grant funding. This keeps quality high. This approach ostensibly tackles issues, but really only in a few places round the country. Once the funding is spent, the project ends, but a new pilot, task-force or grant competition is only a press release away. This results in a similar scheme being funded elsewhere, or a different scheme being set up.

If public money funds a pilot, a sustainability test should be put in place so that it can continue or leave a legacy. It should be clear how it will be funded and how the people will deploy the knowledge they have gained.

A plan provides a parenthesis within which resources can be gathered. If everyone knows the plan, more are able to contribute. The absence of any form of published plan condemns administrations to short-termism, top-down management, waste and, ultimately, failure. Where there is no vision, the people perish.[5]

Of course, the British will always muddle through. Often at the last minute when all other options are exhausted. All a bit ad hoc. The British character can always be relied upon to come through. And then it will be inspiring because everyone will rally together. Dunkirk spirit and all that. There were elements of this type of response during Covid, and it was magnificent and inspiring. Of course, there was a plan to deal with a pandemic, but, like Suvorov said, it didn't survive contact with the enemy.[6]

Were the British always this muddled in their thinking? Something happened as a reaction to the tragedy of two world wars. It was typically British. It was comedy. The people began to laugh at their leaders. Satire brought a new consensus that there was no consensus. And it spawned a new establishment. *That Was The Week That Was* morphed into *The Frost Report* morphed into *Yes, Minister* morphed into *The New Statesman* morphed into *Brass Eye* morphed into *The Thick of It* morphed into *Have I Got News For You* (effectively *Private Eye* magazine for the telly). The '60s created a stain of cynicism that soaked in and spread until consensus itself became fugitive. Everything and everyone was to be laughed at. The wartime generation who never complained about the loss of their lives, their youth, their opportunity and their liberty bequeathed a boom time to the baby boomers, who repaid it in ridicule and irresponsibility. The boomers, in turn, have bequeathed what? Unstoppable climate change? Generational debt? Record inequality? World-class cynicism?

Thus British planning has historically followed a sort of *Dad's Army* model. Pay attention at the back. It starts out with a badly thought out briefing from Captain Mainwaring (the government). It is then implemented wearily and without any commitment by Sergeant Wilson (the civil service), who thinks it rather tiresome. ARP Hodges (the opposition party) tries to sabotage everything. Private Frazer (the House of Lords) foretells disaster. Lance Corporal Jones (the red tops) then tells everyone not to panic in such a way that causes everyone to panic. Private Pike (the BBC) says it will be too much for anyone to bear. Mrs Pike (media celebrities) tells everyone how bad it will be for the vulnerable. The Vicar (the Anglican Church) disapproves of it all. Private Walker (business) makes a bit of money on the side and then Private Godfrey (the great British public) presses on despite his arthritis, cheerfully distributing sandwiches and pineapple upside-down cake made by his sister, Dolly.

Of course, the Nazis don't invade Britain. Captain Mainwaring isn't machine-gunned. Walmington-on-Sea doesn't get turned into Prora. The cast don't get sent off to a labour camp and Private Pike doesn't re-enlist with the Waffen SS (although it's just waiting for Armando Iannucci to write it).[7] In this mash-up of Hašek's *The Good Soldier Švejk* and Clausewitz's *On War*, it's the continuation of the culture of cock-up by other means.[8,9]

This illustrates another feature of the British character. You can be forgiven, loved even, for being a failure (see Henry Cooper, Eddie 'The Eagle' Edwards, Tim Henman, the English/Welsh/Scottish football teams, Del Boy and Rodney etc.). This is because these people are honest failures. British people don't like dishonesty. They don't like being told what to do by people who are not doing it themselves. This might explain why Britain has never had a long-term mission. Individual liberty has been so prized and so fought for that a national characteristic is scepticism about any form of consensus or collectivism and perhaps even of any type of institution. There is even scepticism for well-run, healthy institutions. When they no longer reflect the British character, however, they will be ignored, rejected and eventually bypassed. Here are three examples.

The BBC Director-General George Entwistle was forced to resign in November 2012 after the organisation falsely accused Lord (Alistair) McAlpine of being a paedophile, while harbouring actual offenders Sir Jimmy Savile and Stuart Hall. In 2012, the BBC, having done nothing to investigate Savile or to bring him to justice, were forced to act after a documentary was aired by ITV in October 2012.[10]

During the financial crisis of 2008/09, Parliament cut public services and told everyone to tighten their belts, at the same time that it became known that some MPs were charging the public purse for all sorts of 'sundries'. The same year Labour Party peers were secretly recorded offering to influence public policy in return for consultancy fee payments.

The European Union punishes countries like Greece while allowing other countries like France and Germany to break the rules. It has repeatedly ignored an audit of its own accounts. It lays down rules on public expenditure which its members do not stick to.

Trust varies in institutions according to wealth: the wealthier tend to trust the institutions more.[11] This might explain why a third of the British public persistently do not turn out to vote. The exception is the NHS, which still enjoys a high degree of confidence[12] and which the less wealthy support unconditionally. Trust, therefore, is measured from the bottom and not the top.

The scepticism and reluctance to follow any form of consensus are explained in the two great post-war movements in British politics. First, there was the enforced centralised planning necessitated by the Second World War. This triggered a sudden and massive state intervention, central planning and curtailing of civil liberties. Because it was almost miraculously successful, it created a momentum towards collectivism which carried over into peace time. This was seen with Beveridge, the creation of the welfare state and the NHS. In the three decades following the war, this momentum carried public ownership further than it had ever been intended to go, as telecoms, airlines, banking, car manufacturing, railways and even travel agents became state-owned. The momentum, once established, was unstoppable.

The Labour Party during this time developed a phobia about free markets because it smelled of the very thing they were trying to eradicate: privilege. It was ironic, therefore, that it was a Labour leader, Neil Kinnock, who finally brought this statist movement to an end in his conference speech at Bournemouth in 1985, attacking the left wing of his party and calling for them to end their dogmatic opposition in order to win elections:

> I'll tell you what happens with impossible promises. You start with far-fetched resolutions. They are then pickled into a rigid dogma, a code, and you go through the years sticking to that, outdated, misplaced, irrelevant to the real needs, and you end in the grotesque chaos of a Labour council – a Labour council – hiring taxis to scuttle round a city handing out redundancy notices to its own workers.[13]

At the time, Margaret Thatcher's free market revolution had moved away from state ownership. It created an environment in which the public sector was always seen as bad. Arguably, it carried free enterprise into many areas for which it was unsuitable, in much the same way as the collectivist movement it was reacting against.

The Conservatives during this time developed a phobia about planning because it, too, smelled of the very thing they were trying to dismantle: socialism.

The momentum created by both movements cannot be described as a mission. They were simply a reaction to each other. The sudden and violent movement towards the state was reflected in an equally sharp movement in the opposite direction. There were thirty-five years in each swing.

Tony Blair's 1999 Labour conference speech, again at Bournemouth, echoed Kinnock's fourteen years earlier in attacking dogmatic ideology, but this time it was a dogma of the right:

> And it is us, the new radicals, the Labour Party modernised, that must undertake this historic mission. To liberate Britain from the old class divisions, old structures, old prejudices, old ways of working and of doing things, that will not do in this world of change. To be the progressive force that defeats the forces of conservatism. For the twenty-first century will not be about the battle between capitalism and socialism but between the forces of progress and the forces of conservatism. They are what holds our nation back. Not just in the Conservative Party but within us, within our nation.[14]

Despite Jeremy Corbyn's attempt to reintroduce these old ideas, the politics of socialism and state control have been rejected. This was no triumph of the right; it was a triumph of reality. In much the

same way, it's difficult to argue for the further extension of unregulated free markets after the banking and financial crisis of 2008/09.

The problem is also that no one wants consensus. There are whole
sectors of the economy where income depends on division (or the
appearance of it). No one in the media is interested in hearing that
George and the dragon have come to an amicable damsel-sharing
agreement. The dragon has her Tuesday and Thursday and every
other weekend. That's not going to sell popcorn. uKnight, formerly
known as the Amalgamated Union of Knights, Squires, Pages and
Allied Trades, would call it a sell-out and point to the resulting
job losses. The Royal College of Airborne Ectothermic Squamates
would grab the conch for the 0810 slot on @bbcr4today.

This back and forth of centralisation versus the free market has
characterised British life for most of our adult lives. It's one tribe
against another. What neither side can see is their similarities:
they've both been brought up to define themselves by attacking the
other; they both genuinely want the best for their communities; they
both see the global threats to our way of life; they both fear the other
side would beat them with the olive branch; they both love the fight
so much they've lost sight of the purpose. But perpetuating it leads
to enormous waste in unpicking the previous (or even the same)
parties' plans. The consequence is a decline in trust in Westminster.

This brings us up to the present signalled by Blair. It's no longer
an argument of left or right, but of history and tribe, culture, character and, of course, cock-up. Every party manifesto seems bent on
revenge and rejection. But a mission can't be just about what you
don't want. Brexit rejected European integration, but precious little
was articulated about what it wanted to embrace. Now is our chance
to define what we want the future to look like.

It may be the case that politicians are uniquely unqualified to deliver a unified national mission. They may be too tribal. They may simply find it impossible to reach any agreement with an opposing party member. They may also be just too busy. Politicians have little time to contemplate, let alone look for the elements of national consensus. Politicians are forced overwhelmingly into the tactical domain by the nature of the work they do. Long-term planning is too important a job to leave just in the hands of politicians, but it could be something for an updated House of Lords. Others could have a greater role. Imagine what a reinvigorated House of Lords could do to harness great knowledge and deep regional expertise. This would make use of the experience and wisdom and make a virtue out of the lack of tribalism.

It somehow seems very British not to have a plan. Bertie Wooster never has a plan, although Jeeves does. This hints at planning not being quite *echt*. Planning suggests that we're taking it seriously. As if perhaps we're trying too hard. British leaders – especially Conservative ones historically – are supposed to be effortlessly superior and cool. They don't sweat. They get *condensation*. (In reality, of course, this is not very British at all.) This approach may have worked 100 years ago when Britain had huge resources and was the clear world leader, but it won't work today. The competition is too great. Britain actually has to try. Politicians often talk of rolling up their sleeves during campaigning, but so often government does not operate with the same level of vigour. It campaigns like Captain Mainwaring and governs like Sergeant Wilson.

The underlying assumption used to be that we don't need to be ambitious like other nations. How life has changed. A new generation of ladder climbers has arrived. Having things dropped on them from above doesn't deter them. They keep climbing, hand over hand. They are busy, organised and prepared. They're also unfazed by the ultimate pejorative – that of being *ambitious*. The British people are ambitious, but they're not supposed to admit it. Or so the received wisdom goes.

We need more of these people in leadership. They can come from anywhere, from left or right, but one thing they should have in common is aspiration. Tony Blair and Margaret Thatcher both were unashamed to be aspirant modernisers. It's no accident that they enjoyed two of the largest majorities of the twentieth century, because they reflected the British people – they painted a picture of optimism and positivity.

If Britain is to compete, it needs leaders who are unafraid of graft; indeed, they may have grown up in households dominated by it. Grafters are planners and preparers. They know how to spot opportunity, and good leaders know intuitively how to spot them in return. If you want a job done, give it to a busy woman (or man). They may be a small group, but they are world-class, and we need them if we're going to compete against bigger countries with more resources.

ATTITUDE – WELL WHO CARES, REALLY?

Britain's attitude matters as much as its skills because the latter alone doesn't maximise opportunity. Attitude creates opportunity. There is a great deal of discussion about education and skills, but virtually none about attitude. You can't train people in this because it's about beliefs and expectations. If your expectation is higher than your achievement, misery follows. If it's the other way round, the world transforms. Our global competitors are like Colonel Jessup in *A Few Good Men*: they're not interested in what we think we're entitled to. That's why we need to think carefully and plan our approach.

China has its *Hundred-Year Marathon*,[15] dated from the formation of the Communist Party of China in 1949 taking them out to

2049. We're not saying that Britain needs to think as far ahead as that, but the exercise of doing so couldn't do any harm. It would be better than talking about the last 100 years. As Dwight Eisenhower said, 'Plans are useless but planning is vital.'[16] There are recurring themes and consistencies throughout history which are highly likely to be present in Britain in 100 years' time. Of course, we have seen ten-year plans before. They tend to be associated with Labour governments,[17] for instance John Prescott's ten-year transport plan, which are then subsequently superseded by a Conservative government. Could it be that the tribal nature and mutual suspicion of British politics stop us even attempting to find common ground? Or could it be that the level of mistrust is so high that no consensus is possible? Perhaps now that the divisive nature of Brexit is past, there might be an opportunity for some progressive thinking on both sides.

Britain has had big missions before. The Beveridge Report[18] was a mission to improve welfare, and so was Nye Bevan's drive to form the NHS.[19] Nobody on any side in politics thinks they were a bad idea now. (And if they did, they would never admit to it.) So how might the mission be used to plan Britain's future?

THE CHALLENGER

In business, there are two types of companies: those that dominate and those that challenge. It's the same with countries. Even the most jingoistic of patriots would no longer say that Britain is a dominant power. It is therefore a challenger. The rule for challenger brands is that they must do what dominant players are *unwilling* or *unable* to do. The upshot is that Britain is not free to choose its position. It must pick what America and China simply are unwilling or unable to do. If we don't apply this thinking, we will merely copy the dominant player, at best duplicating efforts, and at worst, inviting unflattering comparisons. This was a strategy pursued by car rental company Avis going up against market leader Hertz. We are not Hertz. We are Avis. We are number two, but we try harder.[20]

If Britain is to find its clear path globally, it must not attempt to do what countries like America and China can do at greater scale. How does a smaller nation compete with a larger one? By studying them and by doing what they are unwilling or unable to do. China has a concept – *Shāshǒujiàn* or 'The Assassin's Mace' – which is not dissimilar. It's basically the idea that China does not seek to be more powerful than its adversaries (at this stage at least). It seeks out their Achilles heel. It looks for vulnerabilities. For instance, it knows that the American military is one of the most technically sophisticated in the world. It relies heavily on satellites, data and telecommunications interdiction. That's the strength but also the weakness. That's where China focuses. It is doing what America is unable or unwilling to. That is the true definition of a challenger brand. It is also one of the reasons that America has reintroduced the subject of celestial navigation back into Annapolis Naval Academy.[21] They have come to expect that satellite navigation might be denied to them in time of war, so they've gone back to learning the old ways. The Royal Navy, by contrast, never stopped teaching it.

TRUST

Britain has a long-term stable position established over hundreds of years. China will be aiming for 2049 as the fulfilment of its hundred-year plan.[22] Trust in China has been eroded by numerous recent events, especially those in Hong Kong, but it is not the only nation to have a trust problem.

Britain has a much longer experience of sovereignty than most other nations. How is this useful? It contributes to trust, which is the primary British brand variable. How is trust useful and how is it established? As His Holiness the Dalai Lama said, 'To earn trust, money and power aren't enough; you have to show some concern for others. You can't buy trust in the supermarket.'[23]

Trust is established in six different ways. First, by reliability and dependability. This can only be built up over time. Those who meet their commitments repeatedly in the long term are trusted. One dictionary definition of trust is 'feeling safe when vulnerable' in the presence of someone with greater power.[24]

Second, transparency of intent and objective also builds trust. This is vested in regular communications. This is especially the case during rapid change. The continuity of institutions is a key point here, especially the judiciary. To invest and plan long term, you need to know that the judiciary is independent of the state. The world sees the British legal system as reliable and fair. Much could be achieved also with transparency and simplification of tax codes, especially with regard to multinationals.

Third, fairness matters in creating trust because it is based upon a genuine altruistic concern for others. Nowhere in the world are the rights of the individual against the system held more highly than in Britain. Fighting for human rights and fair play is key to establishing trust. Life cannot just be about achieving an objective such as making profits. Fairness also means listening to all ideas and encouraging equal contributions.

Fourth, as the Dalai Lama points out, compassion is crucial in building trust. Britain's compassion places the UK at the forefront of international aid and in politics with new ideas and free thinking. It's also why Britain forms long-term trading relationships with many of those countries it has helped.

Fifth, humility is an important quality. If a leader never displays empathy and humility, then many in the team are unlikely to be comfortable sharing their thoughts. Some of the best ideas come from the quieter voices. The sincerity and authenticity of the British character lay it and its institutions open to criticism. The test of all leadership is not found in how well it handles praise, but in how it endures pillory.

Sixth, competency also matters. It doesn't matter how much you like someone or how good someone's intentions are, you won't trust them if they are incompetent. In every town and in every village there are people who are trusted. They might be doctors, vets, accountants, lawyers, butchers, electricians, gardeners, soldiers, landlords, all of whom trade on trust. Many of these learn skills passed to them over generations. Trust promotes efficiency and vice versa.

TRUST AS A MAGNET FOR RISK (AND THEREFORE REWARD)

The world's capital markets seek out large amounts of risk for one good reason: it's correlated with higher levels of return. Risk is like a magnet for money. Of course, though, it's a trade-off. Most investors seek a portfolio of risk. They want high returns but they also want lower risk so they can't lose their shirt.

Trust is therefore useful when it comes to managing risk. Wherever we see large amounts of risk, we find people looking to place their trust in an approach that mitigates it. We see this in physical assets, e.g. insurance and reinsurance, both of which work to defray physical risk. We see it in financial risk, e.g. hedge funds, derivative markets and investment management. We see it in science and research, where there are significant sums of money invested to pursue clinical breakthroughs; in entrepreneurialism and start-ups; in entertainment, defence and especially special forces operations.

For instance, research shows that Germany, Canada and the UK were the most trusted countries for the Covid vaccine. China and Iran came bottom of that research.[25] We see it in reputational management, with some of the world's largest consultancies based in Britain. We see it in all forms of the arts and creativity. Where trust prevails, it makes a higher level of risk manageable and attainable.

This is why Britain has some of the best advertising and creative agencies. They feed on the artists, musicians and designers whose creative minds are open and free to say what they want and to experiment. This is why creativity and credibility go hand in hand. Still too much British creativity needs to go overseas for investment. Britain must learn to take greater risks with its own scientists. A British investment bank similar to the Business Growth Fund (BGF) formed with an organisation like the Royal Society taking minority shares is one idea that has been mooted.

A PLACE WHERE IT'S SAFE TO TRY

Britain is already the home of risk management, but it could go further to become the foremost place globally to manage the risk and reward that capitalism rests upon. We know that higher risks demand greater rewards: that's how the system works. But the reverse part of the equation is also true. Where risks can be minimised then investors are prepared to tolerate lower returns. This can make ideas viable at an earlier stage than in higher-risk regimes. This feeds innovation. Britain is somewhere businesses refer to as STT (Safe to Try). This is one of the reasons Britain has such a great track record of inventions. Or maybe it just rains so much, there's nothing else to do?

If trust is the edifice, then compliance is the foundation. For centuries in Britain, trust has been a matter of culture and behaviour.

In the City of London, for instance, 'my word is my bond' remains the principle of the London Stock Exchange[26] – not my letter or contract, but my spoken word. Britain has never had a written constitution. Why not? Because rights are enshrined in jurisprudence and legal precedent. They are not explicit because the assumption is that they are understood as normal behaviour, as a culture. Some have argued that Britain's lack of a constitutional court makes it more vulnerable to cases being taken to international courts. We seem to think that is a price worth paying.

If Britain positions itself on trust, then it also needs to have both the most trusted political mandate and the most compliant markets and capital system. Britain is known for having lower levels of compliance checks than other markets. For instance, on the London Stock Exchange, the reporting intervals are six months. On a higher-risk (and higher-return) market such as NASDAQ in America, the reporting intervals are quarterly. This imposes an enormous burden of red tape on high-growth companies. Britain's reporting timeline is longer because the companies on the exchange are more trusted by the investors.

Whether investors have confidence is bound up in trust not only in the market but in the institutions that control and service it. When ranked by size, Britain is sixth in the top 100 for number of banks.[27] When ranked by safety, it doesn't have one in the top fifty.[28] Britain needs to work on this. This represents the damage done, for instance, by the collapse of the country's largest bank, RBS.

JUSTICE AND DISPUTE RESOLUTION

Justice starts with human rights. From Magna Carta in 1215 to the 1679 Habeas Corpus Act, the 1689 English Bill of Rights, the 1948 Universal Declaration of Human Rights, the 1950 European

Convention on Human Rights, the 1965 and 1976 Race Relations Acts, the 1998 Human Rights Act, the 2008 UN Convention on the Rights of Persons with Disabilities and the 2010 Equality Act, Britain has been at the forefront of this type of legislation. This is why Magna Carta is displayed side by side with the American Declaration of Independence – they are connected across 500 years of history. For this reason and many more, Britain does better in law firms, with eighteen of the top 100 globally.[29]

MODERNITY

America and China are already modern. Nobody in those countries sees Britain as particularly modern, and within this hides an opportunity. Britain *is* surprisingly modern. Its people are quick to adapt to changed circumstances, but its institutions are not. Britain can choose to modernise them; indeed, it would lack credibility for any future administration to attempt to modernise any aspect of British life without first modernising Parliament.

Britain can, for instance, modernise its infrastructure. It can modernise its universities. It can modernise its legal system. Why is it so uniquely positioned to modernise? Because modernisation involves risk and these institutions are still trusted, despite recent erosion. It retains a high level of residual stability built up over years.

In some respects, successfully modernising old things is exactly what Britain is good at. We saw this in Chapter 1. Britain feels comfortable with London cabs that look like the old ones but which in fact are carbon-free, electrically powered, air-conditioned and Wi-Fi-equipped. This is the perfect analogy for Parliament. It can still hold a special place in people's hearts, even if it is upgraded, modernised and made more fit for purpose.

In some respects, Britain will have modernity forced upon it whatever it does, so why not embrace it? In any case, a secondary effect of Covid and Brexit combined was modernisation. Covid, because it accelerated the move online, thus modernising shopping and work experiences. Ten years of technical change was triggered in ten months. Contactless payments, for instance, rose from £30 to £45 to £100 in one year.[30] It also accelerated and deepened divisions socially, commercially and culturally. Importantly, it tilted the culture towards the internet and news networks competing less on facts and more on entertainment. The result was that feelings became as important as facts, as we learned from 'the stolen election' narrative in America and the Duke and Duchess of Sussex's revelations about the royal family.

Hidden within Brexit, though, are twin warnings. First, we left the European Union citing a lack of democracy. At the same time, the majority of our parliamentarians are unelected. This should be a Chief-Brody-on-the-beach-in-*Jaws* dolly-zoom moment for Parliament, but it probably won't be. Brexit opens up the possibility that people may start to think of Parliament in the same way Brexiteers thought of Brussels. Brexity behaviour thus may become less of an event and more of a process.

Second, it was only by protracted court cases, protest and counter-protest, a change of Conservative leader and a general election that Parliament was forced to obey the people's wishes. Parliament cannot afford to come between the nation and what it wrongly believes is its personal mandate to 'interpret' for its own ends. When it imagines that it has this type of role, it is moving beyond its remit, and it resembles another institution also badly in need of modernisation: the BBC. For both of these reasons, Brexit must lead to the modernisation of Parliament.

The similarity between the BBC and Parliament does not end there. They're both globally recognised institutions. They're each obsessed with the faults of the other. They both criticise each other publicly from time to time. They're both slow-moving, arthritic and under-achieve against public expectations. They've both failed to implement fundamental changes. They're both iconic, at the centre of the British brand. They're both in prime locations in central London and have spent ridiculous amounts refurbishing their buildings and infrastructure. They've both struggled to embrace technology and subsequently been bypassed by it. They've both evangelised standards which they themselves have been unable to uphold. They've both seen their trust eroded[31] as the result of nationwide scandals. In summary, they are becoming less representative of those who fund them. Consequently, they are becoming less relevant to large sections of British society.

HUMAN SCALE

Britain by its very nature, especially after Brexit, is free to take a more personal approach to its neighbours. It can pick and choose. It is not bound to follow the one-size-fits-all relationships of Europe any more unless they are strategically useful. This is an important moment for Britain and for the rest of the world. There is an opportunity for reinvention, resetting and renewing the British brand.

In a world which is increasingly nationalist and retreating behind walls, this open approach is something other large nations couldn't do, either because they are withdrawing or because they've already subsumed their identities within a larger trade bloc. The way to break down this bunker mentality is to point to the benefits of openness in terms of trade, opportunity and the inflow of capital. Many didn't like the EU because it wasn't fair on immigration, it was protectionist on trade and it kept poor countries trapped in poverty within the Eurozone. It was unfair on fishing rights – now in the process of rectification. It allowed escalating youth unemployment in Spain and Italy and the ongoing plight of Greece. It failed to have a comprehensive and competent approach to migration. Its lack of military intervention with European resources undermined its credibility, for instance in failing to honour the promises made to Ukraine. It was weak on organised crime and human trafficking. It proved unable to combat the rise of the far right. It was reluctant to audit the European Commission's budget. All of these aspects undermine trust.

LONDON, UNIQUE IN THE WORLD

London is a key differentiator for Britain. There's nowhere in the world quite like it. One of the peculiar characteristics of Britain is the dominance of the country by London. Paris does not dominate France in the same way, nor Berlin Germany. London's success is down to one unique quality: it is an apex city, a place where everything converges – industry, the arts, academia, politics, the clergy, entertainment, the military, the media, commerce and finance. In America, Los Angeles might be known for its entertainment, San Francisco for its technology and Washington DC for politics. Of course, Paris or Amsterdam have elements of this liminal culture, but nowhere else do worlds collide as in London. This juxtaposition, cross-fertilisation and unique history provide a look across the horizon. It creates situational fluency to see the bigger picture.

It's important to point out here that London is not representative of Britain and it's dangerous to assume it is. It owes its success to its international status. Almost 40 per cent of Londoners were born outside the UK.[32] It is France's sixth largest city; presidential candidates campaign in London for French elections.[33] But there's no reason why other UK cities could not compete internationally. The trust factor, for instance, is universal.

While London is a tremendous asset to Britain, generating 30 per cent of the country's taxes,[34] this concentration in one city also makes Britain more vulnerable, for example if the depopulation of cities caused by Covid continues. Germany, for example, is far more federated and devolved as an economy.

WAITING FOR SOMEONE TO PUT IT TOGETHER

Britain has major assets, but chief among them all is trust. It needs a clearly articulated long-term plan which involves the updating of national institutions. This is the only way it can make the best of its assets and compete against bigger powers. It might be labelled hopelessly naive to search for consensus among warring political parties, but it's been done before. We saw elements of it during the early stages of the pandemic. It's not what the media wants as a spectacle, but it's what the country needs. Rebuilding trust requires us to embark on the following steps.

1. **Recognise the problem**
    Britain needs a clear, long-term mission. There's no reason that we can't have one. So much of government expenditure is un-coordinated in the short term. In the longer term, just looking at the sheer volume of legislation for local democracy in the past twenty years illustrates the waste. By the time you read this, there will have been yet another reorganisation. Britain doesn't need a red reorg or a blue one, it needs a long-term plan, and it must start with the modernisation of democracy. If people can see that Parliament is taking steps to modernise itself, it might go some way towards rebuilding trust. It must be restated: how

democratic can Parliament be when the majority of its representatives are unelected and unaccountable?

This sort of change will need a deep breath from both main political parties, but it will be rewarded by the public later. It can be anticipated that some MPs will not vote to change what for them is a retirement destination. Others might recognise the opportunity to create a chamber which can be a greater complement to the Commons. One which has a better balance of knowledge, skills, backgrounds and geography. One that still provides scrutiny in the here and now, but also helps raise the ambition, forges the partnerships, spots the opportunities, provides continuity and consistency, and fosters necessary common ground. In recent years many in the Lords have taken it upon themselves to do precisely the opposite – to divide the nation, to initiate legislation with no mandate to do so and to frustrate democracy.

The result of that may be the further erosion of the authority of Parliament and a diminished status for all political representation. Modernisation might also motivate and encourage other European nations to follow the same path. In that way Britain could yet be an inspiration as it reinvents itself. We should expect negativity and hostility. When you're rebuilding trust, that will happen at first.

2. **Keep track of what Britain is really good at and celebrate it**
There is a set of crown jewels of British characteristics. We must be aware of them and their importance not just for Britain but globally. Perhaps the most sought-after commodity in a post-industrial, post-truth world is trust. It is the foundation of all collective activity. Enhance this and everything is enhanced. Diminish it and everything is diminished. We don't need

bellicosity about our strengths. We just need to be clear about the facts.

Some of these sectors could do much to revitalise other failing areas. For instance, leading law companies could work to simplify small business law. In a shocking use of mixed metaphors, it could be argued that turkeys don't vote for Christmas, but also poachers often make the best gamekeepers. It would help them win trust. In a similar way, technology companies could work with the education sector to help develop local schemes in depressed areas. This requires that sectors be allowed to cross siloes and work in a joined-up way. All of this is impossible without a long-term planning process and shared vision.

3. **Measure how well sectors perform and show their *entire* contribution**

    If you're trusted, then so is your data. If there's going to be one big problem in the future, it will be the gathering of independent research data from trusted sources. Many British institutions robustly defend themselves from government interference, and rightly so, but involving them in a long-term plan is not seeking to control them. It's making sure that their independence is capitalised on as an asset. Take, for instance, the economic impact of military spending. At present, it is too narrowly measured in terms of return on investment. We need to be able to quantify the qualitative, if that's not a contradiction in terms. We know that the military adds more than just defence. It adds in training, welfare, healthcare, local community engagement, technology development, transport, emergency capacity etc. All of these contributions need to be recognised.

4. **Harness the key assets and modernise them, giving each a plan**

    A modernised Parliament, the BBC, the British military, the

monarchy, our sciences, our universities – there is so much in Britain that can be trusted, but little that doesn't need to be modernised. For instance, until recently if you were a British military planner, every new Strategic Defence and Security Review brought fresh cuts. If you're a teacher, every year brings unexpected changes. This is the same in the NHS. A government which set out on a plan to modernise every institution would create an inflection point for all organisations to review and reinvent. At the end of the Second World War, this process ran through British industry in its entirety. The completion of events allows this to happen. It may be years until Covid is conquered, but it will be. At that point, the world will have changed and learned new ways of doing things. This is the moment ahead which will prove an inflection point.

5. **Build a coalition to find the common ground with allies and opponents**

We cannot be so divided that we do not cooperate among ourselves or with our allies. The United States so often needs British support precisely because the country is trusted and listened to. The democratic nations face so many common threats of dealing with rapid technical change, climate change, security etc. It's not only Britain that needs to plan for a changed world.

Britain should take a more uncompromising stance to modernise world institutions, especially the United Nations. It should not be shy about it. It should do so not because it has any more right but because it is the right thing to do.

Britain could be trusted to do so. Of course, these organisations need consensus to change, but a string of successful examples could help. And if they can't be updated, then Britain must lead the charge to replace them with better ideas.

We need to instigate and build out the D10 group of nations

and work together to combat common threats. The freedom-loving nations are in need of a shot in the arm. The recent divisions in America and Britain cannot have provided much reassurance to other nations. Who can blame the nations of south-east Asia for wanting to hedge their bets against the rise of China when they see so much disarray in the West?

6. **Protect and promote democracy**

Parliament must become the defender of free speech and fresh thinking. This means bringing powerful sanctions to bear against those who abuse or prevent it. This especially means protecting minority voices. It means asking that social media works within laws applicable to other publishers and broadcasters. It also means ensuring that these organisations pay corporation taxes like normal onshore organisations.

7. **Grow the economy**

If the same thought and effort were put into growing the economy as we do into dividing up the revenues, we'd be more successful. Very little thought is given to what really makes an economy grow, but developing specialisms and focusing on them is at the core of it. This also means modernising markets so that they better serve the needs of the community.

The Honours (Prevention of Abuses) Act 1925 was brought in to stop politicians benefitting from the sale of honours. Anyone can nominate another for recognition. Some honours still rely on political patronage, chief among them elevation to the House of Lords. Currently, we have a haphazard system of political patronage. It results in a lack of diversity in experience, skills, geography and background, and a second chamber of limited relevance and capacity.

Why not weight membership more directly to the amount of

public good done? It would certainly be fairer than a hereditary honour. It would be more transparent than political honours. It would be more popular with, well, everybody except perhaps politicians.

8. **Encourage mutuality**

Having an overall plan is not a crime. It actually shows people what you're doing so they can see the bigger picture. Welfare groups attack governments when they think they've been forgotten. Make commitments and stick to them. If public money isn't available, use private money and donations. Nobody minds recognising and honouring those who give money back to their community.

It's not too late for Britain to rediscover a purpose and unity among all the cynicism. It does, however, need a moment to begin it and to lay out the vision. If it doesn't happen then Britain can muddle on for a while. Later, though, when change becomes imperative, it will be so much harder. When change is not allowed to be a process, it can become an event.

PART TWO

OUR MISSION TO MODERNISE

6

MODERNISING THE MANDATES THAT REPRESENT US

Britain's modern democracy is a mixture of ancient statute and precedence. It is embodied in a relic – the Houses of Parliament. Much of the nature of British politics can be learned from the building itself. Walk through the entrance to Westminster Hall and stand to one side. Notice how the eye is drawn upwards, ever upwards through the string course, to the oak-vaulted hammer beams above. It is said that a church architect's first task is to turn the supplicant's face to God.

The Hall was built in 1097 by William the Conqueror's son Rufus as distinct and separate from the older (and adjacent) Westminster Abbey, which had been consecrated just before his father's victory at Hastings in 1066. The Abbey was built by Edward the Confessor, the penultimate Saxon king of England. The Hall was thus designed as a statement of power to consolidate the Norman hold on the country. Bigger and more brutal than the Abbey, in fact bigger than any other enclosed space in the world at the time.

It was a place of litigation as well as consecration. It was the *Curia*

Regis, the King's Court. The great irony of the Norman occupation was that they strengthened the legal system for the citizens so soon after they stole from them. The Hall has seen some of the great trials of history, like that of Charles I, who in 1642 questioned the authority of Parliament itself, and Guy Fawkes, who tried to destroy it in 1605.

The monarch is the nominal authority here. The true power, though, is with the people. In a democracy, power and authority are separate. In Parliament, 'the people', in their political parties, make a case for both the prosecution and the defence. The monarch sits in absentia as an authority, the neutrality ultimately sacrosanct. Her Majesty the Queen never expresses her political views.

The Houses of Parliament may be among the most recognisable buildings in the world, but the fact they were built at all was an accident. Until 1826, the government system of debt finance had been the tally stick. This was a wooden record of debt that was inscribed with the details of borrower and lender. Essentially, it was an ancient form of government bond (hence phrases 'wrong end of the stick', 'tally up', 'keep tally' etc.). By 1834, the sticks were defunct and an order to burn them was made. Not for the first time in Parliament, things got a little out of hand. The fire consumed everything bar the Great Hall, the Jewel House and a few other rooms.

In a sort of architectural arms race, Charles Barry's design aped the extant medieval gothic perpendicular style of the Abbey, itself rebuilt by Henry III in 1245. Thus, Parliament's provenance is previous piety. The recycled gothic style is quasi-ecclesiastical. The message to clergy is clear: we've taken your vestments, your baubles, your stained glass, your vaulted ceilings, your mystery and your 'mad parade'.[1] We, the people, are also an authority. Our building looks like yours, but on steroids. Mother is the more muscular progeny of the Abbey. Barry's architectural broadcast is unmistakable: no difference in deference demanded between church and state.

Since then, Britain has slid from the religious into the secular. Only 38 per cent of Britons now consider themselves Christian.[2] Not Parliament, though. It has its Christian motto carved into its wainscoting like words through Blackpool rock – *Domine dirige nos*, Lord guide us. Its morning prayers are high church, its manner high camp. It was licensed to theologically thrill. Even before Barry. This is Charles Townsend[3] gushing in his 1843 *History of the House of Commons*:

> What intelligent stranger was ever ushered for the first time without a throbbing heart and heightened pulse! Who but has lowered his voice on first entering that room as he felt the genius of the place compelling awe, the deep inspiration of the past! Mighty memories, sublime associations, breathe their subduing spells around the stranger...[4]

This twenty-seven acres of prime central London riverain real estate is about as out of touch with a modern democracy as it's possible to be. Gold-plated, grand, gaudy, overbearing, pompous, procedural, pious, lofty and lavish. It's part museum, part mausoleum. The future is permanently former. Modernity is heresy.

This is arguably the most iconic, most well-known, most (self-) important building in the nation. It says that no other politicians, *no other people*, are as important as the ones within. As a place of domestic democratic demagoguery, only Brodrick's Baroque Revivalist Leeds Town Hall comes close.

Although Barry was the external architect, an ambitious young designer, Augustus Pugin, got the internal job. His imprint is everywhere. In eighteen months, he produced 1,500 designs and motifs, which probably contributed to his over-work, mental illness and premature death at the age of forty. His psychedelic attention to detail was exceeded only by his prurience. Walk through St Stephen's Lobby and notice the lions passant stamped into the floor tiles. Look closer and you'll see the ones in the central thoroughfare have no eyes. Pugin blinded them because he didn't want them up-skirting Victorian visitors. That's detail for you. Paranoid about a pride of printed pervs. No wonder he was carted off.

Near here, Mother's enduring legacy in the world is stamped into the Minton Hollins tiles. Just before Central Lobby, four burnished brass studs attend to the beginning of all parliamentary time. There's no push-button pop-up narrative, no headphones of reverent schoolteacher narrative, nor plaque to mark it. Indeed, the place is treated with the sort of disdain only those rich in history can afford. This is Britain's Babylon, Bethlehem and Golgotha. It's the place where rebellion started in the tradition of Hengist and Horsa and Boudicca. Cromwell, Churchill and Thatcher all recognised it; it's a place where the people said 'no'.

It was here in 1642 that King Charles I stood and demanded the whereabouts of the parliamentary rebels he considered guilty of treason. The Speaker's response was deferential but decisive: 'May it please your Majesty, I have neither eyes to see nor tongue to speak in this place but as this House is pleased to direct me, whose servant I am here.'[5] Following the English Civil War, the country and the king both lost their head. From that point on, the relationship between royalty and politics was never the same. A division was cleft between parliamentarians and aristocrats, players and gentlemen, democrats and despots. The two statues by St Stephen's entrance show this enduring split – Oliver Cromwell and Coeur de Lion, Richard the Lionheart. Commoner and King.

The public ultimately rejected Cromwell's pious, honest, russet-coated reforming, work-rate, self-made, self-improving, self-loathing, Presbyterian puritanical professionals in favour of the romanticism, drinking and debauchery of the restoration. Despite his decapitation, Charles did not vanish from history. Known at Parliament as King Charles 'The Traitor', cross the Thames to Lambeth Palace, the Archbishop of Canterbury's grace-and-favour home, and you'll find him referred to as King Charles 'The Martyr'. One river, two banks, two institutional versions of history. Two power bases both current and very much alive. The line between the ladder climbers and the effortlessly superior, still no less apparent.

The parliamentary anachronisms continue even today in Central Lobby, where the cardinal points are murals of St George for England, St David for Wales, St Andrew for Scotland and St Patrick for Ireland. Needless to say, Parliament predates Irish independence, Welsh devolution and Scottish nationalism. Mother has resisted decolonisation.

From this point, the British constitution can be seen. Face north, there's the Speaker's Chair in the prime chamber, the Commons. Face south, there's the Sovereign's throne in the Lords. In chambers close by, there are entire walls devoted to such scenes as Nelson at Trafalgar and Wellington meeting Blücher on the field at Waterloo. It's not exactly Francophile. Perhaps that's fitting, because it was also up and down these corridors, in the summer of 2019, that the Battle of Brexit was fought. Not the referendum. That had been decided three years earlier. It took three years for these institutions to deliver what the majority of Britons wanted. It took the citizens taking the government to court. It took the executive flexing its muscles. It took the Supreme Court intervening. It took three Queen's speeches and two general elections, yet eventually it produced a result that honoured the referendum.

Old buildings and old processes move slowly, carefully and

gradually. There's just no expectation of precipitate change. It's the price paid for probity. Mother watched the marches, the shouting, the emotion. There were protests outside and in front of broadcasters on College Green. None of this was remarkable, really, not in the context of British history. But how it happened was. Banners representing every possible side of the argument flew side by side. Shouties met each other every day, the tellies gantryed above like sheepskinned John Motsons on FA Cup day. 'Well, if I'm not mistaken, Des, this is only the third time in our history when the electrical retailers of the East Midlands have come together to register such a protest.' There were no *wasserwerfers*, no *sans-culottes*, no Phrygian caps, no riots, no Molotovs, no cars set on fire. But there were beards. Not hipster beards. Big old 'CND' bushy beards. And bobble hats. And Gore-Tex, parkas and kagoules. And there was wit.[6] They waved placards saying things like 'British Tits', with images of the garden birds including 'crested, great, blue, bearded, willow, coal'. Then a picture of David Cameron with the caption 'colossal'. It was like they were trying to stop a bypass being built. It was Twickers without the oggy-oi.

Across the country, most people recognised the need to honour the result – even those who had voted to remain. Despite the political gymnastics, the British public, although exasperated, kept faith that democracy would eventually deliver. Other nations had referendums which did not deliver. They just kept returning to the public, asking until they got the 'right' answer. In the UK, the expectation of the system was stronger.

What does Parliament mean to them? The building and its occupants are certainly a fascination, a *Gormenghast*. To look to the stats, the institution employs more than 2,200 staff.[7] There are 1,000 rooms and three miles of passages.[8] It is responsible for 80 million pages being printed every year. There are 427 seats in the Commons chamber for 650 MPs and 400 seats for more than double that number in the Lords. She is, in every sense, a big Mother, a marvel of over-embellished under-provision.

She also hums: despite the byzantine procedures, there is a huge amount of activity in Parliament, which sits longer than many other legislatures around the world – 155 days in 2018.[9] Reforms have seen the time available to debate in Westminster increase by 43 per cent over recent years.[10] This means that MPs are spending more time sitting in Parliament than they are in their constituencies, in part due to coalition and hung parliaments with fragile majorities. Consequently, they increasingly tend to focus on campaign and media opportunities to reach them.

Each vote in Parliament takes an average of twenty minutes. There can be several a day and they often take place back to back. What if Mother took a leaf out of the Scottish Parliament's book? Electronic voting would speed the process immensely.[11] It was trialled during the Covid pandemic by the House of Commons Commission, which is responsible for the hybrid proceedings in the Commons. It developed a system of remote participation in parliamentary questions and, critically, a remote voting system. A breakdown of what it cost to establish in the Commons is set out below.

The expenses listed relate only to work associated with the Commons and not to Parliament as a whole. The figures show combined implementation/other one-off costs and running costs as at 31 May 2020, and cover committed spend up to that date, not just actual expenditure.

Virtual chamber costs:
Chamber set-up – £31,200
Broadcasting hub set-up – £12,734
Specialist operating team – £176,000

Technical infrastructure hire – £334,000

Remote broadcasting provision for ministers and other key members – £70,000

Additional internet bandwidth – £6,000

Sub-total excluding VAT = £629,934

(*All supplier costs concerned, excluding any capital costs, are VAT recoverable.*)

Virtual chamber capital costs:

Broadcasting equipment – £123,994

Hansard recording equipment – £58,306

Remote voting, balloting and annunciator costs:

Remote voting (development, hosting) – £40,000 approx.

Commons balloting – £12,500

Remote annunciator ('UKParliamentNow') – £33,464 (*Commons share only*)

Sub-total including VAT = £85,964

Virtual committees revenue costs:

Implementation = £29,192 including VAT

Virtual committees capital costs:

Implementation = £396,988 including VAT

Online by-election for Select Committee chairs

Sub-total including VAT = £3,780

Total revenue including non-recoverable VAT = £745,090

Total capital including VAT = £615,748

Grand total = £1,360,838[12]

The internet-based voting system was used for eight days, after which, as Parliament returned, a proxy system was introduced to ensure isolating and shielding MPs were not disenfranchised. A more cost-effective system could increase productivity, bring the provinces closer, help working parents and reduce carbon emissions as well, as MPs would not have to travel repeatedly backwards and forwards between London and their homes. Members might lose time with colleagues or with ministers away from civil servants, but they might also gain time with their constituents or be able to visit other parts of the country. It should be an option. Yet in Parliament, even with a progressive Speaker like Lindsay Hoyle, even such modest modernising is considered radical. The questions remain. Will there ever be permanent electronic voting? Why did it take a pandemic for this option to be trialled? And why was a million-pound system used for only a few days?

Proxy voting is another example of possible change. So is allowing members to use each other's names in the Commons chamber, which might help those watching debates to know who's being referred to. What about allowing Lords and Commoners to share the other's space? At present, they are oil and water. Commoners are not allowed to use the Lords' staircase and Lords are not allowed in the Commons tearoom unless they've previously been members of the Commons. Some of these rules could certainly be rethought to allow for greater cohesion.

In terms of Parliament's professional standards, no one in any other organisation in Britain could get away with calling one of their senior female executives 'a typist'.[13] Nor could they say, with heavy innuendo, that an unmarried female member was angry because she was 'frustrated'.[14] Nor would they be able to mandate equalities legislation without implementing it themselves. All this erodes transparency and respect, as do some of the mysterious mannerisms. Members nod and bob to the Speaker as they go in and out of the chamber and to catch the Speaker's eye when they wish to speak. There are ribbons on the coat hooks for members to hang their swords.

Today, the parliamentary estate has shifted its centre to Portcullis House, with its highly modern, light and airy atrium. And to correct Barry's shortcomings in the older buildings, there are enough ladies' toilets. The outside world, though, is still barely discernible through Miss Havisham's curtains. Skype was introduced in 2019, as was a code of conduct aimed at protecting staff from inappropriate behaviour from members. The facility of enough seats in the chamber is still some way off, however. Likewise seats or shelter from the elements for taxpayers queuing outside to see their representatives. Over the next ten years, the whole estate will be renovated at an estimated cost of £5.6 billion.[15] The optics of this, given other priorities, may be hard to take. Right at the point when Parliament may fail spectacularly to have learned the lesson of Brexit, failed to meet the ambitions of its electorate, it will be spending billions on itself.

Despite the demonstrable decrepitude of Parliament, affection for it remains because the British just like old, familiar things. It was there before them. It will be there after them. Pre-Covid, over a million visited each year[16] and it is the backdrop to some real, though mostly imagined, drama. Its dusty glamour, its confrontation, its traditions and theatrics all draw people in. And since the chamber was first televised in November 1989, hundreds of thousands around the world have watched the parties debate, sometimes with wit but more often with waffle.

But what, beyond this dressing-up box, does Mother represent to people? Journalist Peter Walker, writing in *The Guardian*, said, 'Amid the Brexit chaos, overall public faith in the political system has reached a nadir not previously seen in the sixteen-year history of the Hansard Society's audit of political engagement, lower even than at the depths of the crisis over MPs' expenses.'[17] He went on to say that the audit found 'almost three-quarters of those asked said the system of governance needed significant improvement', and other attitudes emerged that 'challenge core tenets of our democracy'. The majority, it was found, would prefer a return to authoritarianism, or an otherwise strong leader who would be able to ignore Parliament.

Just think about that for a moment. What levels of despair, frustration and exhaustion could lead a nation that has stood for democracy against tyranny and impossible odds to conclude that it really didn't matter any more?

Mother shapes our politics in a wholly anachronistic way. She encourages delusion and mystery. Basic questions need to be asked. What kind of democracy allows the majority of its parliamentarians to be appointed rather than elected? What kind of organisation would fail to do the right thing until compelled by a court of law? Or welch on a contract? Or deliver something that the people did not want? Or dither when faced with a life-or-death decision? Or suggest that democracy should be denied? Our Parliament does and did. And all in recent memory. Quite shockingly, terminating democracy was one of the policies of the Liberal Democrats on the 2019 general election ballot paper. They decided to ignore the result of the referendum.

Mother sees it all – the despots and the democrats, the sacred and the profane, and as if by historical, theatrical, architectural conspiracy to guide our eyes upwards, ever upwards, to the vaulted reverie above, away from reality, away from the *crise du jour*, away from the punters and the shouters outside standing in the rain underneath Cromwell's carroty nose.

Would you wish to be a shareholder of such a firm? Would you continue to be a customer? Strip away the Pugin pedantry from Parliament and what is there to feel affection for? Citizens provide £560.4 million in their annual taxes for this institution.[18] (That's more than the administration budget of the Department for Education and its seventeen agencies, by the way.)[19] The inability of Parliament to deliver Brexit is not an isolated example of inadequacy. That, at least, can be blamed on a lack of majority.

It is widely accepted that the executive and Parliament cannot legislate or regulate at the speed required by business, science and technology. It's repeatedly been unable to support innovation because Parliament is not itself innovative. Nor does it let others innovate. Successful private Bills are rare. A show of public support for an issue can lead to debates on the topic, but not to substantial action. Enabling regulation takes years.

Further to all this, Parliament has also failed to produce long-term answers and consensus to the major challenges facing our country, from social care to climate change, or even to articulate what might be required to tackle these issues. It has not been able to make the nation more productive, nor to grow the economy at the rate the nation needs. It cannot equip our citizens with the long-term technical skills to pursue careers from healthcare to engineering. Its language and traditions entertain but they do not inspire. The equality it demands from others in their own workplaces has often been hypocritically absent at its own door. The House of Lords is an illustration. In the year to March 2019, a report from the *Sunday Times* found the average tax-free payment to peers was

£30,827. This is higher than the median salary of the UK worker, despite the House of Lords sitting for just half a year. The Institute for Government has said the cost of running the House of Lords rose from £99 million in 2017/18 to £117.4 million in 2018/19, during a time of 'austerity'.[20,21]

HOW LORDS ARE MADE

Despite this, Britain is a modern and vibrant economy, one of the top ten on the planet, even. Can the same adjectives be used to describe this country's upper chamber? The House of Lords is the second largest legislature in the world after the National People's Congress in China. There are 750 hereditary lords in the UK, of which ninety-two are allowed to sit in the Lords' Chamber. Their average age is seventy-one[22] and the youngest, Baroness Penn, is thirty-five at the time of writing. Twenty-six members of the Lords are also bishops in the Anglican church. Darren Hughes of the Electoral Reform Society has noted the inbuilt misogyny of the Lords: 14 per cent of it is still reserved for men only. Five of the twenty-six lord bishops are women. However, as hereditary titles still only pass down the male line, many seats in the upper chamber can only have male bottoms filling them.[23]

The House of Lords Appointment Commission is the body that both recommends the appointment of non-party-political life peers and scrutinises all nominations and political appointments. Candidates for membership of the House of Lords can be suggested by anyone, though the Prime Minister must approve the appointment and the Queen give her consent. The Commission boasts that it is independent and separate from the House of Lords. But look closer and you will see that all but one of the committee are members of, you guessed it, the House of Lords.

Elevations are not limited to the Queen's and New Year honours lists. They can be announced on other occasions too, such as when MPs are leaving the Commons, when a Prime Minister leaves office, on the appointment of someone who is not in Parliament as a minister, or, more unusually, at any time at all. Many appointments are political, made with a view to those members regularly attending Parliament and perhaps taking on front-bench work as spokespersons or whips. The Archbishop of Canterbury, who will have been sitting on the bishops' benches anyway, is usually made a life peer on the occasion of stepping down from the role, as are former Speakers of the Commons.

During the Brexit referendum and its aftermath, British politics received a great deal of scrutiny. Many were frustrated at how unaccountable and unresponsive it appeared to be, especially when implementing the decision of the people. This is why Parliament needs to modernise. After all, it would be a supreme irony if a country where the majority of parliamentarians are unelected left the European Union because of a lack of democracy.

The burden of history and tradition that Parliament carries tilts it too far towards the status quo. There is no harm in ribbons for swords on the members' coat hooks, but that cannot be said for other traditions. Pointless procedures that get in the way of an MP being the best they can be should go the way of the tally sticks. With all its history, the building is a receptacle of time itself. The paradox is that it offers its members so little of it. We should not need a pandemic to precipitate progress. Parliament should fear the prospect of becoming polished, privileged and peripheral to the people.

POLITICIANS SPINNING PLATES

Most MPs would see their constituents as their prime concern, and rightly so. This raises the question, though: why are their jobs so chaotic and demanding? One reason is the multiple organisations to which they're accountable. The responsibilities for these organisations can be various, including to vote a particular way, to support a particular campaign, to deliver investments or services, to help a charity group, to stop a development or to provide a tour of the Commons. But there will be asks from others, too. Asks of the national party – fundraising and campaigning, for example. Asks of colleagues – supporting their issues or Private Members' Bills or to attend their events. Asks of government and the Whips' Office – bench duty and time in the chamber or in committee. Asks of the professions – to spend time with them and learn about their issues. Asks of their local party – campaigning, fundraising and going to social events at the weekend. Asks of other local parties – to raise money and speak at events. Asks of sister parties in other nations. Asks of third parties and All Party Groups. Asks of inter-parliamentary organisations. Asks of multilaterals.

Some MPs choose to keep up their professional qualifications and occasionally practise. For example, some are medical professionals, armed forces reservists or special constables. Others devote 10 per cent of their time to charity. While all these asks listed above will be politely acknowledged, 'I know you are enormously busy, but...', none of these competing components will actually be aware of the volume of conflicting demands.

One of the panel from Chapter 2, a businessman, had recently shadowed an MP. He was shocked at what their in-tray included, in that particular instance featuring 'a call from someone whose washing machine had broken down'.

In many respects, politicians can't win. If they do nothing outside, they're accused of being a 'career politician', which is usually intended as an insult. Conversely, if being an MP is just one of their jobs, they're accused of being greedy. Many can still be found working a shift in the NHS, standing guard or attending a charitable board meeting, in spite of this assumption. They would argue they are better MPs as a consequence.

The question is whether we want them to be the best they can. There's no doubt that they want to be, but the dice are loaded against them. Here, ineffective working practices, a lack of flexibility and a ban on innovation meet with little training, no professional development and no preparedness. There are no qualifications required to become an MP, but maybe some formal basic training and support wouldn't go amiss?

The time available to members to carry out their various tasks has also been compressed in recent years. The small or non-existent majorities of recent parliaments have required that MPs are available and no more than eight minutes away from the chamber for most days of the week. As a result, the time in which they would ordinarily be able to do many of the jobs listed above has now been limited to weekends and recesses. In the 2010 coalition, the Commons occupational health service noted a large number of members taking prescription-strength vitamin D due to the fact that they rarely went outside. Reforms to sitting times, designed to be more family-friendly, have in practice actually cut down the hours per day that MPs have available to hold meetings and work. In addition, Parliament now starts earlier on some days, and MPs are often required to be in the chamber, either to ask questions or to listen to and take part in debates. The old method of pairing MPs to avoid the necessity of being present to vote has been used sparingly.

In recent times, post holders have found it hard to hide behind party platforms. Continuous media coverage and a stream of social media commentary mean that 'lines to take' just don't work any more. It's never been more important that MPs are the best pre-pared, situationally aware, informed and capable people for the job.

MPs are not facing the trauma and danger that our emergency services and armed forces face each day, but the pressures can still be significant. There are worries among MPs about the impact on family and children, safety concerns and the emotional demands of dealing with tragedy. Sometimes they must make life-and-death decisions. Consoling, or in some cases being confronted by, the be-reaved is part of the job. It requires resilience. These pressures take their toll both on individuals and on relationships, with the divorce rate among MPs being twice the national rate.[24]

Members have developed ways to cope. They take mindfulness classes. Many exercise. Others hire Cerberean diary secretaries. The role of an MP is demanding, but there are opportunities to indulge interests and meet inspiring people. Each passing week offers the chance to make life better for someone somewhere. Each week too, though, they can be met with as much abuse as gratitude.

DOES PARLIAMENT REPRESENT THE CHARACTER OF THE NATION?

The chief irony of Mother is that she creates 'daddy issues'. Parlia-mentarians cannot escape the slick of anachronism and pomposity. Some even embrace it and become as nineteenth century as the place itself. The problem is that it represents the acme of democracy and the implication is that only Whitehall and Westminster have the answers. Yet many important political figures have never been part of the place. Political thought is not exclusive to MPs. Nor is it confined to councillors, civil servants and devolved assembly mem-bers. Nor is it the exclusive preserve of public and third sector lead-ers, business moguls or even simply adults. Political representation is also about finding leadership in others. The MP's job to ask the questions, not to have all the answers.

There is no real job description for being a politician. You could never write one. If you asked politicians to write their own, each would be different, contingent on each MP's individual communities, manifestos and abilities. There might be some common threads, though. Community leadership, for instance, would surely be one. MPs are ultimately there to bring people together, to convene, to motivate and to inspire. The ability to do that is key, and the criteria required to achieve it are credibility and trust. Yet, trust is shot because politics has been inconsistent with the character of the people. The transcendent British quality – the cornerstone of the brand, if you like – is trust, but this needs to be seen against the timeline of recent parliamentary history.

THE TIMELINE OF TRUST DECAY

To illustrate the problem with trust in Parliament, the timeline below reviews the past twenty years to show some of the key moments.

Since 2001, there have been multiple sexual harassment scandals, resignations and investigations for bribery and corruption, particularly with 'cash for peerages' and 'cash for influence'. In 2009, more than 350 MPs were asked to repay expenses, including the sitting Prime Minister and Speaker of the House. Seven were jailed and many more resigned. The scandal ultimately led to the largest change of Parliament in history at the general election of 2010. One MP had made nineteen claims for horse manure. One claimed £1.50 for an ice cube tray. Another £1.31 for jellied eels. One claimed 59p for a chocolate Santa. Another for a single tin of dog food and a toilet roll holder. Two MPs claimed for three toilet seats. Two others for roof repairs and clearing a moat in their stately homes. Another still for trimming the hedge around their helipad. One claimed for a ride-on lawnmower. In further scandals, another two MPs pleaded guilty for perverting the course of justice. One was arrested five times in five years for multiple offences including assault. One admitted to being 'too drunk to vote'. Another punched a voter live on TV.

In any other organisation, these events would lead to sackings. The expense claims, the sexual harassment and the bribery would simply not be tolerated outside, and individuals would almost certainly be dismissed for gross professional misconduct. The problem is, you can't sack the elected or the appointed on the parliamentary estate. You can recall them, but that involves yet another exercise in democracy. The House does not work to the same standards as the outside world. It is unrepresentative of the organisations and businesses it is there to serve. And those organisations and businesses know it.

The decay of public trust in politicians mirrors that in authority figures elsewhere. Or maybe vice versa. When news of the parliamentary expenses scandal broke in 2009, the financial markets and numerous major brands were also in meltdown. Since then, leadership has been further discredited. The Catholic Church has faced multiple revelations about sex abuse, and both FIFA and Volkswagen have tackled chief executive scandals, for bribery and lying about car emissions respectively. A water utility company covered up polluting its rivers, Oxfam traded aid for sex and the Mossack Fonseca scandals revealed that many business leaders had hidden money offshore for tax reasons. We discuss this further in Chapter 8.

There are multiple ways these examples are at odds with so many British values of fairness, self-sacrifice and playing by the rules. Failing leadership is clearly not the sole preserve of politicians, but

Parliament should have a prime role in representing 'best practice'. It is, after all, supposed to be representative of the nation.

They Appear Not to Be Listening

It doesn't help that the public think MPs are not listening. The signs of this are obvious. They talk over each other in the Commons. They rarely show they are persuaded by another argument. Their Twitter accounts show thousands following and them only following a handful. This is not exactly a model of listening. They have to use template letters.

Politicians have created their own echo chambers by focusing on swing voters and their core areas of support. Many can only do reactive. And all this has happened while the expectations of their constituents have been increasing. 'I can get it on Amazon tomorrow. So why can't I have it now from you?' They want proactiveness. They want competence. They want modernisation. Not just because they want more from their MPs but because many of our citizens want to help, too.

'They're Just Not Like Us'

This is where parliamentary modernisation comes in. The way the Speaker talks to MPs doesn't sound like us. The way people talk to each other in the chamber doesn't sound like us. The way MPs answer questions doesn't sound like us. The way the House operates is unlike any normal administrative centre in the public or private sector. Few organisations are based in buildings that are either historical monuments or designed by ecclesiastical architects. The Houses of Parliament are both. It creates an expectation of flummery, bureaucracy and inaccessibility. It smells institutional and self-important. Probably because it is.

Tony Benn once said that politicians fall into two categories: sign-posts and weathervanes.[25] This has become industrialised. There are politicians who are windsurfers and pressure groups that are wind farms. The signposts are getting blown down.

This could be because of their increasingly similar background. More on this later. It's certainly not because politicians are getting younger. The average age of MPs on election has remained remark-ably consistent at around fifty.[26] But given the need for moderni-sation, that shouldn't be mistaken for a necessarily good thing. As each parliamentary sitting continues, they are serving longer. The trade in MPs over seventy is booming. In the House of Lords, it's even older. Eighty-three per cent of the members are over sixty and the majority are over seventy.[27] It should also be pointed out that this is not ageist; with age comes experience and knowledge. Yet in a country where the average age is forty, it is hardly representative.[28]

How the people are represented matters. If MPs reflect the values of the constituency they're seeking to serve, it helps. And the prob-lems do not simply stop with age and character: privilege is the next big topic.

PRIVILEGES AND PAY

The basic annual salary of an MP in April 2020 was £81,932. The salary for Cabinet ministers is between £134,565 and £141,505, depending on the seniority of their position. The average UK salary is £35,423.[29]

On top of this, MPs are able to claim allowances to cover the costs of running an office, employing staff and maintaining a con-stituency or a London residence. MPs will normally receive a min-imum pension of one-fortieth of their final salary for each year of service.[30] Then, even when MPs leave Parliament, they don't give up their passes. Almost 450 former MPs are currently in possession of a valid pass,[31] giving them many of the benefits and subsidies available to passholders.[32]

So, MPs aren't like the rest of us. They are better paid. They work in London. They are also more mobile than the rest of us. They behave in different ways. More than anything else, they have a different education. That is not to say they haven't had experiences or are devoid of empathy. Each weekend they meet swaths of people from all walks of life. They will undertake surveys. They will join campaigns. They will have had a life prior to Westminster. However, these differences do create a sense of distance from those they serve. Just as the similarities between MPs creates the danger of governing groupthink.

THE RISE OF THE GRADUATE MP

As part of the research for this book, every permanent secretary of every government department and the heads of all government agencies were written to. About one in five responded. They were asked what they thought the skills gaps were among MPs and what was needed to address that. How could their ministers be better prepared to take good decisions? It was clear that many had never even considered the question. But all who replied were keen to help parliamentarians develop their knowledge. The resources aimed at the civil service's continued professional development could also help ministers and potential ministers learn more about how the world works. The Joint Force Development team (Defence Academy and the Royal College of Defence Studies), the Diplomatic Academy and most of the government agencies were volunteered. This was followed up with a discussion with the Institute for Government, which admitted it was largely focused on Whitehall, not the skillsets of MPs.

Although the number of MPs from Oxbridge has declined in recent years, there has been a rise in the number of graduates from all universities. Before 1945, less than 20 per cent of Labour MPs were graduates. This rose to 32 per cent in 1945[33] and since then has climbed further. The majority of the British population does not have a degree,[34] but most of our political representatives do. MPs are better educated than at any stage in the country's history.

Parliament may reflect the country-wide trend of more graduates in leadership. But this is not an industry seeking only specialists. Parliament needs 'join the dots' leaders with a wide range of experience. It doesn't help that the occupations that MPs are drawn from are also narrowing. Of particular interest is the growth in the number of those who were already involved in politics prior to becoming MPs. These figures have more than quadrupled since 1979. The 'Red Wall' Tories are a little more diverse. Of these, eighty are university-educated (several have a politician as a relative) and only seventeen have a technical education or nothing past college.

So, why should this consistently high level of education matter? Well, if we believe that diversity is strength – *e pluribus unum* and all that – it matters greatly. By voting for graduates who did not go to Oxbridge, we think we're getting diversity, but what we might actually be getting is political uniformity.

Diversity matters in government because the constituencies represented are diverse. For instance, it helps in designing services if you've had to be a user of them. If you've experienced the exhaustion of working and caring for three generations of your family, you design services that are easy to use. The more bureaucratic, the less likely they are to be used.

Universities teach a Western reductionist model of thinking: they create experts in rationalising and analysing problems. But perhaps that *is* the problem? They don't teach empathy, humility or integrity. Universities train students to take problems apart, not how to put them back together. They can't join the dots. Or, to put it another way, this model of the world is founded on spotting *difference* rather than *similarity*. Exam questions require that students 'compare and contrast' or 'analyse the causes of'. A problem is analysed – but it is never solved. It is reduced, split into smaller components that themselves are subject to further analysis. It is thinking that goes in one direction only. It struggles to see the whole.

Perhaps the clearest trend in leadership today is the idea that thinking and feeling are two entirely separate entities, and that intellect has become the more dominant of the two. In politics, some believe voters commit only when they understand. No. They commit when they feel understood. That's entirely different. That means we need those who can listen and converse to understand those around them.

Some of the best ideas have a strange way of coming about. They come from conversations or when you are in the midst of doing something else or when you are given time to think. They most often happen when not trying.[35] Or when you can stop. It's almost impossible for politicians to do that. It might explain a lot. The point here is worth labouring. Great thinking doesn't involve either analytical or conceptual processes but *both*.[36] The goal is not to choose between the two approaches but to become more skilled at both. MPs find it difficult to focus on detail while also seeing the bigger picture. This is because of the sheer volume of time expended in administration. Preparing them in some sort of orientation training might help make them more productive.

DEMOCRACY IN DANGER

In 2018, think tank Onward published polling that showed a shift away from policies based on freedom towards those based on 'the politics of belonging'. Security, in a complex and uncertain world, was preferable. Onward's director, Will Tanner, said that summer: 'British politics is undergoing a sea change and it is for security, not freedom. Most voters are not freedom fighters who want more rampant individualism, a small state and lower taxes. They want well-funded public services, security for their family and a strong community in the place they live.'[37]

Parliamentarians may be very much in favour of democracy and free speech. But what if people value security over a freedom that brings only parliamentary paralysis? Then democracy and its parliamentarians become at best frustrating and at worst a complete irrelevance. While support for democracy was still strong at 84 per cent, the Onward poll showed a drift away from liberal democratic forms of government in favour of more authoritarian models. Twenty-six per cent believed that democracy was a bad way to run a country. Eighty per cent wanted experts in charge. Perhaps surprisingly, young voters showed the highest preference for an authoritarian regime, with 66 per cent of 24–34-year-olds[38] favouring strong leaders who 'don't have to bother with Parliament'. Older voters were much more democratic, as the polling showed only 3 per cent of the over seventy-fives think democracy is no good.

Why the difference between the generations? Do younger people take their freedoms for granted? Is it because democracy doesn't seem to be delivering for them? Do their parliamentarians and government look inadequate in their fast-paced and highly responsive world? Did they want more community and less individualism? All these questions remain to be answered. For young people to believe again in democracy, we must show it can be modernised.

CONCLUSIONS

The public perception of MPs is inescapably bound up in Parliament's sweet-wrapper predicament. Churchill was right. The people shape the buildings, and thereafter the buildings shape the people. So, Mother continues to function as a modern democracy despite, rather than because of, her neo-Gothic form. Scotland, Wales and Northern Ireland have their own assemblies and parliaments. England is the only one that hasn't. (Although it does have squatters' rights in the Commons chamber when English-only matters are being discussed and voted on. Then non-English MPs cannot take part.)

The Houses of Parliament, while being a historical wonder, must be improved to facilitate democracy. Of course it is an iconic building, but the cost of antiquity is more than financial. Its procedures need updating to do the basics better, like welcoming members of its own electorate. The Capitol building in Washington DC does an altogether better job of this. Parliament needs to treat the electorate as its customers rather than as tourists, and perhaps then it wouldn't make them queue outside in all weathers. Even enough ladies' toilets (queues every time) would be an improvement. Could Parliament update its systems to include electronic voting and video conferencing to allow MPs to spend more time in their constituencies? It also should adopt the modern standards of business practice and behaviour in its culture and in its customs.

Mother's representatives aren't always that representative. Whether it be in terms of age, mobility, background, earnings, behaviour, education or gender, they don't always look or sound like the constituencies they're serving. They're more middle-class, better educated, wealthier and older. This is especially true of the House of Lords, whose members are wealthier, older, more southern and more male than the people they represent. If the House of Lords was elected, it wouldn't automatically bring democratic account-ability. Only re-elections do that. The coalition reforms promised elections but would have delivered no democracy, just fixed terms of fifteen years and greater politicisation. Once in, that was it. If the UK wants an elected Lords, let's do it properly, too. There could be more emphasis on wider backgrounds and skillsets. The rules on transparency on earnings should be the same as for the Com-mons, with a register of members' financial interests. It would help it in many ways. Their lordships improve legislation, but they also try to initiate and/or stop legislation. No one asked for that and it shouldn't happen.

These changes would enable MPs and their lordships to have a greater connection to a place, by being able to spend more time in their constituency in the former case and with a new geographic role for the latter.

Leaders of all types, especially parliamentarians, need to un-derstand the character of the people they represent. They need to understand that trust has been damaged. The past twenty years of political scandals have eroded public trust in leadership. The Brexit hokey-cokey exacerbated it. Delivering the Brexit mandate will help repair the trust, but the behaviour of our leaders still matters. Those who run for office are motivated to make a difference and serve their community. That which frustrates that aim must be reformed.

Ultimately, the country can be proud of its democratic history. These traditions, however, should not be allowed to erode the ef-fectiveness of a modern working legislature. There are many areas of potential reform, various examples of which have been laid out in this chapter. Arguably, any change brought about by government will take years of patient persistence. It should be done faster. The forces of the future are building up outside Parliament. We should let them flow freely through the place, rather than wash it away.

7

MODERNISING THE MANAGEMENT THAT GOVERNS US

'The only real way to reform the civil service system is to reform the political system, and no government's going to reform the system that put it into power.'

SIR ARNOLD ROBINSON[1]

Given all we've covered, what does government (the Management) need to do now? We can't modernise anything without money, and government is long-term broke. It was broke before Covid, and the finances are even worse now. The government made a clear choice to protect jobs and viable businesses during Covid.

Before we get into more detail, we're acutely aware that this chapter may not be that interesting. So we'll take it in two parts. Problems and solutions. Government is a subject that can drown the reader in terminological, technical tedium. Dullness is part of the problem. You can only talk about government for so long before you're reduced to making only vowel sounds. We're looking at the world through the wrong end of a municipal drainpipe, but it's worth a try.

In the first part of the chapter, we investigate the size, structure and culture of government. How have people tried to simplify it over the years? Why has it changed so many times? How can it contribute to reducing regional inequalities? We look at what needs to happen to bring about change, rather than just the illusion of it.

If we want government to do more, we need to look at the options to make it happen. What are the limits of government spending? How can the money be made to work harder and go further? How can the economy and third sectors be harnessed to produce synergies? How can the government use its convening power to inspire the third sector? How can social entrepreneurs be elevated and liberated within the national framework? The second part of this chapter looks at solutions. Take our advice. Go there now. The first part is too depressing.

PART ONE: PROBLEMS

Government Is Big

Government numbers are big: really, incomprehensibly big. Bigger than Douglas Adams's universe. We can deal with numbers like a thousand, a million, even 50 million. We can understand £25,000 a year. We can even relate to £100,000 a year. But if it's £100 million a year, it becomes harder to comprehend. Most of us live in a financial neighbourhood, a narrow range of numeric parenthesis. When it comes to large numbers, great distances or huge wealth, we are hopelessly parochial.

National government is the biggest thing any of us knows. It employs roughly three million people at the national level and another two in local government.[2] The former has massively overtaken the latter in the past twenty years (see illustration).[3] Despite many governments talking about localism, the centralisation begun by Harold Wilson's 1964 government continues.

UK PUBLIC SECTOR EMPLOYMENT IN LOCAL AND CENTRAL GOVERNMENT, SEASONALLY ADJUSTED
March 1999 to March 2018

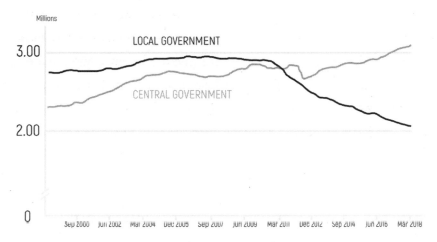

Source: Office of National Statistics, Public sector employment, UK: March 2018
Contains public sector information licensed under the Open Government Licence v3.0.
http://www.nationalarchives.gov.uk/doc/open-government-licence/version/3/

For the avoidance of doubt, in the numbers we're using, a billion is 1,000 million. A trillion is 1,000 billion. There is no such number as a gazillion or bazillion. A Marillion, by contrast, is a British rock group that emerged from the post-punk music scene as a bridge between the styles of punk and classic progressive rock.

Government Is Byzantine

We know Britain likes complicated. We explored that in Chapter 1. It definitely applies to how the country organises itself. Let's start with the basics. There are 5,568 villages in the UK.[45] Seventeen per cent (9.3 million) of the country's population is outside of the urban areas.[6] By subtraction, this means that 83 per cent (45 million) live in urban areas.[7] There are twelve core cities, one in every region of Britain except the east of England. The north-west, Yorkshire and the Humber and Scotland each have two. In between, there are 102 large towns (places with over 75,000 people), 242 medium towns (30,000–75,000), 550 small towns (10,000–30,000) and 567 communities (under 10,000). In total, there are 7,044 'places' across Great Britain, mapped and classified by the Centre for Towns. These places are then divided up into 650 parliamentary constituencies. There are 408 principal (unitary, upper- and second-tier) councils in the UK.[8] Twenty-six county councils, 192 district councils and 190 unitary authorities.[9] England also has 207 clinical commissioning groups, 135 acute trusts and seventeen specialist trusts. There are thirty-nine constabularies and fifty fire services. Wales alone has four health trusts and seven health boards, four police and three fire services.[10] Scotland has fourteen health boards, one police and one fire service. Then there are thirty-eight Local Enterprise Partnerships tasked with economic regeneration in a particular locality. It's big and it's complicated.

Government Is Broke

For 2020, the total amount of planned spending by government was around £874.4 billion, but Covid saw that rise by a further £300 billion.[11] This year, the government will spend more than it takes in revenue. That's called the deficit.[12] Cumulatively, the deficits all add to the national debt, and that figure, at the end of 2020, was £1.82 trillion. Scary stat: it's the highest it's been in peace time. Perhaps more scary stat: it's about the same value as iPhone company Apple.[13,14]

The bad news is that all governments, of every kind, are out of money. Ageing demographics and static economies have forced many countries to live beyond their means. To do more, the economy has to grow. Otherwise, different approaches need to be found.

High Barnet is in north London. It is notable for many things. George Michael, Emma Bunton, Elaine Paige – Trevor Howard, even. It is one of the highest suburbs in the UK. Fancy. It's also famous for the most depressing PowerPoint slide in all local government history (and there are some stiff competitors in this category) – the Barnet Graph of Doom.[15]

THE 'GRAPH OF DOOM'

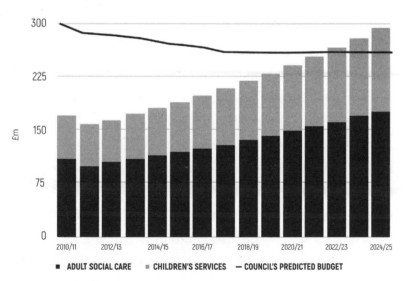

Source: Barnet Council, 'The One Barnet Transformation Programme Presentation 29 November 2011' Andrew Travers, London Borough of Barnet.
https://www.scribd.com/presentation/77279963/The-One-Barnet-Transformation-Programme-Presentation-29-Nov-11

Based on demographic change, the graph suggests that in twenty years, key services for children and adults alone will consume the entire budget.[16] Our society is based on the idea of mutuality – that the strong should help the weak. By doing so, we all become stronger. Given the chart's predictions, it's widely accepted that much of what funds this mutuality will need to be found in new ways.

The Institute for Government estimates in its 'Performance Tracker of 2019' that the government will typically be spending £191.1 billion on just nine public services by 2023/24.[17] These services are GPs, hospitals, adult social care, children's social care, neighbourhood services, the police, prisons, courts and schools. This, of course, rises in line with inflation. The report also noted:

> Over the past nine years of curbs on public spending, most public services have done more with less by limiting staff pay increases and prompting workers to be more productive. But public services will find it difficult to sustain any efficiencies made now the public sector pay cap has been lifted and with many services struggling to recruit and retain staff.

It suggests this will be enough to maintain these services but not to improve them. It highlights particular concerns about violent and ineffective prisons, a strained legal system, adult social care and the future funding of the police. Told you it was depressing. The conclusion of the IfG report is that without perpetual hikes in public spending, there will only be decline. But we will see that is not the only option.

Government Is Bureaucratic

Deep within the bowels of the Treasury building, there's a document that lays out the rules for any government expenditure. It details the approval levels, who needs to be involved and the allowed spending levels. It is gravity-bending in its density.[18] There's a good reason for this. It stops a lot of bad and wasteful projects, but also frustrates innovation and focus. The need for its reform has long been discussed and there has even been some tinkering.

As one Treasury veteran put it:

> I can say that the reality is that pretty much anything can happen if there is political will from the centre. When it comes down to non-centre-driven ideas, however, what creates barriers isn't the Green Book – but a Whitehall culture that seeks to keep barriers up to outsiders, doesn't pay due attention to external expertise, and, most irritatingly, a turf-war mentality that emerges almost immediately when anything genuinely new and innovative emerges. This is because anything new and innovative almost certainly requires collaboration across Whitehall, and thus a pooling of control.

Treasury officials are always seeking improvements to taxation and the other levers they have to raise funds and incentivise particular behaviours and investments, but really big reforms are few and far between. This is partly because it would be complicated to undertake and partly because there hasn't been a big enough majority or a political will strong enough to reform these services in over a decade.

Make no mistake, as long as the Green Book holds sway, there can always be a reason not to do something. The absence of national missions for the country flows into this issue, as does the need to aim high and be aspirational and the need for a large majority to deliver reform.

The main problem is that the book requires every initiative to be evidence-based. If you want to do something with government money, you must be able to prove best practice. But what if you didn't want to use government money? Suppose you wanted to bring in a sovereign wealth fund or create a new national bank that didn't charge interest but only offered tax credits? We need to create an environment in which government doesn't stop new initiatives without good reason. It needs a more organic entrepreneurial approach. Government rarely works in financial partnerships. It never works with other people's money. Working with other people's money is largely limited to that which is collected in tax. Philanthropic organisations that wish to donate substantial sums struggle to engage Whitehall. No matter what the amount, or the expertise and track record of those involved. If it wasn't invested in Whitehall, then Whitehall isn't much interested.

This is not just about the Treasury. There are many who prefer to stymie radical change in favour of administrative incrementalism. There's nothing wrong with that, but it needs to work towards a long-term unified vision.

Chapter 2 of the Green Book gives a useful overview of the appraisal process that must be passed in order for spending to take place.[19] One key step is the assessment of a shortlist of options, in which the expected costs and benefits of each option are estimated and the trade-off is considered. This is done using social cost–benefit analysis (or sometimes social cost-effectiveness analysis). In this process, all impacts of a proposal – social, economic, environmental, financial etc. – should be assessed relative to what might have taken place in the absence of the suggested intervention. But the actual costs of doing nothing are not assessed. The document notes:

'Distributional analysis is necessary where an intervention either has a redistributive objective or where it is likely to have a significant impact on different groups, types of business, parts of the UK or Devolved Administrations. Distributional analysis can include regional, sub-national and local analysis based on geographically defined areas.'

We don't want government to be the Milky Bar Kid, but surely we could make it just a little bit easier? The potential impacts on local government are present elsewhere, too. For instance, the UK must produce enabling regulation more quickly. Currently, data is collected, proposals are drawn up in a Green Paper, a White Paper is produced and consulted on, and then legislation follows. In the meantime, the thing you were trying to regulate has evolved into an entirely different beast. George Freeman, while a transport minister, questioned the idea of regulation coming from Whitehall, given the presence of real-time data. He cited the example of driverless cars. These are more of a concern in cities than in rural communities. So why did the regulations need to be the same across the country?

The main criticism of the Green Book of late is that it does not give enough weight to rebalancing or 'levelling up' regional economies. The rules are blunt and too rigid and there is in-built bias in favour of wealthier areas receiving more infrastructure. In their paper 'The Imperial Treasury: appraisal methodology and regional economic performance in the UK', Diane Coyle and Marianne Sensier proposed: 'Infrastructure investments also need to be based on a strategic view about economic development for the whole of the UK.'[20]

Civil Service World is a notable media outlet. In a piece entitled 'Is Whitehall's obsession with business cases getting in the way of delivery?', former civil servant Andrew Greenway said:

The civil service's approach to business cases is well established. The five-case method set out in the Treasury's Green Book has long been the bible for how things get done. As you would expect, it is on the dense side. The 'short, plain English guide' is nine pages, and includes sentences like: 'The focus in this section of the case is on capital and resource requirements (near-cash or non-cash) and so here VAT and capital charges are included. The financial case is concerned with the impact upon budgetary totals (RDEL, CDEL and AME as explained in Chapter 1 of the Consolidated Budgeting Guidance).' This is a world even hardened technocrats shy away from. Even so, business cases matter. The civil service's dependence on them is one of the suspects in the mystery of why Whitehall often finds it difficult to deliver. Like the *Midsomer Murders* killer that's always fixated on money, business cases are ever-present at the death of major projects. They exemplify how a series of small, sensible suggestions can slowly accrete into a stranglehold ... It is exactly this kind of steady accumulation that typifies a weakness of applying business cases to almost everything.[21]

Government Provides and Polices

One reason the Green Book exists is to prevent corruption. In 2013, the National Fraud Authority estimated that malfeasance was costing the UK £52 billion a year, of which £2.1 billion could be attributed to local government.[22] This covered a wide variety of issues, including housing tenancy, procurement, payroll and council tax fraud. Further examples were granting planning permissions or claiming that such permissions would be granted in return for payment, collusion and bid-rigging on contracts. In the end, the Office of Fair Trading issued penalties totalling £129 million. It may not be big in the scheme of things, but it attracts a lot of attention.[23,24]

The investigation found examples of conflict of interest, such as diverting infrastructure to land owned by a councillor. This also led to the discovery of electoral fraud, such as in the 2004 Birmingham local elections.[25] Tower Hamlets likewise saw 164 allegations of electoral fraud and malpractice during its local elections.[26] The IfG has warned that local government is relying too much on self-regulation.[27,28]

Here we see the administrative morass again. The District Audit Service was founded in 1844, doing its job for 139 years.[29] In 1983, the more general Audit Commission was established, which in turn set up the National Fraud Initiative in 1996. In 2000, a new framework was brought in, doing away with the open committee structure that had existed until that point. Further anti-fraud authorities and frameworks followed in 2008, 2010, 2011, 2012 and 2013. Then the Audit Commission was abolished, to be replaced by a new audit regime: the Fraud, Error and Debt Taskforce. In 2014, the Transparency Code was produced to help this taskforce with its work, requiring that it filed reports on its counter-fraud work.[30]

But these measures have not had the desired effect. A standards board was established under the Local Government Act 2000, with the aim of holding councillors accountable for misconduct.[31] In Wales, there's an ombudsman, and in Scotland, a Commissioner for Ethical Standards in Public Life. There's a notable gap in the scrutiny of England.

This matters not just in terms of the good stewardship of public money but also because fear of corruption has been one of the brakes on devolution. Worries about corrupt local politicians or officials was cited as one of the reasons that John Prescott's regional government reorganisation failed to win the required referendums.

Another problem with the centralisation of power – it draws politicians away from their communities. They think they can do more good by giving out big money centrally than directing small money locally. They assume the centre is where they can make the biggest difference. It's certainly what gets the most attention. Who can blame them? This focus on the centre means there are a large number of uncontested local seats. The Electoral Reform Society said:

> There was a shocking increase in the number of uncontested seats in some English councils up for election in May 2015. The Eden District Council in Cumbria declared twenty-one of its thirty-eight available seats before polling day, meaning that a clear majority of the council (55 per cent) has been returned before the election has even taken place. This is up from 50 per cent of seats in 2011.[32]

If the changes touched on in Chapter 6 came to pass, politicians might make a greater impact closer to home. This trend is illustrated by more current and former MPs like Dan Jarvis and Andy Burnham standing as locally elected mayors.

Government Keeps Changing

All the above detail was true at the time of writing, but by the time you read this, things may have changed. Things *will* have changed. The reorganisation, rearrangement and restructuring of local services is the one thing that has stayed the same for forty years. The structures change as frequently as the people working in them don't.

Whenever you pick up this book in the future, there will be a White Paper mooted/in draft/circulating to reorganise any and all of the organisations mentioned in this chapter.

The nine most dangerous words that can ever be uttered by politicians are: 'I'm from the government and I'm here to help.' Nowhere is this truer than when government tries to sort out government. Local government has been the subject of an almost constant restructuring process that continues to this day.

Eric Pickles (now Baron Pickles), who served as Secretary of State for Communities and Local Government from 2010 to 2015, rumbled in his Bradford brogue: 'Ah 'av a pearl-'andled revolvuh jus waitin' in mah drawuh for the fuhrst civil servunt 'oo suhggests anutha lohcal guvment reorgahnisation.'[33] Words swifter than a weaver's shuttle, has our Eric.

Although various forms of local government existed in Roman, Saxon and medieval times, modern local government dates from the nineteenth century. The Local Government Act of 1888 provided for the creation of sixty-six county councils and a London county council. These councils were run by elected councillors and comprised a chairman, aldermen and councillors.

By the late twentieth century, local government in England had evolved into a complex system in need of modernisation. Consequently, this was simplified to a two-tier system, outlined in the Local Government Act 1972. Under this Act, all local government areas, with the exception of Greater London and the Isles of Scilly, were abolished. In their place, new metropolitan and non-metropolitan counties were created. These, in turn, were divided into districts. Each county was administered by a county council, each district by a district one.

Whole towns thus travelled from one county to another while remaining in the same place. On the Lancashire/Yorkshire border, even today, this border betrayal by the bureaucracy is remembered.

The County of London and the London County Council were abolished and the newt-loving leader's lair of the Greater London Council (GLC) was created in 1965 with thirty-two new London boroughs. In 1986, the GLC was abolished, in turn, for not being Conservative. Then, in 2000, the Greater London Authority (GLA) was created to provide a directly elected strategic administration. The GLA still exists today and shares responsibility for local government services with the thirty-two London boroughs and the City of London Corporation. Ken Livingstone lives on in the form of his 'testicle', the riverside home of the GLA.[34]

Decentralisation can thus result in recentralisation, still conditional on central government approval. There is still continual oversight and few real discretionary powers. Central government staying in control, worried about spending and lack of delivery, sounds similar to a sermon on celibacy from a sex addict.

The IfG has some constructive things to say on this. In its 2017 paper 'All Change: Why Britain is so prone to policy reinvention, and what can be done about it', it looked at the area of policy churn and said, 'Change happens far too often and too casually. New legislation replaces old; organisations are founded and abolished; policies are launched and relaunched; programmes are created and abandoned – all at an alarming rate. This is not merely a facet of ideological change.'[35]

Although some change can certainly be attributed to politics, the paper also pointed to a high level of agreement between parties on the issues. The constancy of change in the UK's local government system has other causes than mere political difference. It appears to be a displacement activity favoured by those unwilling or unable to achieve real organisational change. The consequence is inertia on issues that need real attention, for example social care. The paper went on:

> This churn is a feature of some other persistent weaknesses in our system of government. The poor institutional memory, the tendency to abolish and recreate organisations as a proxy for demonstrating progress, a centre of government that remains too weak at long-term planning and a policy development process that is not as resilient as it could be.

In 1992, it was recommended that some counties should retain their two-tier structures, but that others should change to one-tier unitary authorities. Subsequently, several unitary authorities were created in twenty-five counties between 1995 and 1998. In 2009, further reorganisation created ten unitary authorities on top of that.

Not content with the reorganisation of the structures of local government, the structures of individual councils have also been rehashed. The leader and Cabinet model was introduced following the Local Government Act 2000. The Cabinet is usually formed by the majority party in the local authority where there is one, or by a coalition if not, which comes together to elect a leader. Significantly, this move binned the committee structure, which had made it easy to see what decisions were about to be taken. With this reorganisation there have been changes both to responsibilities and to accountabilities. There must be someone, somewhere, somehow, who finds this all great fun.

In 2010, the new coalition government also pledged to promote decentralisation and passed the Localism Act in 2011, which was designed to reform the role of local government. That Act also included new rights for neighbourhood planning forums. These would give residents in a stated area the ability to write their own local development plans, to be approved in a referendum.

In 2012, Theresa May introduced locally elected police and crime commissioners (PCCs). The impact has been negligible, though. Voter turnouts have been between 10 and 20 per cent and the police commissioners have minimal powers. Now commentators are betting on both PCCs and local plans being swept away with further 'reforms', which will themselves be swept away in due course.

Whenever asked, Britons say they want more local accountability, not less, because their faith in government reduces the closer they get to the centre. An Ipsos MORI poll in 2013 put trust in local government at 79 per cent and that in central government at 11 per cent. So the British people want localism, but with all the checks, balances and standards of central government.

So much of the reform just hasn't worked, for all sorts of reasons. Partly it's due to entrenched politics. Imagine being in a country where you are the monarch, but apart from your ceremonial role, most of the ruling is done by local sheriffs who wish for your downfall. The grand illusion of being the party of government is foiled by local politicians. Never was this truer than in the years of the Thatcher government. Ken Livingstone was the leader of the GLC and took every opportunity to taunt the Westminster government from across the river. This was fondly remembered by all Conservatives in the 1980s and replicated in half a dozen cities.

In a piece entitled 'Someone to Blame, Someone to Sack: Why local government is a failed state', Simon Jenkins wrote: 'Britain hates provinces. It knows and prefers cities and counties. Regions may reflect Whitehall's bureaucratic convenience, but they are poor substitutes for local identity.'[36]

In yet another example of local vs central government disagreements, in 2014 the then Chancellor, George Osborne, seized on Manchester as the base for his Northern Powerhouse,[37] giving it powers and money. This was, of course, provided that the city accepted his new-found fascination with elected mayors. As Jenkins pointed out, in Manchester, at least, this made sense – but soon other cities wanted to reorganise themselves into city regions with elected mayors, too. Osborne was forced to offer everyone more power, until England was on the brink of reordering itself into mini-regions, run by a third tier of local government under mayors, however inappropriate the political geography.

Government's Culture Is Not Business-Like

We're not saying government should be run like a business. But it could be run in a more business-like way. The vast majority of councillors, for instance, cite their motivation as 'serving the community'. These are the local heroes – committed, conscientious, case-sensitive conservative councillors with quiet, national pride and local knowledge. They're a sword with two edges. They miraculously do more with less, but alas cannot make less more. It's ironic that so many local councils used to be called corporations. Local government council is to commercial corporation as fish is to bicycle. Wealth creation and distribution are two full separates.

It gives us some clues as to why wealth does not always percolate to the provinces from its provenance. Burghers beat business people every time. The currency of business is profit, but in local government it's cracker-barrel more often than pork-barrel. It's baksheesh by bonhomie. It's not what you know, it's who. It takes years of real skill and experience. Local government requires more care. They know where you live.

According to the local government census of 2018, councillors are educated to degree or equivalent level (68 per cent, compared with about 40 per cent in the general population in 2018).[38] Only 3 per cent have no qualifications. Their average age is fifty-nine and 63 per cent are male. Almost half are retired and 96 per cent are white.[39] These are pragmatic people aware of local problems and their likely solutions. They hold the key to how to deliver local change cost-effectively.

It's all well and good to suggest methods of reform, but we still need to answer the following question: how can the civil service deliver without money? One way might be a method we have suggested before, of acting centrifugally and pushing more staff to the peripheries of the UK. The distribution of the civil service headcount highlights its London-centric nature.[40] This looks like it will change over time, with a number of departments already announcing relocation.

PART TWO: SOLUTIONS

Prioritise Communities Not Regions

The brunt of the economic hardship in the past twenty years has been borne not by nebulous regions but by specific communities. It's been a gradual dying of the light. It has been a process, not an event. It is true in all Western economies. The issue of how these areas access and create wealth is central to healing division and creating national unity. Fix that, the rest will follow. The hardest-hit areas were the ones that voted for Brexit. They're also the most nationalist areas in Europe. This is an important point: Brexit was not the cause of the division; the division preceded the vote. The referendum just brought the fault lines to national attention.

It's not just jobs that disappear when industries fail. Pride and hope leave as well. Research carried out for the Centre for Towns by Professor Gerry Stoker showed that in many of those regional towns that have suffered economically in recent years, people *believe* that both they and their area are becoming less valued and less relevant.[41]

In his book *Little Platoons*, David Skelton charts the economic and social decline of his hometown, Consett in County Durham.[42] At its peak, Consett Steel produced the hulls of the Royal Navy. There was pride and purpose as well as 6,000 jobs.[43] People felt part of something and this cannot be underestimated. With the closure of the steelworks in 1980, all that went away. It's not an isolated story. The same thing happened on Merseyside, in Middlesbrough, Newcastle and many other cities in those regions. The disparity between the regions is highlighted in the graph below

HOUSEHOLDS IN THE SOUTH-EAST OF ENGLAND HAVE A COMBINED WEALTH OF £2.46TN, COMPARED WITH £368BN IN THE NORTH-EAST

Aggregate household total wealth, £bn

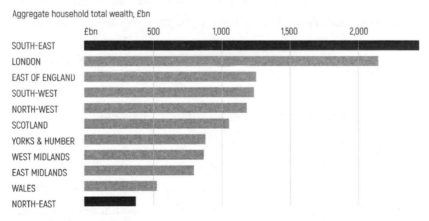

Source: Office of National Statistics, 'Wealth and Assets Survey July 2014 to June 2016. Includes property, belongings, financial assets and private pensions'
Contains public sector information licensed under the Open Government Licence v3.0.
http://www.nationalarchives.gov.uk/doc/open-government-licence/version/3/

In addressing the problems facing the regions in Britain, Skelton notes that many in these areas voted to leave the EU as a solution to their hardship. He concluded that the first priority of post-Brexit Britain must be to turn these towns around.[44,45] He's right, and there is consensus on how to do it.

Good infrastructure and connectivity to major cities are at the heart of it; the re-industrialisation of towns with the combination of R&D investment and high-value manufacturing. This involves the creation of centres of excellence and a clear purpose for a locality, the creation of prosperity hubs, enterprise or opportunity zones. None of this is new.

Trusting local people could energise a community. It would give people a direct stake and encourage them to participate in their communities. Their actions and ideas could really make a difference to establishing a sense of place in the UK, giving them a brand and a connection to their community.

The biggest problem all governments face is delivery. Democracies are inherently weak when it comes to delivering change and reform because they rely on majority consensus. There are three key questions to be asked. First, what reforms are required to allow delegated authority and synergies to be created? Second, who should enact this authority and make good use of it? Third, even if these changes can be enacted – and there is much history of failure – how will they be financed? The problem is, there are limits to the amounts of cash governments can generate, given the conflicting demands the money pool must address.

In theory, the culture of Whitehall is in the way. Central government bemoans the lack of regional talent while simultaneously taking the best for itself. To fix this, Whitehall needs to provide some of the enablers to help turn things around. This could work by introducing

some changes to the civil service fast-track scheme: instead of chan-
nelling the high-flyers to the centre, why not post them to communities where their talent can be used more productively? This would also
allow the mandarins of the future to understand the impact of their
decisions at the local level. It might also engender more local trust if
Whitehall could work with its own future talent at the regional level.

When Whitehall identifies a problem, it always wants to do something to demonstrate that the government of the day is tackling the
issue. But it can't do everything and be everywhere. So, it ends up
just addressing the low-hanging fruit. Or it sets up a pilot fund to
pay for interventions in 10 per cent of places. Or it tackles the issues
in the headlines alone. But reading about progress in a town twenty
miles away is of little use to you if your high street is dying and you
can't find work.

Decentralise Financial Powers and Policy

In 2019, the IfG assessed the economic benefits that devolution had
delivered and concluded they had been 'limited'.[46] The reason again
was that the fiscal and policy levers need to be in local hands. Effectively, geographic disparities are being sustained by lack of fiscal
autonomy and separated by a lack of trust.

In fairness, after the financial crisis of 2009, the level of centralisation increased as the purse strings were tightened. While expenditure increased to deal with the Covid crisis, the decentralisation was
reversed. Nevertheless, the IfG report still highlighted that the UK
is one of the most centralised economies in the world, but it wasn't
always this way. At the start of the twentieth century, the situation
was the reverse, with most taxes raised locally. Growing businesses
and private capital at a local level grew philanthropic capital, too,
and we'll look at this relationship in more detail later.

So, what if we decentralised the finance? What if we localised the Treasury and gave it responsibility and clear targets for improving growth? There are plans to move Treasury officials out of London; could we not embed them in every region? What if we took the same approach to other institutions? What if we created a national bank with local links? This has been done effectively with the Business Growth Fund, a private equity investment bank funded by high street banks that the government bailed out after the crash.[47] By charter, it can only invest minority stakes. This is the sort of thing needed at a regional level. And if it was done in the long term, investors could receive long-term tax credits instead of short-term interest rate returns. What about local stock markets or the creation of sustainable investment funds?

This decentralisation of financial powers and policy could have further benefits. Returning to Skelton, he's scathing of policy that makes British firms more prone to foreign takeovers except those from the US.[48] This should be a strategic as well as an economic concern. For certain sectors, it will be about security and sovereign capabilities, too. Whitehall is ill-equipped to deal with these questions. The Department for Business, Energy and Industrial Strategy has historically had the veto on such issues, but it actually has little situational fluency on what is important to other departments or local communities. There are likewise few Whitehall horizon-scanning tools that can see trouble coming. While ministers can see security briefings, diplomatic telegrams and intelligence reports of every sort in their day-to-day work, they don't get enough information on markets, mergers and financial flows. This needs to be fixed and there have been some recent moves to do so – the National Security and Investment Bill 2020 being one such example.

Trust the People

In the absence of money, the good news is that lots of people want to help. This is key to the very essence of community. A 2017 ONS report into social capital, entitled 'Measuring National Well-Being: an analysis of Social Capital in the UK', reveals a snapshot of the heart of Britain.[49] The report found that 20 per cent of people assist at least one sick, elderly or disabled person, while 53 per cent of people volunteer for and are members of an organisation. There have been increases in unpaid volunteering, too. Among parents, 58 per cent give help to their adult children and 38 per cent receive help from those children in return. Most adults (97 per cent) report having at least one close friend and 84 per cent say they have someone they could rely on if they had a serious problem. As many as 68 per cent regularly talk to their neighbours, and just under half (42 per cent) borrow things from those neighbours – though whether they return them is unreported. The number of people who enjoy a social life with friends or work colleagues at least once a week came in at 61 per cent. As a result of all this, it was reported that just 4 per cent of people living in the UK today are lonely. They are mostly to be found writing books like this.

These connections and networks are what make a community strong. This support is lasting, personal. We saw during Covid how local was always better at identifying unmet need and delivering on it.

Most of this is done without government support and none of these people do what they do for money. A little recognition, though, would be a different thing. It would go a long way to encouraging those involved in such activities and would draw attention to these unsung heroes. This is not a matter for government necessarily, but politicians could up their game. They may not have financial resources, but they do have convening power. It is not so much about what politicians do as opposed to what they are and what they represent. Social enterprise and the third sector have the capacity to help meet the government's budgetary challenges. Enabling that means more than just leaving them to deal with the problem as the state withdraws.

Others have pointed out that civil society is not in good shape. Andy Haldane, the Bank of England's chief economist, said, 'The reason we have the triple threats of disconnection of people from society, mistrust of institutions, and the rising tide of populism is because we have structurally underinvested in civil society.'[50]

There's also a role here for business to create more social enterprises, rather than more corporate social responsibility programmes. Sustainability must become the theme. A social enterprise is defined as 'an organisation that addresses a basic unmet need or solves a social or environmental problem through a market-driven approach'.[51] So, let's be clear then: in this sense, *all* enterprise is social enterprise.

A few good things did happen with the invention of the Big Society. Some charities did get involved in community asset transfers. And Local Enterprise Partnerships, chambers of commerce and trade bodies were asked to embrace social entrepreneurs as equals. There was much scrutiny of the procurement and commissioning practices that had discriminated against the independent sector.

The Big Society got a lot of people excited about the possibilities and the prospect of civic renewal. It actually worked well in areas filled with retired executives or civil servants. In communities with no capacity for setting up a trust or limited company with charitable status, though, it was a different story. The government's new social capital vehicles stalled. Big Society Capital[52] volunteered its services, but the relevant government departments blocked sensible activity.

One example of this was in the care sector. The plan was to close institutions that were no longer suitable for those with mental illnesses and learning disabilities. The initial investment required for building better care settings could have been recouped through the sale of those institutions. To this day, however, hundreds still linger, many in complete isolation.

In another example, the Green Investment Bank found it hard to get local authorities to think creatively about upgrading street lighting using their funds, even when the savings from part-solar-powered lighting would cover the costs of any loan.[53]

The Big Society was a positive idea, but the above examples show how it ran into trouble. Few had enough capacity to enact the suggested changes and even fewer understood the possibilities for improvement. There was progress, but not at the pace required.

This example makes one thing clear: the funds that governments require will always exceed the available sources. Without alternative sources of funding and a different approach, governments of any kind will fail, even if an economy is growing, even when they have a fledgling philosophy like the Big Society. The institutional response will always be unsuccessful unless it uses its powers to convene rather than simply coerce.

The Gap Between Global and Local

The Charities Aid Foundation report 'Giving a Sense of Place' examines the importance of geography and the proximity between a problem and those wanting to provide a solution.[54] Looking to history, it claims that the industrial revolution and urbanisation were two reasons why social problems in the Victorian era began to eat at the consciences of wealthy town dwellers, despite attempts to ensure that the worlds of industry and society rarely collided.

It was true then. It is still so today. Those in positions to do something about an issue are more likely to do so, and to do it better, if they see the situation with their own eyes. The problem is our leaders today tend not to be able to escape unless it's to cut a ribbon. Looking and listening are not considered productive activities – but they should be. If we had more effective and modern working practices in Parliament and Whitehall, how might we free up time for politicians and department directors so they can visit the country outside of their constituencies and Whitehall? This might be one of the spin-off benefits from electronic voting.

Of course, MPs are often in their own patch. Most hold weekly surgeries. However, opportunities to visit elsewhere, to see, learn and listen, are rare due to the demands of Mother, as we've heard.

If we have a sense of our place in the country, will a sense of belonging follow? Onward's 'Politics of Belonging' report[55] shows that two-thirds of people believe communities have become more divided and segregated in recent years. There is a belief, held by 66 per cent, that globalisation has had a detrimental impact on their lives. Again, it is the recurring theme that suggests the government is more interested in the away fixtures than in the home. The report suggests a number of policy shifts to address these concerns. These include restoring a stronger sense of belonging through home ownership, as well as protecting community assets, empowering towns and cities, and prioritising public service investment over tax cuts.

This sense of community and belonging seems to be a recurring theme in such reports. The Centre for Social Justice saw the importance of place in its 'Community Capital' report, for instance.[56] The conclusion is that a sense of belonging is vital to a person's physical and mental well-being. This particular study focused on some of the poorest areas in the UK (Birkenhead, Clacton and the Rhondda Valley) and suggested that we should be monitoring the social fabric across the entirety of the country to shape policy and build community ties. It proposed that there should be a national mission to improve the well-being of the nation and suggested that community assets and facilities will be needed to achieve this. By concentrating on boosting civil society, the Centre for Social Justice notes, we will be directly contributing to the well-being of our communities.

As we've seen, the financial model is unsustainable, so let's look at the options (not necessarily preferences) for how national government funds public services. These are:

1. Tax people more.
2. Do more with less.
3. Grow the economy.
4. Encourage more corporate involvement.
5. Leverage more from the public and third sectors.
6. Shrink the state.
7. Cut public services.

Politicians get fired for the last option, so it could be an even shorter list. We need what the Germans call *Eine Eierlegende Wollmilchsau*[57] – an egg-laying wool milk pig. We know that we need to transfer more resources to the periphery, improve services, involve the community without increasing taxes, and avoid corruption and waste. Let's look more closely at those options:

1. *Tax People More (Especially Locally)*

Taxation of the private sector is the source of all government income. All together now: there is no government money, there is only tax-payers' money. If the government takes an ever-increasing propor-tion of wealth, it will result in the tax take falling. The Institute of Economic Affairs points out that no national government has ever been able to get tax revenues above 40 per cent. Why? Because 28 per cent of ALL income tax is paid by the top 1 per cent and they are highly mobile. They can simply leave and they can take their capital, corporations and consumption elsewhere.[58] Deep pockets don't necessarily mean long arms.

But income tax is only about one-quarter of the tax money raised. There are other sources – see below.

COMPOSITION OF TAX RECEIPTS, 2017-18

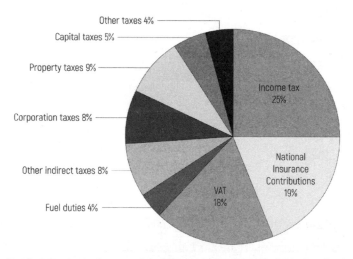

Source: 'Tax revenues: where does the money come from and what are the next government's challenges?' - Helen Miller and Barra Roantree. © Institute for Fiscal Studies. https://www.ifs.org.uk/publications/9178

The taxes need to come from somewhere. You can see the options that might not cost too many votes – capital taxes, corporation taxes and National Insurance contributions. The problem with tax is that people don't like paying it. There are entire industries, professions, lifetimes and lunchtimes spent discussing how to legally avoid the government's gimmes. If we applied the same level of energy to growing the economy, we'd be in a better place.

To dig further into the global changes taking place today, there are several layers of geopolitical change happening across the world. Of course, there is the relative rise and demise of nations, but, within that, nation states themselves are changing. Notwithstanding Covid, cities are becoming more important than the countries in which they exist. For instance, we can see that economic power is being concentrated in these enterprising centres. Globally, 600 cities account for 60 per cent of GDP,[59] and in the US, metropolitan areas contain two-thirds of the population and generate three-quarters of the nation's gross national product. Twenty-five US cities, most of them on the coasts, account for more than half of the US economy. Between 1960 and 1980, economic activity was dispersing across regions, reducing inequality. Since 1980, though, the trend has been in the opposite direction. And since 1960, the number of people living in cities globally has grown from 34 per cent to 56 per cent.[60] More and more people are choosing to live in these hubs of activity, and this looks set to increase as smart cities develop, making them ever more energy-efficient and sustainable.[61]

The places we live are becoming more distinctive. If you're rich, your neighbours are more likely to be rich than they were in the past, and the same is true if you're less financially stable. Poorer neighbourhoods are more cut off, though, socially and geographically, from the sources of economic prosperity, making it harder to bridge the gap.

So, could that taxation be local? Policy work examining a return to greater local taxation has been motivated by the need to improve the financial sustainability of local authorities and create levers for growth.

In 2015, the Centre for Cities published a report on increasing local tax-raising powers to incentivise cities to grow.[62] The report, entitled 'Beyond Business Rates', said:

> UK cities currently lack the ability and incentives to prioritise spending and overcome barriers to local economic growth. Compared to their international counterparts, they have too few financial incentives to take the often difficult decisions required to boost growth, or innovate to deliver more effective and efficient public services. But the funding landscape is changing. The move away from centrally redistributed grants to local government, towards places being more dependent for funding on the business rate revenues they collect locally, provides an opportunity to improve how the system works.[63]

Referred to as 'fiscal devolution', this process of giving places more responsibility to raise and retain their own funding could provide UK cities with incentives to back investment that makes a difference. This could include building new homes, investing in the local skills base or delivering new infrastructure to better connect people to jobs and businesses to customers.

In March 2019, the Institute for Fiscal Studies published a detailed report entitled 'Taking Control: Which taxes could be devolved to English local government?'.[64] It suggested that income tax is the most promising candidate for partial devolution. It proposed a flat rate on all income bands for all councils. In part, this would be a way of mitigating any competition or exacerbation of inequality between local authority areas and minimising administration and compliance costs.

The report noted problems, though, with the idea of giving local authorities new powers over council tax, for example by enabling them to revalue properties in their areas. This would impact the ability to redistribute funding between councils. Instead, the report suggested that 'it is likely to be better to revalue and reform council tax at a national level: this is overdue and could make the tax fairer and raise more revenues'.[65] This is what happens in some states in America, for instance, where a fixed percentage charge is levied on a property's value at the last transaction. As long as there is regional disparity in tax take there will always be a need to redistribute resources. That is not incompatible with a greater shift, over time, to more locally raised and locally administered revenue. For that to happen the budgets administered by Whitehall must shrink.

2. Do More With Less

In figures recorded in 2018, it was found that the US had the highest labour productivity level of all the G7 countries, at $75 per hour worked, followed closely by France and then Germany ($73). The UK is in the middle of the G7 pack at $63, which is 16 per cent below the US and French levels and 14 per cent below Germany's.[66]

The figures regarding labour productivity don't tend to change a great deal from year to year. In comparison, productivity growth from one year to the next can be significant. In recent years, UK productivity growth has been weak, continuing the trend seen since the financial crisis of 2007/08. This trend has also been seen across other advanced economies, although the magnitude of the slowdown in the UK has been stark, moving from one of the highest to one of the lowest of the G7 nations.

The chart below shows total R&D investment as a proportion of GDP in each of the OECD member countries, as well as in several other major economies, such as China.[67]

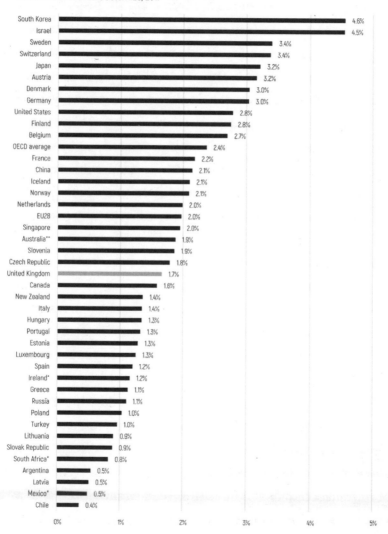

GROSS EXPENDITURE ON R&D AS A % OF GDP
OECD AND SELECTED COUNTRIES, 2017

Country	%
South Korea	4.6%
Israel	4.5%
Sweden	3.4%
Switzerland	3.4%
Japan	3.2%
Austria	3.2%
Denmark	3.0%
Germany	3.0%
United States	2.8%
Finland	2.8%
Belgium	2.7%
OECD average	2.4%
France	2.2%
China	2.1%
Iceland	2.1%
Norway	2.1%
Netherlands	2.0%
EU28	2.0%
Singapore	2.0%
Australia**	1.9%
Slovenia	1.9%
Czech Republic	1.8%
United Kingdom	1.7%
Canada	1.6%
New Zealand	1.4%
Italy	1.4%
Hungary	1.3%
Portugal	1.3%
Estonia	1.3%
Luxembourg	1.3%
Spain	1.2%
Ireland*	1.2%
Greece	1.1%
Russia	1.1%
Poland	1.0%
Turkey	1.0%
Lithuania	0.9%
Slovak Republic	0.9%
South Africa*	0.8%
Argentina	0.5%
Latvia	0.5%
Mexico*	0.5%
Chile	0.4%

Source: House of Commons, 'Briefing for debate on 'Research & Development spending'
© Parliamentary Copyright, 2019

UK R&D investment, equivalent to 1.7 per cent of GDP in 2017, is below both the OECD average of 2.4 per cent and the EU28 average of 2 per cent. The UK also has a lower level of R&D investment than direct competitors like France (which has R&D investment equivalent to 2.2 per cent of GDP), the US (2.8 per cent) and Germany (3 per cent).

In 1984, Britain saw its first retail ethical fund. This was followed seven years later by the first UK Social Investment Forum, and in 2000 the Treasury invited Sir Ronald Cohen to set up the Social Investment Task Force. This at least created a system of sustainable investment, especially in deprived areas of the UK. That year, too, Parliament legislated for responsible investment disclosure requirements for pension funds.

Cohen said: 'Capital has a multiplier effect, by levering in additional funds, by boosting economic activity, by creating role models of entrepreneurial success and by recycling wealth within the community. The private sector, as it is decentralised, can operate swiftly in a community, as a part of it.'[68] His work had a global impact, with Britain being a major player in the G20 to push for more impact funding.

In recognition of this need, the Global Impact Investing Network (GIIN) was formed in 2009.[69] This organisation is the global champion of impact investing, dedicated to increasing the scale and effectiveness of such investment around the world. By convening impact investors, GIIN accelerates leadership and collective action. Ultimately, it reduces barriers so more investors can allocate capital to fund solutions to the world's most intractable challenges. It builds critical infrastructure and develops education and research that accelerate the development of a coherent, impactful investing industry.

Today, Britain is seen as a source of knowledge and experience in this fledgling field of finance. Whether it be start-up capital, a debt finance model, loans to donation schemes or bespoke instruments fitted to a particular situation (disaster recovery, for example), the UK is often the place to find answers, ideas and good practice. The creativity we can find in the UK's financial services sector is world-leading. This needs to be codified and built into plans, so people can see how it works.

In 2013, the Social Value Act came into force, on the face of it allowing government at all levels to encourage social good. It enabled public sector tenders to consider what else a company might bring other than the most competitive bid. But did the venture support the government's objectives? Did it employ disabled people? What did its gender pay gap look like?

There has been much debate on how to measure social value, and the data on what this change has actually delivered is scant. It should improve, though, following a move by the Cabinet Office in 2019 to explicitly evaluate, as opposed to just vaguely considering, social value in all major government procurements. The Young Review and a separate British Council report found that the Social Value Act had delivered better value for money in around £25 billion of public spending.[70]

If we really want to drive up the pay and esteem of social carers then we must look at the profession across all sectors. The findings of the IfG's study on the scale and shape of contracting in the UK are startling – for instance, the parallels that were revealed between the collapse of large private providers and large charities that had grown too quickly and/or saddled themselves with debt. The IfG cites Carillion, 4Children and the Lifeline Project as examples. What is true of one is true of the other: it's unwise for providers to put all their eggs in one basket. A way must be found to enable the smaller, nimbler, community-based organisations to access funding and form transformational partnerships, too. And perhaps this would prevent such large-scale collapse.

Power to Change is a charitable trust, operating in England, created in 2015 with a £150 million endowment from the Big Lottery Fund.[71] The trust is solely concerned with supporting community businesses in England over a ten-year period, after which it will cease operating. It has pointed out the following ways to improve the Social Value Act[72]:

- Lower the financial threshold, to apply to local authority contracts worth less than £170,000.
- Introduce fairer UK charity contracts that demand long-term government support.
- Apply the Act to goods and works, not just services.
- Offer more support for potential providers.
- Explain how social value is measured.
- Encourage councils to take risks.
- Make the Act part of wider social change.

3. Grow the Economy

Every method of increasing taxes takes away from the current economy, overlooking one particular national and international mission: growing the overall economy. If this was prioritised as a target, government could stop tinkering with the policies and know that the overall tax take would increase as the economy increased. So, how do we do that?

The premise of the system is continual growth, as measured by GDP per capita. Economies must grow because if they do not, recession destroys jobs, lives and entire industries. Tax receipts fall, welfare systems fail, everything staggers. Given this fact, it's strange that business isn't more valued by government. When consulted directly for this book, the Confederation of British Industry rated government as giving business 'around six out of ten for importance'. It could not understand why the economy had such a high priority politically and yet so low a priority in terms of MPs' time. One voice suggested that MPs 'prefer talking more to the BBC than they do to business'. Only about a third of MPs have a background in business or wealth creation. When this is the engine room for tax generation and public services, why is economic growth such a low priority?[73,74]

Let's zoom out for a moment. The amalgamation of expertise that exists in the City of London is dazzling. It has resulted in Britain leading solutions for some of the world's greatest headaches. There is, however, a shortage of private and public investment in the world's poorest countries. The additional financing needed to achieve the seventeen UN Global Goals by 2030 is estimated to be $2.5 trillion per year.[75] Current investment levels are less than half that. To fix this, we need an alignment of powerful forces.

The City of London manages over £9 trillion of assets.[76] Little is invested, though, in the world's poorer countries, yet even a small increase would have a huge impact on such economies. For example, if just 1 per cent of the City's assets were directed to investment opportunities in Africa, an additional investment of around 90 billion would be generated. In reality, global aid flows to Africa in 2019 were less than half that sum.[77] In spite of this bleak picture, the City is expanding its role as a financing hub for the developing world, and Theresa May set a new ambition for the UK to be the largest G7 foreign direct investor in Africa by 2022. As a result, a number of African companies have already listed on the London Stock Exchange – 110 at the time of writing – and more are keen to join.[78]

When British investors are struggling to find good returns, these less developed markets can offer good opportunities for pension holders, too. For example, CDC, the UK's prime development investment institution, has achieved a 7 per cent annual return over the past six years while investing in developing countries.[79] This includes older investments in China and Latin America. If done well, the opportunity for British investors is significant. By scaling up investment through CDC and the Private Infrastructure Development Group, the UK is setting a clear ambition to mobilise billions of private investment.[80] Much of these ideas to raise additional capital has come from trying to solve international problems. Perhaps we should also apply it at home? What would it take to transform Britain, to make every community prosperous? How can we lever that in? These are not questions Spending Reviews ponder.

There are more creative ways of encouraging investment in development goals overseas and at home, too. This would be investment that produces growth as well as social good.

There is a growing appetite for knowledge among savers and consumers. Increasingly, they want to hold the companies in which they invest to account. After the Great Depression, Generally Accepted Accounting Principles were developed to ensure that businesses reported their performances consistently and accurately.[81] But that was a century ago, and now, at the start of the twenty-first century, we need new common standards for reporting corporate impact in terms of compassion as well as compliance. The World Benchmarking Alliance developed tools to give consumers, investors and employees the chance to make a difference.[82] The WBA compares companies' performance on the global challenges the world faces.

The move towards private finance as a solution to national and global problems should spark a renewed interest in the creation of wealth funds. The UK has played a key role in raising finance to achieve the UN Sustainable Development Goals. The instruments we have chosen to capitalise, whether at the World Bank or at specialist entities, demonstrate that we are adept at using our expertise overseas. The creation of endowment funds to pay for public goods is a recent trend for the UK government, and the Education Endowment Foundation[83] is a good example. It is, however, a rare example in Whitehall; much more could be done. British investments overseas, made through the country's aid budget, are not set up to generate flexible wealth funds. The returns from the investment can neither be counted towards next year's budget nor taken out of the investment vehicle to pay for services at home, like the NHS or schools. Funds are counted towards the UK's contribution to overseas development assistance when it capitalises an instrument, but not when capital is passed to a development venture. As a consequence, returns on investments become 'trapped' in the instrument. If they are removed, they count negatively against the commitment. Around 2023, it will make sense for the Treasury to change this way of accounting, coinciding with the end of commitments to the EU development budget. This is an opportunity for the UK to build sustainable funds to allow returns for a wider variety of expenditure or to count towards aid commitments.

Economic growth is not the enemy of social good if we are more creative with capital. Indeed, it is only with these investments that we will be able to make progress.

4. Encourage More Corporate Involvement
The private sector is not a democracy. It is free to use its initiative.

It is fast, flexible and imaginative. It can do something quickly. But it can never do what governments can. It doesn't have convening power.

The private sector's job is to grow itself and thus to grow the economy; as businesses create more wealth, a large percentage of this is paid back into the state as taxes for public services. We will turn to corporation tax avoidance later, but for now we want to focus on the charitable giving of these businesses. Enlightened capital that understands the importance of trust and investing back into the community is one of the great win–wins. Customers, employees, shareholders – all of these groups want to support companies that do good. And most companies likewise want to give back. Business and private capital has the potential to contribute much more. Government's job is to convene this support.

The relationship between business and the other sectors has been characterised by charitable giving. This has been facilitated through foundations, partnerships, investments and corporate social responsibility. The relationship has only really become more sophisticated over the past seventy years, though.

Today's arrangements can be traced back 200 years. The growing merchant class of the nineteenth century established trusts, foundations and committees in what was ultimately both the genesis of the public sector and the beginning of regulation in the charity sector. This period also saw individual giving grow at the same time as key changes in the other sectors.

Now the measures for charitable giving are more formalised. FTSE 100 companies together donated £1.9 billion to the third sector in 2015/16.[84] The level had fallen by £655 million since its peak in 2013. The main beneficiaries of private sector donations have been cause-related charities, cultural organisations and the university sector. The latter secured £81 million in 2016/17, excluding corporate foundations. This was a 40 per cent increase on the previous year. Higher education also has the largest share of donations over £1 million.[85]

Some organisations and institutions are rejecting donations. This is likely due to much more thought and caution from both sides of the arrangement. Businesses are partnering with fewer organisations, but they are doing so much more deeply. Charities are also recognising the power of their own brands to 'greenwash' others and to confer respectability.[86] They are becoming more aware that they are custodians of the brand. If these charities disrespect it, then it will lose patronage.

Corporate engagement is likely to increase and become more important as time goes on.[87] There's a simultaneous, building pressure on businesses to demonstrate social purpose, and on the third sector to exhibit a greater understanding of brand value. To succeed, the two must work together. Partnerships are likely to enter into consortia around certain causes and issues. There are big opportunities for governments with a national mission to harness this collective goodwill.

Small businesses are recognising the importance of giving, too. The Federation of Small Businesses surveyed its members and found that 80 per cent gave to charities in various ways. Of those, 38 per cent donated their time and 32 per cent their skills.[88]

Over time, there has been a gradual move from transactional modes of philanthropy towards more complex partnerships. In offering their expert help and knowledge, volunteering and capacity-building now sit alongside fundraising and donations as the most popular methods of corporate giving.

There is huge untapped potential in businesses. To unlock that support, organisations must know they can contribute. They can then decide how. We should also acknowledge the taxes they generate, without which no public service could run.

5. Leverage More from the Public and Third Sectors

The economist and Liberal politician William Beveridge said: 'Co-operation between public and voluntary agencies is one of the special features of British public life.'[89]

The creation of the public sector was inextricably linked with the third sector. In the 1800s, charities grew into partnerships with municipal authorities, with considerable overlap between town clerks and trustees. This period also saw the state take over as welfare and universal provider. Two world wars were the catalyst for the state expanding mutuality. Hitler had proved no match for free markets armed with state planning. There was no end to what we could achieve together. There was no end to what we could endure together. It was miraculous. From state-funded and state-run schools, the NHS and the state pension to local authority community services. This, in turn, changed the remit of the charity sector to that of campaigner as well as provider.

In the post-war period, the public sector has risen from 10 per cent of GDP in 1948 to about 41 per cent in modern times.[90] The targets of the spend, however, have changed dramatically. Currently, the trend is for more of it to be spent on health and support for the elderly.[91]

In the last decade, there was a pause in public spending, but this changed decisively at the 2019 general election. During the previous period of austerity, certain budgets were protected – schools, health, aid and, to a lesser degree, defence. There was little public or political debate about the outcomes. There is equally little discussion, though, about the costs of not doing something.

For instance, training people with learning disabilities[92] increases their employment rate from less than 6 per cent to 86 per cent. What is the cost saving of preventative measures in healthcare? Or in teaching prisoners to read? Or in teaching them a trade? Or allowing them to work in order to save some money? With better support for carers, could we enable them to be economically active, and thus helpful to the community, for longer?

UCL professor Mariana Mazzucato argues that it is public finance that has powered wealth creation.[93] She argues that the way in which the state is perceived should change 'from an inertial bureaucratic "leviathan" to the catalyst for new business investment, from market fixer to market shaper and creator, from simply de-risking the private sector to welcoming and taking on risk due to the opportunities it presents for future growth'.[94]

Whether you agree with her conclusions or not, her work at UCL is important. It's trying to create a framework in which the three sectors can work together and get behind shared objectives or 'missions'. It examines how the public sector needs to develop. It looks at incentives to drive long-term investment and focus. It measures how well we are all doing. Although her work is technical, its rational conclusions chime with the emotional feeling many have that we need to find ways to work together. What is it that we are trying to achieve? It is striking to see just how many organisations and people are coming to the same conclusions, even from different starting points.

There isn't enough money to address all the causes piecemeal, so Britain needs national missions to be codified, like the UN's Development Goals. The mission must appear in every government department and its annual reports. Leaders from every sector should be asked for their thinking on how they could contribute to such aims. Until political leadership says, 'This is what we are going to do, and this is how you can help', we will fail to meet the ambitions of the public.

Even for those with the best vantage point from which to grasp the mission, things are still confusing. Even if we produced a plan or mission for their eyes only, it would help. Take drone technology, for example. Where is Drone HQ in Whitehall? The Department for Transport? The FCDO? The MoD? Each has its own individual R&D with little reference to what others are doing, let alone to anyone who sits outside of government. Even the army, navy and RAF have separate initiatives. How can a Cabinet committee spot something interesting and worthy of further investment if those making the decisions have no idea of the plan?

Two necessary, but not sufficient, conditions for social enterprises and charities to succeed are knowledge and finance. Unfortunately, these are often the most elusive conditions, especially in communities with the least capacity to set up ventures or take over services and facilities. Through initiatives like the central funding portal, and in tackling the bureaucracy involved in pitching for funding or tenders, the government did manage to cut down the administrative burdens on new organisations. Advances in commonly used technology, and in particular social media, have also gone a long way towards building support and information networks for organisations that may be trying to do something somebody else has just achieved elsewhere. But there is more that can be done. Some areas that will require more attention include leveraging greater finance through better coordinated planning between the sectors, ensuring good practice is shared, and confirming that civil servants – both in Whitehall and beyond – understand the sector and how to support it.

To incentivise involvement, local people could have a stake in the regeneration of their area. David Skelton has pointed to the idea of employees being made shareholders in local businesses, but there are other ways, too. Private and philanthropic capital should also be used to build and invest in local communities. There is an opportunity here for direct investment in a philanthropic pool, which could be drawn on by local schemes. Whether funding is provided through a block grant to a city or other area, raised through greater local taxation or through philanthropy, it should be spent on locally designed schemes. There is such connectivity now, making it possible to see the innovation that is happening elsewhere, to learn from that and to compare return, that there can be no reason not to let local people invest in themselves to meet their own needs.

Government investment should incentivise partnerships and co-funding. By that we mean that a project should seek to lever in funds from another sector, not that it is funded from two or more public sector pots. This is how we can get the Jupiter's sling effect – using the power of something existing to accelerate a project.

The government can learn from the charity sector, which tailors its planning cycles to maximise its chance of doing precisely that. Whitehall should tailor its planning, too. Perhaps during the summer every year, any national or local government projects or programmes that might be facing a reduction in public funding should be flagged, and the options for national non-statutory partnerships should be discussed. These projects could then be pitched to the relevant industries and charities for that autumn's planning round. Departments could consult with a small team, too, that has corporate and third sector fundraising expertise, perhaps based in the Cabinet Office. Such teams could include external organisations, such as the Institute of Fundraising, which have particular knowledge to offer. Before changes to funding are announced, government departments should be given a summary of the potential for additional funds to be leveraged. In time, this process could become an established method of facilitation for uniting charities and corporate partners.

If we are to achieve the cultural shift we need, if we are to retain faith and interest in the social sector, then further help for its heroes is required. The approach we've outlined would demonstrate what the sector means not only to the public but to civil servants and local authorities, too. It demonstrates that we don't need a fatalistic attitude to the economic climate: with a little imagination, the goals can be achieved.

Sir Stephen Bubb is a director at the Oxford Institute of Charity. Having mapped the evolution of the third sector, he believes that British philanthropy is the greatest in the world. This is what he says:

Britain has a proud tradition of charity dating back 1,500 years. It's a tradition unparalleled in the rest of the world and the British system has formed the bedrock of charitable endeavour in many other countries. The third sector can help solve many of the big issues of our times like smoking and compulsory car seat belts. These changes came about as a result of highly effective charity campaigns focused on these issues. This is a fact often overlooked by policy makers and government.[95]

Like Roman roads and medieval castles, British charities were built to last, and thousand-year-old educational establishments and charities to aid the poor can be found scattered all across the UK. Today, the charity sector has its own minister, more than ten regulators and its own department: the Office for Civil Society. The sector employs 880,000 staff, which includes 200,000 registered organisations and about 13 million volunteers a month.[96]

Can the public, private and third sectors learn from one another? It's worth taking stock of where communities have been able to flourish and where the obstacles remain. The premise was that using the third sector resulted in higher value for money and more effective delivery of services. Remember the example of commissioning a contract from an Alzheimer's charity; you'd also get an army of volunteers providing support to carers. You might also enable further projects that the charity wanted to undertake, at no further cost. There was something else too: maybe services provided by the beneficiaries would be of better quality.

According to research by the IfG, contracts[97] awarded to the third sector by central government have increased. The gains, however, have been offset by what has happened at a local level. Despite Whitehall embracing the third sector and exhorting commissioners to increase third sector provision, the reality is that the reverse has happened. The obstacles in front of those many individuals and businesses that want to help remain in place.

Many third sector organisations report that their added value is not considered when they respond to a local authority tender. For instance, the fact that some bring carer support as well as competitive services for patients is not a factor in their contracts. Another problem at the local level is risk management. Russell Smith, an entrepreneur with a disability, set up a business pairing social care clients with carers. CarePair[98] was a good idea that enabled carers to stay longer with their clients, suiting both parties. Smith also developed innovative ways to do background checks. But in spite of this, he struggled to get councils to refer social care clients. They had assumed that if something went wrong, they'd be liable. The same councils were happy to refer those in search of a carer to Gumtree, where there was no checking and no duty of care. Due diligence didn't matter. The quality of the carer–client relationship didn't matter. The resulting improvement in care and savings to the health and social care budget didn't matter. What mattered was the councils' risk management register saying no.

There are many other examples of commissioning that is not focused on the outcomes and that doesn't recognise the added value of the third sector. The government has tried to fix this. One such attempt was diversity in provision. This particular scheme was about others stepping in when the state could not provide. But an obvious problem with this approach is that it largely relies on the assumption that communities are capable of stepping in. In some cases they were, but that was not the norm.

The potential of what volunteers can bring is grasped only when there's an understanding between local people of what the problem is and how they can solve it together. For example, the British Red Cross has a scheme in which school children walking to morning classes check in on elderly neighbours.[99] They see that they're up and dressed and that the milk has been taken in. Check-ins on older people teach civic duty to the pupils, break down intergenerational barriers, strengthen communities and reduce emergency healthcare costs, all at zero cost to the taxpayer.

In recent years, there has been real change and regeneration in communities across the UK and there is a pattern forming, revealing the conditions for success. It can be summarised thus: people come together around a common objective and just get on with it. This requires a much closer way of working. It requires knowledge of the sector, shared information and data, agreed missions. Good progress is being made, but if we want to make the most of all our communities have to offer, more focus on removing blockages is needed. To meet the ambition of being the best place to live in the world, we must recognise that government alone cannot deliver. But with all of us working together, we can. How do we know this? Because people are already doing it. Here are some and the lessons we can learn from them.

Details, like people, matter

The most important factors in successful projects are the people involved and the attention to detail.

Lord (Andrew) Mawson is the closest that the Independent People's Republic of Yorkshire has to an ambassador in 'that London'. He is an energetic, enthusiastic, Tigger-like pursuer of lost causes: 'It came down to a biro. Landing on the moon. A biro,' he says. He's fascinated by what creates success:

> It's about the details. Had the first men to walk on the moon accidentally closed the door to the lunar craft, they would have been stuck up there to this day. So many details and any one thing could have destroyed the mission. Without a biro in Buzz Aldrin's pocket and his initiative in using it to mend a broken catch on the craft's door, they wouldn't have been able to take off. Details.

Mawson studies how you get people to work together to deliver for their communities, for the nation and for each other. Perhaps unsurprisingly, he is critical of how Whitehall operates, arguing that it is so unfit for purpose it is now incapable of addressing the needs of the most deprived areas in our country. It was actually over the course of his many regeneration projects across the UK that he developed his format for success. His highly successful model for getting things done galvanised local people to apply a business mindset to sorting out local services and regenerating their communities. He advocates for 'big thinking but small actions'. It's no grand strategy, just getting people together and cracking on with it. It's learning by doing, too.

Whitehall needs to let enterprise and new ideas solve some of its headaches/challenges and let others take the lead on what it is unwilling or unable to do; it also needs to organise itself in a way that encourages others to help. The snail's pace of Whitehall, particularly with regard to enabling regulation, has been criticised by the business and scientific communities alike. The Institute of Economic Affairs has spotted another problem Director-General Mark Littlewood noticed that innovative, disruptive businesses, which were changing the way services were provided, were faltering because Whitehall simply couldn't understand them. Similarly, the consumer was potentially being left without protection.[100] He said, 'Take Airbnb. Is it a hotel? A review site? A booking agency? Which department should be responsible for it? DCMS? Transport? We noticed that many businesses were not able to proceed because Whitehall didn't know how to categorise them.'

The public sector needs to get back to its roots and partner more effectively with the private and third sectors and change some of its practices. That means tax reform, more situational awareness of what's going on across the UK, and a greater cross-government focus on the technologies and solutions that may provide the answers.

6. Shrink the State

Michael Barber, author of *How to Run a Government: So that Citizens Benefit and Taxpayers Don't Go Crazy*,[101] was the founder and first head of the Prime Minister's Delivery Unit under Tony Blair. Currently, he is co-chair of Boston Consulting Group's not-for-profit foundation, the Centre for Public Impact. Remember, Barber had Blair's 100+ majority government behind him – and he still found it challenging. He defines two types of administration:

GOVERNMENT BY SPASM	GOVERNMENT BY ROUTINE
EVERYTHING MATTERS	CLEAR PRIORITIES
VAGUE ASPIRATION	SPECIFICATION OF SUCCESS
CRISIS MANAGEMENT	ROUTINE OVERSIGHT
GUESSWORK	DATA-INFORMED
POST-HOC-EVALUATION	REALTIME DATA
MASSAGED IMPRESSIONS	AN HONEST CONVERSATION
REMOTE AND SLOW	IN TOUCH AND RAPID
PRESENT-FOCUSED	FUTURE-FOCUSED
HYPERACTIVITY	PERSISTENT DRIVE
SOUNDBITES	DIALOGUE
ANNOUNCEMENTS	CHANGE ON THE GROUND
✕	✓

Source: Sir Michael Barber: How to run a Government;
http://www.lse.ac.uk/Events/Events-Assets/PDF/2015/20150316-Sir-Michael-Barber.pdf

Small majority governments tend to focus on the 'spasm' type, but the opportunity for larger majority administrations can be seen in the 'routine' idea on the right of the figure. Barber goes on to say that a government has to be clear about what sort of reform it wants.

FIVE PARADIGMS OF SYSTEM REFORM

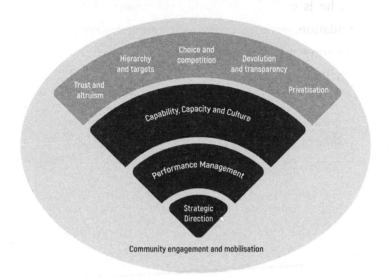

Source: Sir Michael Barber: How to run a Government;
http://www.lse.ac.uk/Events/Events-Assets/PDF/2015/20150316-Sir-Michael-Barber.pdf

Some services can be privatised, but others are better reformed via devolution and transparency. The education sector, for instance, has been subject to more choice and competition. Comparatively, the NHS has had more hierarchy and targets in line with the graph above.

The public sector workforce, as a share of the nation's employed, has declined by about five percentage points in the past two decades. Within those numbers, the NHS and public education workforces have grown steadily.[102]

In some specific areas, there have been big increases in private sector employees delivering services that were historically the domain of the public sector.[103] You have the baby boomers to thank for much of the expansion in nursery care, for instance. It's been driven by private sector expansion, which now constitutes more than 70 per cent of providers.[104,105]

You don't always need public money

On 6 October 2015, Blind Veterans UK (BVUK) celebrated its centenary. Its executives, led by Major-General Nick Caplin (ret.), marked the event with the launch of an ambitious plan. In addition to supporting the nation's blind veterans, the charity decided to establish a research arm and appointed a chief scientific officer, Dr Renata Gomes. Many veterans suffer from body clock disorders as a result of ocular trauma. The research team established key partnerships with academic partners such as Oxford University and a bio-tech spin-off, Circadian Therapeutics. The latter had started looking at circadian disorders among night shift workers and in the airline industry. BVUK then went on to develop Project Gemini, where blind veterans from both the UK and the US shared ideas, learning and comradeship. The US Blinded Veterans Association (BVA) embraced Blind Veterans UK as its sole research partner and established a bilateral Joint Ocular Trauma Task Force for both military and civilian work. This led directly to the formation of a new research group, Bravo Victor, to pool science resources to which royalties from this book are directed.

The resulting venture was more than just academic brilliance. It needed some lateral thinking to make it happen. It's also a clear example of the trust the world puts in British leadership in the knowledge and belief that, together, we can make great things happen. Furthermore, the research advances humanity towards a palliative, if not a cure, for jet lag. This is a good example of what can be done with a charity run with enthusiasm, energy and joined-up thinking.

Social enterprise can make a difference

Following the First World War, there was a need to provide for those who had been disabled in conflict. Enham Place, a 1,000-acre estate in Hampshire, was selected as the site. This was one of the first village centres to be created following the Great War 'for the medical treatment and training of ex-servicemen suffering from the effects of amputations, neurasthenia and shell shock'. Formed with donations from King George V and the Red Cross, it provided homes and employment for hundreds of ex-servicemen. Following the Second World War, a public subscription in Egypt raised £600,000 to thank Britain for its part in ridding Egypt of Axis forces. In recognition, Enham appended the word 'Alamein' to its name and is now known as Enham Alamein. Today, it still provides services, employment and a home to 6,500 people with disabilities, enabling them to live a life of independence, choice and control.[106] Its business model is a combination of enterprise and charity, as volunteers assist those with disabilities on production lines, packaging products that can be found on the shelves of Marks & Spencer and Fortnum & Mason.

Enham Alamein was a trailblazing social enterprise. In 2017, there were an estimated 471,000 such ventures across the UK.[107] There is huge variety in the business models these operations use to remain profitable. The House of St Barnabas[108] is a London private members' club that trains and employs homeless people. Beam[109] is a crowdfunding platform that raises funds and goods in kind for unemployed and homeless people. Different they may be, but what they all have in common is the reality that they are adding value while being sustainable and independently funded.

One final example to note are those organisations that have developed a sophisticated mix of the third and first sectors within their governance structure. Johnson & Johnson is one such example. This is where family-controlled businesses can have an advantage. A significant enlightened controlling interest can make all the difference. There is massive scope here for private finance, business and individuals to do much more to contribute. In order to do so, though, we must be clearer about our ideas as to how they can help, and the obstacles that might prevent or disincentivise them must be removed.

Different communities need different solutions

The EC Roberts Centre in Portsmouth provides services and support for the city's most vulnerable people and families. Carole Damper, the centre's chief executive, said:

> We are best placed to design things for our community. Trying to get what you know needs to be done to fit into a scheme designed by someone who has no concept of what your community needs is terribly frustrating. Let organisations design what they need and then pitch for the funds.[110]

A shift of powers and funding down to a local level will be

uncomfortable for Whitehall. It would have to reverse a trend, as it follows that some functions of central government should be devolved, too. To draw a comparison with the private sector, the operating accounting could be done by those designing, commissioning and delivering services, while the balance sheet could be managed long term by central government. Whitehall's impact might this way be reduced, but the effect could well be positive at a tangible, local level.

Recognise and reward good judgement

Forgotten Veterans UK (FVUK) is a charity which supports more than 600 vulnerable ex-servicemen and women each year. It often finds people at their lowest point, when they are close to suicide, homeless, addicted. It goes further than many statutory services in its efforts to help and takes greater risks to save lives. It has a strong governance structure and oversight from clinicians. Its volunteers will, however, go where statutory services fear to tread: where a life hangs in the balance. Think someone's home at 0300 hours. Think the other end of the country. Of course, in the public sector people care about those in their charge. However, commissioners stop at county boundaries. Risk registers say no. Protocols say, 'Don't get too involved.' FVUK and many other veteran-led organisations are effective because they're focused on the outcome. They go the extra mile and take greater risk. That should be recognised and rewarded.

CONCLUSIONS

Where to begin? Local government needs modernisation, but it really doesn't need any more change. Just reorganising government as a displacement activity will not do. It creates the illusion of change but the reality of retrenchment. So many efforts have been made to change it, with so little effect. The power has been drained away for all sorts of political and pragmatic considerations. If a national mandate is to restore the bridge of trust between the periphery and the centre, it's far from clear that local democracy holds the key to doing so. In any case, it's likely that modernising local government would take two parliaments.

At the core of the British brand is trust, and this draws upon the country's reputation for sound financial management. This obviously took a beating during the global financial crisis, but it has since stabilised. It is possible that there has even been an over-correction in terms of the regulations that must be passed to spend money, making it too difficult to work with the government. As we have noted throughout this book, British thinking has an enviable global reputation. We are known for being generous, inventive, open and far-sighted. The challenge for us is to have that expansive vision and the financial cohesion to match it.

Ultimately, this requires two fundamental admissions. First, that governments of all kinds are financially constrained, unless they fund themselves through engorged deficit spending. Second, that government itself is part of the problem. Its sheer scale and complexity and culture act to inhibit the contributions of the practically minded, if less political, third sector.

We could start off with some quick wins. For instance, fixing a one-sided relationship with HMRC, which currently charges interest on late tax bills but happily holds on to overpayments until the next tax return, with no charge payable. We could produce enabling regulation so that inventions can be developed and manufactured here. There are welcome moves to establish a UK version of a US organisation: the Defense Advanced Research Projects Agency. DARPA operates outside Washington rules. To imitate such a system on UK soil would allow us to fund applied science, support discovery and create the room required for success.

For instance, is the battle against pandemics a health issue or an economic problem or a long-term security and defence threat? The answer is, of course, all of them. The tactical solution is for science to produce a vaccine. The strategic solution is a joined-up science, research and development establishment. It should be remembered that it will be victory over the variants, not a single vaccine, that finally ends Covid. Coming up with one of the first vaccines is one thing. The real global prize will come from the understanding and mastery of the science. Britain already leads in this capacity. We don't just need a vaccine; we need the knowledge and process that can master it. The darkness of the early twenty-first century thus will be lit by four beacons – Democracy, Capitalism, the Law and Science, because without the latter, the former become irrelevant. Any nation that excels in these areas will always have something to say about leadership.

There's a lot of joining up to do. The Prime Minister can, of course, merge and reorganise departments. But we also need to get those departments closer to the people they serve, and we must recognise that our thinking has become too much 'drill down', not enough 'look across'.

We need to listen to third sector experts and look at how their expertise can be harnessed to address the fundamental task at the heart of the UK's future: joining the periphery back to the centre. We need to champion and encourage more social enterprise ventures. If we want more activity, revenue and agency at the local level then Whitehall has to let go and noticeably shrink.

Modernising government might help win back the trust of voters. The public spectacle, though, risks being one set of politicians unpicking the policies, reforms and major infrastructure projects the other set approved at immense cost only a few years ago. There has to be a greater consensus. If that can be achieved, then anything becomes possible.

8

MODERNISING THE MUTUALITY THAT BINDS US

Our instincts are inclined to redress, to protect the vulnerable, to help friends and neighbours, to educate children so they can better themselves, to defend against those that threaten with menaces. We pay our taxes to support the collective good. We are seeing our instinct for equality in the fight against Covid. Our collective sacrifices support those most at risk. What part of this, what part of *any* of this, is not about equality? It's what we came for.

We talk of equality before the law and justice. This is symbolised in Pomeroy's Lady Justice atop the Old Bailey, with scales in one hand and sword in the other. She weighs the balance of innocence and guilt, emotion and reason, and – importantly – the past and the future. Above the main entrance to the courthouse is written: 'Defend the Children of the Poor and Punish the Wrongdoer.'

It's no accident that it features a female in frozen form. The Statue of Liberty is based on the Roman goddess Libertas, and America is represented by another female, Columbia. Britannia is the female personification of Britain and she has been used to symbolise British pride, unity and strength for centuries. She's associated with

Boudicca, the ruler of the Iceni against the might of a European op-pressor. She is, in actuality, based on Minerva, the Roman goddess of the arts, trade, strategy and wisdom. Like so many British icons, she's a mash-up.

Justice is about balance. That's not the same as inertia. A living political system should be constantly adjusting, moving, listening, rebalancing. In recent years, we've seen the young losing faith in democratic politics in greater numbers than any other age group.[1] We've seen growing evidence of the rise of direct action in politics, often from the young. Equalities groups like Disability Rights UK, #MeToo and Black Lives Matter have drawn attention to inequality and injustice in their own fields. Voices are being heard more often, and quite rightly too, frustrated after years of fighting to be heard. These groups appear to be different, but there are similarities. They see no reason to accept standards that previous generations endured; they see a world that has leapt into the future and a political system stuck in the past; they're frustrated by the lack of listening and slow pace of change; unsurprisingly, they see the political system itself as the problem; they want a more modern approach.

There's a reason for repeating the phrase 'they see', because they really do see. It's the first generation to be able to see really clearly the level of wrongdoing. Sure, surveillance capitalism allows those at the top to see into the lives of those below. But what's not always understood by those at the top is that the process is reciprocal. Those at the bottom can see into the lives of those at the top. So, that's where we start in this chapter – the problem as they see it.

The need for modernisation in Britain is at its height in terms of understanding equality and the need for justice and balance. So much has been written about opportunity, equality, diversity, social mobility and discrimination of all types, but it's not just about rights or identity politics. An easily overlooked fact is that attitude matters, too. Attitude attracts opportunity and vice versa. The attitude of individuals actually counts in whether they get opportunities. No amount of legislation or compulsion will right wrongs without persistence, determination and goodwill. But it's not just about the attitude of ordinary people. It matters at the top as well.

THE PROBLEM WITH LEADERSHIP

Since the turn of the century,[2] we've learned that our leaders illegally avoided taxes,[3] rigged interest rates,[4] evaded taxes,[5] laundered drug money,[6] presided over an offshore banking system bigger than anyone thought possible,[7] forced good companies into closure[8] and destroyed pension funds as they themselves grew wealthier.[9] Collectively, they oversaw an unprecedented destruction of wealth and the collapse of the financial system.[10] They watched as life savings placed into investment funds set up by leaders of previously un impeachable integrity turned out to be Ponzi schemes.[11] They sold off reserves of gold to compensate for these exercises in corporate greed, while never once convicting any banker.[12] Our spiritual leaders covered up sex abuse in the Church.[13] Our charity leaders sexually abused the vulnerable.[14] Our child welfare leaders have permitted child abuse.[15] More CEOs are now being forced out of office for ethical lapse than for any other reason.[16] Leaders of the automotive industry[17] lied about emissions,[18] were imprisoned, fled the country while out on bail and remain fugitives.[19] The leaders of our water utilities polluted rivers then tried to cover it up.[20] Global entertainment leaders have faced multiple allegations of sexual harassment and abuse.[21] Britain's leading broadcaster falsely accused political figures of being child abusers,[22] while allowing actual abusers to commit crimes on their premises.[23] Meanwhile, sporting leaders have been caught cheating and doping.[24] Human rights lawyers have been struck off for misconduct and dishonesty.[25] In the US, many of the former president's political advisors have been jailed[26] and he has been subject to impeachment proceedings twice.

From the Mossack Fonseca and the Panama Papers[27] revelations, it's estimated[28] that $8.7 trillion, or 11 per cent, of global wealth resides in tax havens.[29] Large corporations are routinely shielding money, which deprived European governments alone of approximately $170 billion per annum in tax revenue.[30] This offshore tax operation was surprising even to people who were aware of the problem. This was thought to be a *fraction* of the UK economy. It turned out to be a *multiple* of it.

The events listed above sound fantastic, incredible, unbelievable, even impossible, but they all happened. It's the reason so many are angry, not just with political leaders but with *all* leaders.

Partly, this is the fault of leadership models based on the myth of the infallible male leader, whether it's Jesus Christ, Steve Jobs, Moses or Elon Musk. It is individual hero leadership, where the 'leader' is more important than the 'ship'. It has become leadership of the short term, by the short term, for the short term. It is tactical. It is quantitative. It is also highly academically and professionally qualified. It is experienced and data-rich. So why is it failing? Why, with all this experience, qualifications and knowledge, did the above scandals happen? Why, with all this skill, did these leaders fail to do the right thing?

Because competence and confidence are not the same. Because they preferred conquest to consensus. Because they lacked imagination. Because they didn't know right from wrong. Because they were dominated by their markets and not vice versa.

The problem is most of our leaders are drawn from a narrow

background. Their education and training was from the last century, when the world was very different. It was a long-term, male, patient, predictable, factual, planned, heterosexual, white, Christian, Western-orientated, technology-leveraged, deflationary, structured, left-brained, broadcast, top-down, militarily symmetrical world. There was no mansplaining. No white privilege. No colonial historiography. No gender neutrality. No non-binary. No 'sick'. No memes. No fake news. No grievance farmers. No revisionism. No sexting. No transphobia. No YOLO. No FOMO. No TERFs.[31] In the 1970s, only candles were 'lit'. No one was woke. The only trans organisation was an airline owned by Howard Hughes. Gaslighting was something Granny remembered. 'Stan' was a character from *Coronation Street*. A DM was half a bovver boot. 'Who's your daddy?' was a genuine enquiry about your parents. Wicked and dope were bad things. Only machinery was fitted with a filter. A badass followed a curry. Smashing or killing it would've got you locked up. No one vajazzled or twerked and your father was the only mutha you knew.

We now live in an inverted, unreal, amoral, impatient, selfish, spiritual, irrational, gender-fluid, polysexual, strategically multipolar, everywhere-facing, bottom-up, information-soaked, fact-free, multi-racial, androgynous, opinionated, rapidly moving, abusive, asymmetric world. It's all a lot more complicated at one level, but at another it's still about leadership – listening, learning, adapting, understanding.

The emergence of wokery and the desire to rewrite the past must be seen in the context of the available alternatives. There was a time when we still had a future to shape. The present feels like a time when we only have a past to shape. Much easier to fixate on the slave traders of the last century than the plight of young, black, gay men sleeping rough on London's streets. Much easier to talk about 'white privilege' than address why white working-class boys have the worst education attainment of any social group in the UK.[32,33]

This is what happens when there's no narrative or plan for the future. This has been partly caused by the twin uncertainties of Brexit and Covid, which first put the future on hold and then accelerated it wildly. Truth be known, we were lacking a vision before Brexit or Covid were even thought of.

A vision – *any* vision – is better than none because visions are there to be argued over. It's called democratic debate. Argue about them and you argue about the future. We're in danger of spending more time arguing about the past partly because we have no vision of the future.

Some might question why, in a world of total, relentless, nonsensical change, anyone would actually try to embrace this constant movement. A new type of universal conservatism may be emerging among those who just want it all to stop. They want to stop the noise. Stop the change. Stop the bullshit (as they see it). Stop their world being turned upside down. Stop their values and institutions being belittled and patronised. The changes, in their eyes, are a type of catastrophe. They have lost the stars to steer by as slowly, the constants and comforts of their youth have disappeared. The high street has been hollowed out. Their childhood heroes have been debunked and their past rewritten. Local has been replaced with national and international. It all feels overwhelming; their world has been Amazonked.

The paradox of this age is that the technology that has simplified our lives in so many ways has complicated them in so many others. For instance, if we wish to, we can know instantly what's happening anywhere in the world as it actually happens – but the constant interruptions can make it difficult for us to focus on the job at hand. Put another way, the technology that liberates us also creates dependency. It is a force multiplier that makes us more vulnerable.

The rapid change has exposed our leaders as they are repeatedly surprised by the financial crisis, the Brexit vote, Donald Trump's election, the pandemic, etc. The threats are complex, multilateral, asymmetric and constantly changing. It is perhaps the pace of this change that is so bewildering. It's no wonder that national governments, with their bureaucratised and traditional structures, are struggling. The success of all nations, governments and organisations now comes down to one thing: how adaptable their leadership is.

We've touched on some changes when looking at why the equalities argument is so important in mutuality. But it goes further. Ask any leader where they learned leadership. Some will say they learned in the military or on a sports field, but most learn leadership in business school. That's a business school. Not a leadership school. The two are different. As if leadership were a subset of business administration rather than vice versa. They don't teach divinity in business school. Empathy, humility, integrity or ethics are not core components.

Real leadership is not about being the centre of attention. It is about making *everyone else* feel they are the centre of attention. Mo Mowlam was legendary in the Northern Ireland peace process for chatting to people, making them laugh and brewing cups of tea. Leaders create atmospheres that grant permission for people to behave cooperatively.

On a global scale, our leadership has to improve. For Britain, the opportunity created by this moment in time might not recur for a generation. It ranks with 1945 as a pivotal time in history. In the post-Brexit and Covid world, there may be a brief suspension of judgement – a new opportunity for big thinking.

In the early part of the twenty-first century, market leadership has begun to be questioned. This is primarily because it's not working for as many people as before. Below is a graph showing the decline of upwards mobility in America.[34] It's the same in Britain.[35] The problem it illustrates is two-fold. If you're older and have been successful, you're not going to criticise the equality of such a system. If you're younger and you're failing, no one will listen to you because you're a failure. For capitalism to succeed, it needs successful people to critique it and they are few and far between for the reasons above.

THE DECLINE OF UPWARD MOBILITY IN ONE CHART
% of people earning more than their parents

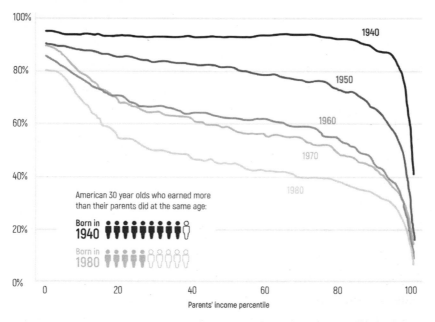

Source: 'The Fading American Dream: Trends in Absolute Income Mobility Since 1940' - Raj Chetty, David Grusky, Maximilian Hell, Nathaniel Hendren, Robert Manduca, Jimmy Narang – December 2016. Opportunity Insights and the US Census Bureau.© https://opportunityinsights.org/wp-content/uploads/2018/03/abs_mobility_paper.pdf

This is why equality is such an important issue to a younger generation. You cannot expect each new generation to support systems like capitalism and democracy when they make them generationally poorer than their parents and grandparents. Equality is providing some redress to the manifest inadequacies of the system. Generational trust is at the heart of this.

We can ask what we should do. But we can also ask who we should be. It is the latter area that can most clearly illuminate both our history and our future. Our national brand is at the core of this. What is it that we and we alone can do? Well, as we explored at the start of this book, Britain is trusted. We must lead on this virtue and we must be first to rebuild it. In doing so, we will perform a service of great global value at a time when the rules-based system is breaking down. Whatever happens next, our global trustworthiness will have a major impact on inbound investment from a global community that is itself looking for leadership.

It might be thought delusional to write about equalities. It's clear, though, that the anger is real enough and the reasons for the failure are equally clear. There are many delusions out there, however, so let's look at some.

THE DOZEN DELUSIONS

1 The UK Is Already Really Good at Equalities

All political leaders say that opportunity and social mobility are central to their mission. Tony Blair said his ambition was to rebuild Britain as 'one nation in which each citizen is valued and has a stake; in which no one is excluded from opportunity and the chance to develop their potential'. Gordon Brown said, 'I want the best of chances for everyone. That is my mission – if we can fulfil the potential and realise the talents of all our people, then I am absolutely sure that Britain can be the great global success story of this century.' David Cameron said, 'We will govern as a party of one nation, one United

Kingdom. That means … giving everyone in our country a chance so that no matter where you're from you have the opportunity to make the most of your life.' Theresa May said she wanted to make Britain a country that works for everyone, adding, 'When it comes to opportunity, we won't entrench the advantages of the fortunate few. We will do everything we can to help anybody, whatever your background, to go as far as your talents will take you.'[36]

Progress *is* being made. Prime Minister Boris Johnson recently committed to 50 per cent of Conservative candidates at the next general election being female.[37] It is recognition that the world is changing. But the progress over the past twenty years has been slow, as we saw in Chapter 2. That's also the conclusion of the Social Mobility Commission's two papers 'Time for change: an assessment of government policies on social mobility 1997–2017'[38] and 'Social mobility in Great Britain – state of the nation 2018 to 2019'.[39]

A 2018 OECD report on the subject measured the number of generations it would take for the descendants of a child born into the lowest 10 per cent of socio-economic groups to earn the national average wage. In Denmark, it was two generations. In the UK, it was five.[40] This report also highlights another factor – the greater the gap between rich and poor, the less opportunity there is for social mobility. We need to close the gap, but you don't make the poor richer by making the rich poorer. It's about responsibility.

You need the economic growth that comes from a concerted campaign to modernise the attitude to success in Britain. This means more ladder climbers in leadership. People who, by definition, still have rungs above them.

For something to really change in this area, it requires the sort of sustained and continuous political pressure often eclipsed by the *crise du jour*. Equality is itself not treated fairly. It appears not as an important opportunity but as an insoluble problem. It's an area where Britain could lead the world, with many spin-off economic and social benefits. It could be a Magna Carta for this millennium.

The truth, however, is that 'equalities' isn't seen as an exciting career choice in government. Treasury, Foreign or Cabinet Office, maybe attractive, but minority groups are seen as awkward, noisy and unpredictable. Disabled people for instance require changes that are seen as tiresome additional costs, not as infrastructure investments. And yet minority achievement is the stuff of which our dreams, history and culture are made. Think Boudicca. Think Elizabeth I. Think Horatio Nelson (a partially sighted amputee). Think Golda Meir. Think Margaret Thatcher. Think Barack Obama. Think Tanni Grey Thompson. Think Marcus Rashford. All achieved against the odds. The message is clear: if a minority can make it, then achievement is open to all. They were and remain important figures because of what they inspired. Many of the most effective politicians who have championed issues such as social mobility and opportunity are so because of who they are, as well as what they do. Harlow MP Robert Halfon is one example. His relentless and un-compromising focus on championing opportunity for those with-out comes from empathy and experience. This is what leadership looks like. He is successful despite and not because of the political machinery around him.

The sad truth is that Westminster itself is the provenance of equalities preaching it does not practise. It undermines its own credibility and trust. When it should be defending disabled groups, it is discriminating against them. Ask any MP who has tried to employ a disabled person on the parliamentary estate.

When it should be simplifying and broadening access, it is conspicuously complicating and narrowing it. When it should be thinking greater, it's acting smaller. There are a host of antiquated parliamentary attitudes and behaviours which span the curiously quaint and quizzical to the cantankerous and questionable. Parliament is not subject to normal. Normal HR. Normal hours. Normal pressures. Normal working practices. Normal interactions. Normal behaviour then gets deviated from, like a wonky shopping trolley.

Equality should be a central mission because of what it says about the nature of politics itself. It should be open to all. Democracy must be made as inclusive as possible; otherwise it becomes a growing irrelevance to be bypassed through direct action. The antediluvian nature of the process described in Chapter 6 has a palpable price. For example, mandating that all MPs are physically present in Parliament to cast votes cuts across many stated policies and not just in the field of equalities. If we want a lower carbon footprint, how does it help to force MPs to travel unnecessarily? If we want levelling up and a greater involvement from the regions, why do we insist that MPs can only exercise their franchise by returning to the centre? If we want equality for working parents with childcare duties, the disabled and those who volunteer for community service, why does the parliamentary process remove so many of them from their families and communities? Things are improving, there are some sign-language facilities at press conferences and easy-read materials to aid citizens with a learning disability, but there is more to do.

#2 Inclusion Is a New Idea

Britain's inclusivity is first found in its physical geography – an island with many natural ports connected by long-navigable rivers. It has always welcomed new people, ideas and trade. This means a constant and incremental process of change. It's one of the reasons for the country's success. Change is the engine room of equality. It is only an issue because the *rate* of change has increased.

Historically, inclusion was a mainstay of a British approach to allow minority groups to become part of something bigger. It's in the richness of our language, comprising a vocabulary of Anglo-Saxon, Celtic, French, German, Italian, Hindi and Roman, among many others. It's in our politics, with the Act of Union between England and Scotland. It's in our institutions. Stand in Parliament's Central Lobby and look up to see regional inclusion Victorian-style. It can be seen in our distinctive flag. It's in the military, with the formation of Scottish, Welsh and Irish regiments, even the Gurkhas. It's in our approach to refugees like the Ugandan Asians.[41] More recently, three million Hong Kong residents have been offered the chance to settle in the UK and apply for citizenship.[42] If you have a bigger vision than just your narrow, selfish goals, you can attract people to your cause.

You can treat those agitating for change as rebel platoons and expend a great deal of energy stopping them. Alternatively, you could see them for what they really are – groups that are fighting for inclusion in your dream, because it's theirs as well. It's not just individual equality that is worthy of consideration here: it's our whole philosophy. 'Wider still and wider'[43] can be interpreted as embracing ideas, scientific investigation and knowledge.

Inclusion is an old idea which has served Britain well. Successfully navigating the change that has come with it could even be argued to be one of the country's greatest achievements. If we're in search of a reason to love the Union of the United Kingdom, there's one right there.

#3 Gender Equality Is a Left-Wing Conspiracy That Will Make Businesses Less Competitive

Not true. Some of the most pro-free market organisations are in favour of it. Yes, it's a matter of social justice, but for those that understand, it's about business efficiency as well. There's clear evidence of gender inequality in the workplace. Only 7 per cent of the FTSE 100 companies have female CEOs, for example.[44] The UK's Gender Equality Monitor clearly shows that the gender pay gap starts at the beginning of working life and it rises steeply as women have children and take time out.[45] It continues to increase as women approach fifty and it peaks for those aged fifty to fifty-nine, the prime age for caring for both children and elderly relatives. The gap continues to rise and then turns into a pensions pay gap. Men are projected to have significantly higher income on average than women in their first year of retirement.[46,47]

Investors are also waking up to the inequalities and demanding that firms recruit more widely. In 2018, BlackRock, the world's largest asset manager, said that it would divest from firms that have fewer than two women on their boards.[48,49] Firms with women in key leadership positions are more profitable.[50]

Why does this really matter to growing our economy? Well, what is the fastest-growing entrepreneurial group in America? It's not middle-aged white men.[51] It's African-American women. The number of businesses they own has increased more than threefold since 1997. Where employers are unwilling or unable to create flexible jobs, these women step in to take responsibility. They are re-engineering lives through free enterprise. They are resourceful, determined, self-sufficient and energetic. If we want entrepreneurship then we need to start thinking more widely about how we define it.

America shows what's possible. The number of women-owned

businesses grew by 74 per cent between 1997 and 2015. This is one and a half times the national average, according to the American Express *State of Women-Owned Businesses Report 2019*. Women now own 39 per cent of all businesses in the US[52] – some 11.6 million firms. Furthermore, African-American women control 19 per cent of those companies, or an estimated 2.2 million businesses.[53] Increasing women's productivity and employment to those of men could add 35 per cent to GDP or £600 billion to the UK economy.[54]

There's something else in the gender equality debate that deserves closer scrutiny. What did the scandals at Enron, Oxfam, Volkswagen, the Catholic Church, Bernie Madoff and the major banks have in common? Could it be that reckless overconfidence is behind so many leadership failures? Or because they couldn't even imagine what might go wrong? More of this later.

Professor Tomas Chamorro-Premuzic, from University College London (UCL), has written about how confidence can mask incompetence. He said in an interview in 2014 for *Harvard Business Review*: 'Confident people tend to be more charismatic, extroverted, and socially skilled, which in most cultures are highly desirable features ... in virtually every culture, confidence is equated with competence.' So, we automatically assume that confident people are also more skilled or talented. He went on to point out that 'competent people are generally confident, but confident people are not generally competent. They're good at hiding incompetence and insecurities ... mostly because they are self-deceived themselves, so they generally think that they are much better than they actually are.'[55]

Imagine a world where doctors, teachers, engineers and pilots are selected on the basis of their confidence as opposed to their actual ability.

Premuzic believes this preference for the over-confident will continue to make it hard for women, he says, because they are usually both humbler and more competent than men. As far as the gender debate is concerned, he thinks the problem is not that women lack confidence, it's rather that men have too much of it. He also says that the criteria we use to evaluate men are different than those we use for women. When men come across as confident or even arrogant, for example, we assume that they are good at what they do and we call them charismatic. When women behave in the same way, though, he says, 'We tend to see them as *psychopathic* or a threat to society or an organisation. So, society punishes manifestations of confidence in women, and rewards them in men – which only reinforces this natural difference between the genders.'[56]

To suggest that this is the only thing holding women back from leadership positions is too simplistic. What if inequality was a symptom of something wider? What if the culture of leadership has become so attuned to analytical thinking that it is simply blind to a more joined-up view of the world? Could it be that short-term, tactically focused, quantitatively obsessed, qualitatively blind, drill-down, academically qualified, 'data-driven' thinking has come to be considered as the only legitimate type of intelligence? If so, we're in real trouble. We cannot afford to be prejudiced against leadership thinking because of its provenance.

One conclusion we might draw from Premuzic's work is that reliance on too narrow a type of thinking can cause inequalities because talent cannot progress unless it conforms. In other words, excellence is made of diversity. It takes different types of thinking, academic as well as pragmatic, local as well as global, male as well as female, to harness the potential of people. Diversity results in stronger, more effective organisations, growth in the economy and fairness in society. In short, maybe when it comes to leadership, we need to focus less on the 'leader' and more on the 'ship'?

#4 Politics Is All About the 'Silent Majority'

Listening is more important now than at any time since the Second World War. This is a time of significant national threat. We must encourage dialogue despite our disagreements. This is not helped by 'cancelling' those with a different view or declaring them beyond the pale.

The importance of minority views has been underlined by recent events. They foretold 9/11, the banking crisis, the rise of nationalism, the climate change movement, the coming of Brexit and the rise of Donald Trump. It wasn't a lack of data that hid these issues; it was an inability to read the mood. Communication is not the same as conversation. They don't teach that at university. Graduates may say that data is the new oil, but stock markets are moved as much by sentiment as they are by statistics. Looking at statistics will not help you understand sentiment. Britain may be doing well in aggregate, but the experience in the regions can feel very different.

Britain has always been an open country and culture. In the future, as Britain reaches out globally to new partners and opportunities, this will be more important than ever. Britain must be the best place for big ideas to be burnished or blended. It will require flexibility, imagination, sensitivity and empathy. Knowledge as well as experience.

#5 Equality Is an Easy Problem to Solve

One of the great problems with equality is that it's difficult to gauge progress. So often, the measures we use to measure quality are in actual fact measures of quantity. So, for instance, a firm might increase the number of female apprentices, which might also increase the gender pay gap.

In boardrooms, you can increase the number of women. But so often equality isn't just about the maths; it's about the mood. It's no use having more women in boardrooms if they just behave like the men they replaced. The point about equality is that it should change the way an organisation feels. So, you need to measure different things. This could be the level of collaboration, consultation or communication. Not everything that counts can be counted. Not everything that can be counted counts.

We need to understand that representation is about feeling as well as thinking and that credibility increases with proximity to the coalface. If MPs can be closer to their constituents physically, culturally and emotionally, the connection and understanding are likely to be strengthened.

Second, Britain talks about its levelling up, public service modernisation, equality, productivity and leadership failures as if, somehow, they are unrelated items. If Britain is to be successful, however, it has to draw upon all the skills available to solve what are multidimensional problems. Who better to overcome multidimensional challenges than those who have already done so? Why do you think that a quarter of government funding to start-ups went to disabled entrepreneurs? They are the most creative problem-solvers around.[57]

#6 More Education Leads to Greater Diversity of Thought

The idea of inclusive thinking starts in education. We give marks for competition not collaboration, for deduction not determination, for industry and not integrity, and for enterprise rather than empathy. When individual skills are prioritised over collective ones, we fuel the inability to produce inclusive leadership. There are

ever-increasing numbers of graduates coming through into industry and into political representation. This means teaching people
to look across the shared experience and not just drill down into
ever-more-reductive analysis. We need to see the bigger picture.

The majority of us are not graduates, and it's important for those
who are to see that their way of looking at the world is not necessarily
representative. Graduates are far more likely to be in employment,
to have a much narrower background of life experience, to earn
more and to be in debt – a major disincentive to non-graduates.

That's also the view of Sir Anthony Seldon, historian, biographer
and former vice-chancellor of the University of Buckingham. What
sets Buckingham apart is that it's the UK's only not-for-profit private university. Seldon makes the point that if you don't teach wider
issues such as ethics and morality, pupils won't learn them:

> We have a situation where Gradgrind is running most education
> systems around the world. Anybody who says you can reduce
> the purpose of education to the passing of tests is guilty of
> adopting that approach. Exams and tests matter but they're not
> all that matters and the problem is they are seen by many to be
> all-embracing.[58,59]

We need leaders who can think, not just pass exams. The purpose
of education is not solely to get a job. It should be much more than
that. Robert P. George is an American legal scholar and political
philosopher at Princeton University. So he's not exactly under-
educated himself. This is an extract from his concluding statement
at an American academic conference, Education 20/20:

> You're sending us students who are diverse in myriad ways and

yet alike in their viewpoints and perspectives and prejudices. Students who have absorbed what I sometimes call the *New York Times* view of the world. They think what evidently they think they are supposed to think. They seem to have absorbed uncritically progressive ideology, and they embrace it zealously, obediently, and alas, dogmatically, as a faith, as a kind of religion... Challenging its presuppositions and tenets is regarded not merely as wrong, or even heretical, but as in many cases quite literally unthinkable.[60]

Our education is not teaching independent thought. Nor is it always value for money. In an education select committee report, degree student Sam Brook described what you get for your money:

Personally, I think value for money in higher education is about what costs I received at university. I went to Warwick and studied Economics. Spending £9,000 a year there got me 250 hours of contact time, which was often shared with 349 other students. Some simple back-of-the-envelope statistics: that equates to a one-hour lecture costing £18,000 to deliver.[61]

No wonder he'd started to question the return on his investment.

Britain is a country of experiences as well as knowledge. For instance, you could study hunger. You could discuss it in a seminar; you could even get a degree in it. You could go on the telly and comment on it. You could be awarded prizes for your insights. But could you ever really understand hunger or pain or poverty without directly or indirectly experiencing it? Following the public inquiry into poor care at Mid Staffordshire NHS Foundation Trust in 2013,[62] there was a move among healthcare professional bodies to emphasise values and attitude when recruiting to the profession. You can teach skills, but you can't teach someone to care. How can you measure tenderness, patience, love? Understanding is not achieved only by knowing facts. You cannot understand without experience. Rationality can only do so much. We must avoid our representatives becoming 'intellects whose desires have outstripped their understanding'.[63,64]

Most people can detect someone with similar experience. This is why police officers, the military, nurses and other front-line workers feel so unusually bonded. They know the difference between what the media calls a crisis and a real one. Indeed, those who face a common threat often form a strong local community. They may not be graduates but they are expert citizens who are often helping to maintain – even transform – their communities and tackle big issues. Furthermore, they know they can contribute to solving problems on local, national and global levels. Wide and diverse experience, background and education will result in catalytic processes.

The 'cancel culture' of university education also tends towards the binary result of the 'right' answer. Experience knows that there can be several right answers. We must understand that even the perception of inclusion is important in driving sustainable results. This is an academic culture that permeates the political professions and, importantly, the civil service. As much as intelligence and precision are needed, there is also a need to simplify Whitehall's language. The more complex and opaque we make the issues, the less people can contribute to solving them.

The lingua franca of academia includes words like ontological, epistemological and pedagogical. In such language systems, mystery and value have a linear relationship. This is a culture that rewards the complicated, the hieroglyphic, the cryptic and the abstract. The language that graduates in general and in Whitehall in particular are taught is designed to be divisive in its derivation. It is designed secretly to signal to the similarly indentured. Civil service Sir Humphreys baffle unsuspecting Jim Hacker in uncomfortably familiar parody. MPs may be as educated as civil servants, but they are not always experienced public administrators. Maybe all MPs should have training in this area?

Another narrowing aspect of contemporary education is that so often becoming a graduate means leaving home, never to return. This is at the heart of what David Goodhart in his book calls 'Anywhere' people.[65] Graduates are told to aspire to be the best, then told the best is at the end of a Coriolic plughole spiral. Then other graduates ask why our regions are not attracting investment. Money follows talent and vice versa. Graduates make London an unreal city where 60 per cent of the population has a degree. If we believe in the power of democracy to enrich the regions, then education must set an example.[66,67]

America has an approach that anticipates this. It can be seen in its state university systems. The University of California (UC) is an example. Each major city has a branch which is effectively a university in its own right. There are ten of them: UC Berkeley, UC LA, UC SF, UC Santa Barbara, UC San Diego, UC Irvine, UC Davis, UC Santa Cruz, UC Riverside and UC Merced. Although they cater for the brightest students, they have localism baked into the selection process and charge vastly reduced fees for in-state students. As a result, 70 per cent of the UC intake comes from California, which is an all-time high.[68] The state also has community colleges that operate at a more practical level as part of this system, designed for candidates who wish to work part time as well as plan to go to university. When students complete a two-year programme in community college, they are then allowed to choose which of the UCs they go to. The UCs are mandated to accept them, subject to grades. In total, 37 per cent of UC students come from low-income families.[69]

Why can't this be done in the UK regions? It would cut the cost of education by keeping it local, it would reduce our carbon footprint and perhaps make it more likely that talent would find regional opportunities after graduation. Have we got the balance right between creating centres of excellence for particular subjects and sustaining communities?

No one would say we need less education. But we do need more diversity within it. All too quickly, the unreal university cloistering comes to an end. Mid-Covid, this could result in over-educated, over-indebted under-achievement, and a tragic recalibration of expectation.

People should have the option to put down roots, to build a community where they have family. If we want to level up, then a more even spread of where students are studying around the UK would be helpful.

Universities have traditionally focused on building centres of excellence for particular disciplines. One thing Covid has taught us is that such centres need not be physical ones. The university sector in the UK needs to think hard about these challenges and opportunities.

#7 There's No Science to Equality, Only Politics

Part of the problem with discrimination is that it is hardwired. We may not even be aware that we are affected by it. Take height, for example. It is associated with authority and loudness, with confidence. In *Blink*, Malcolm Gladwell suggests that most powerful people are tall, their height over other people giving them an advantage.[70]

The average height of men in the US is 5ft 9 in., whereas American women are, on average, 5ft 4 in. Gladwell found that most male CEOs were a shade under 6ft tall – or, in other words, most male bosses are three inches taller than other men.

> Most of us, in ways that we are not entirely aware of, automatically associate leadership ability with imposing physical stature. We have a sense, in our minds, of what a leader is supposed to look like, and that stereotype is so powerful that when someone fits it, we simply become blind to other considerations.[71]

Loudness, too, is correlated with confidence, and men have deeper, louder voices than women.[72,73,74]

We can't avoid looking at how these issues affect leadership because a lack of inclusivity is also implicated at the heart of leadership failure. After the collapse of so many famous brands and trusted institutions, what has been learned? In the financial crisis, leaders were not short of intelligence, experience, data or confidence. They had those in spades. The imagination to see the potential catastrophe comes from empathy, humility and a deeper field of vision... well, these were less obvious. This is not to say that you should rid the markets of 'animal' spirits but that you should enlighten them. In this way, diversity and greater representation can help avoid another banking catastrophe. It would help to improve the balance of short- and long-term goals, quantitative and qualitative outcomes. Greater inclusion in capitalism and greater inclusion in democracy go together. They ensure our children grow up thinking that both systems remain relevant.

Writing in *Psychology Today*, Dan Goleman asked, 'Are women more emotionally intelligent than men?' Emotional intelligence (EI) has four parts: self-awareness, managing our emotions, empathy, and social skill. Goleman indicated that in many tests of emotional intelligence, women tend to have an edge over men. In leadership roles, this is a critical skill.

Goleman says women differ from men where the other person is upset, or if their emotions are disturbing. Female brains tend to stay with those feelings, sitting with them and experiencing them, but male brains do something else. They sense the feelings for a moment, then they tune out of the emotions and switch their focus to other areas of the brain, which try to solve the problem that is creating the disturbance.[75,76]

Empathy is a key skill for leadership. Again, it's not taught in universities or business schools. There are three kinds: cognitive empathy regards understanding how the other person sees things; emotional empathy is about feeling what the other person feels; and empathic concern considers being ready to help someone in need. In general, women tend to be better at emotional empathy than men. This is an important leadership skill because it fosters rapport and chemistry in a team. People who excel in emotional empathy make good counsellors, teachers and group leaders because of this ability to sense, in the moment, how others are reacting.

Other research showed something stranger. When women were injected with testosterone, they became more egocentric and less attuned to the needs of the group. The hormone actually disrupted their ability to work together. 'Egocentricity bias is the degree to which people over-weight their own opinion. If you are more egocentric, you are more likely to think you are right,' said study researcher Nicholas Wright, of UCL. 'These women were more likely to say they were right when they were on testosterone than when they were on placebo.' In short, the testosterone led women to make more selfish decisions that were less in the interests of the group. It made them behave like men. Blimey.[77]

This isn't just a story about gender wage gaps; it's a story about motivation. In manufacturing and other complex processes, teamwork is vital. It's not enough to focus on making women feel confident. It's also key to make over-confident men modify their behaviour.

According to research, women are more likely to agree with the statement 'being a good team player means helping all of my colleagues with what they need to get done'. In contrast, men are more likely to agree with the statement 'being a good team player is knowing your position and playing it well'. While both perspectives are valid, they lead to different patterns of collaboration.

Not only are women less likely to carve out time for their own work, they're more likely to give it for free. They're also more likely to feel guilty about ignoring a request or declining a meeting in order to prioritise their own work. Social scientist Benjamin Voyer explains why that might be: 'Guilt is an "other-focused emotion"[78] – an emotion that involves thinking about others, which research indicates is typically a female trait.'

Competing on a global scale means harnessing as much talent as we can. This is especially the case when it comes to maximising collective talent in teams. This is why we need to understand the issue of gender. If we're going to get to the heart of greatness in this country, we need modernity, aspiration and representation. And what part of that is not served by the greater diversity of thinking that comes alongside gender equality? This is frequently framed as a matter of justice for women. It certainly is that, but we should also note that to continue without it wastes so much human potential.

Are gender traits embodied in Western reductionist thinking? Premuzic's work would suggest that the drill-down, short-term, tactical, quantitative, left-brain approach might be associated with masculine behaviour. Conversely, big-picture, compassionate, empathetic, qualitative, right-brain thinking might be considered more feminine behaviour. But what is wrong with teaching both? If the two types of approach are like water and oil, then we need to create an emulsion.

#8 Everyone Gets a Fair Say in the News and Social Media

Just as men dominate the discussions in boardrooms across the UK, they also dominate the conversation on comment boards across the internet – especially when they can post under a pseudonym, according to one study. Dr Fiona Martin of Sydney University took a sample of comments from fifteen major websites and analysed the genders of the commenters. She categorised people as male, female or ambiguous. On international sites, men accounted for as many as 79 per cent of the commenters. While women were more likely to comment on local news sites than international ones, reaching 35 per cent on one publication, men still appeared to dominate the conversations.[79,80]

The findings echo work done by Emma Pierson, who reviewed 1 million comments left on the *New York Post*'s website in 2014 and concluded that men left 75 per cent of the comments, despite accounting for only 56 per cent of the readership. Looking at the results of the study, Dr Martin speculated that the discrepancy could be explained by the higher rate of unpaid work that women do: 'They simply don't have as much time to spend commenting on news websites.'[81] She suggests that online commentary is a microcosm of the everyday difficulties women face in getting their voices heard: 'It appears our experience of online conversations is reflecting our gendered experiences of the world at large. Just like in face-to-face public conversations, like meetings or forums, women are being put off by male voices being adversarial, dismissive and sometimes abusive.'[82]

In 2015, Adam Grant (Wharton Business School) and Sheryl Sandberg (Facebook) teamed up to write an opinion piece in the *New York Times* entitled 'Speaking while female'. In it, they listed several studies that show how the spoken contributions of women in the workplace are consistently undervalued. It's not just that women are interrupted more frequently than men; it's that their ideas, contributions and data are more likely to be discounted entirely. Across environments as diverse as the television industry, politics and business corporations, there are similar patterns.[83]

#9 Racial Discrimination Is Just About Prejudice Alone

It is not. Racial discrimination is the greatest human injustice, made greater by the fact that it attracts so many other injustices. In March 2018, Sajid Javid, then Communities Secretary, pointed out that 770,000 people living in England speak little or no English.[84] Seventy per cent of that group are thought to be women. Javid referred to his own mother, for whom he had to work as an interpreter. It didn't stop her raising her family, but it made it harder. He was speaking as the government launched an Integration Green Paper, which subsequently became the Integrated Communities Action Plan (2019) under James Brokenshire. Javid noted that the figures, which were derived from census data, were critical, because 'if you don't speak English then there is no way you can take full advantage of the opportunities that modern Britain has'. Surely, though, the same is true in reverse? Britain cannot take full advantage of the skills that such non-fluent speakers have to offer.

Sometimes, this notion of inclusion is reflected in the detail that only minority groups notice. It was almost two decades ago that New York entrepreneur Michael Panayiotis created Ebon-Aid, 'the bandage exclusively designed for people of color'.[85] By late 2002, out of an original lot of 1 million boxes, he had sold only around 20,000. After losing his original $2 million investment, his company folded. The issue was subsequently revisited when the head of research of American equalities group Race Forward tweeted about it in 2019. His tweet was liked 520,000 times. The experience here illustrates a problem. To operate at economic scale, manufacturers and retailers will ignore minority requirements. Hopefully, changing technologies and the demand for better representation will change this.[86,87]

Young people from black, Asian and other minority ethnic backgrounds are 47 per cent more likely to be on a zero-hours contract, according to the Carnegie Trust, University College London.[88] Douglas White from the organisation said:

> Good work can have a really positive impact on people's wellbeing – but we need to tackle the inequalities in who has access to good-quality jobs. This report highlights that young people from BAME communities are particularly likely to enter into precarious forms of work. We need policy and practice to recognise and respond to this to ensure that good work is available to all.[89]

Inequality is an issue not just at the bottom rungs of the ladder. In a February 2020 investigation, the British Medical Association (BMA) found that while minority groups comprise 40 per cent of medical undergraduates nationwide, only 13 per cent of teaching staff were from non-white backgrounds. In an attempt to address the issue, the BMA issued guidance to medical schools on racial harassment. Chaand Nagpaul, the BMA's chair of council, said: 'Two-fifths of medical students are from black, Asian or other minority ethnic (BAME) backgrounds. They experience greater levels of undermining behaviour, micro-aggressions and racial harassment. Such behaviour damages self-esteem and confidence, affects learning, and contributes to the ethnic attainment gap that emerges through medical education and training.' The effects are cumulative.[90]

In some circles, the mere mention of micro-aggressions prompts ridicule. But is it the neologism they object to or is it the principle? If you were born British and black, how many times could you put up with being asked what country you were from? Micro-aggressions are just a series of indignities incurred by minorities. You may not think they're real but ask a disabled person about the routine indignity they suffer as a result of insufficient toilet facilities. Or about how many times people literally talk over their head and assume that being in a wheelchair means you're also a bit dim and/or hard of hearing. Or being lectured about their condition by complete strangers. Sam Renke, actress and disability activist, was once given some advice about her brittle bone condition: 'Have you tried drinking more milk, eating more cheese?'[91] It all mounts up. Is being considerate too much to ask?

Lord (Victor) Adebowale, former chief executive at Turning Point, a social care organisation, echoed Nagpaul, saying, 'Academia is about relationships. If you're black, you're not in the loop. Medical schools need to be put under the same levels of scrutiny that we put other organisations under.'[92] Jyoti Baharani, a London-based consultant in nephrology, tweeted that it was a 'pity we still have to debate this in 2020. But unfortunately, racism in medicine still exists. Try being a coloured female doctor in the NHS sometime.'[93] According to the NHS's Workforce Race Equality Standard 2019 report, white job applicants are still more likely to be shortlisted compared with minority applicants.[94] This is the NHS, the greatest pragmatic manifestation of equality we are supposed to have.

The point here is that a lack of racial and ethnic diversity leads to situations where the discrimination is compounded. As per Sajid Javid's point above, you're more likely to suffer discrimination if you cannot speak English, and even more so if you're a woman. You're more likely to be in precarious employment as a minority and also more likely to have mental ill-health. This is why we cannot look at diversity issues solely in isolation. They have knock-on effects that need to be viewed holistically. Covid has brought this problem even more sharply into focus.

#10 Equality and Social Mobility Are the Same Thing

There's a lot of confusion about equality, diversity and social mobility. Let's use an automotive analogy. Economic growth is to social mobility as fuel is to cars. Without it, a lot more pushing is required. Without equality, however, the car cannot be steered. That's why the first priority in all equality movements is economic growth. You need economic growth to move the car forward, but you also need equality to ensure it is steered. There's no point steering a stationary car.

When an economy is weakened, it is the weakest that suffer. That's why the first job of government in regard to protecting minority groups is to maintain the economy. This is especially the case where there is layered disadvantage. It is so easy to forget about inequality when you are privileged. That's why it needs to be at the centre of our thinking, if we believe strongly in aspiration. The strong tend to stick together. It's a natural instinct and there's nothing wrong with that. But if you are strong, you have one purpose: to serve others who are not so advantaged. This is more than a matter of political policy, more than a matter of dialectic discipline; it should be a matter of personal principle.

#11 Equality Is a Minority Issue

It is not. Everyone is affected. Women make up 51 per cent of the country and 47 per cent of the UK workforce.[95] Understanding how to release the potential of this group and all other minorities is clearly not a minority issue.

There are also a lot of men who want a more modern, aspirant and representative society. They have wives, sisters, mothers and daughters. The American civil rights movement was helped by white democrats including President Kennedy. The colour-blind ethos of Martin Luther King highlighted not just the relevance to all of mankind, but the responsibly of all to fight for it.

Minority groups should understand that you don't have to be a victim of injustice to want to fight it. Men have a role in fighting for women's equality. For instance, the person who has done most in Parliament to champion female entrepreneurs is a man, Craig Tracey MP, who chairs both the All Party Parliamentary Group (APPG) for Women and Enterprise and co-chairs the APPG for Breast Cancer.

So often men sound like the enemy of equality, but demonising men is not only unjust, it's also counterproductive. If you seriously believe that no one at all, anywhere, should be judged by their gender, race, age or for any other reason, then you shouldn't be using phrases like 'pale, male and stale'. There's no doubt that some men are prejudiced, involved in sexual harassment and consider all displays of feminism to be a threat. Those men might never be convinced, but they will, eventually, be eclipsed by others that do.

The grand aphorism that 'the first duty of government is the defence of the realm' is loved by politicians, but really inequality takes more lives than wars do in the long term. So if we're looking for a national mission, then there's one right here. Government is there to ensure equality of opportunity, not outcome. To ensure the presence of the positive, we first have to ensure the absence of the negative.

HOUSEHOLDS IN THE SOUTH-EAST OF ENGLAND HAVE A COMBINED WEALTH OF £2.46TN, COMPARED WITH £368BN IN THE NORTH-EAST

Aggregate household total wealth, £bn

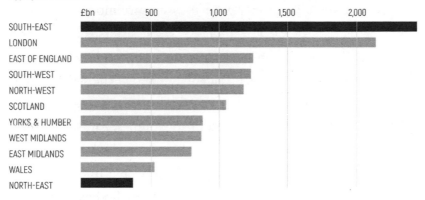

Source: Office of National Statistics, 'Wealth and Assets Survey July 2014 to June 2016. Includes property, belongings, financial assets and private pensions'
Contains public sector information licensed under the Open Government Licence v3.0.
http://www.nationalarchives.gov.uk/doc/open-government-licence/version/3/

Regional inequality, too, was a key underlying issue at the 2019 general election. Superficially, the villages and towns of Britain appear to be similar, but the economic inequality between them is stark.[96] This is illustrated by the relative differential in the tax take between the areas. London and the south-east dominate, as you'd expect, followed by the east of England, the south-west and the north-west. Scotland has a higher wealth per household than Yorkshire. Surprisingly, perhaps, the East and West Midlands have only a slightly higher income than the north-east of England.

Low-Income Constituencies

The scale of the challenge in transforming the peripheries can be seen in the differing levels of wealth throughout the UK. This, after all, is what the levelling-up agenda is about. How many constituencies have a lower average wage than the national average wage? According to the House of Commons library, it's almost a quarter – 161 constituencies have a median gross weekly wage for resident full-time employees at below 90 per cent of the national average.[97]

To get by on a low wage, you have to be energetic, disciplined and creative. This is the last thing you are inclined to be if you've been on a low income for any length of time. Emotional, physical and spiritual exhaustion are the shadow of financial difficulties. Horizons become narrowed, the view becomes tactical. Sometimes the level of energy required to get through the bureaucracy is self-defeating to those in need. Simply making it easier for these people to access government services would minimise the effort that people at the end of their rope need to make. That doesn't need legislation, only more efficiency.

Government would design better services if it had more experience of a life lived day by day, but our lives are becoming more distinctive. If you're rich, your neighbours are more likely to be in the same boat than in the past. The same is true if you're less financially stable. There's less mixing. Poorer neighbourhoods are more cut off socially and geographically from the sources of economic prosperity, making it harder to bridge the gap.[98] Liz Truss MP has recognised this and the Government Equalities Office is one of the first parts of Whitehall to be moved closer to the people it serves.

#12 Equality Is No Laughing Matter

Unsurprisingly, much of the debate about equality is centred on gender. One of the cul-de-sacs is single-sex discussions. If men are to understand the issues, they must hear the effects of their behaviour first-hand. Invite them. Let them in. Every church needs sinners.

Equalities thinking produces neologisms and sometimes the language of equality is itself discriminatory. Take the instance of a Conservative candidate selection board that asked a woman, 'Will we be having children, then?', to which the candidate replied, 'It's all a bit quick, sir. We've only just met.'

Or the case of an 85-year-old widow who, while accessing council services, was asked to respond on a form to multiple questions about her sexuality. She'd never been exposed to words such as heterosexual, lesbian, bisexual. She selected the latter, then enquired of one of the authors later whether she'd got it right: 'I thought bisexual sounded closest 'cos there was always two of us,' she said sheepishly. She was mortified when brought up to date. She remains, to our knowledge, the only octogenarian bisexual bus-pass holder in her district.

There's a serious point here. She was a pillar of her community. Gave to charity. Supported neighbours. She worked for years as a military auxiliary and wanted to join the army full time but had domestic priorities. So she sacrificed her career for her family. She might not have known the latest equalities terminology, but she could recognise opportunity and the difficult choices it brings for women when she saw it.

The language and fixation on equality are important to a metropolitan mind. To an elderly rural lady trying to manage the basics, it's a minefield. If we want to help people into opportunities, then it doesn't help to do so with language that excludes them.

Finally, it should be remembered that politics itself is a minority pursuit. Not everyone is interested in politics, but they do care about fairness, justice and their communities.

A RESPONSIBLE STATE NEEDS A RESPONSIBLE ADULT

Of course, the more responsible people are the better, but when it comes to it, life isn't that simple. The ways in which we're infantilised are many-fold. In football, the *Lord of the Flies* chanting. The 'on my head, *son*, the *boy* dun good, take a bow *son*' (© Andy Gray c. 1993). Crowds of any sort infantilise. So do relationships. Babe, sweetheart, sugar daddy. And fascists, with their mother country, mother tongue and Fatherland. Fascism and infantilism are in (goose) step. It's in religion, too. O heavenly Father, all God's children, *Il Papa*, Mother Superior. The state cannot manufacture responsible adults. Only an individual can choose to be so. It can, however, recognise that the ways the state infantilises are no less proscriptive, with its means-testing, risk-assessing, CRB-OCD box-ticking, form-filling, credential-wearing, neighbour-snitching, net curtain-twitching, recycling bin-checking, stationery-armed, your-reference-my-reference, gimcrack-engineered, self-important, three-piece Presbyterian, inappropriately named busybodies. The really busy are the opposite of the administratively promiscuous.

If we want people to take responsibility, we must understand the ways in which we prevent it. Why do so many willingly abandon responsibility? Frankly, because it's easier and because we don't always reward it in any case. This is tied up with our notion of leadership because to lead is to take responsibility. It is not only leaders who can lead. Leadership can exist at any level. What drives responsibility comes from within. It is the decision to own outcomes and accept their consequences. Do adults want responsibility? They want authority, but that's not the same. Unfortunately, the former and latter usually come together. And this applies to the wealthy, too. They also have to take responsibility for outcomes.

Responsibility is never given; it is always taken. It cannot be induced by the state, only deduced by the individual. There are many paths to this deduction – all are personal. Victim or victor? Whatever you decide, you're right. These are big questions, not easily discussed or addressed by busy, distracted, overloaded people under all sorts of pressures.

Responsibility is usually triggered by the desire to protect another – a child, a parent, a sibling, a partner, a cause. It is done for the cause of equality and you don't pick your cause. It picks you. Wherever we see this, we should celebrate it. That's the sort of leadership we should be focused on.

Those who can be responsible should be and this applies to the wealthy and large corporates, as well. Nothing is more important to the future of this nation. Britain has much strength, but it serves no end unless the strong defend the weak. Not accepting responsibility has the opposite effect. To make another responsible is to become powerless. The state ultimately makes a poor protector without the personal touch. A responsible state needs a responsible adult. A responsible state should reward responsible adults: the savers, the self-employed, the entrepreneurs and employers, the carers, the defenders and protectors. Taking responsibility is a prerequisite to equality. It has to be taken. It cannot be given.

CONCLUSIONS

Equality cannot be seen as a minority or single-issue matter any longer. It is central to a modernising agenda and is at the core of progressive economic and social policies.

Only 53 per cent of disabled people are in employment, compared with 82 per cent of able-bodied people. Just 18 per cent of disabled people with learning difficulties are in work.[99] LGBTQ+ people are at a higher risk of being homeless or sleeping rough. Of those who are homeless, the majority have mental health needs. Of the 30 per cent of women who were in low-paid jobs in 2006, the majority were still stuck on low pay a decade later.[100] People from black African, Bangladeshi and Pakistani ethnic groups are still the most likely to live in poverty, deprivation and sickness.[101]

If leadership is to serve the community in the long term, it needs to understand the values that bring us together. This requires empathy, sensitivity and compassion. It also needs the action, aggression and energy to defend us against those who would do us harm.

To get there, to really make this country as good as it can be, we need to draw upon the skills of as many different people as possible. There's no doubt that many want to help but find the current approach outdated, inefficient and frustrating. It's not just about gender. We don't need a man or a woman to lead. We need a blend of skills that can be present in any person of any gender, race or background. Our institutions, businesses, public services and communities need diversity to thrive. We need much greater, more effective and consistent focus on enabling talent to reach its full potential. Modernity, aspiration and representation are the qualities that can inspire minorities. So, if it helps, think less about the notion of 'equalities' and more about how we make our country a place of shared ambitions. That way, the future we're fighting for will be about all of us.

This book is about us. It is about our shared values. There are ten chapters in this book, but really only one that, if we get it wrong, could cost us the country. We must know the values we have in common. For Britain to seize opportunities ahead, it must recognise that we need to work together.

An attitude of self-reliance, self-confidence and responsibility is just as important as extending opportunity. If you can be self-reliant, then you should be.

Social mobility is not just a nice-to-have; it's an essential for Britain's success. Instead of being focused on it, we're in danger of creating a culture war. To cut through, leaders must resist fanning those flames. They must change minds. They must bring people together. They must focus on the values we all share. We need to ask activists the following questions. Is your cause one that unites or divides? Does it seek to understand or cancel? Is it colour-blind? Are you destroying another's property? Are you taking responsibility, for yourself and for others? Are you shouting down someone else's point of view? Or demanding they agree with yours? Do your actions champion free speech and open debate? Are you listening? Are you humble? Do you care? Do you have a dream you can share? Are you prepared to admit that you just might be wrong? Or do you have the sort of certainty that can only be the provenance of mediocrity and ignorance? Do you want to understand? Do you want to be understood? Establishing shared values starts with being prepared to defend them. Our nation, our mutuality, our Union and its future success depends upon it.

9

MODERNISING THE MARKETS THAT SERVE US

To ask people to keep faith with capitalism, democracy and leadership, we need to recognise that the glue that holds them together is trust. In this chapter, we look at the deep and complex relationship between democracy and free markets. We explore the origins of economic success and the role that democracy played in the development of capitalism. How can we modernise capitalism to better serve democracy and vice versa? When capitalism is global, how can the nation states scale alongside it? Is it possible that capitalism would prefer to fragment democracy through the application of nationalism? All the time the nation state is pinned back to its geographic remit, capitalism can effectively bypass it. This is illustrated in offshore finance and corporate tax avoidance. We also look at the other variations of capitalism that can be found around the world, in China, Japan and Germany. Finally, we ask how capitalism can survive if no one believes in it. Let's start by analysing where economic success comes from.

GEOGRAPHY, TRADE AND HUMAN RIGHTS
First and foremost, Britain is economically successful because it is

fantastically well connected. It is connected to both the world and itself. Nowhere in Britain is far from the sea, thus nowhere is far from trade, new ideas and diversity. It is inclusive by nature. Britain's rivers and oceans were the internet before the internet. These ancient watery synapses bestowed a collective identity and a clearly defined realm bounded by the seas. Today, Britain is at the centre of the global business day. You can fly anywhere in the world direct from Heathrow. Whether your luggage will arrive with you is another matter.

Tim Marshall, author of *Prisoners of Geography: Ten maps that tell you everything you need to know about global politics*,[1] has pointed out that nations bounded by physical geography have strong identities. If there's a relationship between a physical boundary and a strong identity, then the reverse must also be true – nations with no physical borders have a weaker identity. Good neighbours maintain fences because they respect each other. They're confident in their identity, but they're different from their neighbour. This matters because trade only occurs between people who have different resources, different skills and different identities.

Britain was founded upon trade. Trade took a strong natural infrastructure and enhanced it with a man-made one.

There's a difference between trade and plunder. The latter is unsustainable. Trade requires free will, justice, government, finance, insurance, labour and capital. From trade springs democracy and the law, science and innovation. It incentivises the flow of ideas. In economic terms, connection and trade enable centralisation, standardisation, economies of scale. Trade allows specialisation in education, administration, agriculture. It ultimately brings government, protection, security. There was a time when trade and science were the national mission.

It's no surprise that Britain's first commercial ventures were infra-structure-based. All infrastructure creates trade. Britain financed, designed and built ships, roads and canals to transport coal, timber and grain. It built bridges, viaducts, railways and ports and it developed new technologies in iron, steel and transportation itself. The development of steam power, smelting and longitude science, the Greenwich meridian, were all driven by trade. The investment in science and infrastructure continues, and to this day some of the largest projects in the world are in Britain.[2] This history can all be seen in the Science Museum.[3] It is one of the world's largest museums, with over seven million objects from every continent. When you can see where you've been, it's easier to see where you're going.

Britain has rain. So, it has rivers. Water played an important role. Unsurprisingly, Britain has the best merchant marine sector in the world and the Royal Navy is still seen as the prototype to emulate. British maritime history is filled with sailors, oceanographers, cartographers, hydrographers, innovators and adventurers. All this was mastery with a mission. For instance, Sir Stamford Raffles invented the concept of a free port in Singapore – a place where people could come and go without paying a national tariff. It had all the utility of a port with none of the political problems of sovereignty. His idea allowed the UK to beat other trading nations competing for use of the deep waters of Keppel Harbour. It was a gift the world would value, securing British interests.[4]

The mastery of the oceans was not limited to the British, of course. France, for instance, has almost three times as many ports, but a merchant fleet of only a sixth of the size. Britain's fleet is the tenth largest in the world. The Netherlands, Portugal and Spain all produced excellent mariners and many colonies, yet none was as strongly connected to trade. Trade forms a large part of Britain's character. Trade brings understanding, compromise, sustainability and stability. As a result, change comes naturally and incrementally.

Infrastructure, commerce and justice are the ingredients of success because they help create stability. They are universal, but wherever they are combined, they create success. This should not be forgotten – long-term success and stability cannot be sustained without these three key ingredients. Two out of three won't do.

For this reason, Britain has enjoyed almost 1,000 years of uninterrupted sovereignty. This continuity is embodied in Parliament. It is personified in Her Majesty the Queen. Monarchy is itself founded upon trade. It owes its position and continuity to it, thus the relationship between administrative stability and capitalism is linear. Capital thrives on human rights because the latter are fundamental to transactional laws. In turn, democracy thrives on free markets because the most common first sign of dissent is not political but economic. This can be traced all the way back to 1215, when Magna Carta first separated authority and power. It said that power can only be wielded with consent and this can only be given by the people. In other words, no one is above the law. It established the rights of free citizens to own and inherit property. It allowed them to be protected from excessive taxes. It outlined the principles of due process and equality. It contained provisions forbidding bribery and official misconduct. It also created the rights of widows not to remarry, in the first example of gender equality legislation.

CAPITALISM AND DEMOCRACY

The light cast by democracy and free speech serves many purposes. It illuminates the darkened path ahead. It enlightens and refreshes politics. It allows us to orientate ourselves as we move forward and, importantly, it identifies challenges as they move towards us from the future. It shows us where we are and, just as important, it shows others where we are and what we stand for. Our systems are not perfect, though. The beacon has been burning bright in Britain for a thousand years. Democracy is its light. Capitalism is its heat. It needs careful stewardship, and we will discuss its failings. What other nation is better qualified for the task of protecting capitalism and democracy? What other nation has the centuries-long heritage of those twin engines of human progress? In defending one, you enhance the other. They are central to the notion of free speech.

Britain should be proud of this track record. It should also be bold in its promotion of democracy both at home and abroad, for instance in Hong Kong. By doing so, it reminds the world not just of British values but of those of humanity. Britain has a duty to help those trapped in totalitarian regimes. The largest movements of people in human history have always been towards democracy and away from totalitarian systems. Through long experience, the British know that the size and power of the state must be held in check. This is because everyone is equal before the law – the state included.

Capitalism is the lifeblood of any government because it provides the fuel for the mutuality that binds us. Without taxation, there are no government funds. Capitalism is the music to which suppliers and consumers move, and politicians and central bankers are the conductors of the band. It is not enough to say that capitalism simply channels resources to meet consumer needs. It does more than that. It links those suppliers and consumers voluntarily and freely. They are the ones who decide when to dance and to what tune. Sure, the better educated and resourced might choose the best tunes, but democracy and capitalism cannot be coerced. They both rely on elective, individual, voluntary cooperation.

Capitalism is full of paradoxes, and this has been a feature of capital markets since their inception. The most obvious of these paradoxes is that for something so individualistic, the system creates and facilitates large amounts of collectivism. This includes shareholders, employees and other stakeholders. It's powerful stuff, and the reason for all this joining together is partly that capitalism is dangerously disinterested in human outcomes. For capitalism to serve us, not vice versa, it needs democracy to control its worst excesses. Britain knows what China has yet to learn.

There are further contradictions, too. For something so local, it is now a global system. For something so apolitical, capitalism is the central pivot of the entire political system. It is political folly to despise it, because the very means of economic redistribution lies within.

It's nothing new to want to control and manage capitalism. The guilds of London, associations of craftsmen or merchants designed for mutual aid, were established in every trade to teach skills, maintain standards and monitor market conditions. Often, these were accompanied by patronage from royalty too, to help regulate the markets. Trade unions followed in the footsteps of the guilds to provide the power of collective bargaining to the labour forces, in what is ultimately another type of market mitigation.

It is a central idea of this book that capitalism and democracy are reflexive and reciprocal. Some believe they can exist without one another, and that may be true in the short term, but such independence of ideas has never been tried in the long term. There is simply no evidence that capitalism can be sustained without democracy. Capitalism is like fire: it's a good servant but an evil master. It can warm your house. It can cook your food. It can light the darkness. But it can burn and blind you, too. Capitalism must be directed and guided by democracy. They feed on each other. Democracy is the fire brigade.

When democracy works *pro bono publico*, it creates the conditions under which capitalism can be sustained. People in democracies are healthier, they live longer and they have stronger human rights. Governments in democracies are also able to increase their public services in direct proportion to the performance of the economy, because as the economy expands (and with healthier citizens it will), more tax can be raised. Louis XIV's finance minister, Jean-Baptiste Colbert, noted that 'the art of taxation consists in so plucking the goose as to obtain the largest possible amount of feathers with the smallest possible amount of hissing'.[5] Or you could just get a bigger goose?

BEVERIDGE AND HAYEK

Communists go on about capitalism in the rubric of Millwall criticising Manchester United. Many are sold communism's utopian vision despite and because of the fact that in most places, communism has died. It just ran out of a) dictators who were madder than 'Mad Jack' McMad, winner of last year's Mr Madman contest, and b) people who were madder than that and willing to support the madness.[6] This is not to say that capitalism does not have its mad men. It thrives on them. But it's much easier to criticise capitalism because its shortcomings are all around us. Communism is mysticised by its antediluvian nature. Few have any direct experience of it. Those who do are already mentally or physically fugitive. Or dead.

It would be easier to take communism seriously if it had worked well, but it didn't. It was miserable and murderous and grey and petty and paranoid and bureaucratic and Rosa Klebb bossy and heartless and maniacal and hierarchical and unfair and inefficient and, worst of all, boring. Really, really boring. Capitalism is not perfect, but it's never dull.

Red, blue, left, right, in, out, north, south, east, west, discussions engorged so many conversations of the late twentieth century. You remember conversations. When there were polite exchanges over dinner, rather than heavy mortaring from either end of the table. Arguing about capitalism is two fleas arguing about who owns the dog that has done a big job that everyone's stepped in. It provides a displacement activity for those of the Maginot Line mentality. Absolute, fixed, unbreakable, unswerving, rock-solid, middle-management certainty separated on either side by a high prophylactic fence topped with broken dogma that prevents any form of perspective. Some get to quite like it. It becomes how they graduate into economics and politics. Most never venture that far. That world remains hermetically sealed off from the rest of normal humanity who have more pleasurable recreational pastimes, like going water skiing, wearing a furry hat, walking the dog, riding a bicycle, going to the pub, stroking a cat or baking a cake.

In essence, though, this comes down to a balance between markets and mutuality – or, put another way, between individual freedoms and what is best for the collective or the state. Both systems rely upon each other. An illustration of this understood symbiosis is the relationship between what would now be photonegatives from a philosophic point of view.

Austrian wonder boy Friedrich Hayek was the economist's economist, although he also held doctorates in law and political science. William Beveridge, by contrast, was a liberal, progressive, interventionist colleague of Sidney and Beatrice Webb, parents of modern trade unionism. All his life he worked to expand the role of the state in social outcomes.

Hayek was praised by John Maynard Keynes and invited by Beveridge to become a professor at the London School of Economics

(LSE) in the 1930s.[7] This was when the left and right were focused on the problem in hand, rather than on mutual homicide.

Beveridge and Hayek were the Odd Couple of 1930s economics. The LSE had been founded by Fabians in 1895 and had developed a reputation for socialism. Yet by the 1930s, in a period of experimental economic cross-dressing, it had embraced liberalism – just at the time when Hayek's native country was turning towards fascism. Being different in almost every way from the democracy of Britain, perhaps it is the crushing conformity of communism and fascism that destroys individual excellence, and hence progress and enlightenment. In any case, fascism resulted in one of the best minds in history coming to Britain.

And here's the thing. Hayek was Austrian at a time when that nation had just recently been an enemy. Yet still the UK embraced him. He was the most vocal critic of Keynes's work. Without going into too much detail, Hayek argued that Keynes's solutions would not solve the slump of the time but would instead institutionalise inflation. Yet still Beveridge and Keynes embraced him. What Hayek experienced must come close to the very essence of Britishness. Countries and institutions that understand John Stuart Mill's tyranny of the majority are always bound for success.[8]

It's hard to imagine figures from the left and right collaborating in such a manner today. Perhaps it was the parenthesis of greater evils – the First World War and the rise of Nazism – that allowed it. Contemporary political differences are puffed up by protagonists precisely because their positions are so proximate.

Hayek was beloved by Margaret Thatcher because he knew his place. To him, economists and policymakers went astray when they presumed to have more knowledge than they actually did, or even than they could ever possibly have. Hayek's comparative insistence on intellectual humility, according to the economist Russ Roberts, can be found in the Talmud.[9] The modern economic theories of specialisation and the development of *Halakhah* (the Way) itself mirror the Hayekian notion of 'emergent order', which appreciates the thousands of people who must come together to achieve one thing. This philosophy was all about placing yourself as an individual within a system: you have your own ends, of course (to earn a wage, for instance), but you are at the same time a cog in the larger structure.[10,11]

Hayek warned of the danger that results from government control of economic decision-making through central planning: 'A claim for equality of material position can be met only by a government with totalitarian powers.'[12] And, perhaps most famously, when referring to dictators: 'From the saintly and single-minded idealist to the fanatic is often but a step.'[13] Democracy stands in the way of this top-down control. Democracy is imperfect. But the system at least gives us the ability to change it if we want. All the time, the safety valve of consent moderates democracy.[14]

But Hayek left us with a question: what is the right balance between individual liberty and state planning? The same questions are asked by every generation. Now, though, it's not the answers that are different but the questions. The internet is unleashing a massive acceleration not only in transactions and the velocity of money but in individual choice. No matter how extreme your flavour, you can find it on the internet. Incidentally, this partly explains the fragmentation of the franchise into identity politics. Broader political messages have become so diluted as to be transparently vacuous. So, alternative options that are closer to and more congruent with a person's individual ideologies are chosen instead. Increasingly, the individual has the power to dictate our direction, and capitalism has had its role to play in that.

Either way, capitalism is not the enemy for any serious modern politician. It's there to be steered, not stifled. Democracy and government create opportunities for capitalism, but Hayek showed us that the same is true vice versa. Active at around the same time, Churchill's metaphor-laden view of capitalism was this: 'Some regard private enterprise as if it were a predatory tiger to be shot. Others look upon it as a cow that they can milk. Only a handful see it for what it really is – the strong horse that pulls the whole cart.'[15]

Government needs capitalism in the same way that the Catholic Church needs confession. Free will is at the heart of fair markets and this is what links them closely to politics. Any reduction of human rights diminishes capitalism; extinguish human rights and you undermine capitalism because, fundamentally, it relies on a faith in the longer term.

We've established that democracy needs capitalism in order to thrive. Capitalism needs democracy to keep it in check, but global capital has accelerated ahead of democracy. This is why a more modern, revitalised democracy is vital.

We saw in Chapter 8 that there is a need to rebuild trust in a global system. It may not sound like a priority, but when cracks are appearing in the structure of a house, it's usually due to problems in the foundations. By rebuilding global trust in democracy, we can rebuild capitalism at the same time. The economic crisis of 2008 undermined trust and belief. If we boost the latter, the former must benefit – but it depends on the quality of leadership.

Of course, our leaders must be drawn from the community they serve. They are human, they suffer the same failures and flaws as everyone else, and the reasons for their failures are identifiable. The difference now is that the stakes are higher financially, commercially and politically, because the world has never been more connected and yet more divided.

POLICING CAPITALISM

Markets are amoral; they are efficient but also brutal in the process. So, we must mitigate them or risk losing mutuality. You can direct them and you can regulate them, but if capitalism is going to work effectively, it needs to be harnessed and focused. This means a sea change in leadership, not a tsunami of regulation.

We've been trying for quite some time to regulate one of capitalism's primary battlegrounds with democracy: tax avoidance. Let's look at the approach of some of the world's largest corporations. The growth in supranational companies has enabled tax avoidance on a large scale, and we should note that the majority of these companies are American. In 2018, an analysis of the financial filings of the Fortune 500 was carried out by the Institute on Taxation and Economic Policy (ITEP). It found that sixty of that nation's biggest corporations *didn't pay anything* in federal income taxes in 2018, on a collective $79 billion in profits. Specifically, the ITEP reported that giants Netflix and Amazon paid no federal taxes, while other companies on this list included Chevron, Delta Airlines, Eli Lilly, General Motors, Gannett, Goodyear Tire and Rubber, Halliburton, IBM, JetBlue Airways, Principal Financial, Salesforce, US Steel, and Whirlpool.[16]

This is something that Britain, with its huge experience of both professional services and taxation, could work on together with the US. Both countries have a vested interest in tackling this problem. The beneficial stewardship of capital is not just confined to taxation.

It also knocks on to security, defence and international aid. Terrorist organisations feed on a lack of compliance. Some £50 billion annually disappears from African economies due to corruption. This is equivalent to the combined total of aid spent there each year.[17] According to the report:

> These companies avoided taxes by employing a variety of legal tax breaks. Accelerated depreciation allows companies to write off the cost of their investments much faster than these investments wear out. This break accounted for hundreds of millions in tax write-offs. Chevron alone, for example, reported $290 million in accelerated depreciation and Halliburton reported $320 million.

The report was damning, noting that stock options were providing a dubious tax break that allowed several corporations to write off expenses far in excess of the cost they reported to investors. As indicated above, it named companies directly, saying that Amazon, Netflix, Salesforce and a number of others appeared to use this tax break to write off millions of dollars that were owed to the state. Tax credits and subsidies also provided hundreds of millions in write-offs.

The report added: 'These tax loopholes allow many profitable corporations to avoid paying a single dime in taxes, but it should also be noted that many other profitable corporations are also using these special breaks to pay far less than the 21 per cent statutory federal income tax rate.' The report was clear about the consequences of this tax avoidance: 'We cannot pretend that corporate tax avoidance has no cost. Corporations zeroing out their tax bills or paying single-digit federal tax rates mean a substantial loss in federal revenue. Calls to cut critical programs and services in the wake of these corporate tax cuts are absolutely connected.'

Let's be clear. One reason tax remains uncollected from the largest companies in the world is the lack of political will allied to international cooperation. When this is allowed to happen, the implications are huge and, ultimately, the reputation of capitalism is at stake. This short-term, arrogant, selfish approach may appear smart, and if capitalism is the prioritisation of money, it certainly achieves that goal. The avoidance of funding public services, though, should be a matter for shame. It undermines trust not just in these companies but in the capital system. Those companies involved in this avoidance should be warned. They serve communities that are the source of all the success they enjoy, and you cannot serve a community while simultaneously undermining it. Those who care about capitalism (and, as we have seen, this by definition also means those who care about democracy) should be embarrassed by this behaviour. Other leading capitalists need to police the outliers in the same way that any other group leaders would look after their community values. It needs capital leaders to wake up and recognise the problem.

If capitalism is to avoid being rejected by a new generation, then there are two choices. Either capitalism can police itself, or governments will have to. At present, neither of these is adequate. Supranational companies are more powerful than governments, so they don't feel obliged to keep in step. This may change, however, with the new, and rising, global consciousness of corporate wrongdoing. The same lack of imagination that we've seen in so many historical corporate failures is stalking the boardrooms of these firms. If they aren't worried, their shareholders and employees should be. And actually, this is where government can help. What would it cost for the tax authorities to say thank you and congratulate companies for their tax contributions? Would it be a problem to point out exactly how many nurses, schools or police they have funded? Each of these services is costed by government, so it wouldn't be hard to do, and the positive outcomes could be enormous, allowing companies to tell their consumers in real terms the social good that the money they spend on coffee each day is helping to achieve. Why could this not be included in an annual report and accounts? Not just profit and loss, but community value.[18]

Boardrooms need to recognise that it isn't a lack of intelligence, wealth or experience that brings corporations down; it is a shortage of imagination, often topped up by over-confidence that borders on recklessness. For boardrooms not to recognise the ethical problem with tax avoidance is not just a failure of corporate compliance, it is corporate negligence in the face of a known threat. How many systemic failures and cries of 'We just didn't see it coming!' do we need to hear before company boards faintly recognise their responsibility to seek out moral hazard, model it and codify their actions accordingly? There may come a time when only this type of audit trail will save their personal reputations.

Another way of ensuring compliance with our taxation laws is for global government to seek to mitigate its worst effects. To do this will require cooperation among the largest capital democracies and it will take time. However, there is now little doubt that governments will need to apply greater legislation in this sector. There is little doubt, too, that these enormous corporations will employ even bigger teams of lawyers to combat these new laws.

It's possible that the solution may come from the application of both. What governments lack in resources, they make up for in convening power. For instance, they are able to influence accounting and audit standards authorities to change the way they report on 'fair and accurate' accounts. An example of this is the Generally Accepted Accounting Principles, which are the rules that allow investors to check whether companies and their directors are discharging their fiduciary duties. This raises three possibilities. First, that statute law may be applied to any accounting and audit firm. Second, that it could be applied to the managing partners, personally. And third, that the law could also be applied to the company's clients and their corporate officers, again personally. These moves may take time and several test cases to apply, but they would begin to change the level of tax avoidance that is deemed acceptable. Shareholding boards would not tolerate drunkenness, sexual harassment or drug abuse in their businesses – tax avoidance must be added to this list.

We should spare a word here to address the argument that government is inefficient in the way it uses tax money. Such a point is ultimately irrelevant. Yes, governments are less efficient than corporations, but that goes back to what we have said before: it is because they run on democracy. A system in which all voices must be heard will never be the quickest, but it will be the fairest, *in the long term*. Businesses aren't democracies, but while they exist in a truly capitalist system, they are still bound by its rules.

Why does this need to be done now? Because this is just the beginning. There's an opportunity to correct this while the internet, and its consequent effect on globalism, is still, relatively speaking, in its infancy.

Implementing measures like those described above carries the risk of being labelled 'business-unfriendly'. Any company required by its country to implement such procedures unilaterally would likely also become a target for other competitor nations, which might lower their taxes to compete further. Business is much more mobile than government and it can react to changes of environment much more quickly as a result, playing the economic climate to its advantage. Consequently, without a coordinated effort across the globe, governments can be picked off and divided. No government wants to be branded with that business-unfriendly label – but then no government wants to see public services eroded either. That's why it would be altogether better if business was to police itself.

Professor Syed Kamall of the Institute of Economic Affairs has said:

> One option we would like to see explored in the future is to abolish corporation tax and make owners of shares pay tax on their earnings per share. This should lead to a situation where it does not matter where the company is domiciled; it is where the owners live that matters.[19]

Another way that government can encourage fair play on tax is by flexing its muscles as a customer. This could be done under existing legislation, too, such as the Social Value Act of 2012. This could also be encouraged by going further down the supply chain.

Sceptics about the merits of social value in contracting are concerned that the public purse will just end up paying more for contracts. However, that charge cannot be levied when social value includes tax paid.

A NEW ACCELERATION OF CAPITAL?

As we hinted in the introduction to this book, there is a strong link between infrastructure and wealth. The faster the communication channels, the greater the link to market, and we can see this re-flected in the UK's movement from navigable rivers and waterways to roads, railways and airports. Our methods of connection are getting quicker, and at every stage of speeding up the flow of goods and services, we've seen GDP grow too.[20]

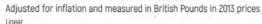

GDP PER CAPITA IN ENGLAND SINCE 1270
Adjusted for inflation and measured in British Pounds in 2013 prices
Linear

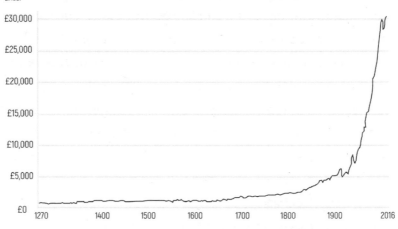

Source: Broadberry, Campbell, Klein, Overton and van Leeuwen (2015) via Bank of England (2020)
Published online at OurWorldInData.org. Retrieved from: https://ourworldindata.org/economic-growth

In the past twenty years, GDP has continued to accelerate further still. Infrastructure has improved. It is about to accelerate again.

There are two main types of market infrastructure globally: one is based on data, the other on physical goods. The former is overtaking the latter. According to McKinsey:

Conventional wisdom says that globalisation has stalled. But although the global goods trade has flattened and cross-border capital flows have declined sharply since 2008, globalisation is not heading into reverse. Rather, it is entering a new phase defined by soaring flows of data and information. Remarkably, digital flows which were practically non-existent just fifteen years ago now exert a larger impact on GDP growth than the centuries-old trade in goods.[21]

The world is becoming more connected than ever. The nature of its connections, though, has changed in a fundamental way. Cross-border bandwidth has grown forty-five times since 2005. It's projected to increase an additional nine times over the next five years as flows of information (searches, communication, video, transactions and intracompany traffic) continue to grow. Virtually every type of cross-border transaction now has a digital component. Director of the Institute of International Monetary Research Dr Juan Castañeda has pointed out:

> The Internet facilitates trade and expands the market. If anything, it reduces transaction costs and therefore enhances trade and economic activity. In this vein, rather than inflationary, what it does is to increase the availability of goods and services in the overall market (be it the traditional 'onsite' markets or online). In the end what will determine the rate of inflation/deflation is the rate of growth of the amount of money relative to the rate of growth of the supply of goods and services. Further developments on the Internet will only be deflationary if they manage to increase trade and the amount of money does not increase accordingly.[22]

We're at the start of a new and emerging global market for goods and services driven by data. You might not think this applies to physical goods, but what are these goods except solidified data? With the growth of 3D printing,[23] we're already beginning to see the data blueprint for many products transmitted across borders and printed out or assembled locally. The question of how governments will charge import duties on data remains, but it's a question that should be answered sooner rather than later. Here are just some items that can be 3D printed: musical instruments, food via open-sourced 'growbots', quick-build homes, body parts/prosthetic limbs, electric vehicles, firearms, plastic components.[24]

From time to time throughout the centuries, governments, whether they admit it or not, have inflated their way out of debt. This first happened in 1694 to finance William III's war against France, and it was achieved with the introduction of banknotes. It happened in America, too, to finance the War of Independence, and after the Napoleonic wars with the burning of the tally sticks. In the past fifty years, it happened during UK decimalisation and during the switch to the euro in 1992. It also happened after the dot-com crash and again after the 2009 financial crisis. Each time, it was a conscious decision made by the government of the time. It is about to happen again.[25,26]

Another effect of the internet is that the control of money has passed from central banks to other, less recognisable, and perhaps less reliable, providers. This creates an unprecedented opportunity for those who wish to 'get off the grid', for compliance or criminal reasons, for instance. This is the case with new digital technologies such as bitcoin, which use blockchain security. Blockchain offers an ultimate lock for a transaction, providing transparency and clarity as to the provenance and destination of funding. In this instance, it could be argued that one of the reasons that banking has been slow to adopt technologies like this is precisely because it provides the ultimate in terms of transparency. Some banks may prefer the plausible deniability of more old-fashioned methods.

Such technologies may also create opportunities for countries that are not even on the grid. The internet is supranational and therefore can be policed only with global agreements.

The new, global, internet-driven economy will pose fresh challenges for democratic government. National treasuries will no longer be able to control the flow of money or taxation because the internet already has its own currencies. We know that harnessing the power of digital will be a priority for policymakers and business everywhere. If our leaders can embrace these new ways of working, it will lead to more cross-border e-commerce by addressing the ease of payments systems, the coordination of tax issues, and integrated logistics.

The large amount of data generated by the new systems will also create opportunities. For one thing, education output will need to change to develop talent to code and manage big data. Some have even said that data will be the new oil. If that's true, it will be extracted from each and every one of us, provided that global systems are set up to exploit it safely. And in the UK provided also that it has our consent.[27,28]

In the years ahead, companies and economies everywhere can overcome constraints in their local geographical markets and connect with global customers, suppliers, capital and talent. It is for this reason that nation states no longer need to be allied to those geographically adjacent. The infrastructure we have available to us today renders such narrow alliances obsolete.

All this means that many firms are now using technology both for automation and to shorten supply chains, especially where labour costs are no longer the biggest concern. This transition from the physical to the virtual would seem to favour the United States.

As the world's leading producer of digital platforms and content, it accounts for more than half of the online content consumed in every region of the world except Europe.[29,30]

This could have huge implications for China, too, if it continues to sit behind the great firewall, not engaging with this global free flow of data. Data drives creativity and innovation, but also dissent. If humanity is going to address some of its greatest challenges to date, we cannot afford to discriminate against the provenance of the solutions. Are we seriously saying that ideas will be legitimate only if they have been accepted and authorised by a controlling political party?

If the growth of the internet is an important opportunity to reform capitalism, we should address the idea that it presents the same opportunity for democracy, too. There's a big difference between running a government like a business and running it in a business-like way. There's simply no reason for us to continue with outdated methods or lower standards than would apply elsewhere. The internet allows huge opportunities for efficiencies, even in the area of democratic machinery itself. Perhaps we should follow Estonia's lead, for instance, where all citizens already have the right to vote electronically. Emerging countries could also be helped by the technology.[31]

DEBT AND INFLATION

Global debt is now three times the level of global GDP. To be specific, as of the fourth quarter of 2020, the debt stood at 365 per cent of global GDP, or some $277 trillion.[32] By the time you read this, it will be bigger still. The horrifying facts are constantly repeated in the press and by international organisations. The Institute of International Finance, for example, said that China's debt levels ballooned to 300 per cent of GDP in 2019. There is also evidence that 60 per cent of American workers are so indebted they don't have $500 in savings to cover an emergency.[33] A study by the Royal Society of Arts echoed this, showing that around 70 per cent of British workers are chronically broke, with some 32 per cent having less than £500 in savings.[34]

Such economic hardship is why inflation is one of the themes of the moment all across the globe. If the stimulus of quantitative easing wasn't working, the increased defence expenditure, Trump's presidential tax cuts, China's Belt and Road Initiative (BRI) and spiralling Chinese wages certainly are. China is investing trillions of dollars in global infrastructure with the BRI, but that injection of capital is not necessarily picked up by traditional monetary aggregate measures because it's being spent overseas. Where once China was exporting deflation, it's now exporting inflation.

Forbes also points out that until the credit crisis, tens of millions of people each year were joining the middle class on a worldwide scale. Between 2003 and 2007, the growth of the American economy alone exceeded the size of the entire Chinese economy. In fact, China's growth rates were higher, but it was starting from a much smaller base. *Forbes* states, 'Along with bringing prosperity to millions, democratic capitalism has undermined political tyranny and promoted democracy and peace between nations of the world. It is, without doubt, the world's most moral system.' Not bad for something so amoral.[35]

China is at an interesting point. The uneasy partnership of state-run industry, repressed liberties and entrepreneurialism are being thrown into focus, but there is a bigger malaise, too: that of the tariff war with the US. Chinese entrepreneurs are leaving China. According to a survey conducted by China Merchants Bank and

Bain & Company, 27 per cent of entrepreneurs worth over 100 million yuan (US$15 million) have already emigrated, and 47 per cent are considering moving abroad.[36] Speaking to *Asian Entrepreneur* magazine, Huang Song, secretary-general of the Finance Industry and Development Research Centre at Peking University, noted an apparently neglected reason behind the emigration:

> There are many reasons why entrepreneurs choose to emigrate. Public opinion is usually concerned with two reasons: first, they do not have confidence in China's future; second, they are trying to escape from something illegal they have done. But there's a very important reason often ignored, that is, the large number of government restrictions and barriers to overseas investment and financing. First, due to the control of foreign exchange under the capital account, overseas investment by Chinese enterprises needs to be approved by the Foreign Exchange Management Department. And although the investment policies have become more relaxed than the past, there are still a lot of limitations and financial investment is still strictly managed. Second, overseas investment has to be approved by the Development and Reform Department, which brings a lot of uncertainty to projects.[37]

China's financial system really only supports state-owned and large enterprises. For small and medium-sized enterprises, it's difficult to get loans, and even more difficult to obtain public or issue bonds. Less than 6 per cent of Chinese shares are foreign-owned.[38] In comparison, the NYSE records 20 per cent of equities as owned by foreigners and 42 per cent of bonds. US stock markets are worth $29 trillion in market capitalisation, whereas China's stock market is worth around $4.7 trillion.[39] In addition, more than half of Americans hold shares in their stock exchange; this figure is only about 7 per cent in China. In recent years, the performance of the Shanghai exchange against the Nasdaq tracker has been disappointing.

SHANGHAI STOCK EXCHANGE VERSUS NASDAQ STOCK EXCHANGE

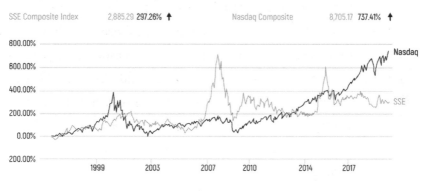

Source: Generated using Google Finance

In the US, due to accountability, more people are prepared to invest in the stock market, which in turn invests in companies. This does not happen to the same extent in China. Instead, the Chinese typically invest heavily in property – but this does not recirculate the cash in quite the same way as equities.

Until very recently, Asian workers have been enjoying the highest wage increases anywhere in the world,[40] and according to *Forbes*, Chinese wages now equal or exceed those in parts of Europe.[41] Today, the only major emerging market that undercuts China on wages is Mexico. There, wages are lower than China with quality control that is American standard.[42] Many American businesses now have manufacturing operations in Mexico.

The loss of competitiveness in low-value goods has forced China to move up the ladder into products that can better sustain long-term economic growth. This explains the move into superfast trains and the railways associated with them, as well as small nuclear plants. On top of this, China is investing $3 trillion in the BRI – another major injection of inflationary capital into the world's economy.

THE BIGGEST INFRASTRUCTURE PROJECT IN THE WORLD

Infrastructure is geopolitics. Many leaders have not truly understood the magnitude of the Belt and Road Initiative, President Xi Jinping's plan to build a 21st-century silk road between Asia, Africa and Europe, because it's happening in far-off places. Leaders might easily dismiss it because new infrastructure in, say, Kazakhstan is irrelevant (partly because they don't know where it is). According to *The Economist*, though, the BRI 'is the kind of leadership America has not shown since the post-war days of the Marshall Plan in Western Europe'. In fact, the BRI is seven times larger financially.[43]

The BRI is not really a plan. It is a series of discrete infrastructure deals with different purposes, financing arrangements and participants. This provides infrastructure links which literally solidify political alliances. Together, they add up to one massive network. Specific routes have been built or improved, to include, for instance:

- A railway link from Yiwu in eastern China to London and Madrid via Kazakhstan, Russia, Belarus, Poland, Germany, Belgium and France. This link connects Yiwu with Rotterdam via Moscow and Ürümqi in China and with regional railway networks, such as those in south-east Asia.
- Trains from Kunming, China, will link to Vietnam, Laos, Thailand, Cambodia and Myanmar. In East Africa, the BRI will

connect Ethiopia, Djibouti, South Sudan, Kenya, Tanzania, Uganda and Rwanda. In each case, ports are also being built or upgraded.

- In the Himalayas, China is building railway and highway links in both Pakistan and Bangladesh to connect China to the sea via both countries, using Pakistan's Economic Corridor and the Bangladesh–China–India–Myanmar Corridor.[44] The Himalayan Economic Rim project will connect Nepal, India, Bhutan and Tibet.[45]

- In the Middle East, China is financing links between Turkey, Lebanon, Syria, Iraq, Iran and Jordan in a new Silk Road.[46] The railway routes in the region will be supplemented by new or upgraded ports in places like Oman, all the way to Athens.

- A proposed new port will be built on the west coast of Mexico at Lázaro Cárdenas.[47] This is expected to be bigger than the Port of Long Beach in California (the second largest in America). This will allow Chinese ships to bypass US West Coast ports. Some suggest that as much as a quarter of the approximately 60 million tons of cargo that the Los Angeles and Long Beach ports handle each year could be diverted. Mexico will get new ports, too, and upgraded railways and highways in the effort to ensure that commerce from the East and West Coasts of North America can reach China ever more easily.

- This will be matched with another two proposed Panamax-sized canals, the first in Nicaragua – the Grand Nicaragua Canal – and the second across the Kra Peninsula in Thailand – the Thai Canal.[48] China is also moving closer to Malaysia in its BRI projects and has invested $14 billion (US$10 billion) in the Melaka Gateway project, a port that could replace Singapore as the main entry point in the region.[49]

- In Latin America, the BRI takes the form of an ocean railway from Brazil to Chile and the Trans-Amazonian Highway across Brazil.[50]
- The Arctic aspect of the BRI is a maritime route that runs from Dalian in eastern China through the Arctic Circle to Rotterdam and then south through the Suez Canal back to China.[51] The widening of the Suez Canal to accommodate two-way traffic and Panamax-size tankers is one of the biggest projects of all within the BRI.[52]

All this investment will add at least a further $5 trillion to global investment.[53] When you add this to the $18 trillion already invested by global central banks,[54] you can see that this is significant in terms of both scale and risk. The BRI is ambitious, even inside China. According to the English-language newspaper *China Daily*, 'Twenty-nine of China's thirty-one provinces and regions are now served by high-speed rail, with only the regions of Tibet and Ningxia in the northwest yet to be connected.'[55]

China has built out the BRI anticipating the supremacy of trade in physical goods. In reality, though, as we noted earlier, the value of data and ideas seems to be eclipsing this as the prevailing form of infrastructure across the globe.[56] As James Sproule has pointed out, sea lanes are changing to e-lanes.[57]

Can China continue to succeed with its current attitude towards human and intellectual property rights? Or have we seen this all before?

THE JAPANESE MODEL

In the 1980s, the Japanese model, which featured lifetime employment and cross-ownership to shield companies from shareholder pressures, seemed the way to go. Then, in 1992, the asset price bubble burst.[58] The Japanese experience sounds the warning for China. Initially, the consequence was just a standard downturn following a stock market decline. This was compounded dramatically, though, by inept intervention. Things got worse when people began to save more, pulling their savings out of the Japanese private banking system. The result of all this was economic stagnation and a lost decade.

When governments get it wrong, the results can be disastrous. In this particular case, the government overestimated the amount of fiscal stimulus. In total, around 23 trillion actual yen was injected into the Japanese economy in 1992–97, but at the same time, the government took more than double that out of the economy.[59] When the government raised the national consumption tax by 2 per cent in 1997 and contracted government spending, confidence was finally destroyed. The economy is just beginning to recover today.[60]

THE RHINELAND MODEL

And then, of course, there's the German model.[61] Much of the beauty of capitalism lies in its ability to be crafted to suit different cultures, times and contexts. Post-war European consensus, for instance, is embodied in the idea of Rhineland capital. The irony of Europe's capital model is that it only really works in European countries beginning with G. This specific example involves long-term state involvement in policing business and highly regulated labour markets.

German capitalism mixes seemingly impossible ingredients, like strong trade unions and efficiency, high-cost workers that also compete in manufacturing, and generous unemployment benefits alongside low levels of unemployment. It also has a strong base of independent, small and medium-sized family-run manufacturers called the *Mittelstand*. (Literally, the middle class.) This is partly the reason that Germany overtook China in 2017 with the world's largest trade surplus.[62]

Germany's economic strength is a result of its own particular circumstances. In the mid-1990s, it suffered with the twin problems of high debt and high unemployment. The country's labour costs were the largest in the industrialised world, while unemployment had rocketed in the former East Germany. The German government responded with the Hartz reforms, which strengthened the hand of employers in negotiations with unions. For instance, one of the reforms was to allow companies in difficulties to opt out of union contracts and shorten working weeks. Unions thus became less demanding. Germany still suffered an economic contraction in 2009, but job losses were minimised due to flexibility schemes. The *Kurzarbeit* (short-time working) programme subsidised 1.5 million German workers through the worst of the recession.[63]

Some other European countries have tried to copy the German system. For instance, with soaring youth unemployment at 33 per cent in 2019, Spain was looking to boost German-style apprenticeship programmes – but it hasn't worked.[64] Perhaps German policies function well because they are designed specifically to work in Germany.

The point of exploring these models is to show that the world doesn't need a one-size-fits-all approach. Each of the above models works well for its own country. Each area has its own specific requirements based on local characteristics. What works in the Rhineland won't necessarily work in the Thames Valley. In a fast-moving world, economic systems depend on flexibility and adaptability for their success.

THE NEED FOR CHANGE

One enduring irony of a system that champions competition is how it finds itself in a monopoly position as far as political philosophies are concerned. No other system has been as effective as capitalism at turning scarcity into abundance. Although capitalism has been the world's most successful economic system in history, it has not been above criticism.[65] In their book *How Capitalism Will Save Us*, Steve Forbes and Elizabeth Ames said:

> We all know the Rap on capitalism: That it is fundamentally greedy and immoral. That it enables the rich to get richer at the expense of the poor. That open markets are Darwinian places where the most ruthless unfairly crush smaller competitors and where the cost of vital products and services like health care and energy are almost beyond the reach of those who need them. Capitalism has also been blamed for a range of social ills from air pollution to obesity.
>
> Not only have educated, successful people bought into capitalism's bad Rap, but the Rap is taught in our schools. It has moulded the thinking and analyses of our most influential opinion leaders, writers, thinkers, and policy makers of both political parties. Long before the stock market meltdown, before AIG executives and automotive CEOs were being tarred and feathered by Congress, Democrats and Republicans alike regularly blamed overpaid executives and Wall Street greed for the problems ailing America's economy.[66]

The authors make a good point. It's important to bear in mind, though, that the security of our beliefs is vested not in how much we praise them but the opposite. We criticise the best ideas because they are robust.

Forbes has a point about politicians, though. They habitually point to what they have spent, not what they have made for the country or how they've grown the economy.

HOW EFFICIENT IS CAPITALISM?

There's no doubt capitalism has its shortcomings. It is often said to be a more efficient way of allocating resources, but the scale of waste is also worth a look. It's true, for instance, that the investment community may expect to lose some money in order to make bigger returns elsewhere. In fact, *Techcrunch* found that 96 per cent of all start-ups backed by venture capital firms were 'somewhere between breaking even and downright losing money (remember to adjust for inflation)'.[67]

VC FUNDS - RETURN ON INVESTMENT

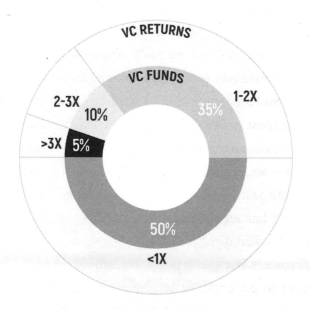

Source: Money Talks, Gil Ben-Artzy, UpWest Labs. LinkedIn SlideShare:
https://www.slideshare.net/gilbenartzy/money-talks-things-you-learn-after-77-investment-rounds

You can see from the figure that at least one-half of all investments return less than the money invested in them. Another third return only the original funding and up to twice more. Only 5 per cent earn back more than three times the original money.

This goes to the heart of the social good done by capitalism. The vast majority of new jobs are created by companies employing fewer than fifty people. These companies account for 99.9 per cent of the business population (6 million businesses). The Federation of Small Businesses says these 6 million small businesses in Britain employ 61 per cent of the total UK workforce. Stock markets don't invest in these small companies. They want to chase higher returns. The largest pool of savings, usually in the form of pensions, doesn't find its way to these small companies. We entrust these funds to professional investing institutions. This isn't because these investments are risky. It is because they don't generate big enough returns for professional investors.[68]

THE IMPORTANCE OF THE FUTURE ORIENTATION

Capital investment makes a set of presumptions, that tomorrow will be different, and probably better, than today. This future orientation is one of the most striking hallmarks of a drive to modernity. Some may say it creates an uncertain future, but all futures are uncertain. The only way we can tell whether this is true, paradoxically, is by looking to the past.

Capitalism has enjoyed a profound inflexion since 1700, and this can be tracked directly to the enlightenment and the application of science.[69] For the majority of human history, a belief that life is going to get better would have been mad. We now live in times, though, when life is immeasurably better than it was 300 years ago.

Capitalism's forward-looking nature is essential to its success. If the promise of a better future starts to fade, a vicious cycle sets in. Why save? Why sacrifice? Why stick at education for longer? If our belief in better things to come fails, then the entire system fails, too. To some extent, then, investment and savings are political manifests, and we could posit that a forward-looking nature is thus at the heart of all political leadership. If people believe they will be better off, they will invest, and consequently they – and the country they live in – will be better off. It's the same story in the stock market, as all shares are assessed on their forward-looking price–earnings ratios. In the period following a global financial collapse, one of the primary reasons capitalism starts to fail is because people *believe* it is failing. The biggest threat to capitalism is not socialism; it is pessimism. As we learned in Chapter 2, the British can be world-class cynics. Or they could be if they had an ounce of self-belief.

You see, cynicism is sophisticated, supercilious, saturnine, feline and conditional. Stroke me and I might purr. The British don't really have fun. At best, they pass the time. Andy Murray is a sort of master of morose. Doctor Dour himself. If you end up that happy after winning Wimbledon, then God help any failures.

Optimism is simple, naive, canine, unconditional and wind-down-the-window-so-I-can-stick-my-head-out joyous. Americans don't just enjoy themselves, they have a blast. The difference between Britain and America is shown in local news broadcasts. In Britain, it would be about the depth of misery. In America, the size of pizza. America is successful, partly because it believes it will be.

Economic progress spans the generations, as parents see their children's standard of living surpass their own, and their children experience the same in turn. The thing is, that endless expectation of a higher income than your parents is unsustainable without economic expansion. We're hardwired for 'loss aversion', to experience more pain from loss than pleasure from gain. In an example of this, after wages, workers rank job security as one of the qualities they most value in a workplace.[70] It is the lack of understanding of this factor that has been so costly to free marketeers. They advocate its benefits – and there are many – but are less keen to see or mitigate for its downside, especially through the eyes of the workforce. Workers displaced by automation have been treated as effectively disposable by businesses and political leaders alike. There are questions to be asked. For instance, if we have a national insurance scheme, why isn't it being used to secure wage payments in conjunction with actual insurance policies to compensate for downward shocks, as happened during Covid? Why does our welfare system disincentivise the self-employed to insure themselves?

Another question is why governments settle for a very small range of economic growth. If we hit growth stretch targets, we could also set spending targets in line with them. For instance, if we all knew that we were working for a specific goal, e.g. for hospitals or schools, wouldn't that make it easier to achieve?

This is why aspiring to better things matters. People have got to know that there's room at the top and that they can climb the rungs of the ladder. In order to keep faith in the system, we must actively look for examples of aspiration. If people believe they will be worse off than their parents, of course that affects the ethos of capitalism. We have to ensure that capitalism is delivering for all groups because, if the economy isn't growing, this affects mobility for everyone.

PEOPLE LIVING ALONE BY AGE GROUP IN THE UK 1996-2017

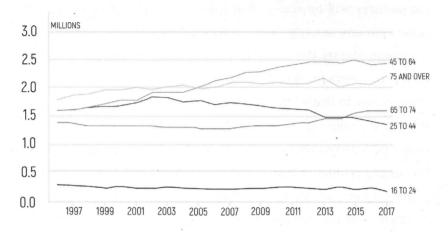

Source: Office for National Statistics, 'Labour Force Survey'
This is licensed under the Open Government Licence v3.0.
https://www.nationalarchives.gov.uk/doc/open-government-licence/version/3/

Social trends affect personal wealth as well. More people living on their own might mean more household costs and less shared income to support them. After all, it costs the same to heat a household for one as it does two. For this reason, the family remains the most efficient economic unit, but statistics suggest this mode of living is becoming less common. If you're older you're more likely to be living on your own (see graph above). The real issue for capitalism is not necessarily the actuality of being better off. What matters is whether people *believe* they will be better off.

ARE THERE LIMITS TO CAPITALISM?
The environmental lobby puts this idea front and centre, and many would argue that it seems a counterpoint to capitalism. But is it? The only way of addressing the carbon footprint is to harness the same power that caused it (capitalism) in its removal. For instance, what would capitalism prefer? The destruction of the entire air

travel industry or the invention of emissions-free aircraft? The airline industry will have to pay to clean up the planet based on the future cash flow of carbon-free (and guilt-free) travel.

Some might say that capitalism has a limit because having been active consumers for decades, we now have all we need. Well, if you could choose to live longer, would you? If you could travel first class rather than economy, would you? Of course you would. Our ideas of comfort change. Once considered a luxury by most Britons, central heating is today seen as a necessity, and it features in 95 per cent of households.[71] The same is true of holidays. More Britons travelled abroad in 2018 than any other nationality, according to official data from the international trade body for aviation: 126.2 million passengers were British – totalling 8.6 per cent, roughly one in twelve of all international travellers.[72]

Capitalist growth has its foundations in the idea that it doesn't have an end point. However, maybe this could be enhanced with distributive targets. For instance, why doesn't government set regional economic growth targets as well as national ones?

A second reason that the idea of limits doesn't fit with capitalism is that the system is intrinsically growth-orientated. Markets don't work well in a stationary state; they are like sharks, either moving or dead. It hardly needs to be stated that to this day nobody has satisfactorily described a no-growth market-based model. It should also be noted that this idea of limited capitalism always seems to come from elite thinkers, who decide that enough is enough; many of their fellow citizens, looking up at them, might reasonably feel differently.

One of the most remarkably far-sighted (and terrifying) reports on the limits of capital growth was written in 1972. A presentation of the work of no fewer than seventeen researchers, 'The Limits to Growth' introduced the world to the concepts of resource limitation,

atmospheric carbon and global warming, arguing that the deple-
tion of natural resources would stop capitalism in its tracks. It was
wrong about some key areas, such as oil reserves and consumption
and the ability of food production to scale. It was, however, right
that environmentalism would become a major political issue. Many
people today care more about handing over a better planet to their
children than having a bigger wallet.[73]

If capitalism takes to cleaning up the environment with the same
energy, enthusiasm and imagination it employed to pollute it, this
could be its finest hour. There's already plenty of evidence that it
can. In fact, it will be able to do it faster and more efficiently. Government, though, needs to do its part to incentivise and direct this.

CONCLUSION

The question now is whether the leadership can be found to change
capitalism against a backdrop of nationalism and protectionism.
This needs to be led by nations like the US and the UK, in the same
spirit that was shown during the 1930s and in the post-war years.[74]
This will require confident Bretton Woods-style thinking,[75] bringing together today's pre-eminent minds to collaborate with vision
and coordination to plan ahead. This should be an appealing area
both for Britain and for America because of the inherent trust that
accompanies their democratic systems.

Democratic political and capitalist economic systems share the
important and attractive feature of vicarious power. Every vote
counts equally. Every pound does, too. Politicians and companies
are obliged to serve *all* people, no matter who they are or what
opinions they hold. This especially applies to the young and the as
yet unborn. If we allow cynics to drain faith from the future, then
of course the system won't function for them. And what will they

be left with? The truth remains that no other economic system has delivered as much as capitalism.

If the past ten years have shown anything, it's that relatively small activist groups (e.g. Brexiteers and climate change campaigners) can have large impacts on global geopolitics and economics. As we go forward to form our country's national mission, Britain must be situationally fluent in its understanding of geopolitics and economics. We can be successful and regain competency, but we must rethink our institutions if they are going to retain popular support. Underpinning democracy and capitalism, trust is at the core of this. The British brand is one to be trusted, and this is exactly what capitalism needs if it is to have a sustainable, viable future.

10

WHAT *IS* BRITAIN?

What it means to be British is being tested again. Can Britain reinvent itself as it has so many times before? Will Britain turn inward just to solve its own problems? Is the government structured in a way that makes this possible? Capitalism has flourished and become more powerful, but democracy and political institutions have lagged, either baulking at the boundaries of the nation state or finding themselves bypassed by direct action. Will the British political system allow fresh thinking and a new age of bipartisan consensus? The analytical, drill-down, there's-only-one-right-answer approach has not saved us from capital collapse or ethical scandal. In each of these failures, Britain should recognise the opportunity to provide leadership. We've never been more dependent on those in power to make good choices, but trust is at an all-time low. Could we ever reach consensus on Britain's role in the world or even what our national missions should be? Or on what unifies us? In this final chapter, we answer these questions and draw together some of the key themes.

PIÑATA POLITICS

The world has accelerated to become fast-paced, opaque and

increasingly joined up, with complex relationships between health, economics, technology and the environment. We're being surprised more than ever.

Frustration with politics is partly about people wanting their representatives to do better. The people know how things can be done better, but the levers are out of reach for them. They want to take action, too. Hence, we've seen a rise in direct democracy: the number of referendums has shot up, with just over 600 having been held since 1973.[1] This, though, has not addressed the single great sterile political cleavage. It can be summarised thus: the left think the right is evil. The right think the left is stupid.

People on the right identify with a different set of ideas; people on the left, with a different identity. The latter really matters, because for Britain to be a challenger as outlined in Chapter 4, it must do what the competition is unwilling or unable to do. If we can't work out who 'we' are, then we'll remain a set of ever-narrower warring tribes. Both main parties know how damaging this can be.

This tribalism has defined seventy years of post-war politics. In this political knees-up, the right knee-jerks against regulation, the left against free markets. It's head versus heart played out, re-enacted, perpetuated and enshrined for the benefit of zealots on both sides. The media encourages and thrives on such conflict because it sells popcorn. It's idealism versus experience. Reds versus blues. United versus City. Beatles versus Stones. Unions versus bosses. Male versus female. North versus south. Old versus young. Rich versus poor. The net result is to focus on our differences. Without clear national missions, government presides in the form of a giant political *piñata* to be strung up and periodically pounded until the pennies pour out.

We have to think through this and be positive. This is not going to be universally welcomed. If you're trying to do good and you get criticised, well, do it anyway. Do not do it because you are right. Do it because it's the right thing to do. Bear in mind that when trying to unify, two rules apply: that no good deed goes unpunished; and the road to hell is paved with good intentions. Those organising #FestivalUK2022 will be aware of this. The *Financial Times* referred to it as 'FUK 2022', which neatly supports the points we've made earlier about the scepticism of the British. Makes you proud either way, really.[2,3]

This is not to be confused with jingoism or nationalism. Love is none of those things. The answers are not all logical. Some solutions will come from joining the dots and looking across at seemingly unrelated siloes. Is it skills a country needs or is it attitude? What is it, for instance, that gives a country confidence? More celebration of our successes would help. Britain has reinvented itself countless times, but it remains dogged by periodic bouts of pessimism and introspection.

BRITAIN'S ROLE IN THE WORLD

One of the things that haunts Britain is its role in the world. Let's deal with that here.

Addressing the West Point Military Academy in 1962, former United States Secretary of State Dean Acheson observed that 'Great Britain has lost an empire but not yet found a role'.[4] In an age of worlds, it was calculated to wound. It did, but not in the way he intended. It said more about Acheson than it did about Britain. It was like a grandchild criticising a grandparent for their archaic argot, no longer being physically strong or wearing fashionable clothes. Like all grandparents, Britain indulged him in the fullest knowledge that the American people were, and remain, bigger than Acheson would ever become.

His comments did, however, reflect a contemporary zeitgeist. The 'world' was on everyone's minds because humanity had just emerged from half a century of 'world' conflict. You had to have a 'role'. It wasn't enough to have been on the right side. During the succeeding forty-year Cold War, despite the proximity of immediate death, *because* of the proximity of immediate death, 'world' powers plotted and manoeuvred in a way they always had but without such terminal consequences. In that particular past future, American men drove ever-bigger American rockets and ever-bigger American cars with ever-bigger American tail fins, while ever-bigger bosomed, ever-bigger beehived American women were still in charge of baking and babies. Nostalgics complain about the past never staying the same due to revisionism, but 'past' futures are no more reliable.

Wannabe Britain engaged enthusiastically in its own way. It couldn't afford real cars or even real actors, so it made toy cars and puppets that still reflected the British class system in its final death throes. Lady Penelope was driven everywhere by Parker in a not yet camp pink Rolls-Royce pregnant with explosive projectiles. He was a sort of Jeeves for the atomic age, armed with an abundance of British pluck (of course), improvisation, unfeasibly squirrel-tailed eyebrows and risible non-U pronunciation. 'Yes, Milady' became his catchphrase in response to every request from Lady P, thus powering several smutty saloon bar sniggers through the '60s. Gerry and Sylvia Anderson's Cinzano Bianco-induced optimism captured the mood.[5]

In this theatre of 'worlds', technology development was anticipated as eagerly as gender equality and racial representation weren't. Then, modernism was exciting; it meant no outside khazi, no slums, no smoke, no soot, no measles, no coal in the bath, no nits, no Victorian death-cult architecture, no immolating Havishams. It was fifty shades of filth. The really dirty version.

Modernism was bright and colourful and exciting. The world, too, was an 'exotic' word, as alien to the over-sixties then as 'bonking' is to the under-thirties now. Britain was trying its best to be exotic. Fry's Turkish Delight was exotic – 'Full of Eastern Promise'. It was made in Bristol. Old Jamaica chocolate had rum and raisins. It was made in Birmingham. Babycham, a 'champagne' perry, was made in Shepton Mallet. The Scandinavian-inspired Skol lager was from Alloa, Scotland. The single channel of commercial TV enabled customers to be cudgelled into compliance. The public were programmed with an age of slogans: 'Beanz Meanz Heinz' and 'Trebor mints are a minty bit stronger', which was much improved by the demotic rejoinder 'stick 'em up your arse and they'll last a bit longer'.

The world then meant foreign travel, jet aircraft, sangria, consequence-free sexual intercourse, rope donkeys and El Beatle. They'd seen the pa-pa pa-pa papapa Pearl & Dean ads at the movies. It meant *Any time, Any place, Anywhere / there's a wonderful world you can share / it's the bright one / it's the right one / that's Martini*. The world was the ultimate in social parenthesis. It was an enchanted, colourful youtopia beyond these cold, grey, rain-streaked, Victorian lavatory walls. The media reflected this obsession with worlds. After two world wars, it was perhaps inevitable that the franchise would be extended beyond conflict. The World Bank was born in 1944, the World Health Organization in 1948, and contestants at Miss World (1951 on) wanted an end to world poverty and a start to world peace (whatever the hell that was). The *Guinness Book of Records* was established in 1955, the World Wildlife Fund in 1961, the World Trade Center in 1970, Disney World and the World Economic Forum in

1971, UNESCO World Heritage Sites in 1972, the World Tourism Organization in 1974, the World Wide Web in 1989, *Wayne's World* in 1992 and finally the World Trade Organization in 1995. It was in advertising with *Probably the best lager in the world* (Carlsberg 1973) and *I'd like to buy the world a Coke* (itself a cover of the New Seekers' 'I'd Like to Teach the World to Sing') in 1971. British Airways told us it was *The world's favourite airline* in 1983. In entertainment, Cat Stevens (as he then was) sang 'Wild World' in 1970, David Bowie sang 'The Man Who Sold the World' in 1971 and Liza Minnelli sang 'Money Makes the World Go Round' in 1972. There was 'We Are the World', a peculiarly American anthem for Africa in 1985. Groups went on 'World Tours'.

World in Action (1963) was the sort of angry campaigning journalism that angry Ray Gosling-types would make about how angry they were. It was an unsmiling, grimy, back-to-back world of hard men with hard stares and even harder vowels. It did not feature the world. It featured gritty black-and-white stories (in every sense) about slum clearance scandals in the north of England, where evil landlords preyed on victim tenants. This was literally another world to the 'Terry and June' Home Counties. It also covered stories on what was not yet then called the Third World, way before editorialising reporters embroidered it with catastrophe.

Jeremy Isaacs' *The World at War* (1973) was a documentary series of the Second World War that wearily anticipated the start of the Third. Throughout the twenty-six instalments, Laurence Olivier delivered as many moods of melancholy as the Inuit have words for snow.[6] It was mainly made from recycled footage and quirky music, all reverse-leavened by its narrator. It was of its time.[7]

There was *Whicker's World* in 1978, where a curiously (even then) old-fashioned ex-military officer, Alan Whicker, investigated bare breasts on the beaches of Malaga and Rio in the name of 'world' reporting. Out of super-charged expenses by way of Jersey-based tax-exile status, he was equipped with an old-school tie installed beneath a detuned Murray Walker voice. *Whicker's World* was certainly possessive, but hardly definitive. Its lamentable lasting legacy lies in its contribution to the cockney rhyming slang for ladies' underwear.

Weekend World with Brian Walden made no pretence of being about the world at all. Walden was an aquiline inquisitor, ITV's answer to Robin Day. He was a Labour MP for a Birmingham constituency called All Saints, before it was demolished to make way for the international pop group of the same name. What he lacked in diction he more than made up for in dissection. He was famous for trapping Margaret Thatcher leg before wicket in a TV interview. One of the few who ever did.

In *World of Sport* (1965–85), the world was blue collar – the world of wrestling, horse racing (and betting) from Sandown Park, football (scores, never action), athletics and, er, more betting, this time from Uttoxeter. It was fronted by spoonerising Scouser Dickie Davies, who became famous for transforming Cup Soccer into Cock Sucker – another 'world' first at the time.

There were other worlds. There was an appropriately French frogman who presented *The Undersea World of Jacques Cousteau*, where your new colour telly was turned into a sort of aquarium. Gateau, chateau, Clouseau, Cointreau, Cocteau, Moreau, Cousteau – everything French was cool. (The British take on the French was summed up by Kenneth Williams singing 'Ma Crepe Suzette'.)[8] In the *Mysterious World* of Arthur C. Clarke, another former military officer dressed in a pastel safari suit navigated his way around the universe and questions about his own sexuality.

There was *Tomorrow's World*, which evangelised technology that was more promise than performance. It told us how lives would be made so much better – again technologically not socially – by ignoring the rules of what not to do on live television. This usually involved demonstrations – it worked perfectly in rehearsal – of machines that caught fire/exploded/spewed and chewed/said all the wrong things and basically became the electronic equivalent of the baby elephant on *Blue Peter*. Frustrating or deeply reassuring, depending on your age.

The world had its own newspapers – 'When *The Times* speaks, the world listens.' There was the *News of the World*, which reached sales of 8.5 million copies at its peak but contained no real news about 'the world'. Unless of course the world was 'cunt and crime', as the paper was known by some in Fleet Street, itself an expert on the twin genres.

There was the First World, a Brave New World, the Free World and the Third World, but by 1980 the world-famous world had become world-weary. As if to mark a valediction, there was the appropriately named *Disappearing World*, made by ITV. This was ostensibly about environmental change but ironically disappeared itself around 1993, when other programmes with 'World' in the title also largely disappeared.

The BBC's World Service and the Radio 4 programmes *World at One* (1967), *The World Tonight* (1970) and *Gardeners' World* (1968) are the survivors of the age of worlds. In Britain, age and affection are linear relationships.

The concept of the world came to symbolise an optimistic, sunny horizon for so many – a place in which everything was possible. You could go up in the world with Trans World Airlines. The world was your lobster (Arthur Daly c.1979). There was no British disease, no industrial decline, no three-day week, no class system, just an over-whelming excitement at modernity and possibility. Why? Because the imminent threat of destruction had made an unambiguous world with defined edges and no moral relativism. It was a simpler time. It was an age before confusion. The world was emerging, fun and there to be tasted.

The age of worlds has come to an end. An age of values has now begun. Geography has been eclipsed by technology, simplicity by complexity, resources by ideas, and trust has become the world's scarcest commodity.

THE RISING THREAT OF TOTALITARIANISM

Of course, there are many issues that Britain faces, but one, above all others, that threatens life on this planet. This is the rise of more totalitarian regimes that stamp out free speech, invade other countries and annexe swathes of ocean to call their own. These are the regimes which deny truths, violate treaties, engage in espionage to steal scientific and industrial secrets, and seek to undermine free religious worship with the threat of imprisonment. Countries that arrest young political representatives and sentence them to hard labour need to understand that not only will this approach fail, but all attempts to destroy democracy by totalitarianism will fail. What are they afraid of? Ideas? If Britain was looking for a cause to defend then it is the same one it has always defended – freedom and de-mocracy. We take this all for granted, but it has been won in living memory and at great cost.

Acheson was wrong. Britain doesn't need to worry about its role in the world; it just needs to be itself. Economist Paul Collier points out that some of Britain's main problems come down to self-confidence: 'As a country, Britain should have a greater sense of ambition. It should stop selling itself short by allowing the nation's narrative to be dominated by negative individuals and groups with no belief in the true potential of its people.'9

In his books, Collier looks at how we can restore ethics to the state, the firm, the family and the world, and create an inclusive society. There was a time when politicians grasped problems and came up with practical solutions, but somehow the ethical foundations of social democracy became corroded. What started in the cooperative movement of the nineteenth century grew into a great understanding of why we should act in our mutual interests.

The post-war cultural shift weakened obligations. Of employers to employees. Of citizens to society. Of capitalists to capitalism. Of debate to democracy. The dark cloud of the pandemic may have a silver lining of relearned lessons. That the hospital is the centre of society. That the school matters as much as the stock market. That neighbours make the neighbourhood. That science is superior to superstition. That money should never be the only reason for undertaking a task. That one day all of us will be a minority. That the people's purpose is not just personal profit.

Our country can change its narratives, laws, taxes and benefits to restore the ethical family and firm. We can create the common space in which to communicate (we've tried to do so in this book). We can rid ourselves of the divisive narratives of belonging that claim national identity for some to the exclusion of others. Communicating this commonality should be at the core of our future leadership. Shared identity and common purpose are the foundation for the far-sighted mutuality found in social welfare systems. Shared values are the basis of the obligations to others. We are not defined just by what we do but who we collectively are.

For the country to recover its ethical bearings, it needs to rebuild trust by modernising its institutions to be more respected. The last word to Collier: 'We can do better: we once did so, and we can do it again.'

HOW DO WE REINVENT US?

The problem with national division is that it poisons all levels. If everyone and every idea is seen as red or blue, then reinvention is impossible. Cooperation and collaboration need goodwill. In the aftermath of the Conservative victory and Labour humiliation at the end of 2019, both sides need to work at bringing the country together, especially the winners. We need a sort of mini-Marshall Plan to provide aid to the peripheries of the UK. It needs generosity, imagination and a genuine affection for the people.

Human imagination and goodwill must be the standard for public services, not the limits of the Treasury. And so, these qualities must be applied to its funding. Whitehall encourages low expectations. It's not focused on the citizen as a customer. It can identify problems; but solutions? That's a bit trickier. Civil servants want to be responsible only for what they can control, so they prefer to be judged on their activities rather than on the unpredictable outcomes. That's not to say public servants aren't interested in social care. Many are. They also have a stake in it. But who wants targets knowing you will probably miss them? It's not career enhancing.

In order to tackle problems, Whitehall creates activity. It runs pilots and creates steering committees. It will set up a grants programme to learn from sites across the UK. There will be roundtables and taskforces. But the result of short-term budgeting, political flux and the lack of a national mission has been to reduce Whitehall to something demeaning: a displacement activity. We need national missions to turn the ambiguity into ambition and practical reality, in part because government resources can't deliver on it alone.

Today, the more government departments are involved in an issue, the less likely it is to be resolved. This is a reason pensioners, the disabled and the abused suffer: they fall between departments of local government, education, health and work. The departments are designed to look after their own areas. They don't necessarily fix the problem. If reinvention is required, it must start with joining things up.

IS IT BECAUSE GOVERNMENT IS JUST TOO BIG?

Listed below are the world's Top 10 companies, alongside the UK and US governments, together with the number of people they employ.[10] Don't forget this is revenues, not market capitalisation. Apple has $265 billion of revenues[11] but a market cap of $1.3 trillion[12] (to find this you multiply the number of the company's shares by its price and you get a much more accurate estimation of the company's value). In comparison with Apple, Walmart has revenues of $524 billion and a market capitalisation of $432 billion.[13] It makes more in terms of revenue but is worth less as a company. Apple is the other way round.

Anyway, the point is that Walmart has a clear operating structure, with a business plan and annual report.[14] Of course, the UK government is not a business, but it could still produce a clear plan, a set of national missions and a discussion of the problems faced, just like every other large organisation across the globe.

	2020 revenues	Headcount
Walmart	$524,000,000	2,200,000
Sinopec	$407,000,000	400,000
State Grid China	$384,000,000	913,000

China Petroleum	$379,000,000	4,00,000
Shell	$352,000,000	83,000
Saudi Aramco	$330,000,000	79,000
BP	$283,000,000	70,000
Amazon	$280,000,000	1,200,000
Toyota	$275,000,000	360,000
US government	$3,500,000,000	20,200,000
UK government	$850,000,000	5,424,000

As the table shows, the UK government is big, but not that much bigger than some of the largest companies and not so big that it can't be managed in a more business-like way. Not like a business – in a more business-like manner. For instance, if governments could offer up clear, articulated visions for their countries, investors could be presented with a more investable, business-like approach. It would bring together clarity of purpose and planning, so third-party groups could easily see areas of mutual interest. Large organisations are waking up to the requirement to show value beyond the bottom line. Why haven't governments set the standards for delivery and given them a geographic or sector focus? This might also act as a signal for the third-sector providers.

WHO ARE 'WE'?

'If you believe you are a citizen of the world, you are a citizen of nowhere.' When Theresa May uttered these words at the Tory Party conference in 2016, there was uproar. The then Prime Minister was targeting the liberal establishment, who flit from Mayfair to Monaco, from Davos to Doha; those in positions of power, who, as May put it, 'behave as though they have more in common with international elites than with the people down the road'.[15]

But for another group, May's words resonated. These are the

people identified by David Goodhart.[16] It is those who feel genu-inely rooted in their communities, who feel the strongest sense of solidarity with those who share their history, language and other elements of a common culture. These people often feel that they are sneered at as nationalists, or worse as bigots, by those who do not understand that the nation state is the natural expression of a group identity. This is of course deeply personal, but universal stuff. Everyone has an identity, but it seems this is no longer a matter of fact; it's increasingly a matter of personal choice.

In his book *The Once and Future Liberal*, Mark Lilla points out that there can be no liberal politics without a sense of 'we'.[17] But what if the only thing we share is citizenship? Likewise, in *Prosperity Without Growth*, Tim Jackson notes that it is incumbent on us to set aside tribalism in the search for solutions.[18] To take a leaf out of Deng Xiaoping's notebook – who cares what colour the cat is as long as it catches mice?[19]

THE BRITISH BRAND

As we have noted throughout this book, trust is at the core of Brit-ain's role in the world. This points to moral leadership in promoting and arguing for human rights, democracy, fairness and justice. But it should also be vested in compassion and care, for instance with a revitalised and robust third sector that leads by example. It should be about cultural leadership in exporting our brand and our values, not just in arts and culture but in enterprise and innovation. It should be about leadership in climate change, too, both by example and by global cooperation.

The key to this, then, is recognising that focusing solely on our-selves is the road to hell. It's about the values shared by humanity and about what Britain offers in this cause to the world. It's what makes us greater together than on our own. Britain is at its greatest when it's pointed outwards at collective goals and in so doing meets its internal goals, too. If we're true to ourselves, our domestic and geopolitical goals should align. In any case, the latter cannot be achieved without the former.

The GREAT campaign[20] is the government's most ambitious and consistent international marketing campaign, promoting the very best the whole nation has to offer, in order to encourage the world to visit, study in and do business with the UK. The campaign is highly visible and is active in 144 countries. It attracts partnership and ambassadorship and generates significant returns. The campaign brings it all together – our culture, our heritage, our creativity, our science and tech, our countryside, our universities and schools, our businesses and our exports. It has led to a greater awareness and understanding of who the British are everywhere in the world except Britain.

SYMBOLS OF IDENTITY

It is a great mistake to dismiss and belittle patriotism in this country, because to do so insults our sense of identity. Politicians should beware: the issue even cost Labour MP Emily Thornberry her job in 2014 when she tweeted a photo of a house in Rochester adorned with English flags.[21] Flags extoll the merits of belonging. They require no literacy. They are, in a modern sense, accessible. They are also a construct of an age of belonging and identity.

The British flag is unusual in many respects. Like other flags it uses colour and shape to tell its story. However, it is three flags in one.

At its core is a vertical red cross on a white background. This symbolises both the courage and purity of St George. He is thought to have been a high-ranking Christian officer in the Roman army killed around 303AD.[22] The Roman Emperor Diocletian had him tortured to make him deny his faith. William Shakespeare was born and died on St George's Day (23 April) in 1564 and 1616, respectively. The red cross is superimposed onto the diagonal cross of St Patrick, patron saint of Ireland.

Another big constituent of the flag is the Saltire, Scotland's national flag. Legend has it the flag originated in battle. An army of Picts fought a larger force of Angles and Saxons under King Athelstan. The Picts' King led prayers for deliverance and a cloud formation of a white saltire appeared against a blue sky. (The apostle St Andrew, the brother of St Peter, had been crucified on a diagonal cross.) The king vowed that if, with the saint's help, he gained the victory, Andrew would thereafter be the patron saint of Scotland.

The flag of Wales is the Red Dragon (*Y Ddraig Goch*). It is based on an old royal badge used by British kings and queens since Tudor times. The flag is claimed to be the oldest national flag still in use. It is not represented because Wales was part of the Kingdom of England when the Union flag was designed.

Altogether, the British flag is a graphic emblem of England's union with Scotland and Northern Ireland. Its correct name is the Union Flag, except in Canada, where it's known as the Royal Union Flag, and when it's on a ship, in which case it is known as the Union Jack. Wales is not represented. But somehow this doesn't matter. Why not? The meaning of the flag is that we're stronger when we stand together, when we focus on what unites us. Many feed on division for their own ends, but you can't lead with hatred. Every group is diverse. Leadership's job is to unite people in a common cause. The flag does this graphically. The Queen embodies it, too. She wears tartan; her son is the Prince of Wales, who learned to speak Welsh ahead of his investiture address; her husband is the

Duke of Edinburgh; one of her sons is named after the patron saint of Scotland. Globally, she remains the most popular and respected royal on earth.[23] She's dignified, dedicated, hard-working, selfless and long-suffering. She's the longest-reigning of any monarch and remains the only current head of state to have served in the Second World War. 'She's played a blinder,' as Danny Dyer might put it.

Across the globe, flags command respect and love – but we should acknowledge that, perhaps strangely, this is not so for the British flag. At least not universally. Depending on your view, discussion of the flag can invite suspicion of nationalism or patriotism. There are xenophobes and racists who wrap themselves up in it. But these plastic patriots know nothing of British culture and history. If you love a shared set of values and you're prepared to work and fight for them, who cares what your gender, ethnicity or religion is? Most of us don't have flags or statues in our homes. We have values. That's what we should be fighting for.

Maybe it would help if British organisations fought for it, too? But it's no longer fashionable. The BBC used to respect the union daily in its 'UK Theme', which was played on Radio 4 every morning between 23 November 1978 and 23 April 2006, immediately followed by the shipping forecast. The tune included excerpts from 'Danny Boy', 'What Shall We Do With the Drunken Sailor?', 'Scotland the Brave', 'Rule Britannia', 'Men of Harlech', 'Greensleeves', 'Londonderry Air' and 'Early One Morning'. It was an orchestral arrangement of traditional British and Irish airs. The five-minute theme was composed by a Jewish refugee, Fritz Spiegl, who came to the UK in 1939 after his family fled fascist persecution. It was a love song to those that took him in. It was terminated by the BBC on St George's Day, 23 April 2006. It was a move designed by its timing to hurt. It did.

The decision to drop the theme was made by the controller of Radio 4 at the time, Mark Damazer, to make way for what he said would be a faster news briefing. But why the timing? It was done without notice or consultation. It caused controversy in the British media, and even in Parliament. Prime Minister Tony Blair was urged to intervene on behalf of the theme. In response, he joked: 'Obviously, my influence with the BBC is legendary. But I know they will be aware of the very strong feeling that is expressed by you and by many others, I am sure, in the House and across the country.'[24]

Labour MP Austin Mitchell told the station's *Today* programme the BBC was 'crazy' to want to drop the theme. What he then went on to say could have been said of the union itself: 'It's very cleverly welded together. For most people, it isn't an everyday experience. Each time it comes with a fresh joy, the shock of the new. It's lovely.'[25]

Then *Newsnight* presenter Jeremy Paxman also criticised the decision: 'We've no idea what the head of Radio 4's playing at – we're thinking of using it every night,' he told viewers.[26]

Damazer later admitted the mistake. He had misread a report and thought mere hundreds of people were listening at 5.30 a.m., rather than hundreds of thousands. Still, the decision was not reversed. Damazer later stood down after six years in charge of Radio 4 to become head of St Peter's College, Oxford. He has always defended his decision to axe the medley, though he later admitted to underestimating listener sensitivities: 'I don't regret it but I think I underestimated the fact that I was causing some people considerable pain,'[27] he said unconvincingly.

If you don't invest in relationships, can you be surprised if they atrophy? The 'UK Theme' was exactly that sort of investment. You'd think the BBC would get this. It has nested identities, too; it can be

Scottish, British and European all at the same time. Just like the rest of us.

THE BRITISH IDEA

At its heart, the British Idea is no more than a collection of multiple universal values, shared experiences and aspirations. British thinking always was international and outward-looking, because Britain was America *before* America. And perhaps British ideas are so exportable because so many of them came from elsewhere.

Always spreading and developing the rule of law, the British Idea has outlived the dictatorships. It has soared above communism. Why should a country with a thousand years of unbroken sovereignty take lessons from any other governmental system? If it's going to listen to criticism, let it be constructive. Let it be from within.

We face new threats, that much is clear. The biggest threat of all, though, is not the Russians or Daesh, but potentially our own political thinking in military matters. Throughout history it's been the same. The stagnation of the Western Front in the First World War; the folly of fixed defences in the Second World War; the move from air-launched, strategic deterrents to submarine-based ones; the combined services operations in recovering the Falkland Islands. For each generation, the lesson must be learned: our forces implement our political thinking on the battlefield. If that thinking is outdated, then strategy, doctrine and weapons will be, too. When we're not operating in a 'hot' era, we lose the emphasis on adaption and innovation. We must ensure that even in 'cooler' times, we continue to learn and drive towards becoming even more effective and prepared for what the future holds.

There are some who say the military should not have a political point of view. But it is naive to believe it doesn't, especially of those that put their lives at risk for their country. Democracy is, after all, what they're fighting for. They defend us. All of us. And the deal is that we defend them in return. That's why there's no room for injustice in the way the military is treated: they must be defended from spurious, commercially motivated legal claims.

British forces may not be political, but they are geopolitical. They defend the rule of law, they defend the rights of the individual against the system, they defend the weak against the bully, they defend the flag and they are prepared to die for it. Remember this the next time you criticise them.

SERVICE

'What does love look like? It has the hands to help others. It has the feet to hasten to the poor and needy. It has eyes to see misery and want. It has the ears to hear the sighs and sorrows of men. That is what love looks like.'

St Augustine

This is not necessarily about the Christian ethos. It is about the primacy of the heart. It's the idea that there is something indivisible or infinite. A custodial responsibility for our time here. If science is driven to divide us, then divinity seeks singularity. St Augustine of Hippo embraced this notion. By focusing solely on our own needs, we are directed inwards, but St Augustine pointed out that at the heart of man there existed a 'God-shaped hole', a desire for fulfilment that no amount of money, food, sex and drugs could ever fill. If we were to go looking for true leaders, they would not be those acting for personal gain; they would be those acting in service.

Why does Britain have so many charities? Is it compassion? Empathy? Guilt, even? What was it that motivated Sir Bob Geldof to found Live Aid? The cynical mind might accuse him of career opportunism, but that would not have sustained such an enterprise. The notion that artists in a notoriously competitive and cut-throat industry would cooperate was ridiculed. But it worked. It was a big idea and it grew bigger. The resulting concerts raised £150 million for those in need in Ethiopia.[28] This sort of cause unifies; it brings people together for a higher reason; it motivates and it removes division.

This is not confined to rock stars, though. The whole of Britain has a big heart. Why does all this happen? What is it that causes people to work together in such a way? Many complain that it is a weak-minded government that encourages overseas aid, but government, in many instances, is just following the people's lead. It's not the other way round.

Big ideas don't come from the head. There are stirring, all-powerful, unstoppable, popular movements more powerful than logic. To do something for others is the antidote to so-called rational behaviour. Economic theory would have it that we behave rationally: we earn money so we can spend it – why would we give it away? That's not logical. But truly great ideas transcend logic: we *know* the best course of action. Have you ever just known something to be true? Or has everything had to be proven to you? If you decide to do the morally right thing, is that just logic? Or is it something more powerful? This is what St Augustine was driving at. Great thinking is not just logical; it is *intuitive*.

This philosophy is at the heart of enduring institutions. They may inhabit grand buildings, but above all else they represent values. Britain has a 'to do' list but should remember that it can't *do* reassuring, inspiring or visionary; it can only *be* them. Great thinking involves having a clear set of values, knowing what you stand for, knowing who you are and knowing that you are not here only for yourself. It is enough to serve.

The logical mind asks questions like: What do you want to achieve in your life? Where do you want to be in five years? What will you do in the first six months? We ask these questions of our leaders, too. But we do not ask who they are. Why not?

So, let's apply this to the question of who we are as a nation. If we ask logically, it will probably describe us or tell us about our history. Language and location will also come into it. It might tell us what we own or how we rank against others, as we saw in Chapter 2. It might throw out some numbers: GDP, the size of the economy, population, industries, ethnicities and contributions. But logic will never talk about values. The point of this book is to say that we need to remember our values: again, it's not what we're here to do, it's about who we are.

Service and compassion are the provenance of one part of great thinking. What might these ideas illuminate about our values? Those who care for others are not just in it for themselves; they see further, they see connections and they are there to do good. Ultimately, they know that the pursuit of logic alone might lead to unfair outcomes.

THE MADNESS OF DEMOCRACY

To consider democracy, we must first address the fact that we give our mandate to individuals who might be grossly under-qualified for the role. The job of MP is open to anyone aged eighteen years or above. You need to pass no test and you don't have to be a registered elector or even live in the country. You can be a drunk and you can be bankrupt. Member of Parliament is the one profession that requires no professional qualifications. In fact, the role is open to absolutely anyone *except* those with certain qualifications. Those who cannot stand to be MPs include the following: those convicted for more than a year, civil servants, judges, serving members of the military, police constables, bishops, government-nominated directors of companies, Lords Lieutenant, high sheriffs and the poor old governor of the Isle of Wight.[29]

Next, we allow voters to decide whether they're actually going to vote or not. Some countries, like Australia, actually fine people for not voting.[30] There are others who think not all votes should be equal, or, more specifically, that some people's votes should count for more. François Fillon, Prime Minister of France from 2007 to 2012, declared that the young should have two votes, for example. Jacqueline Fehr, a Swiss Social Democrat politician, proposed extending this double dipping to anyone aged between eighteen and forty.[31] Many asking for a second referendum openly justified their ask because, they said, only the stupid or gullible could have voted for Brexit. There are some who think we should stop 'stupid people' voting. In a piece entitled 'Should We Stop Dumb People from Voting?', Stephen Masty said:

The universal franchise, whereby every adult can vote who wishes to, is a ticket to the asylum. It is, to borrow a phrase from PJ O'Rourke, 'like giving your dog a credit card'. So how can we stop it before it is too late? Unfortunately, it may already be too late. Not only do our morons vote, in numbers roughly equalling the rest, but mob rule expands daily; as every outraged tweet or text from unidentified people who may be hydrocephalic is quoted as a legitimate news source, ranking alongside of the dean of Washington's National Cathedral, a well-informed scholar or even a professional football player who is at least a known entity. So, if we wish to cut the idiots out of democracy we need their approval. That can be done. One fact about idiots is they are not very bright.[32]

One person's idiot is another's genius, and 'bright' and 'stupid' are about as useful as 'good' and 'evil' when it comes to classifications. We may not be able to allow definitions of bright and stupid, but until recently, mental illness was a different category. In 2012, MPs voted to end discrimination that stopped the mentally ill serving in public life. This came via a rare Private Members' Bill introduced by then Conservative backbencher (now Lord) Gavin Barwell and it was backed by the House of Commons. It also relaxed the rules on jury selection and company directorships as they apply to mental illness. In a rare show of unity in the House of Commons, the Mental Health (Discrimination) Bill was passed without a vote. Those with mental illness also have opinions and perspective and experience which we value.

Some could easily say that it's stupid to allow crowds to make a decision. Crowds do really dumb things and they are often made up of stupid people who don't listen. Surely logic would dictate that only the highly educated should be allowed to decide great matters of state? You know, the sort of matters that really, erm, *matter*. Like life and death. Like everything you've ever worked for. Like all you believe in – the greatest risk possible. It's almost inconceivable that the great institutions of state would even contemplate such stupidity. These are the people we trust everything to, and they risk it all. Democracy is a ridiculous process participated in by people who, in many cases, couldn't even name the policies or personnel of the party to which they give their vote. The voters are people who bet on horses or who go to Blackpool for their holidays. People who get drunk. People who don't read *The Guardian*. People who can't answer a single question on *University Challenge*. Members of the English Defence League and Tommy Robinson supporters. People who watch *Strictly*. Who don't listen to Radio 3. Or, horrifyingly, even Radio 4. It doesn't bear scrutiny. It's not logical, it's not sensible, but it is more durable than any other system humans have yet tried. Why? Because it means, ultimately, that we trust each other as equals. It is the ultimate in mutuality.

Totalitarianism cannot understand this. In order to ensure proper equality, there are some that must ordain it. It is a system built on the logic of dominance, on the threat of compliance or violence. It does not recognise consent – or even its sister, consensus. Fascism celebrates Darwinian theory. Nazism thrived on the logic that strength should prevail, that dissent was disease and that the weak were worthless. It had no compassion. It had no empathy. It had no law. It was built on vectored hate. This is the paradox at the heart of fascism and its bundle of sticks. The sticks may be weak, and bundling them may make them feel stronger, but they're sticks. They're not people. People are not sticks to be bundled. If they are weak, they're not made stronger by trimming them all to the same length. Their diversity and weakness *is* their strength. Democracy is a great idea. It lives in *e pluribus unum*. Out of the many, come one. It lives in *Honi soit qui mal y pense*: evil be to him that evil thinks.

This idea is as hard to grasp as it is to live by the values. But it's like the Union: if we don't celebrate or recognise it, then we can easily lose it. The point of values is that you can't achieve them. You have to regularly demonstrate them. To exist, they need to be shown regularly in who you are, showing that you're prepared to keep shared values alive from one generation to the next. One such example is the Battle of Britain Memorial Flight (BBMF). Every year, these old aircraft are kept flying in air shows in what could be considered a tremendous waste of money. It costs millions of pounds. Logically, the aircraft don't contribute to the defence of the realm. You can describe a Lancaster in a book, you can even see it in movies. You can gain knowledge about its payload, wingspan and aerial capabilities. But without seeing it for yourself, you will not understand it, or what the sky looked like when filled with hundreds of them, or how vulnerable they appear to be or how small they are when compared with a Boeing 747.

The BBMF is not a collection of aircraft; it is a flying set of values. It goes beyond logic and beyond money. It doesn't belong to Britain; it represents British values. Yes, ingenuity. Yes, technology. Yes, logistical know-how. But the qualities we all admire, too, like courage, selflessness and service. Such values are why people served this country in the past, it's why they serve today and why they will continue to do so in the future. It is an idea and it's more powerful than any weapon yet devised.

We remember yesterday to remind us of who we are today. We have grandparents to tell us where we've been, but this history can also tell us where we're going. This is not a physical destination but a set of values. The country does not go anywhere. Half of its success is in standing for what it has always stood for. This is the great tension between what a country does and what it actually is.

Fine words butter no parsnips. You can't feed people on philosophy, so we'd better find some practicalities. Our values need to be baked into national missions, not just to do and achieve things, but to amplify what we are. To signal what we're trying to achieve so everyone can lend their help. Because what lies ahead is a battle of ideas every bit as big as we've seen in the past, but hopefully without such disastrous consequences. No one ever persuades the other side with force, only with shared values.

CONCLUSIONS

Great thinking still resides in Britain today, and in the next decade it will be highly visible both at home and abroad as other countries watch what we do with our new freedom. We seldom stop to think about who we are, but this point in history should be one of those moments. To be born in Britain is still to win the lottery of life. We should recognise there are freedoms and privileges granted to us that are denied to so many. We should have self-respect, we should be proud of our people and our processes, but we should not be complacent.

There is serious work to be done. We need to modernise our democracy. We need to modernise so many areas. We need to become less amateur, especially in public administration. We need to do more with less (we're actually quite good at that). We need to behave in a way that will make our children proud. But in spite of all this need for change, there is much for us to laugh at, too.

We're not better than the rest of humanity, but if we collectively recognise the opportunities just ahead, we can showcase the very best of it. What does it mean, for example, to be free? What practical benefits does it have? This is where St Augustine again is at his finest. Because freedom is connected with trust. If someone is free to make the choice not to help you, and yet they still choose to, you can draw conclusions about that person. Without freedom, there can only be compulsion and coercion; without freedom, there can be no dissent – this is tantamount to admitting that the provenance of good ideas is uniquely in the state or the controlling power, rather than in individuals. This is to deny human nature. It is to deny the human spirit. Without freedom, individuals are denied their potential. It is inefficient, of course. And it is also only ever temporary. The human spirit can be suppressed – history is peppered with examples of this – but it can never be denied. Britain has used its freedom well.

The British are creative, compassionate, intelligent, hard-working, educated and funny. No other country has done as much to defend freedom and free speech. It has bankrupted itself to defend its democratic values. The money expended bought something priceless – integrity and trust in the post-war environment. This was the platform on which the country transformed itself with imagination and determination and became a beacon of capitalism and democracy. Britons risked their lives for this country. Now people routinely risk their lives to get into Britain by any means. If America is ever again temporarily unwilling or unable to lead, then the nations of the earth can rely upon Britain to uphold the combined values of humanity. Its people on the balance of probability turn out to have heroism stamped into their souls. Sometimes these are the heroes who win medals. Sometimes they are heroes who lie unadorned in northern France. Sometimes they are the everyday heroes no one notices. If you're a politician in the making, do not make your heroes Marx or Engels or Thatcher or Ayn Rand: make them those that no one ever notices or remembers because, in reality, that's where you'll find the majority of heroism.

With a rich and detailed past which catalogues the experience of humanity and distils it into one language, one experience, one view, Britain stands ready for whatever the future has in store. How can anyone be so sure about this? Because no other nation has done it for so long, so consistently and contributed so much to the advance of humanity. Britain doesn't always *do things right*, but if you had to gamble on any nation and place your trust in it to *do the right thing*, then this attitude, this country, these people would be top of the list.

Our greatest narratives are the forces of the individual versus the incumbent. The more we looked, the more we saw. It's in our movies, our minorities, our songs, our books, our daily newspapers, our heroes and our villains. Freedom is the optimal human condition, philosophically, morally, economically, emotionally. To deny it is to guarantee failure because it removes hope. Individuals who create hope have been among the greatest of the great thinkers. Perhaps, then, this is the very definition of what it means to become greater. It bestows, promotes, preserves and amplifies hope.

Some British citizens are the best in the world at what they do. Many of them are 'routine' heroes and deserve respect and celebration. They live in a country where the present is no longer predictable, where the past just won't sit still any more and where the future has been constrained by Covid. These are difficult times, but nothing compared with what previous generations faced. They fought for freedom, not just for them but for the whole of humanity. You can face anything with freedom. It is the light through which the human soul sees and it is the very essence of us.

SURPRISING FACTS

- Britain is the most attractive country for young people across the G20.[1]
- Britain ranks fifth of the World's Top Nations, according to US News & World Report.[2]
- Britain is the largest recipient of investment in Europe (and Top 3 globally).[3]
- Britain is the fifth biggest exporter in the world.[4]
- Britain is the fifth most innovative country, according to the Global Innovation Index.[5]
- Britain is the largest exporter of financial services in the world.[6]
- The British pound sterling is the oldest currency still in use in the world.[7]
- The NHS is the fifth largest employer in the world.[8]
- The NHS is ranked No. 1 healthcare system in the eleven wealthiest countries.[9]
- Britain is the largest foreign investor in America.[10]
- Britain is the home of global motorsport.[11]
- Britain has the highest grossing football league in the world.[12]
- Britain is the global leader for professional maritime services.[13]

- Britain is the fifth largest military power.[14]
- Britain ranks in the Top 10 with thirty-two UNESCO World Heritage Sites.[15]
- Britain reduced carbon emissions more than any G20 country in three years.[16]
- Britain leads the world in renewable energy through offshore wind.[17]
- Britain has the largest aviation hub in the world.[18]
- London has the second most highly rated public transport system in the world.[19]
- London has more Indian restaurants that Mumbai and Delhi combined.[20]
- Britain leads the world in animal welfare standards.[21]
- Britain has four of the top ten universities, according to the QS survey of Top Universities.[22]
- Britain ranks best country in the world for education, according to Study International.[23]
- Britain has half of the top ten law firms.[24]
- Britain leads the world in 'soft power'.[25]
- Britain ranks sixth (above America) as one of the best countries in which to live in the world.[26]
- Britain is listed among the top ten most charitable nations and overseas aid donors.[27]
- Sixty-four per cent of British people volunteered for a charity in 2018.[28]
- British people spend more money shopping online than any other nation.[29]
- The British Library is the largest in the world.[30]
- The British government is the most transparent and open with its data.[31]

- Britain has the world's oldest scientific academy, the Royal Society, with 1,600 fellows.[32]
- Britain has the second largest number of Nobel laureates.[33]
- Britain has only ever had one Prime Minister with a science degree, Margaret Thatcher.[34]
- London has ranked as the World's Best City for the past five years.[35]
- Britain has the first billionaire book author, J. K. Rowling.[36]
- Britain has twelve of the top fifty bestselling recording artists of all time.[37]
- Britain has the largest theatre-going audience in the world.[38]
- Britain ranks fifth in the world for dental health (not aesthetics).[39,40]
- British people are the sixth most obese in the world.[41]
- The worst quality of the British, according to the British Council, is 'they drink too much'.[42]
- Britain is one of the worst countries in the world to live as an expat.[43]
- The House of Lords is the largest unelected parliamentary chamber of any democracy.[44]
- The 2019 general election turnout was the fifth lowest in 100 years.[45]
- Young British graduates are less likely to vote than those with no qualifications.[46]

A PERSONAL NOTE

By Penny Mordaunt

I wanted to write this book because Britain has given me so much. All it demands is that you pick yourself up after a setback. I've seen it bounce back from wars, from economic crises and even from the pandemic. In so many ways, the ups and downs of our country are reflected in our own lives.

This is still a country where you can rise to high office no matter where you're from. No matter that you're from a single-parent family. No matter that you become a primary carer at an early age. No matter that you work in a factory. No matter that you're from the wrong end of town. No matter that you have no connections. No matter that you have no money. No matter that no one in your family ever went to university. And no matter that you have a learning disability.

For decades, I suffered headaches and tripped over words. Reading was an ordeal. It came to a head writing this book. The intense research and drafting aggravated the symptoms. Experts performed a number of tests and diagnosed dyslexia. While it was a shock, it was also a relief. I am grateful to everyone who works and helps combat this condition. When I left office in 2019, I wanted to write this book to learn more about my country. In so doing, I also learned more about myself.

ACKNOWLEDGEMENTS

Thanks go to Sarah Aitchison, Sarah Aitchison and Sarah Aitchison, Sir Ben Ainslie, Helen Alderson, Beth Armstrong, Mohamed Amersi, Kate Andrews, Lord Ashcroft, Anne Aslett, Admiral Sir Jonathon Band, Sir Michael Barber, Olivia Beattie, Sue Beavis, Sinclair Beecham, Simon 'Bilbo' Billington, Professor Jeremy Black, George Blacklock, Tony Blair, Yvonne van Bokhoven, Irena Boostani, Liam Booth, Sir Graham Brady, Professor David Brown, Richard Johnstone-Bryden, Sir Stephen Bubb, Alex Burghart, Alistair Burt, Major-General Nick Caplin, Dr Juan Castañeda, Alex Chisholm, Viv Church, Celia Clark, Professor Paul Collier, Professor Sir Cary Cooper, Phyllis Costanza, Michael Crone, John Cullen, Richard Curtis, Iain Dale, Ruth Davidson, Edward Davies, Professor Francis Davis, Mrs Margaret Dawson (Mrs D), Lord Michael Dobbs of Wylye, Umang Dokey, Bryher Dunsby, Noah Dye, Helen Ellis, Tobias Ellwood MP, Dame Carolyn Fairbairn, Simon Finkelstein, Ken Ford, Professor Russell Foster, Steve Frampton, Gemma Freeman, George Freeman, Andrea Fuller, Bill Gates, Alan Gemmell, Michael Gove, Peter Pereira Gray, Baroness Sally Greengross, Josh Grimstone, Chris Heaton-Harris, Trudie Harrison,

Lord Peter Hennessy, Neil Heslop, Karin von Hippel, Asif Husain, Christina Ioannou, Lucinda Jamieson, Sir Elton John, the Rt Hon. Boris Johnson MP, Ambassador Robert 'Woody' Johnson, Sir Robin Knox-Johnston, Edmund King, Gerard LaFond, Cherylyn Harley LeBon, Richard Levick, Jo Lewis, Georgia Lewis, Pip Lewis, Mark Littlewood, Jorge López, Julian Lyon, Declan Lyons, Andrew Mace, Gemma Martinblower, Martin Matthews, Jim Mattis, Lord Andrew Mawson, Dominic McVey, Ella Miller, Anne Milton, Agnieszka Mordaunt, Edward Mordaunt, James Mordaunt, John Mordaunt, Sylvia Mordaunt, John Morgan, Fallon Murray, Leslie Myrell, Robert New, Mark Norbury, Inez Odom, James Oehlcke, Isabel Oswell, James Palmer, Tony Palmer, Rear Admiral Chris Parry, Wes Paul, John Penrose, Beth Perry, Su Pollard, Alex Pomphrey, Oliver Preston, Alan Priddy, Dominic Raab, Kelly Redding, Rachel and Tim Redfern, Steven Reilly, Sir Malcolm Rifkind, the Rt Hon. Lord Robertson of Port Ellen, (the late) Sir Ken Robinson, Sarah Robinson, Jacqueline de Rojas, Jo Ruxton, Matthew Rycroft, Dominic Sandbrook, Suzanne Sangster, Sir Anthony Seldon, John Paul Schutte, Peter Shaw, Imogen Sinclair, David Skelton, Jonathan Slater, Libby Smith, Dame Cilla Snowball, Alex Stephany, James Stephens, Admiral Rob Stevens, Baroness Philippa Stroud, Will Tanner, Ellis Taylor, Julian Thompson, Bill Thornhill, Brig Gen, USAF (Ret.), Kenneth Todorov, Pamela Tor Das, Liz Truss, Francis Tusa, Andrew Tyrie, Daniel Wemyss, Hillary Werronen, the Rt Hon. Lord David Willetts, Andres Wittermann and Faril Yeo.

An independent group has been established to discuss and promote the ideas raised in this book. Please see Gogreater.org.

NOTES

PROLOGUE

1   Sadly, they themselves both disappeared in January 2021 and May 2020 from cancer and Covid respectively.
2   http://www.bbcamerica.com/anglophenia/2013/10/10-places-brits-love-to-live-in-america
3   https://www.businessinsider.com/british-expats-most-population-destinations-2015-9#4-spain--381025-expats-spain-is-still-high-on-the-list-where-brits-go-for-the-cheap-booze-sunny-weather-and-relatively-easy-integration-into-the-culture-14

INTRODUCTION

1   http://www.eiu.com/topic/democracy-index
2   https://www.economist.com/schools-brief/2018/08/04/against-the-tyranny-of-the-majority
3   https://www.carnegieuktrust.org.uk/blog/never-doubt-a-small-group-of-committed-individuals-can-change-the-world/
4   https://www.worldatlas.com/articles/highest-immigrant-population-in-the-world.html
5   https://www.weforum.org/agenda/2017/11/these-are-the-countries-migrants-want-to-move-to/
6   https://www.thetimes.co.uk/article/uk-will-fall-to-7th-in-gdp-rankings-say-experts-288h5g8qq
7   https://blogs.ncvo.org.uk/2018/07/26/new-volunteering-data-out-today/
8   https://www.cafonline.org/about-us/media-office-news/uk-is-one-of-the-top-10-most-generous-countries-in-the-world
9   https://www.topuniversities.com/university-rankings-articles/world-university-rankings/top-universities-world-2019
10 https://www.theguardian.com/science/datablog/2016/oct/08/which-countries-have-had-the-most-nobel-prize-winners
11 https://www.ft.com/content/54e31212-17f1-11e4-b842-00144feabdc0
12 https://www.theguardian.com/society/2018/jul/02/is-the-nhs-the-worlds-best-healthcare-system
13 https://www.kingsfund.org.uk/publications/whats-happening-life-expectancy-uk
14 https://www.bbc.co.uk/news/uk-47637378
15 Steven Pinker, Enlightenment Now: The Case for Reason, Science, Humanism, and Progress https://www.amazon.co.uk/Enlightenment-Now-Science-Humanism-Progress/dp/0525427570
16 https://www.youtube.com/watch?v=iXczSof201U

17 https://www.bbc.com/future/article/20161110-the-name-for-britain-comes-from-our-ancient-love-of-tattoos

18 https://medium.com/daliaresearch/who-has-the-most-tattoos-its-not-who-you-d-expect-1d5ffff66of8

19 https://www.youtube.com/watch?v=LPNH8uMbaH4

CHAPTER 1: WHO ARE WE?

1   https://www.amazon.co.uk/England-Elegy-Roger-Scruton/dp/0826480756

2   Ronnie Corbett was 5 ft 0, Charlie Drake was 5 ft 1, Dudley Moore was 5 ft 3.

3   Technically 1971.

4   https://www.chapterhousedesign.co.uk/garden-folly-kits-26-c.asp

5   Included with the kind permission of JRM himself.

6   https://www.youtube.com/watch?v=koHKquVNbnc

7   https://www.statista.com/statistics/281713/us-bars-taverns-und-nightclubs-industry-establishments/

8   https://www.christianitytoday.com/news/2017/september/how-many-churches-in-america-us-nones-nondenominational.html

9   https://www.statista.com/statistics/310723/total-number-of-pubs-in-the-united-kingdom/

10 https://www.theguardian.com/commentisfree/2015/oct/22/churches-survive-church-of-england-religion-buildings

11 https://www.google.com/search?client=firefox-b-d&q=average+life+expectancy+uk

12 https://www.seattletimes.com/nation-world/british-rail-companies-have-a-message-were-sorry-very-sorry-apologies/

13 https://yougov.co.uk/topics/lifestyle/articles-reports/2015/07/01/oh-sorry-do-british-people-apologise-too-much

14 https://www.amazon.co.uk/Watching-English-Hidden-Rules-Behaviour/dp/0340818867

15 https://www.facebook.com/watch/?v=512389702820097

16 https://www.telegraph.co.uk/finance/personalfinance/7182362/Return-of-original-Fairy-Liquid-bottle-for-John-Noakes-generation.html

17 Chaired by Victoria Coren-Mitchell, the thinking man's fentanyl.

18 https://www.imdb.com/title/tt0037367/

19 https://www.telegraph.co.uk/news/newstopics/howaboutthat/5052956/Britons-spent-six-months-queuing.html

20 https://www.telegraph.co.uk/news/newstopics/howaboutthat/5052956/Britons-spent-six-months-queuing.html

21 https://www.who.int/westernpacific/emergencies/Covid-19/information/physical-distancing

22 https://www.bbc.co.uk/news/business-52874615

23 He became big in Albania.

24 https://www.imdb.com/title/tt1083452/

25 http://www.aceldama.com/~tomr/media/dalek/blueprints/dal2_.gif

26 https://www.telegraph.co.uk/culture/tvandradio/11653529/Blakes-7-the-low-budget-late-70s-British-sci-fi-is-now-a-genuine-classic.html

27 http://www.thefa.com/football-rules-governance/lawsandrules/laws/football-11-11/law-11---offside

28 https://www.taxpayersalliance.com/new_research_the_length_of_tolley_s_tax_guides

29 https://www.britannica.com/place/London-Eye

30 https://www.telegraph.co.uk/culture/art/3574331/Pull-down-the-London-Eye.html

31 https://www.ons.gov.uk/peoplepopulationandcommunity/wellbeing/bulletins/socialcapitalintheuk/may2017

CHAPTER 2: WHAT ARE WE GOOD AT?

1   https://www.gov.uk/government/news/uks-creative-industries-contributes-almost-13-million-to-the-uk-economy-every-hour

2   https://budstars.com/martinprosperity/Global-Creativity-Index-2015.pdf

3   https://www.culturepartnership.eu/en/article/global-creativity-index-2015

4   https://www.bloomberg.com/news/articles/2020-01-18/germany-breaks-korea-s-six-year-streak-as-most-innovative-nation

5   https://www.legit.ng/1368477-uk-tops-list-top-5-countries-a-career-in.html

6   https://www.independent.co.uk/news/business/indyventure/uk-one-best-places-world-start-business-a6717886.html

7   https://www.oecd.org/social/soc/Social-mobility-2018-Overview-MainFindings.pdf

8   https://www.edp24.co.uk/news/business/salad-growers-hail-success-of-pick-for-britain-campaign-1551484

9   https://www.bbc.com/worklife/article/20200710-the-remote-work-experiment-that-made-staff-more-productive

10   http://www3.weforum.org/docs/GCR2018/05FullReport/TheGlobalCompetitivenessReport2018.pdf

11   https://www.ons.gov.uk/employmentandlabourmarket/peopleinwork/labourproductivity/articles/ukproductivityintroduction/julytoseptember2019

12   https://www.independent.co.uk/news/education/education-news/job-skills-jobs-councils-local-government-association-lga-careers-a9285371.html

13   https://www.cityam.com/skills-shortages-continue-to-hit-growth-as-uk-employers-struggle-to-find-the-right-talent/

14   http://www.oecd.org/education/skills-beyond-school/41529765.pdf

15   https://www.wired-gov.net/wg/news.nsf/articles/5+million+adults+lack+basic+literacy+and+numeracy+skills+30082016131500?open

16   https://www.telegraph.co.uk/news/2019/01/05/millions-british-adults-functionally-illiterate-problem-ignored/

17   https://www.theguardian.com/education/2019/mar/03/literacy-white-working-class-boys-h-is-for-harry

18   https://www.statista.com/statistics/275999/household-internet-penetration-in-great-britain/

19   https://www.speedtest.net/global-index

20   https://www.worldbank.org/en/publication/human-capital#data

21   https://www.usnews.com/news/best-countries/articles/2020-01-15/us-trustworthiness-rating-dives-in-2020-best-countries-report

22   https://www.accountancydaily.co/uk-ranked-eighth-world-ease-doing-business

23   https://www.ipsos.com/sites/default/files/ct/publication/documents/2019-09/ipsos-thinks-trust-the-truth.pdf

24   https://www.cafonline.org/docs/default-source/about-us-publications/caf_wgi2018_report_webnopw_2379a_261018.pdf?sfvrsn=c28e9140_4

25   https://www.sciencealert.com/the-most-empathetic-countries-in-the-world-have-just-been-ranked

26   https://worldjusticeproject.org/our-work/wjp-rule-law-index/wjp-open-government-index/global-scores-rankings

27   https://ceoworld.biz/2018/02/14/the-top-25-countries-with-the-best-healthcare-systems-the-world-in-2017/

28   https://newsroom.fmglobal.com/releases/fm-global-unveils-updated-country-rankings-in-the-2019-fm-global-resilience-index

29   https://www.countryliving.com/uk/wildlife/countryside/news/a2467/britain-funniest-country-europe-new-survey/

30   https://www.weforum.org/agenda/2016/02/which-countries-are-most-optimistic/

31   http://www.emmc-imae.org/wp-content/uploads/Map-of-countries-where-English-is-an-official-language.pdf

32   https://www.usnews.com/news/best-countries/slideshows/10-countries-that-are-most-connected-to-the-world-ranked-by-perception?slide=10

33   https://assets.publishing.service.gov.uk/government/uploads/system/uploads/attachment_
      data/file/340601/bis-13-1082-international-education-accompanying-analytical-narrative-
      revised.pdf

34   https://www.usnews.com/news/best-countries/power-rankings

35   https://www.prosperity.com/rankings

36   https://www.ons.gov.uk/peoplepopulationandcommunity/wellbeing/bulletins/
      measuringnationalwellbeing/april2019tomarch2020

37   https://www.bbc.com/news/uk-41901297

38   https://www.usnews.com/news/best-countries/best-green-living

39   https://assets.publishing.service.gov.uk/government/uploads/system/uploads/attachment_
      data/file/48128/2167-uk-renewable-energy-roadmap.pdf

40   https://www.iqair.com/blog/report-over-90-percent-of-global-population-breathes-
      dangerously-polluted-air

41   https://www.gov.uk/government/publications/25-year-environment-plan

42   http://worldpopulationreview.com/countries/murder-rate-by-country/

43   https://metro.co.uk/2018/08/31/uks-safest-and-most-dangerous-cities-are-
      revealed-7901267/

44   https://www.ons.gov.uk/peoplepopulationandcommunity/crimeandjustice/articles/
      domesticabuseprevalenceandtrendsenglandandwales/yearendingmarch2019

45   https://www.cps.gov.uk/sites/default/files/documents/publications/CPS-Hate-Crime-
      Annual-Report-2018-2019.PDF

46   https://www.tuc.org.uk/news/disability-pay-gap-day-disabled-people-work-2-months-
      year-free-says-tuc

47   https://www.gov.uk/government/publications/national-lgbt-survey-summary-report/
      national-lgbt-survey-summary-report

48   https://www.cps.gov.uk/sites/default/files/documents/publications/CPS-Hate-Crime-
      Annual-Report-2018-2019.PDF

49   https://www.telegraph.co.uk/politics/2020/04/02/number-paedophiles-uk-surges-
      300000-police-chiefs-warn-online/

50   https://www.bbc.co.uk/news/uk-48343369

51   https://www.instituteforgovernment.org.uk/publications/performance-tracker-2020

52   https://www.vox.com/2020/1/28/21074386/health-care-rationing-britain-nhs-nice-
      medicare-for-all

53   https://read.oecd-ilibrary.org/social-issues-migration-health/oecd-reviews-of-health-care-
      quality-united-kingdom-2016_9789264239487-en#page42

54   https://www.nhs.uk/news/cancer/uk-cancer-survival-rates-below-european-average/

55   https://cles.org.uk/wp-content/uploads/2016/11/Due-North-Report-of-the-Inquiry-on-
      Health-Equity-in-the-North-final.pdf

56   https://www.ons.gov.uk/peoplepopulationandcommunity/birthsdeathsandmarriages/
      lifeexpectancies/bulletins/nationallifetablesunitedkingdom/2016to2018

57   https://www.independent.co.uk/life-style/health-and-families/features/1-3-women-have-
      abortion-and-95-don-t-regret-it-so-why-aren-t-we-talking-about-it-10392750.html

58   https://worldpopulationreview.com/country-rankings/abortion-rates-by-country

59   https://www.kingsfund.org.uk/projects/time-think-differently/trends-workforce-overview
      NHS is 1.4m of Britain's 27.1m workforce.

60   https://www.kingsfund.org.uk/projects/public-satisfaction-nhs

61   https://www.centreforsocialjustice.org.uk/core/wp-content/uploads/2016/08/addictionpr.pdf

62   https://www.drugwise.org.uk/how-many-people-use-drugs/

63   https://alcoholchange.org.uk/alcohol-facts/fact-sheets/alcohol-statistics

64   https://cy.ons.gov.uk/peoplepopulationandcommunity/healthandsocialcare/druguse
      alcoholandsmoking/bulletins/opinionsandlifestylesurveyadultdrinkinghabitsingreat
      britain/2005to2016

65   https://digital.nhs.uk/data-and-information/publications/statistical/statistics-on-obesity-physical-activity-and-diet/statistics-on-obesity-physical-activity-and-diet-england-2019/part-3-adult-obesity

66   https://www.ageuk.org.uk/latest-press/articles/2019/november/the-number-of-older-people-with-some-unmet-need-for-care-now-stands-at-1.5-million/

67   https://www.bigissue.com/latest/social-activism/how-many-people-are-homeless-in-the-uk-and-what-can-you-do-about-it/

68   https://www.ons.gov.uk/peoplepopulationandcommunity/personalandhouseholdfinances/incomeandwealth/articles/financialresilienceofhouseholdstheextenttowhichfinancialassetscancoveranincomeshock/2020-04-02

69   https://www.smf.co.uk/press-release-financial-fragility-of-workers-is-impacting-uk-productivity/

70   https://www.ons.gov.uk/peoplepopulationandcommunity/personalandhouseholdfinances/incomeandwealth/articles/persistentpovertyintheukandeu/2017

71   https://www.ons.gov.uk/peoplepopulationandcommunity/personalandhouseholdfinances/incomeandwealth/bulletins/pensionwealthingreatbritain/april2016tomarch2018

72   https://www.ft.com/content/14cda94c-5163-11e5-b029-b9d50a74fd14

73   https://www.sharesoc.org/investor-academy/advanced-topics/uk-stock-market-statistics/

74   https://themoneycharity.org.uk/money-statistics/

75   MHCLG figures show the UK built 251,820 properties in 1980, and in 2015 just 152,440.

76   https://homebuildingfund.campaign.gov.uk/

77   https://www.ifs.org.uk/publications/13940

78   https://www.disabilityinnovation.com/

79   https://www.ons.gov.uk/peoplepopulationandcommunity/housing/articles/ukperspectives2016housingandhomeownershipintheuk/2016-05-25

80   https://www.ons.gov.uk/peoplepopulationandcommunity/housing/articles/ukperspectives2016housingandhomeownershipintheuk/2016-05-25

81   https://www.abi.org.uk/globalassets/sitecore/files/documents/publications/public/2016/keyfacts/keyfacts2016.pdf

82   https://www.centreforsocialjustice.org.uk/core/wp-content/uploads/2017/04/CSJJ5159_Back_banking_roundtable_paper_WEB.pdf

83   https://www.theguardian.com/money/2019/apr/22/britons-without-bank-account-pay-poverty-premium

84   https://www.bbc.co.uk/news/uk-england-29880995

85   https://www.telegraph.co.uk/news/newstopics/howaboutthat/12046445/Which-nationalities-are-most-confrontational-and-which-are-the-most-emotional.html

86   https://www.thinkbox.tv/research/barb-data/top-programmes-report/

87   http://viz.co.uk/2015/02/28/rogers-profanisaurus-deansgate-tornado/

88   https://www.sciencedaily.com/releases/2000/11/001120072759.htm

89   https://www.youtube.com/watch?v=VyWN5017wD8

90   https://www.theguardian.com/uk-news/2018/dec/02/revealed-the-stark-evidence-of-everyday-racial-bias-in-britain

91   https://assets.publishing.service.gov.uk/government/uploads/system/uploads/attachment_data/file/686071/Revised_RDA_report_March_2018.pdf

92   https://www.theguardian.com/world/2019/may/20/racism-on-the-rise-since-brexit-vote-nationwide-study-reveals

93   https://www.bsa.natcen.ac.uk/latest-report/british-social-attitudes-30/personal-relationships/marriage-matters.aspx

94   https://www.bbc.com/news/uk-43782241

95   https://yougov.co.uk/topics/international/articles-reports/2020/03/11/how-unique-are-british-attitudes-empire

96   https://docs.cdn.yougov.com/z7uxxko71z/YouGov%20-%20British%20empire%20attitudes.pdf

97   https://www.gov.uk/government/news/uk-aid-to-protect-7000-commonwealth-veterans-of-the-british-armed-forces-from-extreme-poverty

98   https://www.dailymail.co.uk/debate/article-9348551/SIR-KENNETH-OLISA-Queens-black-Lord-Lieutenant-not-believe-royals-racist.html

99   https://www.thestage.co.uk/features/breaking-out-of-constraints

100   https://www.theguardian.com/politics/2019/nov/25/george-the-poet-rejected-mbe-pure-evil-british-empire

101   'Reformed Honours System', Select Committee on Public Administration: Fifth Report, 13 July 2004.

102   https://publications.parliament.uk/pa/cm200304/cmselect/cmpubadm/212/212.pdf

103   https://www.theguardian.com/commentisfree/2019/dec/29/rebecca-long-bailey-labour-party-britain

104   https://www.newstatesman.com/politics/uk/2019/12/win-again-labour-must-embrace-radical-patriotism

105   https://www.telegraph.co.uk/politics/2019/12/21/labours-mission-must-britains-real-middle-class/

106   https://www.politics.co.uk/comment-analysis/2019/04/15/polling-analysis-the-full-extent-of-britain-s-division-bruta

107   https://yougov.co.uk/topics/politics/articles-reports/2019/11/07/which-issues-will-decide-general-election

CHAPTER 3: HOW DID WE GET HERE?

1   https://www.theguardian.com/politics/2015/sep/11/jeremy-corbyn-leader-uk-labour-party

2   https://www.bbc.co.uk/news/av/election-2019-50768605

3   https://www.independent.co.uk/news/uk/politics/eu-referendum-bookies-have-always-made-a-remain-vote-favourite-and-the-odds-continue-to-shorten-a7093971.html

4   https://www.youtube.com/watch?v=f2zJ8vaB5jo

5   http://www.bbc.co.uk/newsbeat/article/36392621/heres-how-unlikely-donald-trumps-success-once-seemed

6   https://www.youtube.com/watch?v=G87UXIH8Lz0

7   https://www.thesun.co.uk/news/6632462/how-project-fears-dire-warnings-about-the-dangers-of-brexit-havent-come-true-two-years-on-from-the-referendum/

8   https://www.theguardian.com/politics/2018/jan/29/brexit-could-leave-patients-unable-to-access-new-drugs

9   https://www.bloomberg.com/news/articles/2019-10-08/no-deal-brexit-could-hit-fruit-and-vegetable-supply-u-k-warns

10   https://www.goodhousekeeping.com/uk/food/a27942196/you-gov-survey-british-food/

11   https://www.dailymail.co.uk/femail/food/article-2980788/Author-travels-UK-eating-pastries-700-days-search-Britain-s-best.html

12   https://news.sky.com/story/cameron-personally-requested-obamas-back-of-the-queue-brexit-warning-11423669

13   https://www.telegraph.co.uk/news/2017/01/05/bank-england-admits-michael-fish-moment-dire-brexit-predictions/

14   https://www.europeanmovement.co.uk/monthly_membership

15   https://www.bbc.co.uk/news/world-europe-46944358

16   https://uk.reuters.com/article/uk-britain-eu-autos-germany/german-carmakers-warn-hard-brexit-would-be-fatal-idUKKCN1PA173

17   https://ec.europa.eu/eurostat/web/products-eurostat-news/-/DDN-20190830-1

18   https://www.statista.com/chart/18794/net-contributors-to-eu-budget/

19   https://www.thesun.co.uk/news/6745786/nato-contributions-country-who-pay-most-least-2-percent-gdp-target-trump/

20   https://www.amazon.co.uk/Short-History-Europe-Pericles-Putin/dp/0241352509

21 https://www.theguardian.com/commentisfree/2017/jun/08/election-landslides-labour-tory-majority

22 https://researchbriefings.files.parliament.uk/documents/SN04252/SN04252.pdf

23 https://www.democraticaudit.com/2014/03/13/in-britain-people-with-higher-educational-attainment-are-less-likely-to-vote-because-they-are-younger/

24 https://www.hepi.ac.uk/wp-content/uploads/2014/12/Do-students-swing-elections.pdf

25 https://www.theguardian.com/commentisfree/2019/nov/01/middle-aged-swing-voters-age-class-political

26 https://www.britishelectionstudy.com/

27 https://www.bbc.com/mediacentre/2020/creative-diversity-plan

28 https://www.amazon.com/Made-Scotland-Grand-Adventures-Country/dp/178594374X

29 https://www.amazon.com/Brit-ish-Race-Identity-Belonging/dp/1911214284

30 https://www.theatlantic.com/international/archive/2017/03/martin-mcguinness-ian-paisley/520257/

31 https://www.bbc.com/news/uk-wales-32919137

32 https://www.amazon.com/Watching-English-Hidden-Rules-Behavior/dp/185788616X

33 https://www.amazon.com/England-Elegy-Roger-Scruton/dp/0826480756

34 Leeds United supporters sometimes refer to themselves as the Yorkshire Republican Army. https://www.facebook.com/YRA-Yorkshires-Republican-Army-204956969537411/

35 https://www.royal-irish.com/stories/lieutenant-colonel-tim-collins-eve-of-battle-speech

36 https://www.ratebeer.com/Story.asp?StoryID=275

37 https://www.sustainweb.org/realbread/bread_list/

38 https://englishbreakfastsociety.com/british-sausage.html

39 https://cheese-store.com/history-of-british-cheese/

40 https://www.bbc.com/news/uk-northern-ireland-50391731

41 https://www.scottishrefugeecouncil.org.uk/wp-content/uploads/2019/10/Refugees-in-Scotland-after-the-Referendum-PDF-summary.pdf

42 https://commonslibrary.parliament.uk/insights/migration-statistics-how-many-asylum-seekers-and-refugees-are-there-in-the-uk/

43 https://www.theguardian.com/world/2018/feb/16/japan-asylum-applications-2017-accepted-20

CHAPTER 4: WHO DO WE COMPETE WITH?

1 Antietam remains the largest daily death toll of any American military engagement.

2 https://www.cnn.com/2021/01/07/us/capitol-confederate-flag-fort-stevens/index.html

3 https://www.nytimes.com/2015/07/08/business/economy/germanys-debt-history-echoed-in-greece.html

4 The Bilderberg Group 'is defined as bolstering a consensus around free market Western capitalism and its interests around the globe. Participants include political leaders, experts from industry, finance, academia, and the media.' It is not to be confused with The Build-A-Bear Group, which is a store that facilitates the building of teddy bears. The only sinister connection appears to be capitalism.

5 https://www.weforum.org/agenda/2017/05/despite-the-decline-of-printed-papers-theres-one-place-that-is-bucking-the-trend

6 Symbols either side of the Speaker's Chair in Congress feature Roman symbols, most notably the fasces. This is an ancient symbol of power carried by lictors in front of magistrates, a bundle of sticks featuring an axe, indicating the power over life and death.

7 Held at the National Archives in Washington: https://www.foxnews.com/world/only-us-copy-of-magna-carta-featured-in-new-museum-gallery

8 https://psycnet.apa.org/record/1989-14051-001

9 https://www.thesun.co.uk/tvandshowbiz/9529653/tv-show-rainbow-sex-secrets-behind-the-scenes/s

10 https://www.theguardian.com/culture/tvandradioblog/2008/mar/18/isbasilbrushracist

11   Now curiously retro over-dubbed onto the contemporary recordings: https://www.youtube.com/watch?v=siHsGTyw1Pk

12   https://metro.co.uk/2018/06/11/milky-bar-kid-jailed-robbery-died-leaving-prison-got-hooked-spice-7621118/

13   https://www.amazon.co.uk/Plague-Penguin-Modern-Classics/dp/0141185139

14   https://www.amazon.com/Hundred-Year-Marathon-Strategy-Replace-Superpower/dp/1250081343

15   https://www.railway-technology.com/features/timeline-165-years-history-indian-railways/

16   https://www.investopedia.com/articles/markets-economy/090516/10-countries-most-natural-resources.asp

17   https://www.unenvironment.org/news-and-stories/press-release/china-outpacing-rest-world-natural-resource-use

18   https://countryeconomy.com/countries/compare/china/usa?sc=XE23

19   https://worldpopulationreview.com/country-rankings/countries-by-density

20   https://www.history.com/this-day-in-history/china-ends-one-child-policy

21   https://www.uscc.gov/sites/default/files/Research/10_26_11_CapitalTradeSOEStudy.pdf

22   https://www.msn.com/en-us/money/markets/28-incredible-made-in-china-innovations-that-are-changing-the-world/ss-BBRWnlD#image=3

23   https://www.nytimes.com/2015/12/23/world/asia/air-pollution-china-india.html

24   https://www.reuters.com/article/us-china-swinefever-smithfield-foods-foc/at-smithfield-foods-slaughterhouse-china-brings-home-u-s-bacon-idUSKBN1XF0XC

25   https://nationalinterest.org/blog/the-buzz/chinas-not-so-great-wall-debt-28-trillion-counting-18537

26   https://www.investopedia.com/articles/investing/092415/chinas-stock-markets-vs-us-stock-markets.asp

27   https://www.macrotrends.net/countries/GBR/united-kingdom/military-spending-defense-budgethttps://www.ted.com/talks/yasheng_huang_does_democracy_stifle_economic_growth?language=en

28   https://www.mylifeelsewhere.com/country-size-comparison/china/united-states

29   https://en.wikipedia.org/wiki/List_of_countries_by_median_age

30   https://www.macrotrends.net/countries/USA/united-states/birth-rate

31   https://www.macrotrends.net/countries/CHN/china/birth-rate

32   https://www.nsenergybusiness.com/features/electricity-consuming-countries/

33   https://www.nsenergybusiness.com/features/electricity-consuming-countries/

34   https://www.theglobaleconomy.com/China/gasoline_consumption/

35   https://www.macrotrends.net/countries/USA/united-states/military-spending-defense-budget

36   https://www.defensenews.com/global/europe/2019/12/19/uk-government-to-launch-radical-assessment-of-britains-place-in-the-world/

37   https://www.sipri.org/sites/default/files/2020-04/fs_2020_04_milex_0_0.pdf

38   https://educationdata.org/number-of-college-graduates

39   https://www.pewresearch.org/fact-tank/2019/06/20/u-s-women-near-milestone-in-the-college-educated-labor-force/

40   https://www.statista.com/statistics/227272/number-of-university-graduates-in-china/

41   https://en.wikipedia.org/wiki/Government_spending_in_the_United_States

42   https://www.bloomberg.com/news/articles/2020-03-13/unraveling-the-mysteries-of-china-s-multiple-budgets-quicktake

43   https://www.bp.com/content/dam/bp/business-sites/en/global/corporate/pdfs/energy-economics/statistical-review/bp-stats-review-2019-natural-gas.pdf

44   https://www.eia.gov/environment/emissions/carbon/

45   https://www.worldometers.info/co2-emissions/china-co2-emissions/

46   https://www.indexmundi.com/factbook/compare/china.united-states

47   https://www.ucsusa.org/resources/each-countrys-share-co2-emissions

48 http://www.eiu.com/topic/democracy-index

49 https://www.theguardian.com/notesandqueries/query/0,5753,-2036,00.html

50 https://www.bbc.com/news/world-asia-india-48347081

51 https://www.pewresearch.org/fact-tank/2020/11/03/in-past-elections-u-s-trailed-most-developed-countries-in-voter-turnout/

52 https://qz.com/1605690/european-election-belgiums-voter-turnout-rate-is-an-outlier/

53 https://www.statista.com/statistics/1050929/voter-turnout-in-the-uk/

54 https://thecommonwealth.org/about-us

55 https://news.cgtn.com/news/3d3d674d78456a4d33457a6333566d54/index.html

56 https://foreignpolicy.com/2020/06/10/g7-d10-democracy-trump-europe/

57 https://www.visualcapitalist.com/100-most-spoken-languages/

58 https://www.forbes.com/sites/dominicdudley/2018/01/13/renewable-energy-cost-effective-fossil-fuels-2020/#226572fd4ff2

CHAPTER 5: WHAT SHOULD WE BE DOING?

1 https://www.usnews.com/news/best-countries/articles/2020-01-15/us-trustworthiness-rating-dives-in-2020-best-countries-report

2 https://www.gov.uk/government/publications/industrial-strategy-the-grand-challenges/missions

3 https://marianamazzucato.com/wp-content/uploads/2019/01/iipp-pb-04-the-green-new-deal-17-12-2018_0.pdf

4 https://www.conservativehome.com/platform/2015/02/francis-maude-mp-what-weve-done-to-improve-value-for-money-in-government-and-what-we-plan-to-do-next.html

5 King James Bible, Proverbs 29–18.

6 Suvorov: 'No plan survives contact with the enemy.' Suvorov was an eighteenth-century Russian general. He fought sixty-three major battles and won them all. He emphasised detailed planning and careful strategy. He communicated with his troops in clear and understandable ways. Pedants may point out that it was Field Marshal Helmuth Karl Bernhard Graf von Moltke, chief of the Prussian general staff, who said it. But he was a century after Suvorov. Originator of the phrases 'train hard, fight easy' and 'fight the enemy with the weapons he lacks'. No matter. Both were splendid buggers when it came to planning.

7 https://www.cnbc.com/2017/06/17/a-nazi-era-resort-town-redeveloped-and-open-for-business.html

8 https://www.amazon.com/Good-Soldier-Svejk-Fortunes-Classics/dp/0140449914

9 https://www.clausewitz.com/readings/OnWar1873/TOC.htm

10 https://www.theguardian.com/media/2012/oct/04/jimmy-savile-television

11 https://www.independent.co.uk/news/uk/home-news/poorer-britons-significantly-less-likely-trust-institutions-survey-reveals-a6819816.html

12 https://www.england.nhs.uk/2019/07/nine-out-of-10-patients-have-confidence-and-trust-in-their-gp/

13 http://www.britishpoliticalspeech.org/speech-archive.htm?speech=191

14 http://www.britishpoliticalspeech.org/speech-archive.htm?speech=205

15 https://www.amazon.co.uk/Hundred-Year-Marathon-Strategy-Replace-Superpower-ebook/dp/B00IWUI7B4

16 https://www.oxfordreference.com/view/10.1093/acref/9780191826719.001.0001/q-oro-ed4-00004005

17 http://news.bbc.co.uk/1/hi/magazine/8465383.stm

18 http://www.nationalarchives.gov.uk/pathways/citizenship/brave_new_world/welfare.htm

19 https://www.theguardian.com/society/2016/jan/18/nye-bevan-history-of-nhs-national-health-service

20 https://slate.com/business/2013/08/hertz-vs-avis-advertising-wars-how-an-ad-firm-made-a-virtue-out-of-second-place.html

21 https://www.militarytimes.com/news/your-military/2015/11/01/naval-academy-reinstates-celestial-navigation/

22 https://www.amazon.co.uk/Hundred-Year-Marathon-Strategy-Replace-Superpower-ebook/dp/B00IWUI7B4
23 https://twitter.com/dalailama/status/1068452282109386753?lang=en
24 https://www.forbes.com/sites/dennisjaffe/2018/12/05/the-essential-importance-of-trust-how-to-build-it-or-restore-it/?sh=67f9b5064fe5
25 https://yougov.co.uk/topics/health/articles-reports/2021/01/15/how-much-difference-does-it-make-people-where-covi?utm_source=twitter&utm_medium=website_article&utm_campaign=vaccine_origin_perceptions
26 https://www.londonstockexchange.com/discover/lseg/our-history?lang=en
27 https://www.statista.com/statistics/940867/number-of-banks-in-europe-by-country/
28 https://www.gfmag.com/magazine/november-2019/worlds-safest-banks-2019
29 https://en.wikipedia.org/wiki/List_of_largest_law_firms_by_revenue
30 https://www.bbc.com/news/business-56263582
31 https://www.pressgazette.co.uk/robert-peston-itv-says-declining-trust-in-bbc-is-bad-for-all-impartial-news-providers/
32 https://en.wikipedia.org/wiki/Ethnic_groups_in_London
33 https://www.france24.com/en/20170222-france-uk-macron-takes-presidential-campaign-london-meets-theresa-may
34 https://www.centreforcities.org/press/london-generating-30-uk-economy-taxes-serious-implications-post-brexit-britain/

CHAPTER 6: MODERNISING THE MANDATES THAT REPRESENT US

1 The Authors are grateful to Pistoleros Cook, Jones, Lydon and Matlock for the loan of the phrase.
2 https://www.christianpost.com/news/only-38-brits-identify-christian-lowest-proportion-in-polls-history.html
3 https://www.amazon.com/History-Commons-Convention-Parliament-Passing/dp/B07R333YWV
4 https://catalog.hathitrust.org/Record/007703785
5 https://www.parliament.uk/business/publications/parliamentary-archives/explore/archives-highlights/archives-speakerlenthall/
6 https://www.boredpanda.com/funny-anti-brexit-protest-signs-london/?utm_source=google&utm_medium=organic&utm_campaign=organic
7 https://www.parliament.uk/site-information/foi/foi-and-eir/commons-foi-disclosures/human-resources/staff---numbers-2017/
8 https://www.bbc.co.uk/news/uk-politics-31049249
9 https://www.bbc.co.uk/news/uk-politics-31049249
10 https://www.instituteforgovernment.org.uk/publication/parliamentary-monitor-2018/time
11 https://webrootsdemocracy.org/2018/01/19/mps-clamour-for-electronic-voting/
12 HoC library.
13 https://www.theguardian.com/politics/2016/feb/06/who-needs-house-of-lords-meet-peers-rattling-the-commons
14 https://www.theguardian.com/politics/2011/sep/07/nadine-dorries-david-cameron-quip
15 https://www.bbc.com/news/uk-politics-parliaments-42908222
16 https://www.visitbritain.org/annual-survey-visits-visitor-attractions-latest-results
17 https://www.theguardian.com/politics/2019/apr/08/uk-more-willing-embrace-authoritarianism-warn-hansard-audit-political-engagement
18 https://www.instituteforgovernment.org.uk/publication/parliamentary-monitor-2020/cost-administration
19 https://www.instituteforgovernment.org.uk/publication/parliamentary-monitor-2020/cost-administration
20 https://www.thetimes.co.uk/article/house-of-lords-expenses-spiral-out-of-control-36w0cbq5s
21 https://www.express.co.uk/news/politics/1323184/house-of-lords-peers-expenses-cost-voting-debates-electoral-reform-society

22   https://www.parliament.uk/about/faqs/house-of-lords-faqs/lords-members/

23   https://www.electoral-reform.org.uk/latest-news-and-research/publications/house-of-lords-fact-vs-fiction/#sub-section-3

24   https://www.dailymail.co.uk/news/article-2375700/MP-Mark-Pritchard-My-marriage-latest-list-20-Tories-split-spouses.html

25   https://labourlist.org/2014/07/labour-need-more-signposts-not-weathervanes/

26   https://commonslibrary.parliament.uk/house-of-commons-trends-the-age-of-mps/

27   https://researchbriefings.files.parliament.uk/documents/CBP-7483/CBP-7483.pdf

28   https://www.statista.com/statistics/275394/median-age-of-the-population-in-the-united-kingdom/

29   https://www.ons.gov.uk/employmentandlabourmarket/peopleinwork/earningsand workinghours/datasets/allemployeesashetable1

30   https://en.wikipedia.org/wiki/Salaries_of_Members_of_the_United_Kingdom_Parliament

31   https://www.parliament.uk/site-information/foi/transparency-publications/hoc-transparency-publications/former-mp-passes/

32   http://www.w4mp.org/library/researchguides/welcome/access-to-refreshment-facilities-in-the-palace-of-westminster/

33   https://www.parliament.uk/business/publications/research/olympic-britain/parliament-and-elections/representatives-of-society/

34   https://www.theguardian.com/higher-education-network/blog/2013/jun/04/higher-education-participation-data-analysis

35   https://www.amazon.co.uk/Too-Fast-Think-Creativity-Hyper-connected/dp/0749478861

36   Iain McGilchrist, 'The Divided Brain and the Making of the Modern World', TED, October 2011.

37   https://www.politicshome.com/news/article/boris-johnson-faces-election-wipeout-unless-he-rejects-rampant-individualism-new-poll-warns

38   https://www.ukonward.com/thepoliticsofbelonging/

CHAPTER 7: MODERNISING THE MANAGEMENT THAT GOVERNS US

1   (Cabinet Secretary, Yes, Minister)

2   https://www.ons.gov.uk/employmentandlabourmarket/peopleinwork/publicsectorpersonnel/bulletins/publicsectoremployment/march2018

3   https://www.ons.gov.uk/employmentandlabourmarket/peopleinwork/publicsector personnel/bulletins/publicsectoremployment/march2018

4   2014/5 data

5   https://www.centrefortowns.org/our-towns

6   https://www.gov.uk/government/publications/rural-population-and-migration/rural-population-201415

7   https://www.gov.uk/government/publications/rural-population-and-migration/rural-population-201415

8   https://lgiu.org/local-government-facts-and-figures-england/

9   https://www.politics.co.uk/reference/local-government-structure

10 https://gov.wales/nhs-wales-health-boards-and-trusts

11 https://www.ukpublicspending.co.uk/government_expenditure.html

12 https://www.ukpublicspending.co.uk/uk_national_deficit_analysis

13 https://www.ukpublicspending.co.uk/uk_national_debt_analysis

14 https://www.ft.com/content/45163e43-1b21-4353-9a0e-ba03ee886075

15 https://www.theguardian.com/society/2012/may/15/graph-doom-social-care-services-barnet

16 https://www.theguardian.com/society/2012/may/15/graph-doom-social-care-services-barnet

17 https://www.instituteforgovernment.org.uk/publications/performance-tracker-2019

18 https://assets.publishing.service.gov.uk/government/uploads/system/uploads/attachment_data/file/685903/The_Green_Book.pdf

19 https://www.gov.uk/government/publications/consent-the-green-book-chapter-2

20 http://hummedia.manchester.ac.uk/schools/soss/economics/discussionpapers/EDP-1901.pdf

21 https://www.civilserviceworld.com/articles/opinion/whitehalls-obsession-business-cases-getting-way-delivery

22 https://assets.publishing.service.gov.uk/government/uploads/system/uploads/attachment_data/file/206552/nfa-annual-fraud-indicator-2013.pdf

23 https://www.theguardian.com/politics/2020/oct/07/fears-grow-over-uk-firms-ability-to-repay-covid-business-loans

24 https://assets.publishing.service.gov.uk/government/uploads/system/uploads/attachment_data/file/206552/nfa-annual-fraud-indicator-2013.pdf

25 https://www.telegraph.co.uk/news/uknews/1487145/Labour-activists-had-vote-rigging-factory-to-hijack-postal-votes.html

26 https://www.thetimes.co.uk/article/tower-hamlets-faces-vote-fraud-claims-tk7bxw09j

27 https://assets.publishing.service.gov.uk/government/uploads/system/uploads/attachment_data/file/503657/Fighting_fraud_and_corruption_locally_strategy.pdf

28 https://www.transparency.org.uk/publications/corruption-in-uk-local-government-the-mounting-risks/

29 https://ecpr.eu/Filestore/PaperProposal/0b9ff538-85e4-480a-b43e-e7c0f6febfd3.pdf

30 https://www.gov.uk/government/publications/local-government-transparency-code-2015

31 https://en.wikipedia.org/wiki/Standards_Board_for_England

32 https://www.electoral-reform.org.uk/campaigns/local-democracy/

33 https://www.conservativehome.com/localgovernment/2008/12/eric-pickles-th.html

34 Livingstone gave it the name: http://traquo.com/visiting-london-what-is-kens-bollock/

35 https://www.instituteforgovernment.org.uk/sites/default/files/publications/IfG_All_change_report_FINAL.pdf

36 https://www.theguardian.com/commentisfree/2016/apr/27/local-government-failed-state-mayors-george-osborne-unpopular-plan

37 https://northernpowerhouse.gov.uk/

38 https://www.local.gov.uk/sites/default/files/documents/Councillors%27%20Census%202018%20-%20report%20FINAL.pdf

39 https://www.local.gov.uk/sites/default/files/documents/Councillors%27%20Census%202018%20-%20report%20FINAL.pdf

40 https://www.instituteforgovernment.org.uk/sites/default/files/blog/wp-content/uploads/2015/11/1-Headcount-bar.png

41 https://ukandeu.ac.uk/towns-cities-and-brexit/

42 https://www.amazon.com/Little-Platoons-Englands-forgotten-political/dp/1785905120

43 http://www.bbc.co.uk/nationonfilm/topics/steel/background.shtml

44 https://www.amazon.com/Little-Platoons-Englands-forgotten-political/dp/1785905120

45 https://www.theguardian.com/inequality/2018/sep/05/qa-how-unequal-is-britain-and-are-the-poor-getting-poorer

46 https://www.instituteforgovernment.org.uk/sites/default/files/publications/has-devolution-worked-essay-collection-FINAL.pdf

47 https://www.bgf.co.uk/

48 https://www.theguardian.com/business/2011/oct/13/mergers-and-acquisitions-autonomycorporation

49 https://www.ons.gov.uk/peoplepopulationandcommunity/wellbeing/bulletins/socialcapitalintheuk/may2017

50 https://www.theguardian.com/society/2019/may/22/andy-haldane-bank-of-england-voluntary-sector-civil-society-technological-age

51 https://socialenterprise.us/about/social-enterprise/

52 https://bigsocietycapital.com/

53 https://www.greeninvestmentgroup.com/news/2016/gib-helps-finance-major-local-authority-streetlighting-project.html

54 https://www.cafonline.org/docs/default-source/about-us-policy-and-campaigns/giving-a-sense-of-place---philanthropy-and-the-future-of-uk-civic-identity.pdf

55   https://www.ukonward.com/thepoliticsofbelonging/

56   https://www.centreforsocialjustice.org.uk/library/community-capital-how-purposeful-participation-empowers-humans-to-flourish

57   https://www.google.com/search?client=firefox-b-d&q=eierlegende+wollmilchsau&spell=1&sa=X&ved=2ahUKEwjE1pyfrZfnAhWEKVAKHYZHAnoQBSgAegQIARAm&biw=2413&bih=976

58   https://fullfact.org/economy/do-top-1-earners-pay-28-tax-burden/

59   https://www.mckinsey.com/featured-insights/urbanization/urban-world-mapping-the-economic-power-of-cities

60   https://data.worldbank.org/indicator/SP.URB.TOTL.IN.ZS

61   https://www.citylab.com/equity/2012/03/us-urban-population-what-does-urban-really-mean/1589/

62   https://www.centreforcities.org/publication/beyond-business-rates-how-fiscal-devolution-can-incentivise-cities-to-grow/

63   https://www.centreforcities.org/publication/beyond-business-rates-how-fiscal-devolution-can-incentivise-cities-to-grow/

64   https://www.ifs.org.uk/publications/13991

65   https://www.ifs.org.uk/publications/13991

66   https://stats.oecd.org/Index.aspx?QueryId=95561

67   https://www.oecd-ilibrary.org/science-and-technology/main-science-and-technology-indicators_2304277x

68   https://www.philanthropy-impact.org/inspiration/personal-stories/sir-ronald-cohen

69   https://thegiin.org/

70   https://www.pioneerspost.com/news-views/20180718/why-the-social-value-act-needs-another-push

71   https://www.wired-gov.net/wg/news.nsf/articles/150m+endowment+will+give+communities+the+Power+to+Change+23012015122104?open

72   https://www.theguardian.com/voluntary-sector-network/2017/aug/15/seven-ways-improve-social-value-act

73   Panel interview with Matthew Fell, chief UK policy director, CBI.

74   https://researchbriefings.files.parliament.uk/documents/CBP-7483/CBP-7483.pdf

75   https://www.un.org/sustainabledevelopment/sg-finance-strategy/

76   https://www.theglobalcity.uk/industries/asset-management

77   https://www.oecd.org/dac/financing-sustainable-development/development-finance-data/Africa-Development-Aid-at-a-Glance-2019.pdf

78   https://www.lseg.com/resources/companies-inspire-africa/companies-inspire-africa-2019/london-stock-exchange-group-africa

79   https://www.devex.com/news/financial-returns-likely-to-go-down-over-next-5-years-says-cdc-chair-92943

80   https://www.pidg.org/

81   https://corporatefinanceinstitute.com/resources/knowledge/accounting/gaap/

82   https://www.worldbenchmarkingalliance.org

83   https://educationendowmentfoundation.org.uk/

84   https://www.civilsociety.co.uk/news/ftse-100-donations-to-charity-fall-by-655m-in-three-years.html

85   From Transactional to Transformative: The Future of Corporate Partnerships. © More Partnership, 8 May 2018.

86   https://www.nytimes.com/2015/10/18/business/energy-environment/social-responsibility-that-rubs-right-off.html

87   https://www.morepartnership.com/library/The_Future_of_Corporate_Partnerships.pdf
      Its surveys show that over 90 per cent of charities and 85 per cent of businesses have a view that corporate partnerships will be more important in the next three years.

88   Small Business, Big Heart: bringing communities together
      https://www.fsb.org.uk/resource-report/small-business-big-heart-communities-report.html

89   https://charityfutures.org/wp-content/uploads/2019/01/history-of-charity-lecture-online-copy-30-6.pdf

90   https://www.cbpp.org/blog/is-government-spending-really-41-percent-of-gdp

91   https://www.ageuk.org.uk/Documents/EN-GB/For-professionals/Research/The_Health_and_Care_of_Older_People_in_England_2016.pdf?dtrk=true

92   https://www.jrf.org.uk/sites/default/files/jrf/migrated/files/1859352413.pdf

93   https://www.amazon.co.uk/Entrepreneurial-State-Debunking-Private-Economics/dp/0857282522

94   https://www.amazon.co.uk/Entrepreneurial-State-Debunking-Private-Economics/dp/0857282522

95   Interview with the authors, January 2020.

96   https://nfpsynergy.net/free-report/facts-and-figures-uk-charity-sector-2018

97   https://www.instituteforgovernment.org.uk/news/latest/one-third-governments-spending-contractors

98   https://www.carepair.co.uk/

99   https://www.redcross.org.uk/about-us/what-we-do/uk-emergency-response/Covid-and-the-power-of-kindness

100   https://www.vox.com/2019/11/14/20961972/airbnb-scam-how-to-stay-safe-reset-podcast

101   https://www.amazon.com/How-Run-Government-Citizens-Taxpayers/dp/0141979585/ref=sr_1_1?keywords=michael+barber+government&qid=1574274608&s=books&sr=1-1 https://www.ifs.org.uk/bns/bn145.pdf

102   Together, these two functions made up 23 per cent of the public sector workforce in 1961, 42 per cent in 1991 and around 57 per cent in 2013.

103   In the mid-1990s, private sector nursery nurses and assistants accounted for around 40 per cent of the nursery workforce, but this figure increased to more than 70 per cent by 2010.

104   For personal care, a similar story can be told. The number of care sector workers in the public sector has been largely flat since the mid-1990s, while numbers in the private sector have more than doubled since the mid-1990s and accounted for around three-quarters of care sector workers by 2010.

105   https://www.ifs.org.uk/bns/bn145.pdf

106   https://www.enhamtrust.org.uk

107   https://assets.publishing.service.gov.uk/government/uploads/system/uploads/attachment_data/file/644266/MarketTrends2017report_final_sept2017.pdf

108   https://hosb.org.uk/

109   https://beam.org/

110   http://www.robertscentre.org.uk/latest-news/roberts-centre-ceo-carole-damper-cited-in-centre-for-social-justice-report-on-welfare-dependancy/

CHAPTER 8: MODERNISING THE MUTUALITY THAT BINDS US

1   https://www.thetimes.co.uk/article/the-times-view-on-millennial-attitudes-to-government-and-morality-on-liberty-qn6zj7lvt

2   The Leadership LAB 2018, reproduced with the kind permission of Kogan Page Ltd.

3   http://fortune.com/2017/11/06/apple-tax-avoidance-jersey/

4   https://www.reuters.com/article/us-deutschebank-libor-settlement/deutsche-bank-fined-record-2-5-billion-over-rate-rigging-idUSKBN0NE12U20150423

5   http://www.bbc.com/news/business-31248913

6   https://www.theguardian.com/business/2012/jul/17/hsbc-executive-resigns-senate

7   https://www.forbes.com/sites/kenrapoza/2017/09/15/tax-haven-cash-rising-now-equal-to-at-least-10-of-world-gdp/?sh=556f93d970d6

8   https://www.theguardian.com/business/2016/nov/08/rbs-facing-400m-bill-to-compensate-small-business-customers

9   https://www.ft.com/content/87f72e9e-bafb-11e7-9bfb-4a9c83ffa852

10   https://www.theguardian.com/business/2008/dec/28/markets-credit-crunch-banking-2008

11   http://www.businessinsider.com/how-bernie-madoffs-ponzi-scheme-worked-2014-7

12   https://www.forbes.com/sites/greatspeculations/2019/05/03/20-years-since-the-uks-massive-gold-sales-heres-the-big-lesson-for-gold-investors/#51fb3a932ac6

13   https://www.cnn.com/2017/06/29/world/timeline-catholic-church-sexual-abuse-scandals/index.html

14   http://www.bbc.co.uk/news/uk-43121833

15   http://www.bbc.com/news/education-11621391

16   https://www.pwc.com/ee/et/publications/pub/sb87_17208_Are_CEOs_Less_Ethical_Than_in_the_Past.pdf

17   https://www.bbc.co.uk/news/business-34324772

18   https://www.theguardian.com/environment/2015/oct/09/mercedes-honda-mazda-mitsubishi-diesel-emissions-row

19   https://edition.cnn.com/2019/12/30/business/carlos-ghosn-lebanon/index.html

20   https://www.bbc.co.uk/news/business-48755329

21   http://www.bbc.co.uk/news/entertainment-arts-41594672

22   https://www.theguardian.com/media/greenslade/2014/feb/19/newsnight-lord-mcalpine

23   https://www.telegraph.co.uk/news/uknews/crime/jimmy-savile/12172773/Jimmy-Savile-sex-abuse-report-to-be-published-live.html

24   http://www.bbc.co.uk/sport/athletics/43301116

25   https://www.theguardian.com/law/2017/feb/02/iraq-human-rights-lawyer-phil-shiner-disqualified-for-professional-misconduct

26   https://www.theguardian.com/us-news/2018/aug/22/how-many-of-trumps-close-advisers-have-been-convicted-and-who-are-they

27   https://www.icij.org/investigations/panama-papers/

28   https://www.bostonglobe.com/ideas/2018/01/20/trillions-dollars-have-sloshed-into-offshore-tax-havens-here-how-get-back/2wQAzH5DGRwomFH0YPqKZJ/story.html

29   https://www.visualcapitalist.com/80-trillion-world-economy-one-chart/

30   https://uk.reuters.com/article/us-davos-meeting-eu-tax/tax-avoidance-evasion-costs-eu-170-billion-euros-a-year-says-poland-idUKKBN1ZL1H4

31   https://www.theguardian.com/commentisfree/2018/nov/29/im-credited-with-having-coined-the-acronym-terf-heres-how-it-happened

32   https://stonewallhousing.org/wp-content/uploads/2018/09/FindingSafeSpaces_StonewallHousing_LaptopVersion.pdf

33   https://www.telegraph.co.uk/news/2016/11/10/white-working-class-boys-perform-worst-at-gcses-research-shows/

34   https://www.visualcapitalist.com/the-decline-of-upward-mobility-in-one-chart/

35   https://www.theguardian.com/society/2020/jan/21/social-mobility-decline-britain-official-survey-finds

36   https://assets.publishing.service.gov.uk/government/uploads/system/uploads/attachment_data/file/622214/Time_for_Change_report_-_An_assessment_of_government_policies_on_social_mobility_1997-2017.pdf

37   https://www.thetimes.co.uk/article/johnson-says-half-of-mps-should-be-women-vdgnw2gpx

38   https://assets.publishing.service.gov.uk/government/uploads/system/uploads/attachment_data/file/622214/Time_for_Change_report_-_An_assessment_of_government_policies_on_social_mobility_1997-2017.pdf

39   https://www.gov.uk/government/publications/social-mobility-in-great-britain-state-of-the-nation-2018-to-2019

40   https://www.oecd.org/social/broken-elevator-how-to-promote-social-mobility-9789264301085-en.htm

41   https://www.bbc.com/news/world-africa-36132151

42   https://www.bbc.com/news/uk-politics-53246899

43   https://assets.publishing.service.gov.uk/government/uploads/system/uploads/attachment_data/file/413347/Music_in_schools_wider_still__and_wider.pdf

44 https://www.statista.com/statistics/685208/number-of-female-ceo-positions-in-ftse-companies-uk/

45 https://assets.publishing.service.gov.uk/government/uploads/system/uploads/attachment_data/file/814080/GEO_GEEE_Strategy_Gender_Equality_Monitor_tagged.pdf

46 https://www.telegraph.co.uk/women/work/just-who-are-the-7-women-bosses-of-the-ftse-100/

47 https://www.bloomberg.com/gei/

48 https://www.wsj.com/articles/blackrock-companies-should-have-at-least-two-female-directors-1517598407

49 https://www.bloomberg.com/news/articles/2018-02-02/blackrock-asks-companies-to-explain-dearth-of-women-on-boards

50 https://hbr.org/2016/02/study-firms-with-more-women-in-the-c-suite-are-more-profitable

51 https://fortune.com/2015/06/29/black-women-entrepreneurs/

52 https://www.nawbo.org/resources/women-business-owner-statistics

53 https://www.nawbo.org/resources/women-business-owner-statistics

54 https://www.womensbusinesscouncil.co.uk/wp-content/uploads/2017/02/DfE-WBC-Two-years-on-report_update_AW_CC.pdf

55 https://www.intheblack.com/articles/2016/08/01/challenging-the-myth-that-self-confidence-equals-success

56 https://hbr.org/2014/07/the-dangers-of-confidence

57 https://researchbriefings.files.parliament.uk/documents/SN05878/SN05878.pdf

58 https://www.telegraph.co.uk/culture/charles-dickens/9048771/Gradgrind-My-favourite-Charles-Dickens-character.html

59 https://www.independent.co.uk/news/education/education-news/sir-anthony-seldon-historian-says-test-obsession-wrecks-education-a6779891.html

60 https://www.youtube.com/watch?v=7UfRLFTFDJ4&feature=youtu.be

61 Value for money in higher education, Seventh Report of Session 2017–19, House of Commons Education Committee, 5 November 2018.

62 https://www.theguardian.com/society/2013/feb/06/mid-staffs-hospital-scandal-guide

63 https://www.ifs.org.uk/bns/bn145.pdf

64 https://allauthor.com/quotes/63585/

65 https://www.amazon.com/Road-Somewhere-Populist-Revolt-Politics/dp/1849047995

66 https://www.bbc.co.uk/news/education-25002401

67 https://www.amazon.co.uk/Road-Somewhere-Populist-Revolt-Politics/dp/1849047995

68 https://www.universityofcalifornia.edu/press-room/uc-admission-california-students-all-time-record-high

69 The UC system, University of California, available at: https://www.universityofcalifornia.edu/uc-system

70 https://www.amazon.com/Blink-Power-Thinking-Without/dp/0316010669

71 https://www.amazon.com/Blink-Power-Thinking-Without/dp/0316010669

72 http://journals.sagepub.com/doi/full/10.1177/147470491201000314

73 https://www.sciencedirect.com/science/article/pii/0092656673900305

74 https://www.nbcnews.com/health/mens-health/deep-masculine-voice-not-you-ladies-n569631

75 https://www.psychologytoday.com/blog/the-brain-and-emotional-intelligence/201104/are-women-more-emotionally-intelligent-men

76 https://www.psychologytoday.com/basics/emotional-intelligence

77 https://www.livescience.com/18231-testosterone-collaborative-decisions-women.html

78 https://www.telegraph.co.uk/women/womens-life/10467289/Guilt-do-women-really-have-more-to-feel-guilty-about-than-men.html

79 https://www.telegraph.co.uk/men/thinking-man/11544484/Why-are-most-online-commenters-male.html

80 https://www.telegraph.co.uk/men/thinking-man/11544484/Why-are-most-online-commenters-male.html

81   Ibid.
82   Ibid.
83   https://www.nytimes.com/2015/01/11/opinion/sunday/speaking-while-female.html
84   Sajid Javid: 770,000 people in England unable to speak English well, *The Guardian*, 14 March 2018. https://www.theguardian.com/politics/2018/mar/14/sajid-javid-770000-people-in-england-not-able-to-speak-english
85   https://www.theatlantic.com/health/archive/2013/06/the-story-of-the-black-band-aid/276542/
86   https://www.raceforward.org/about
87   https://twitter.com/ApollonTweets/status/1119399823587758081
88   Young ethnic minority workers more likely to be in unstable jobs – study, BBC, 2 March 2020. https://www.bbc.co.uk/news/business-51700408
89   https://www.bbc.com/news/business-51700408?ocid=socialflow_twitter
90   British ethnic minority students racially harassed: BMA, Aljazeera, 14 February 2020. https://www.aljazeera.com/news/2020/02/british-ethnic-minority-students-racially-harassed-bma-200214090309387.html
91   https://disabilityhorizons.com/2020/01/samantha-renke-on-disabled-toilets/
92   https://www.aljazeera.com/news/2020/2/14/british-ethnic-minority-students-racially-harassed-bma
93   https://twitter.com/renalpages?lang=en
94   NHS Workforce Race Equality Standard, NHS Equality and Health Inequalities Council, 31 July 2014. https://www.england.nhs.uk/about/equality/equality-hub/equality-standard/
95   https://www.ifs.org.uk/uploads/BN234.pdf
96   https://www.centreforcities.org/wp-content/uploads/2015/07/15-07-06-Mapping-Britains-Public-Finances.pdf
97   https://researchbriefings.parliament.uk/ResearchBriefing/Summary/CBP-8456
98   https://www.businessinsider.com/millionaire-study-neighborhood-house-affects-building-wealth-2019-1
99   https://www.ons.gov.uk/peoplepopulationandcommunity/healthandsocialcare/disability/bulletins/disabilityandemploymentuk/2019
100 https://www.brookings.edu/blog/the-avenue/2019/11/21/low-wage-work-is-more-pervasive-than-you-think-and-there-arent-enough-good-jobs-to-go-around/
101 https://www.ons.gov.uk/peoplepopulationandcommunity/healthandsocialcare/conditionsanddiseases/articles/whyhaveblackandsouthasianpeoplebeenhithardestbycovid19/2020-12-14

CHAPTER 9: MODERNISING THE MARKETS THAT SERVE US

1   https://www.amazon.co.uk/Prisoners-Geography-Everything-Global-Politics/dp/1783961414
2   https://www.brookings.edu/research/trends-in-the-information-technology-sector/
3   https://blog.sciencemuseum.org.uk/nine-things-you-didnt-know-about-the-science-museum/
4   https://en.wikipedia.org/wiki/Stamford_Raffles
5   https://www.sbs.ox.ac.uk/sites/default/files/2020-06/Shaviro-D-Whatareminimumtaxesandwhyonemightfavorordisfavorthem.pdf
6   The nation thanks Rowan Atkinson, Richard Curtis and Ben Elton for their genius.
7   https://blogs.lse.ac.uk/politicsandpolicy/keynes-hayek-nicholas-wapshott/
8   https://www.pbs.org/wgbh/commandingheights/shared/minitext/prof_friedrichvonhayek.html
9   https://mosaicmagazine.com/picks/history-ideas/2018/04/the-common-insights-of-economics-and-judaism/
10   https://medium.com/newco/what-do-economists-know-199bf5793ae6#.gqky9w6dw
11   https://mosaicmagazine.com/picks/history-ideas/2018/04/the-common-insights-of-economics-and-judaism/
12   https://www.amazon.com/equality-material-position-government-totalitarian/dp/B08LNJLKRY

13   https://www.citatum.org/book/The_Road_to_Serfdom?r=6

14   Op. cit.

15   https://winstonchurchill.org/publications/finest-hour/finest-hour-118/wit-and-wisdom-10/

16   https://itep.org/60-fortune-500-companies-avoided-all-federal-income-tax-in-2018-under-new-tax-law/

17   https://www.un.org/africarenewal/magazine/december-2013/africa-loses-50-billion-every-year

18   https://www.ifs.org.uk/publications/9178

19   https://www.wsj.com/articles/tax-competition-works-for-europe-1416511643

20   https://ourworldindata.org/economic-growth

21   https://www.mckinsey.com/business-functions/mckinsey-digital/our-insights/digital-globalization-the-new-era-of-global-flows

22   https://www.youtube.com/watch?v=GTG2VvvIs10

23   https://www.newscientist.com/article/2110280-what-can-we-3d-print-everything-here-are-8-awesome-examples/

24   https://all3dp.com/1/3d-printing-materials-guide-3d-printer-material/

25   https://www.bbc.com/news/business-40189959

26   https://www.theguardian.com/business/2013/sep/10/banknotes-history

27   https://www.economist.com/leaders/2017/05/06/the-worlds-most-valuable-resource-is-no-longer-oil-but-data

28   https://www.wired.com/story/no-data-is-not-the-new-oil/

29   https://datareportal.com/reports/digital-2019-global-digital-overview

30   https://www.oecd.org/internet/ascendancy-digital-trade-new-world-order.htm

31   https://e-estonia.com/solutions/e-governance/i-voting/

32   https://www.cnbc.com/2020/11/19/Covid-drives-global-debt-to-a-new-record-high.html

33   https://money.cnn.com/2017/01/12/pf/americans-lack-of-savings/index.html

34   https://www.theguardian.com/money/2018/jan/25/uk-workers-chronically-broke-study-economic-insecurity

35   https://www.forbes.com/2009/11/03/capitalism-greed-recession-forbes-opinions-markets.html?sh=366619087f32

36   https://www.forbes.com/sites/gordonchang/2011/06/05/chinese-entrepreneurs-are-leaving-china/?sh=5beba7d41dfe

37   https://www.asianentrepreneur.org/why-are-rich-chinese-entrepreneurs-leaving-china/

38   https://www.investopedia.com/articles/investing/092415/chinas-stock-markets-vs-us-stock-markets.asp

39   https://www.investopedia.com/articles/investing/092415/chinas-stock-markets-vs-us-stock-markets.asp

40   https://www.ilo.org/wcmsp5/groups/public/---dgreports/---dcomm/---publ/documents/publication/wcms_650553.pdf

41   https://www.forbes.com/sites/kenrapoza/2017/08/16/china-wage-levels-equal-to-or-surpass-parts-of-europe/#5f4a34d53e7f

42   https://napsintl.com/manufacturing-in-mexico/mexico-vs-china-manufacturing-comparison/

43   https://www.economist.com/special-report/2020/02/06/china-wants-to-put-itself-back-at-the-centre-of-the-world

44   https://thediplomat.com/2017/05/reviving-the-comatose-bangladesh-china-india-myanmar-corridor/

45   https://thediplomat.com/2016/08/tibet-and-chinas-belt-and-road/

46   https://globalshippersalliance.org/wp-content/uploads/2018/01/Study_EP_IPOL_STU2018585907_EN.pdf

47   https://www.mhlnews.com/global-supply-chain/article/22042478/more-competition-for-us-west-coast-ports

48   https://www.bangkokpost.com/business/2001843/controversial-thai-canal-back-in-spotlight

49   https://www.smithsonianmag.com/science-nature/new-canal-through-central-america-could-have-devastating-consequences-180953394/
      https://www.forbes.com/sites/wadeshepard/2020/01/31/inside-the-belt-and-roads-premier-white-elephant-melaka-gateway/?sh=6cb8f63266ee
50   https://www.coha.org/the-twin-ocean-project-south-americas-transcontinental-railroad/
51   https://www.reuters.com/article/us-china-arctic/china-unveils-vision-for-polar-silk-road-across-arctic-idUSKBN1FF0J8
52   https://www.eia.gov/todayinenergy/detail.php?id=18011
53   https://www.csis.org/analysis/how-big-chinas-belt-and-road
54   https://www.bloomberg.com/markets/fixed-income
55   https://www.reuters.com/article/us-china-railway-yunnan/china-completes-high-speed-rail-links-from-southwest-yunnan-idUSKBN14I07I?il=0
56   http://oecdobserver.org/news/fullstory.php/aid/5565/The_ascendancy_of_digital_trade:_A_new_world_order_.html
57   https://www.cps.org.uk/media/press-releases/q/date/2020/07/27/the-uk-must-be-the-champion-of-global-entrepreneurship-/
58   https://www.japantimes.co.jp/news/2009/01/06/reference/lessons-from-when-the-bubble-burst/
59   https://www.piie.com/commentary/testimonies/some-background-qa-japanese-economic-stagnation
60   https://www.forbes.com/sites/yuwahedrickwong/2019/04/10/japans-richest-2019-pm-abes-aim-is-true/#355e961c77a6
61   https://qz.com/452076/this-just-in-german-capitalism-has-won/
62   https://www.thelocal.de/20170130/germany-overtakes-china-as-worlds-richest-exporter
63   https://www.foreignaffairs.com/articles/germany/2017-09-11/germany-after-hartz-reforms
64   https://tradingeconomics.com/spain/youth-unemployment-rate
65   https://www.forbes.com/2009/11/03/capitalism-save-us-opinions-forbes_land.html#34045425258c
66   https://www.amazon.com/How-Capitalism-Will-Save-Us/dp/0307463095?ie=UTF&tag=capbookedit-20
67   The Meeting That Showed Me the Truth About VCs by Tomer Dean, TechCrunch, 1 June 2017.
68   https://www.fsb.org.uk/uk-small-business-statistics.html
69   https://www.visualcapitalist.com/2000-years-economic-history-one-chart/
70   https://www.shrm.org/resourcesandtools/hr-topics/employee-relations/pages/jobsecurityandbenefits.aspx
71   https://www.statista.com/statistics/289137/central-heating-in-households-in-the-uk/
72   https://www.independent.co.uk/travel/news-and-advice/british-travellers-iata-world-air-transport-statistics-a9029366.html
73   http://www.donellameadows.org/wp-content/userfiles/Limits-to-Growth-digital-scan-version.pdf
74   https://www.theguardian.com/commentisfree/2019/aug/21/contemporary-capitalism-liberal-democracy-policies
75   https://www.federalreservehistory.org/essays/bretton-woods-created

CHAPTER 10: WHAT *IS* BRITAIN?

1   https://www.theguardian.com/news/2019/mar/11/referendums-who-holds-them-why-and-are-they-always-a-dogs-brexit
2   https://www.theguardian.com/politics/2021/mar/25/a-festival-to-heal-the-scars-of-brexit
3   https://www.ft.com/content/38aaed34-e6d0-477d-a3a6-d42c2c1a2f51
4   https://www.jstor.org/stable/2639732?seq=1
5   Penny Mordaunt is named after HMS *Penelope*, a Leander class frigate. Penny remains grateful to the HMS Penelope Association for the loan of the original Lady Penelope puppet. Although she returned somewhat worse for wear from their annual shindig. The puppet, we mean, of course. http://www.hms-penelope.com/

6   https://readable.com/blog/do-inuits-really-have-50-words-for-snow/

7   The Vietnam anti-war culture was profound at the time. The period is notable for many remarkable anti-war films like *Catch-22* (1970), *Johnny Got His Gun* (1971) and *Slaughterhouse-Five* (1972).

8   https://www.youtube.com/watch?v=6MbZjzIg5w8

9   https://www.amazon.co.uk/s?k=the+future+of+capitalism&adgrpid=56946435281&gclid=EAIaIQobChMIzr2A5YSa5wIVjuJ3Ch2YBgU6EAAYAiAAEgJHwPD_BwE&hvadid=259097718950&hvdev=c&hvlocphy=9045896&hvnetw=g&hvpos=1t2&hvqmt=e&hvrand=8069021772559257504&hvtargid=aud-857384558300 percent3Akwd-504789622312&hydadcr=24431_1748949&tag=googhydr-21&ref=pd_sl_804a8mwxdf_e

10   https://qz.com/1331995/walmart-is-the-worlds-biggest-company-apple-isnt-in-the-top-10/

11   https://www.statista.com/statistics/265125/total-net-sales-of-apple-since-2004/#:~:text=Apple's%20revenue%20worldwide%202004%2D2020&text=Apple's%20total%20net%20sales%20amounted,in%20the%20last%20ten%20years.

12   https://www.investopedia.com/news/apple-now-bigger-these-5-things/#:~:text=Key%20Takeaways-,Apple%20Inc.,the%20GDP%20of%20most%20countries.

13   https://www.macrotrends.net/stocks/charts/WMT/walmart/market-cap

14   https://s2.q4cdn.com/056532643/files/doc_financials/2019/annual/Walmart-2019-AR-Final.pdf

15   https://www.telegraph.co.uk/news/2016/10/05/theresa-mays-conference-speech-in-full/

16   Op. cit.

17   https://www.amazon.co.uk/Once-Future-Liberal-Identity-Politics/dp/0062697439

18   https://www.amazon.com/Prosperity-Without-Growth-Economics-Finite/dp/1849713235

19   http://www.chinadaily.com.cn/a/201808/02/WS5b728ae4a310add14f385b4a.html

20   https://www.greatbritaincampaign.com/

21   https://www.theguardian.com/politics/2014/nov/20/emily-thornberry-resigns-rochester-tweet-labour-shadow-cabinet

22   https://www.historic-uk.com/HistoryUK/HistoryofEngland/St-George-Patron-Saint-of-England/

23   https://yougov.co.uk/topics/politics/explore/public_figure/Queen_Elizabeth_II

24   http://news.bbc.co.uk/2/hi/entertainment/4644630.stm

25   Ibid.

26   Ibid.

27   https://www.theguardian.com/media/2010/oct/12/mark-damazer-uk-theme-radio-4

28   https://www.thisdayinmusic.com/liner-notes/live-aid-lineup/

29   https://www.electoralcommission.org.uk/sites/default/files/pdf_file/UKPGE-Part-1-Can-you-stand-for-election.pdf

30   https://www.aec.gov.au/FAQs/

31   https://www.amazon.co.uk/Twilight-Elite-Prosperous-Periphery-Future/dp/0300233760

32   https://theimaginativeconservative.org/2015/08/should-we-stop-dumb-people-from-voting.html

SURPRISING FACTS

1   https://www.britishcouncil.org/research-policy-insight/insight-articles/UK-most-attractive-country-G20

2   https://www.usnews.com/news/best-countries/united-kingdom

3   http://www.oecd.org/investment/FDI-in-Figures-October-2019.pdf

4   https://www.thetimes.co.uk/article/uk-will-fall-to-7th-in-gdp-rankings-say-experts-288h5g8qq

5   https://www.wipo.int/edocs/pubdocs/en/wipo_pub_gii_2019.pdf

6   https://www.lovemoney.com/galleries/70588/25-things-the-uk-leads-the-world-in?page=4

7   http://news.bbc.co.uk/2/hi/programmes/bbc_parliament/7090665.stm

8   https://www.bbc.com/news/magazine-17429786

9   https://www.bbc.com/news/health-40608253
10   https://www.uschamber.com/international/europe/us-uk-business-council/us-uk-trade-and-investment-ties
11   https://www.autosport.com/asi/news/133624/how-did-the-uk-become-the-centre-of-racing
12   https://sportmob.com/en/article/897583-richest-football-leagues-in-the-world
13   https://londoninternationalshippingweek.com/new-maritime-london-report-outlines-steps-to-grow-uks-6bn-maritime-businesses/
14   https://www.theguardian.com/commentisfree/2010/jan/25/britain-world-role-europe-us
15   https://www.thewholeworldisaplayground.com/countries-with-most-unesco-world-heritage-sites/
16   https://www.edie.net/news/9/Report--UK-leading-G20-countries-in-global-low-carbon-transition/
17   https://assets.publishing.service.gov.uk/government/uploads/system/uploads/attachment_data/file/48128/2167-uk-renewable-energy-roadmap.pdf
18   https://www.internationalairportreview.com/article/32311/top-20-busiest-airports-world-passenger-number/
19   https://www.farandwide.com/s/public-transit-systems-ranked-c5d839d8a48d4da3
20   https://timesofindia.indiatimes.com/home/sunday-times/deep-focus/India-beats-China-in-UK/articleshow/17633302.cms
21   https://www.nfuonline.com/sectors/animal-health/animal-health-news/uk-leads-the-way-in-animal-welfare/
22   https://www.topuniversities.com/university-rankings-articles/world-university-rankings/top-universities-world-2019
23   https://www.studyinternational.com/news/the-uk-is-the-best-country-in-the-world-for-education-says-study/
24   https://en.wikipedia.org/wiki/List_of_largest_law_firms_by_revenue
25   https://softpower30.com/wp-content/uploads/2018/07/The-Soft-Power-30-Report-2018.pdf
26   https://www.usnews.com/news/best-countries/overall-rankings
27   https://www.cafonline.org/about-us/media-office-news/uk-is-one-of-the-top-10-most-generous-countries-in-the-world
28   Ibid.
29   https://www.lovemoney.com/galleries/70588/25-things-the-uk-leads-the-world-in?page=6
     https://www.trbusiness.com/regional-news/international/uk-consumers-spend-the-most-online-per-household/118733
30   https://www.ibtimes.com/what-largest-library-world-20-things-know-about-british-library-london-2434774
31   2019 data, https://opendatabarometer.org/?_year=2017&indicator=ODB
32   https://www.theguardian.com/science/datablog/2016/oct/08/which-countries-have-had-the-most-nobel-prize-winners
33   https://en.wikipedia.org/wiki/List_of_Nobel_laureates_by_country
34   https://www.chemistryworld.com/opinion/the-iron-lady/5028.article
35   https://www.bestcities.org/rankings/worlds-best-cities/
36   https://www.guinnessworldrecords.com/world-records/first-billion-dollar-author
37   https://www.businessinsider.com/best-selling-music-artists-of-all-time-2016-9#50-dave-matthews-band-345-million-units-1
38   https://www.ft.com/content/54e31212-17f1-11e4-b842-00144feabdc0
39   https://www.bbc.com/future/article/20150602-do-the-british-have-bad-teeth
40   https://www.orchardscottsdental.com/10-countries-whose-citizens-have-healthy-teeth/
41   https://www.marketwatch.com/story/the-us-is-the-most-obese-nation-in-the-world-just-ahead-of-mexico-2017-05-19
42   https://www.britishcouncil.org/contact/press/best-and-worst-british-eyes-world
43   https://www.internations.org/expat-insider/

44 https://blogs.lse.ac.uk/politicsandpolicy/the-unreformed-house-of-lords-is-already-the-largest-parliamentary-chamber-of-any-democracy/

45 https://www.statista.com/statistics/1050929/voter-turnout-in-the-uk/

46 https://www.democraticaudit.com/2014/03/13/in-britain-people-with-higher-educational-attainment-are-less-likely-to-vote-because-they-are-younger/

INDEX